TV SEASON
74-75

Compiled and Edited
by
NINA DAVID

ORYX PRESS

Operation Oryx, started more than 10 years ago at the Phoenix Zoo to save the rare white antelope — believed to have inspired the unicorn of mythology — has apparently succeeded .

An original herd of nine, put together through Operation Oryx by five world organizations, now numbers 34 in Phoenix with another nine farmed out to the San Diego Wild Game Farm.

The operation was launched in 1962 when it became evident that the animals were facing extinction in their native habitat of the Arabian peninsula.

Copyright © 1976 by
The Oryx Press
3930 E. Camelback Road
Phoenix, Arizona 85018

Printed and Bound in the United States of America

Library of Congress Card No. 76-22622

ISBN 0-912700-20-3

Shows Cancelled During 1974-1975 Season

Adam-12 30
The Addams Family 32
Apple's Way 83
The Brady Bunch 164
The Bugs Bunny Show 174
The Girl in My Life 434
Goober and the Ghost Chasers 451
Gunsmoke 472
How to Survive a Marriage 519
Ironside 558
Jeannie 576
Jeopardy! 578
The Jetsons 581
The Joker's Wild 589
Kung Fu 614
Lassie's Rescue Rangers 624

Mannix 684
My Favorite Martians 748
Name That Tune 752
The Newlywed Game 780
Now You See It 805
The Odd Couple 809
Password 840
The Reasoner Report 903
Split Second 1022
Star Trek 1025
Superfriends 1051
What's My Line? 1179
Winning Streak 1206
Yogi's Gang 1229
Zoom 1239

New Shows 1974-1975

The ABC Saturday News with Ted Koppel 21
AM America 57
Baretta 105
Barney Miller 107
Big Blue Marble 130
Celebrity Sweepstakes 218
Cher 226
Chico and the Man 229
Consumer Reports 257
Devlin 312
The Diamond Head Game 313, 314
Dinah! 318
Evening at Symphony 373
Friends of Man 418
The Harlem Globetrotters Popcorn Machine 481
Harry O 486
Hong Kong Phooey 513
The Hudson Brothers Razzle Dazzle Show 522
The Jeffersons 577
Jeopardy! 579
Land of the Lost 621
Little House on the Prairie 651
Lorne Greene's Last of the Wild 656
The Magnificent Marble Machine 671
Masquerade Party 695
Monty Python's Flying Circus 733
Movin' On 736

Musical Chairs 745
Name That Tune 753
NBC News Update 763
The New Adventures of Gilligan 774
The New Candid Camera 775
The New Treasure Hunt 777
Paul Hornung's Greatest Sports Legends 841
Petrocelli 851
Police Woman 864
Rhoda 913
Rhyme and Reason 914
The Rockford Files 921
Run, Joe, Run 934
Ryan's Hope 939
S.W.A.T. 1053
Sammy and Company 946
Shazam! 984
Showoffs 988
Take Kerr 1056
That's My Mama 1070
These Are the Days 1073
To Tell the Truth 1087
Tony Orlando and Dawn 1094
U.S. of Archie 1141
Valley of the Dinosaurs 1146
Vaudeville 1148
Villa Alegre (Happy Village) 1156
Weekend 1169
Wheel of Fortune 1184
You Don't Say! 1230

New Shows, Cancelled During 1974-1975 Season

Amy Prentiss 70
The Big Showdown 132
Blank Check 144
Blankety Blanks 145
The Bob Crane Show 149
Born Free 160
Caribe 189
Feeling Good 393
Feeling Good (new format) 394
Get Christie Love! 433
Hot l Baltimore 515
Karen 597
Khan! 603
Kodiak 611
Korg: 70,000 B.C.! 613
Lucas Tanner 661
The Mac Davis Show 665
The Manhunter 683

The Money Maze 730
Nakia 751
The New Land 776
The Night Stalker 794
Paper Moon 837
Partridge Family: 2200 A.D. 839
Paul Sand in Friends and Lovers 842
Planet of the Apes 858
Sierra 989
The Smothers Brothers 1003
The Sonny Comedy Revue 1010
Sons and Daughters 1011
Spin-Off 1021
Sunshine 1047
We'll Get By 1170
Wheelie and the Chopper Bunch 1185

Summer Shows 1975

The ABC Summer Movie 23
Almost Anything Goes 55
Conversations with Eric Sevareid
    268
Dan August 287
The Dick Cavett Show 315
Gladys Knight and the Pips 441
The Jim Stafford Show 582

Joey & Dad 584
Keep on Truckin' 600
The Manhattan Transfer 682
Moses the Lawgiver 735
Summer Semester 1044
The Texas Wheelers 1066
The Zoo Gang 1238

EMMY AWARDS

Presented by the
NATIONAL ACADEMY OF TELEVISION ARTS AND SCIENCES
for programs shown
March 18, 1974–March 10, 1975

ιe 1974–1975 annual prime-time awards were presented on May 19, 1975 at the ɔllywood Palladium; the 1974–1975 annual daytime awards were presented on ay 15, 1975, on board the Hudson River Dayliner in New York Harbor. All minations are listed for each category; winners are starred.

THE CATEGORIES
Entertainment Program and Individual Achievements

UTSTANDING COMEDY SERIES

The Mary Tyler Moore Show James L. Brooks and Allan Burns, Executive Producers; Ed Weinberger and Stan Daniels, Producers (CBS)

*M*A*S*H* Gene Reynolds and Larry Gelbart, Producers (CBS)

All In The Family Don Nicholl, Executive Producer; Michael Ross and Bernie West, Producers (CBS)

Rhoda James L. Brooks and Allan Burns, Executive Producers; David Davis and Lorenzo Music, Producers (CBS)

UTSTANDING DRAMA SERIES

Upstairs, Downstairs Masterpiece Theatre; Rex Firkin, Executive Producer; John Hawkesworth, Producer (PBS)

The Streets Of San Francisco Quinn Martin, Executive Producer; John Wilder and William Robert Yates, Producers (ABC)

Police Story Stanley Kallis and David Gerber, Executive Producers; Chris Morgan, Producer (NBC)

The Waltons Lee Rich, Executive Producer; Robert L. Jacks, Producer (CBS)

Kojak Matthew Rapf, Executive Producer; Jack Laird and James McAdams, Producers (CBS)

UTSTANDING COMEDY-ɅRIETY OR MUSIC SERIES

The Carol Burnett Show Joe Hamilton, Executive Producer; Ed Simmons, Producer; Carol Burnett, Star (CBS)

Cher George Schlatter, Producer; Cher, Star (CBS)

OUTSTANDING LIMITED SERIES

★*Benjamin Franklin* Lewis Freedman, Executive Producer; George Lefferts and Glenn Jordan, Producers (CBS)

McCloud, NBC Sunday Mystery Movie; Glen A. Larson, Executive Producer; Michael Gleason and Ronald Satlof, Producers (NBC)

Columbo, NBC Sunday Mystery Movie; Roland Kibbee and Dean Hargrove, Executive Producers; Everett Chambers and Edward K. Dodds, Producers (NBC)

OUTSTANDING SPECIAL — DRAMA OR COMEDY

★*The Law*, NBC World Premiere Movie; William Sackheim, Producer. Shown October 22, 1974 (NBC)

The Missiles Of October, ABC Theatre; Irv Wilson, Executive Producer; Herbert Brodkin and Buzz Berger, Producers. Shown December 18, 1974 (ABC)

Queen Of The Stardust Ballroom Robert W. Christiansen and Rick Rosenberg, Producers. Shown February 13, 1975 (CBS)

Love Among The Ruins, ABC Theatre; Allan Davis, Producer. Shown March 6, 1975 (ABC)

QB VII (Parts 1 & 2), ABC Movie Special; Douglas S. Cramer, Producer. Shown April 29 & 30, 1974 (ABC)

OUTSTANDING SPECIAL — COMEDY-VARIETY OR MUSIC

★*An Evening With John Denver* Jerry Weintraub, Executive Producer; Al Rogers and Rich Eustis, Producers; John

Denver, Star. Shown March 10, 1975
(ABC)
Lily Irene Pinn, Executive Producer; Jane
Wagner and Lorne Michaels, Producers;
Lily Tomlin, Star. Shown February 21,
1975 (ABC)
*Shirley MacLaine: If They Could See Me
Now* Bob Wells, Producer; Shirley
MacLaine, Star. Shown November 28,
1974 (CBS)

OUTSTANDING CLASSICAL MUSIC PROGRAM (for a special program or for a series)

★*Profile In Music: Beverly Sills,* Festival '75;
Patricia Foy, Producer; Beverly Sills,
Star. Shown March 10, 1975 (PBS)
Rubinstein, Great Performances; Fritz
Buttenstedt, Executive Producer;
Helmut Bauer and David Griffiths,
Producers; Artur Rubinstein, Star.
Shown October 16, 1974 (PBS)
Bernstein At Tanglewood, Great
Performances; Klaus Hallig and Harry
Kraut, Executive Producers; David
Griffiths, Producer; Leonard Bernstein,
Star. Shown December 25, 1974 (PBS)
Evening At Pops William Cosel, Producer;
Arthur Fiedler, Star; Series (PBS)

OUTSTANDING LEAD ACTOR IN A COMEDY SERIES

★Tony Randall, *The Odd Couple* (ABC)
Alan Alda, *M*A*S*H* (CBS)
Jack Albertson, *Chico And The Man*
(NBC)
Jack Klugman, *The Odd Couple* (ABC)
Carroll O'Connor, *All In The Family* (CBS)

OUTSTANDING LEAD ACTOR IN A DRAMA SERIES

★Robert Blake, *Baretta* (ABC)
Karl Malden, *The Streets Of San Francisco*
(ABC)
Barry Newman, *Petrocelli* (NBC)
Telly Savalas, *Kojak* (CBS)

OUTSTANDING LEAD ACTOR IN A LIMITED SERIES

★Peter Falk, *Columbo;* NBC Sunday
Mystery Movie (NBC)
Dennis Weaver, *McCloud;* NBC Sunday
Mystery Movie (NBC)

OUTSTANDING LEAD ACTOR IN A SPECIAL PROGRAM — DRAMA OR COMEDY (for a special program; or a single appearance in a Drama or Comedy Series)

★Laurence Olivier, *Love Among The Ruins;*
ABC Theatre; shown March 6, 1975 (ABC)

Richard Chamberlain, *The Count of Monte
Cristo;* Bell System Family Theatre;
shown January 10, 1975 (NBC)
William Devane, *The Missiles Of October;*
ABC Theatre; shown December 18, 197
(ABC)
Charles Durning, *Queen Of The Stardust
Ballroom;* shown February 13, 1975
(CBS)
Henry Fonda, *IBM Presents Clarence
Darrow;* shown September 4, 1974
(NBC)

OUTSTANDING LEAD ACTRESS IN A COMEDY SERIES

★Valerie Harper, *Rhoda* (CBS)
Mary Tyler Moore, *The Mary Tyler Moore
Show* (CBS)
Jean Stapleton, *All In The Family* (CBS)

OUTSTANDING LEAD ACTRESS IN A DRAMA SERIES

★Jean Marsh, *Upstairs, Downstairs;*
Masterpiece Theatre (PBS)
Angie Dickinson, *Police Woman* (NBC)
Michael Learned, *The Waltons* (CBS)

OUTSTANDING LEAD ACTRESS IN A LIMITED SERIES

★Jessica Walter, *Amy Prentiss;* NBC Sunda
Mystery Movie (NBC)
Susan Saint James, *McMillan & Wife,* NB
Sunday Mystery Movie (NBC)

OUTSTANDING LEAD ACTRESS IN A SPECIAL PROGRAM — DRAMA OR COMEDY (for a special program; or a single appearance in a Drama or Comedy Series)

★Katharine Hepburn, *Love Among The
Ruins;* ABC Theatre; shown March 6,
1975 (ABC)
Jill Clayburgh, *Hustling;* Special World
Premiere ABC Saturday Night Movie;
shown February 22, 1975 (ABC)
Elizabeth Montgomery, *The Legend Of
Lizzie Borden;* Special World Premiere
ABC Monday Night Movie; shown
February 10, 1975 (ABC)
Diana Rigg, *In This House Of Brede;* GE
Theater; shown February 27, 1975 (CBS
Maureen Stapleton, *Queen of The Stardus
Ballroom;* shown February 13, 1975
(CBS)

OUTSTANDING CONTINUING PERFORMANCE BY A SUPPORTING ACTOR IN A COMEDY SERIES (for a regular or limited series)

★Ed Asner, *The Mary Tyler Moore Show* (C

Rob Reiner, *All In The Family* (CBS)
Ted Knight, *The Mary Tyler Moore Show* (CBS)
Gary Burghoff, *M*A*S*H* (CBS)
McLean Stevenson, *M*A*S*H* (CBS)

OUTSTANDING CONTINUING PERFORMANCE BY A SUPPORTING ACTOR IN A DRAMA SERIES (for a regular or limited series)

Will Geer, *The Waltons* (CBS)
Michael Douglas, *The Streets Of San Francisco* (ABC)
J. D. Cannon, *McCloud;* NBC Sunday Mystery Movie (NBC)

OUTSTANDING CONTINUING OR SINGLE PERFORMANCE BY A SUPPORTING ACTOR IN VARIETY OR MUSIC (for a continuing role in a regular or limited series; or a one-time appearance in a series; or a special)

Jack Albertson, *Cher.* Shown March 2, 1975 (CBS)
Tim Conway, *The Carol Burnett Show.* Shown November 23, 1974 (CBS)
John Denver, *Doris Day Today.* Shown February 19, 1975 (CBS)

OUTSTANDING SINGLE PERFORMANCE BY A SUPPORTING ACTOR IN A COMEDY OR DRAMA SPECIAL

Anthony Quale, *QB VII, Parts 1 & 2;* ABC Movie Special. Shown April 29 & 30, 1974 (ABC)
Ralph Bellamy, *The Missiles Of October,* ABC Theatre. Shown December 18, 1974 (ABC)
Trevor Howard, *The Count of Monte Cristo;* Bell System Family Theatre. Shown January 10, 1975 (NBC)
Jack Hawkins, *QB VII, Parts 1 &2;* ABC Movie Special. Shown April 29 & 30, 1974 (ABC)

OUTSTANDING SINGLE PERFORMANCE BY A SUPPORTING ACTOR IN A COMEDY OR DRAMA SERIES (for one-time appearance in a regular or limited series)

Patrick McGoohan, *By Dawn's Early Light;* Columbo; NBC Sunday Mystery Movie. Shown October 27, 1974 (NBC)
Lew Ayres, *The Vanishing Image;* Kung Fu. Shown December 20, 1974 (ABC)
Harold Gould, *Fathers And Sons;* Police

Story. Shown October 1, 1974 (NBC)
Harry Morgan, *The General Flipped At Dawn;* M*A*S*H. Shown September 10, 1974 (CBS)

OUTSTANDING CONTINUING PERFORMANCE BY A SUPPORTING ACTRESS IN A COMEDY SERIES (for a regular or limited series)

★Betty White, *The Mary Tyler Moore Show* (CBS)
Julie Kavner, *Rhoda* (CBS)
Nancy Walker, *Rhoda* (CBS)
Loretta Swit, *M*A*S*H* (CBS)

OUTSTANDING CONTINUING PERFORMANCE BY A SUPPORTING ACTRESS IN A DRAMA SERIES (for a regular or limited series)

★Ellen Corby, *The Waltons* (CBS)
Nancy Walker, *McMillan & Wife;* NBC Sunday Mystery Movie (NBC)
Angela Baddeley, *Upstairs, Downstairs;* Masterpiece Theatre (PBS)

OUTSTANDING CONTINUING OR SINGLE PERFORMANCE BY A SUPPORTING ACTRESS IN VARIETY OR MUSIC (for a continuing role in a regular or limited series; or a one-time appearance in a series; or a special)

★Cloris Leachman, Cher; shown March 2, 1975 (CBS)
Rita Moreno, Out To Lunch; shown December 10, 1974 (ABC)
Vicki Lawrence, The Carol Burnett Show; shown November 9, 1974 (CBS)

OUTSTANDING SINGLE PERFORMANCE BY A SUPPORTING ACTRESS IN A COMEDY OR DRAMA SPECIAL

★Juliet Mills, *QB VII – Parts 1 & 2,* ABC Movie Special; shown April 29 & 30, 1974 (ABC)
Charlotte Rae, *Queen Of The Stardust Ballroom;* shown February 13, 1975 (CBS)
Lee Remick, *QB VII – Parts 1 & 2;* ABC Movie Special; shown April 29 & 30, 1974 (ABC)
Eileen Heckart, *Wedding Band;* ABC Theatre; shown April 24, 1974 (ABC)

OUTSTANDING SINGLE PERFORMANCE BY A SUPPORTING ACTRESS IN A COMEDY OR DRAMA SERIES (for a one-time appearance in a regular or limited series)

★Cloris Leachman, *Phyllis Whips Inflation;* The Mary Tyler Moore Show; shown January 18, 1975 (CBS)

★ Zohra Lampert, *Queen Of The Gypsies,* Kojak; shown January 19, 1975 (CBS)

Shelley Winters, *The Barefoot Girls of Bleecker Street;* McCloud; NBC Sunday Mystery Movie; shown September 22, 1974 (NBC)

OUTSTANDING DIRECTING IN A DRAMA SERIES (for a single episode of a regular or limited series with continuing characters and/or theme)

★Bill Bain, *A Sudden Storm;* Upstairs, Downstairs; Masterpiece Theatre; shown December 22, 1974 (PBS)

Harry Falk, *The Mask Of Death;* The Streets Of San Francisco; shown October 3, 1974 (ABC)

David Friedkin, *Cross Your Heart And Hope To Die;* Kojak; shown December 1, 1974 (CBS)

Telly Savalas, *I Want To Report A Dream . . .;* Kojak; shown March 9, 1975 (CBS)

Glenn Jordan, *The Ambassador;* Benjamin Franklin; shown November 21, 1974 (CBS)

OUTSTANDING DIRECTING IN A COMEDY SERIES (for a single episode of a regular or limited series with continuing characters and/or theme)

★Gene Reynolds, *O.R.;* M*A*S*H; shown October 8, 1974 (CBS)

Hy Averback, *Alcoholics Unanimous;* M*A*S*H; shown November 12, 1974 (CBS)

Alan Alda, *Bulletin Board;* M*A*S*H; shown January 14, 1975 (CBS)

OUTSTANDING DIRECTING IN A COMEDY-VARIETY OR MUSIC SERIES (for a single episode of a regular or limited series)

★Dave Powers, *The Carol Burnett Show* (with Alan Alda); shown December 21, 1974 (CBS)

Art Fisher, *Cher* (with Bette Midler, Flip Wilson and Elton John); shown February 12, 1975 (CBS)

OUTSTANDING DIRECTING IN A COMEDY-VARIETY OR MUSIC SPECIAL

★Bill Davis, *An Evening With John Denver* shown March 10, 1975 (ABC)

Robert Scheerer, *Shirley MacLaine; If T. Could See Me Now;* shown Novembe 28, 1974 (CBS)

Dwight Hemion, *Ann-Margret Olsson;* shown January 23, 1975 (NBC)

OUTSTANDING DIRECTING IN A SPECIAL PROGRAM — DRAMA OR COMEDY

★George Cukor, *Love Among The Ruins;* ABC Theatre; shown March 6, 1975 (ABC)

John Badham, *The Law;* NBC World Premiere Movie; shown October 22, 1974 (NBC)

Sam O'Steen, *Queen Of The Stardust Ballroom;* shown February 13, 1975 (CBS)

Tom Gries, *QB VII – Parts 1 & 2;* ABC Movie Special; shown April 29 & 30, 1974 (ABC)

Anthony Page, *The Missiles Of October,* ABC Theatre; shown December 18, 1ᵗ (ABC)

OUTSTANDING WRITING IN A DRAMA SERIES (for a single epis₠ of a regular or limited series with continuing characters and/or theme

★Howard Fast, *The Ambassador;* Benjami Franklin; shown November 21, 1974 (CBS)

Robert Collins, *Robbery: 48 Hours;* Poli₠ Story; shown September 24, 1974 (NB

Alfred Shaughnessy, *Miss Forrest;* Upstairs, Downstairs; Masterpiece Theatre; shown November 3, 1974 (P▶

Loring Mandel, *The Whirlwind;* Benjami₠ Franklin; shown December 17, 1974 (CBS)

John Hawkesworth, *The Bolter;* Upstairs Downstairs; Masterpiece Theatre; sho▶ December 22, 1974 (PBS)

OUTSTANDING WRITING IN A COMEDY SERIES (for a single episode of a regular or limited serie with continuing characters and/or theme)

★Ed Weinberger and Stan Daniels, *Mary Richards Goes To Jail;* The Mary Tyl₠ Moore Show; shown September 14, 1₠ (CBS)

David Lloyd, *Lou And That Woman;* Th▶ Mary Tyler Moore Show; shown October 5, 1974 (CBS)

Norman Barasch, Carroll Moore, David Lloyd, Lorenzo Music, Allan Burns, James L. Brooks and David Davis, *Rhoda's Wedding;* Rhoda; shown October 28, 1974 (CBS)

OUTSTANDING WRITING IN A COMEDY-VARIETY OR MUSIC SERIES (for a single episode of a regular or limited series)

★Ed Simmons, Gary Belkin, Roger Beatty, Arnie Kogen, Bill Richmond, Gene Perret, Rudy DeLuca, Barry Levinson, Dick Clair and Jenna McMahon, *The Carol Burnett Show* (with Alan Alda); shown December 21, 1974 (CBS)

Digby Wolfe, Don Reo, Alan Katz, Iris Rainer, David Panich, Ron Pearlman, Nick Arnold, John Boni, Ray Taylor and George Schlatter, *Cher* (with Raquel Welch, Tatum O'Neal and Wayne Rogers); shown February 16, 1975 (CBS)

OUTSTANDING WRITING IN A COMEDY-VARIETY OR MUSIC SPECIAL

★Bob Wells, John Bradford and Cy Coleman, *Shirley MacLaine: If They Could See Me Now;* shown November 28, 1974 (CBS)

Sybil Adelman, Barbara Gallagher, Gloria Banta, Pat Nardo, Stuart Birnbaum, Matt Neuman, Lorne Michaels, Marilyn Miller, Earl Pomerantz, Rosie Ruthchild, Lily Tomlin and Jane Wagner, *Lily;* shown February 21, 1975 (ABC)

OUTSTANDING WRITING IN A SPECIAL PROGRAM — DRAMA OR COMEDY — ORIGINAL TELEPLAY

★James Costigan, *Love Among The Ruins;* ABC Theatre; shown March 6, 1975 (ABC)

Jerome Kass, *Queen Of The Stardust Ballroom;* shown February 13, 1975 (CBS)

Stanley R. Greenberg, *The Missiles Of October;* ABC Theatre; shown December 18, 1974 (ABC)

Fay Kanin, *Hustling;* Special World Premiere ABC Saturday Night Movie; shown February 22, 1975 (ABC)

Joel Oliansky, Story by William Sackheim and Joel Oliansky; *The Law;* NBC World Premiere Movie; shown October 22, 1974 (NBC)

OUTSTANDING WRITING IN A SPECIAL PROGRAM — DRAMA OR COMEDY — ADAPTATION

★David W. Rintels, *IBM Presents Clarence Darrow;* shown September 4, 1974 (NBC)

Edward Anhalt, *QB VII – Parts 1 & 2;* ABC Movie Special; shown April 29 & 30, 1974 (ABC)

OUTSTANDING ACHIEVEMENT IN CHOREOGRAPHY (for a single episode of a series or a special program)

★Marge Champion, *Queen Of The Stardust Ballroom;* shown February 13, 1975 (CBS)

Alan Johnson, *Shirley MacLaine: If They Could See Me Now;* shown November 28, 1974 (CBS)

Dee Dee Wood, *Cher* (with Freddie Prinze and The Pointer Sisters); shown March 9, 1975 (CBS)

OUTSTANDING ACHIEVEMENT IN MUSIC COMPOSITION FOR A SERIES (for dramatic underscore for a single episode of a regular or limited series)

★Billy Goldenberg, *The Rebel;* Benjamin Franklin; shown January 9, 1975 (CBS)

Pat Williams, *One Last Shot;* The Streets Of San Francisco; shown September 12, 1974 (ABC)

OUTSTANDING ACHIEVEMENT IN MUSIC COMPOSITION FOR A SPECIAL (for dramatic underscore)

★Jerry Goldsmith, *QB VII – Parts 1 & 2;* ABC Movie Special; shown April 29 & 30, 1974 (ABC)

Billy Goldenberg, Alan and Marilyn Bergman; *Queen Of The Stardust Ballroom;* shown February 13, 1975(CBS)

OUTSTANDING ACHIEVEMENT IN ART DIRECTION OR SCENIC DESIGN (for a single episode of a comedy, drama or limited series)

★Charles Lisanby, Art Director; Robert Checchi, Set Decorator; *The Ambassador;* Benjamin Franklin; shown November 21, 1974 (CBS)

Michael Baugh, Art Director; Jerry Adams, Set Decorator; *Playback; Columbo;* NBC Sunday Mystery Movie; shown March 2, 1975 (NBC)

OUTSTANDING ACHIEVEMENT IN ART DIRECTION OR SCENIC DESIGN (for a single episode of a comedy-variety or music series; or a comedy-variety or music special)

★Robert Kelly, Art Director; Robert Checchi, Set Decorator; *Cher* (with Bette Midler, Flip Wilson and Elton John); shown February 12, 1975 (CBS) Ken Johnson and Dwight Jackson, Art Directors; *An Evening With John Denver;* shown March 10, 1975 (ABC)

OUTSTANDING ACHIEVEMENT IN ART DIRECTION OR SCENIC DESIGN (for a dramatic special or a feature length film made for television)

★Carmen Dillon, Art Director; Tessa Davies, Set Decorator; *Love Among The Ruins;* ABC Theatre; shown March 6, 1975 (ABC)

Jack DeShields, Art Director; Harry Gordon, Set Decorator; *The Legend Of Lizzie Borden;* Special World Premiere; ABC Monday Night Movie; shown February 10, 1975 (ABC)

Ross Bellah and Maurice Fowler, Art Directors; Audrey Blesdel-Goddard and Terry Parr, Set Decorators; *QB VII – Parts 1 & 2;* ABC Movie Special; shown April 29 & 30, 1974 (ABC)

OUTSTANDING ACHIEVEMENT IN GRAPHIC DESIGN AND TITLE SEQUENCES (for a single episode of a series; or for a special program. This includes animation only when created for use in titling)

★Phill Norman, *QB VII – Parts 1 & 2;* ABC Movie Special; shown April 29 & 30, 1974 (ABC)

Rick Andreoli, *The Tonight Show Starring Johnny Carson;* shown November 12, 1974 (NBC)

Susan Cuscuna, *The Tonight Show Starring Johnny Carson;* shown December 10, 1974 (NBC)

OUTSTANDING ACHIEVEMENT IN CINEMATOGRAPHY FOR ENTERTAINMENT PROGRAMMING FOR A SERIES (for a single episode of a regular or limited series)

★Richard C. Glouner, A.S.C., *Playback; Columbo;* NBC Sunday Mystery Movie; shown March 2, 1975 (NBC)

William Jurgensen, *Bombed;* M*A*S*H; shown January 7, 1975 (CBS)

Vilis Lapenieks, A.S.C. and Sol Negrin, A.S.C., *Wall Street Gunslinger;* Kojak; shown October 6, 1974 (CBS)

OUTSTANDING ACHIEVEMENT IN CINEMATOGRAPHY FOR ENTERTAINMENT PROGRAMMING FOR A SPECIAL (for a special or feature length program made for television)

★David M. Walsh, *Queen Of The Stardust Ballroom;* shown February 13, 1975 (CBS)

Howard Schwartz, A.S.C., *Sad Figure, Laughing;* Sandburg's Lincoln; shown February 12, 1975 (NBC)

Paul Beeson and Robert L. Morrison, *QB VII – Parts 1 & 2;* ABC Movie Special; shown April 29 & 30, 1974 (ABC)

Michael Chapman, *Death Be Not Proud;* Tuesday Movie of the Week; shown February 4, 1975 (ABC)

OUTSTANDING FILM EDITING FOR ENTERTAINMENT PROGRAMMING FOR A SERIES (for a single episode of a comedy series)

★Douglas Hines, *An Affair To Forget;* The Mary Tyler Moore Show; shown December 21, 1974 (CBS)

Stanford Tischler and Fred W. Berger, *The General Flipped At Dawn;* M*A*S*H; shown September 10, 1974 (CBS)

OUTSTANDING FILM EDITING FOR ENTERTAINMENT PROGRAMMING FOR A SPECIAL (for a special or film made for television)

★John A. Martinelli, A.C.E., *The Legend Of Lizzie Borden;* Special World Premiere; ABC Monday Night Movie; shown February 10, 1975 (ABC)

★ Byron "Buzz" Brandt and Irving C. Rosenblum, *QB VII – Parts 1 & 2;* ABC Movie Special; shown April 29 & 30, 1974 (ABC)

Jerry Young, *Attack on Terror: The FBI Versus The Ku Klux Klan;* Parts 1 & 2; shown February 20 & 21, 1975 (CBS)

OUTSTANDING FILM EDITING FOR ENTERTAINMENT PROGRAMMING FOR A SPECIAL (for a special or film made for television)

★John A. Martinelli, A.C.E., *The Legend Of Lizzie Borden;* Special World Premiere; ABC Monday Night Movie; shown February 10, 1975 (ABC)

★ Byron "Buzz" Brandt and Irving C. Rosenblum, *QB VII – Parts 1 & 2;* ABC Movie Special; shown April 29 & 30, 1974 (ABC)

Jerry Young, *Attack on Terror: The FBI Versus The Ku Klux Klan;* Parts 1 & 2; shown February 20 & 21, 1975 (CBS)

OUTSTANDING ACHIEVEMENT IN FILM SOUND EDITING (for a single episode of a regular or limited series; or for a special program)

★Marvin I. Kosberg, Richard Burrow, Milton C. Burrow, Jack Milner, Ronald Ashcroft, James Ballas, Josef Von Stroheim, Jerry Rosenthal, William Andrews, Edward Sandlin, David Horton, Alvin Kajita, Tony Garber, and Jeremy Hoenack, *QB VII – Parts 1 & 2;* ABC Movie Special; shown April 29 & 30, 1974 (ABC)

Donald Isaacs, Don Higgins, Larry Kaufman, Jack Kirschner, Dick LeGrand, Gary Vaughan, Gene Wahrman, Frank White, and Harold Wooley, *The Legend Of Lizzie Borden;* Special World Premiere; ABC Monday Night Movie; shown February 10, 1975 (ABC)

OUTSTANDING ACHIEVEMENT IN FILM OR TAPE SOUND MIXING (for a single episode of a regular or limited series; or for a special program)

★Marshall King, *The American Film Institute Salute to James Cagney;* shown March 18, 1974 (CBS)

Doug Nelson, *The Missiles Of October;* ABC Theatre; shown December 18, 1974 (ABC)

Doug Nelson and Norm Schwartz, *California Jam;* Wide World In Concert, shown May 10, 1974 (ABC)

OUTSTANDING ACHIEVEMENT IN VIDEO TAPE EDITING (for a single episode of a regular or limited series; or for a special program)

★Gary Anderson and Jim McElroy, *Judgment: The Court-Martial Of Lt. William Calley;* ABC Theatre; shown January 12, 1975 (ABC)

Nick V. Giordano and George Gurunian, *California Jam;* Wide World In Concert; shown May 10, 1974 (ABC)

Jerry Greene, *The Missiles Of October;* ABC Theatre; shown December 18, 1974 (ABC)

OUTSTANDING ACHIEVEMENT IN TECHNICAL DIRECTION AND ELECTRONIC CAMERAWORK (for a single episode of a regular or limited series; or for a special program)

★Ernie Buttelman, Technical Director; Jim Angel, Jim Balden, Ron Brooks, and Art LaCombe, Cameramen; *The Missiles Of October;* ABC Theatre; shown December 18, 1974 (ABC)

Heino Ripp, Technical Director; Jon Olson, Bob Keys, John James, and Kurt Tonnessen, Cameramen; *IBM Presents Clarence Darrow;* shown September 4, 1974 (NBC)

Heino Ripp, and Lou Fusari, Technical Directors; Roy Holm, Tony Yarlett, Rick Lombardo, Bob Keys, and Ray Figelski, Cameramen; *The Perry Como Christmas Show;* shown December 17, 1974 (CBS)

OUTSTANDING ACHIEVEMENT IN LIGHTING DIRECTION (for a single episode of a regular or limited series, or for a special program)

★John Freschi, *The Perry Como Christmas Show;* shown December 17, 1974 (CBS)

Lon Stucky, *IBM Presents Clarence Darrow;* shown September 4, 1974 (NBC)

OUTSTANDING CHILDREN'S SPECIAL (for specials which were broadcast during the evening)

★*Yes, Virginia, There Is a Santa Claus* Burt Rosen, Executive Producer; Bill Melendez and Mort Green, Producers; shown December 6, 1974 (ABC)

Be My Valentine, Charlie Brown Lee Mendelson, Executive Producer; Bill Melendez, Producer; shown January 28, 1975 (CBS)

Dr. Seuss' The Hoober-Bloob Highway David H. DePatie, Executive Producer; Friz Freleng and Ted Geisel, Producers; shown February 19, 1975 (CBS)

It's The Easter Beagle, Charlie Brown Lee Mendelson, Executive Producer; Bill Melendez, Producer; shown April 9, 1974 (CBS)

OUTSTANDING SPORTS EVENT (which, when broadcast, was not edited)

★*Jimmy Connors vs. Rod Laver Tennis Challenge* Frank Chirkinian, Executive Producer; shown February 2, 1975 (CBS)

NFL Monday Night Football Roone Arledge, Executive Producer; Don Ohlmeyer, Producer; shown September 16, 1974 (ABC)

NCAA Football Roone Arledge, Executive Producer; Chuck Howard, Producer; shown September 7, 1974 (ABC)

ABC Championship Golf Roone Arledge, Executive Producer; Chuck Howard, Producer; shown May 4, 1974 (ABC)

NBA Championship Game Chuck Milton, Producer; shown May 10, 1974 (CBS)

National Football League Game – Washington vs. Dallas Chuck Milton and Tom O'Neill, Producers; shown November 28, 1974 (CBS)

Jackie Gleason Inverrary Classic John Koushouris, Executive Producer; Joe O'Rourke and Herb Kaplan, Producers; Shown March 1 & 2, 1975 (HTN)

Andy Williams San Diego Open John Koushouris, Producer; Shown February 15 & 16, 1975 (HTN)

Madison Square Garden Events Jack Simon, Producer; Shown September, 1974; March, 1975 (HTN)

1974 World Series Scotty Connal, Executive Producer; Roy Hammerman, Producer; Shown October 12–17, 1974 (NBC)

NBC Monday Night Baseball Scotty Connal, Executive Producer; Roy Hammerman, Producer; Shown April 8, 1974 (NBC)

AFC Football Playoffs Scotty Connal, Executive Producer; Don Ellis and Ted Nathanson, Producers; Shown December 21, 1974 (NBC)

Spalding International Mixed Doubles Tennis Championship Ron Devillier, Executive Producer; Renate Cole, Producer; Shown January 4–5, 1975 (PBS)

National Bicycle Track Championships Alf Steele, Executive Producer; Shown July 31–August 3, 1974 (PBS)

ATP Summer Tennis Tour Greg Harney, Executive Producer; Shown July 22–August 12, 1974 (PBS)

World Football League Championship Edward Einhorn, Executive Producer; Joe Gallagher, Producer; Shown December 5, 1974 (TVS)

UCLA-Notre Dame Basketball Edward Einhorn, Executive Producer; Howard Zuckerman, Producer; Shown January 25, 1975 (TVS)

NCAA Basketball Edward Einhorn, Executive Producer; Howard Zuckerman, Producer; Shown March 20, 1975 (TVS)

OUTSTANDING SPORTS PROGRAM (for a program which, when broadcast, contained edited segments)

★*Wide World Of Sports* Roone Arledge, Executive Producer; Doug Wilson, Ned Steckel, Dennis Lewin, John Martin and Chet Forte, Producers; Shown April 14, 1974 (ABC)

The Superstars Roone Arledge, Executive Producer; Don Ohlmeyer, Producer; Shown January 5, 1975 (ABC)

The American Sportsman Roone Arledge, Executive Producer; Neil Cunningham, Pat Smith, Curt Gowdy, Bob Duncan, Neil Goodwin, Producers; Shown April 28, 1974 (ABC)

CBS Sports Spectacular Frank Chirkinian, Executive Producer; Perry Smith, Producer; Shown March 2, 1975 (CBS)

NFL On CBS William Fitts, Executive Producer; Tom O'Neill, Producer; Shown December 1, 1974 (CBS)

NBA On CBS Perry Smith and Chuck Milton, Producers; Shown March 9, 1975 (CBS)

The Baseball World of Joe Garagiola, Gates Brown — Parts 1 & 2; Joe Garagiola, Executive Producer; Don Ellis, Producer; Shown July 8 & 15, 1974 (NBC)

The Baseball World of Joe Garagiola Old Ball Parks; Joe Garagiola, Executive Producer; Don Ellis, Producer; Shown May 27, 1974 (NBC)

Super Bowl IX Pre-Game Show Scotty Connal, Executive Producer; Dick Auerbach, Producer; Shown January 12, 1975 (NBC)

The Way It Was Gerry Gross, Executive Producer; Shown October 3–December 26, 1975 (PBS)

Victor Awards, David Marmel, Executive Producer; Lou Rudolph, Producer; Shown June 13, 1974 (TVS)

USA-China Basketball Highlights Edward Einhorn, Executive Producer; Howard Zuckerman, Producer; Shown January 25, 1975 (TVS)

OUTSTANDING SPORTS BROADCASTER

★Jim McKay, *Wide World Of Sports;* Shown April 14, 1974 (ABC)

Howard Cosell, *Monday Night Football;* Shown September 16, 1974 (ABC)

Keith Jackson, *NCAA Football;* Shown September 7, 1974 (ABC)

Frank Gifford, *Monday Night Football;* Shown September 16, 1974 (ABC)

Chris Schenkel, *ABC Championship Golf;* Shown May 4, 1974 (ABC)

Vin Scully, *Jimmy Connors Vs. Rod Laver Tennis Challenge;* Shown February 2, 1975 (CBS)

Pat Summerall, *NFL Football* (CBS)

Brent Musburger, *NBA Basketball* (CBS)

Jack Whitaker, *NBA All Star Game;* Shown January 14, 1975 (CBS)

Ken Squier, *CBS Sports Spectacular;* Shown July 21, 1974 (CBS)
Curt Gowdy, *AFC Football Playoffs;* Shown December 21, 1974 (NBC)
Don Meredith, *Super Bowl IX;* Shown January 12, 1975 (NBC)
Joe Garagiola, *The Baseball World of Joe Garagiola;* Gates Brown — Parts 1 & 2; Shown July 8 & 15, 1975 (NBC)
Jim Simpson, *Wimbledon Tennis;* Shown July 6, 1974 (NBC)

Tim Ryan, *1974 Stanley Cup Playoffs;* Shown May 19, 1974 (NBC)
Budd Collins, *Spalding International Mixed Doubles Tennis Championship;* Shown January 4–5, 1975 (PBS)
Judy Dixon, *Spalding International Mixed Doubles Tennis Championship;* Shown January 4–5, 1975 (PBS)
Curt Gowdy, *The Way It Was;* Shown October 3– December 26, 1975 (PBS)

THE AREAS

SPECIAL CLASSIFICATION OF OUTSTANDING PROGRAM AND INDIVIDUAL ACHIEVEMENT (An Award for unique program and individual achievements, which does not fall into a specific category, or is not otherwise recognized)

★*The American Film Institute Salute To James Cagney* George Stevens, Jr., Executive Producer; Paul W. Keyes, Producer; Shown March 18, 1974 (CBS)
The American Film Institute Salute To Orson Welles George Stevens, Jr., Executive Producer; Paul W. Keyes, Producer; Shown February 17, 1975 (CBS)
★ Alistair Cooke, Host, *Masterpiece Theatre;* Series (PBS)
The Dick Cavett Show, John Gilroy, Producer; Dick Cavett, Star; Series (ABC)
That's Entertainment: 50 Years Of MGM ABC Wide World of Entertainment; Jack Haley, Jr., Executive Producer; Jimmie Baker, Producer; Shown May 29, 1974 (ABC)
86th Annual Pasadena Tournament Of Roses Parade Dick Schneider, Producer; Shown January 1, 1975 (NBC)
Tom Snyder, Host, *Tomorrow;* Series (NBC)
Jack Stewart, Art Director; John Hueners, Set Decorator, *Bicentennial Minutes;* Series (CBS)

OUTSTANDING ACHIEVEMENT IN SPECIAL MUSICAL MATERIAL (for a song (which must have both music and lyrics), a theme for a series, or special material for a variety program providing the first usage of this material was written expressly for television)

★Alan and Marilyn Bergman, and Billy Goldenberg, *Queen Of The Stardust Ballroom;* Shown February 13, 1975 (CBS)
★ Cy Coleman and Bob Wells, *Shirley MacLaine: If They Could See Me Now;* Shown November 28, 1974 (CBS)
Morton Stevens, *Police Woman;* Theme; Series (NBC)
Earl Brown and Billy Barnes; *Cher* (with Bette Midler, Flip Wilson and Elton John); Shown February 12, 1975 (CBS)
Jose Feliciano and Janna Merlyn Feliciano; *Chico and The Man;* Theme; Series (NBC)

OUTSTANDING ACHIEVEMENT IN COSTUME DESIGN (for a single episode of a series; of for a special program)

★Guy Verhille, *The Legend Of Lizzie Borden;* Special World Premiere; ABC Monday Night Movie; Shown February 10, 1975 (ABC)
★ Margaret Furse, *Love Among The Ruins;* ABC Theatre; Shown March 6, 1975 (ABC)
Bruce Walkup, *Queen Of the Stardust Ballroom;* Shown February 13, 1975 (CBS)
Bob Mackie, *Cher* (with Bette Midler, Flip Wilson and Elton John); Shown February 12, 1975 (CBS)
Ret Turner, *The Sonny Comedy Revue* (with McLean Stevenson and Joey Heatherton); Shown September 29, 1974 (ABC)

OUTSTANDING ACHIEVEMENT IN MAKE-UP (for a single episode of a series; or for a special program)

Harry Blake, Stan Winston, Jim Kail, Ralph Gulko, Bob Ostermann, Tom Cole and Larry Abbott; *Masquerade Party* (SYNDICATED)

Mark R. Bussan, *The Ambassador;*
Benjamin Franklin; Shown November
21, 1974 (CBS)
Dan Striepeke and John Chambers, *Twigs;*
Shown March 6, 1975 (CBS)

OUTSTANDING ACHIEVEMENT IN ANY AREA OF CREATIVE TECHNICAL CRAFTS (An Award for individual technical craft achievement which does not fall into a specific category, and is not otherwise recognized)

★Edie Panda, Hairstylist; *The Ambassador;*
Benjamin Franklin; Shown November
21, 1974 (CBS)
★ Doug Nelson and Norm Schwartz, *Wide World In Concert;* Double System Sound Editing and Synchronization For Stereophonic Broadcasting Of Television Programs; Series (ABC)
Larry Germain, Hairstylist; *If I Should Wake Before I Die;* Little House On The Prairie; Shown October 23, 1974 (NBC)

OUTSTANDING INDIVIDUAL ACHIEVEMENT IN SPORTS PROGRAMMING (for individuals who may be directors, writers, cinematographers, technical directors and electronic cameramen, sound mixers, film editors, video tape editors, lighting directors and graphic designers — for graphic design and title sequences)

★Gene Schwartz, Technical Director; *1974 World Series;* Shown October 12–17, 1974 (NBC)
★ Herb Altman, Film Editor; *The Baseball World Of Joe Garagiola;* Shown May 27, 1974 (NBC)
★ Corey Leible, Len Basile, Jack Bennett, Lou Gerard and Ray Figelski, Electronic Cameramen; *1974 Stanley Cup Playoffs;* Shown April 9–May 19, 1974 (NBC)
★ John Pumo, Charles D'Onofrio, Frank Florio, Technical Directors; George Klimcsak, Robert Kania, Harold Hoffmann, Herman Lang, George Drago, Walt Deniear, Stan Gould, Al Diamond, Charles Armstrong, Al Brantley, Sig Meyers, Frank McSpedon, George F. Naeder, James Murphy, James McCarthy, Vern Surphlis, Al Loreto, Gordon Sweeney, Jo Sidlo, William Hathaway, Gene Pescalek and Curly Fonarow, Cameramen; *Masters Tournament;* Shown April 13 & 14 1974 (CBS)

Larry Kamm, Lou Volpicelli, Brice Weisman, Ned Steckel, Andy Sidaris and Chet Forte, Directors; *Wide World of Sports;* Shown April 14, 1974 (ABC)
Werner Gunther, John Broderick and John Irvine, Technical Directors; Andy Armentani, Drew DeRosa, Jim Heneghan, John Morreale, Joe Nesi, Mike Rebich, Jack Hinnelfarb, Steve Ciliberto, Jesse Kohn, Joe Stefanoni, Stu Goodman, Joe Schiavo, Bob Hammond, Art Peffer, Dick Spanos, Art Ferrare, Gene Wood, Roy Hutchings, Bill Karvelas, Ronnie Sterckx, Joe Sapienza, Bob Wolfe, John Cronin, Carl Brown, Robert Copper, Dick Kerr, Mort Levin, Bob Bernstein, Jerry Doud and Jack Dorfman, Cameramen; *U.S. Open;* Shown June 14, 1974 (ABC)
William Morris and Werner Gunther, Technical Directors; Andy Armentani, Drew DeRosa, Jim Heneghan, John Morreale, Joe Nesi, Mike Rebich, Jack Himelfarb, Steve Ciliberto, Jesse Kohn, Joe Stefanoni, Stu Goodman, Joe Schiavo, Bill Sullivan, Steve Nikifor, Jack Dorfman and Bob Lopes, Cameramen; *Indianapolis 500;* Shown May 26, 1974 (ABC)
John Peterson and Tony Zaccaro, Film Editors; *Wide World Of Sports;* Shown April 14, 1974 (ABC)
John Croak, John DeLisa, Chester Pawlak, Marv Gench, Alex Moskovic, Jack Hierl, Tony Greco, Erskine Roberts, Art Volk and Harvey Beal, Video Tape Editors; *Wide World Of Sports;* Shown April 14, 1974 (ABC)
John Croak, John DeLisa, Art Volk, Ron Ackerman, Marv Gench, Alex Moskovic and Nick Mazur, Video Tape Editors; *The Superstars;* Shown January 5, 1975 (ABC)
Pat Smith, Writer; *The American Sportsman;* Shown April 28, 1974 (ABC)
Jack Simon, Director; *New York Mets Baseball* (HTN)
Jack O'Rourke, Director; *Professional Championship Golf;* Shown February–March 1975 (HTN)
Harry Coyle, Director; *1974 World Series;* Shown October 12–17, 1974 (NBC)
Ted Nathanson, Director; *AFC Football Playoffs;* Shown December 21, 1974 (NBC

Howard Neef and Barry Winnik, Cinematographers; *The Baseball World Of Joe Garagiola;* Gates Brown — Parts 1 & 2; Shown July 8 & 15, 1974 (NBC)
Murray Vecchio, Bill Tobey, Bill Rose, John O'Connor, Videotape (Slow Motion) Editors; *Orange Bowl;* Shown January 1, 1975 (NBC)

Sandy Bell, Frank Vilot, Chuck Franklin, Jim Angerami and John Burkhart, Technical Directors; Dick Douglas, George Klimcsak, Al Diamond, Frank McSpedon, John Lincoln, Phil Walsh, Stan Gould, Mike English, Robert Heller, David Graham, Walt Deniear, Robert Chandler, Harold Hoffman, Gene Savitt, Dave Levenson, George Erickson, Curly Fonarow, Tom McConnell, Fred Dansereau, Bob Faeth, George Drago, Jim Murphy, George F. Naeder, Jo Sokota, Pat McBride, Al Loreto, Dave Leavel, Jerry Weaver, Bob Chaney, Fred Schultz, Tony Butts, Danny Ireland, Cameramen; *NBA Basketball* (CBS)

Angelo J. Gulino, Bob Brown, Ed Dahlberg, Dick Ohldacker, Sam Lane, Tom Duffy and Frank Hicks, Sound Mixers; *NBA Basketball* (CBS)

Pete Reed, Sound Mixer; *Jimmy Connors Vs. Rod Laver Tennis Challenge* (CBS)

Sandy Grossman, Director; *NBA Basketball* (CBS)

Bob Dailey, Director; *Jimmy Connors Vs. Rod Laver Tennis Challenge;* Shown February 2, 1975 (CBS)

SPECIAL AWARDS

OUTSTANDING ACHIEVEMENT IN ENGINEERING DEVELOPMENT

★*Columbia Broadcasting System* for spearheading the development and realization of the Electronic News Gathering System

★ *Nippon Electric Company* for development of digital television Frame Synchronizers Citation to *The Society Of Motion Picture* *And Television Engineers* for the technical development of the Universal Video Tape Time Code

TRUSTEES AWARDS

★Elmer Lower, Vice President, Corporate Affairs, American Broadcasting Companies, Inc.

★ Dr. Peter Goldmark, President, Goldmark Laboratories, Stamford, Connecticut

THE NATIONAL AWARD FOR COMMUNITY SERVICE

Awards Presented April 7, 1975

★*The Willowbrook Case: The People Vs. The State Of New York* WABC-TV, New York, New York

Breast Surgery: Rebirth Or Betrayal WXYZ-TV, Detroit, Michigan

Focus 30 KYTV, Springfield, Missouri

Grandpeople WPBT (Educational Station), No. Miami, Florida

The Occupant In The Single Room WNET (Educational Station), New York, New York

Senality, A State Of Mind KSL, Salt Lake City, Utah

Smoke And Steel WKY-TV, Oklahoma City, Oklahoma

Trouble In The Ghetto WAGA-TV, Atlanta, Georgia

Why Me? KNXT, Los Angeles, California

Without Fear WKYC-TV, Cleveland, Ohio

DAYTIME PROGRAM AND INDIVIDUAL ACHIEVEMENTS

OUTSTANDING DAYTIME DRAMA SERIES

★*The Young and the Restless* John J. Conboy, Producer; William J. Bell and Lee Phillip Bell, Creators (CBS)

Days of Our Lives Mrs. Ted Corday, Executive Producer; Ted Corday, Irna Phillips and Allan Chase, Creators; Jack Herzberg, Producer (NBC)

Another World Paul Rauch, Executive Producer; Joe Rothenberger and Mary E. Bonner, Producers; Irna Phillips and William J. Bell, Creators (NBC)

OUTSTANDING DAYTIME DRAMA SPECIAL

★*The Girl Who Couldn't Lose* ABC Afternoon Playbreak; Ira Barmak, Executive Producer; Lila Garrett, Producer; Shown February 13, 1975 (ABC)

The Last Bride Of Salem ABC Afternoon Playbreak; Robert Michael Lewis, Executive Producer; George Paris, Producer; Shown May 8, 1974 (ABC)

OUTSTANDING GAME OR AUDIENCE PARTICIPATION SHOW

★*Hollywood Squares* Merrill Heatter and Bob Quigley, Executive Producers; Jay Redack, Producer (NBC)

The $10,000 Pyramid Bob Stewart, Executive Producer; Anne Marie Schmitt, Producer (ABC)

Jeopardy! Robert H. Rubin, Executive Producer; Lynette Williams, Producer (NBC)

Let's Make A Deal Stefan Hatos, Exceuive Producer; Alan Gilbert, Producer (ABC)

OUTSTANDING TALK, SERVICE OR VARIETY SERIES

★*Dinah!* Henry Jaffe and Carolyn Raskin, Executive Producers; Fred Tatashore, Producer (SYNDICATED)

The Mike Douglas Show Jack Reilly, Executive Producer; Woody Fraser, Producer (SYNDICATED)

Today Stuart Schulberg, Executive Producer; Douglas P. Sinsel and Gene Farinet, Producers (NBC)

OUTSTANDING ENTERTAINMENT CHILDREN'S SPECIAL

★*Harlequin* The CBS Festival Of Lively Arts For Young People; Edward Villella, Executive Producer; Gardner Compton, Producer; Shown April 10, 1974 (CBS)

Ailey Celebrates Ellington The CBS Festival Of Lively Arts For Young People; Herman Krawitz, Executive Producer; Bob Weiner, Producer; Shown November 28, 1974 (CBS)

What Makes A Gershwin Tune A Gershwin Tune? New York Philharmonic Young People's Concert; Roger Englander, Producer; Shown September 29, 1974 (CBS)

OUTSTANDING ENTERTAINMENT CHILDREN'S SERIES

★*Star Trek* Lou Scheimer and Norm Prescott, Producers (NBC)

Captain Kangaroo Jimmy Hirshfeld, Producer (CBS)

The Pink Panther David H. DePatie and Friz Freleng, Producers (NBC)

OUTSTANDING ACTOR IN A DAYTIME DRAMA SERIES

★Macdonald Carey, *Days Of Our Lives* (NBC)

John Beradino, *General Hospital* (ABC)

Bill Hayes, *Days Of Our Lives* (NBC)

OUTSTANDING ACTOR IN A DAYTIME DRAMA SPECIAL

★Bradford Dillman, *The Last Bride Of Salem;* ABC Afternoon Playbreak; Shown May 8, 1974 (ABC)

Jack Carter, *The Girl Who Couldn't Lose;* ABC Afternoon Playbreak; Shown February 13, 1975 (ABC)

Bert Convy, *Oh! Baby, Baby, Baby . . .;* ABC Afternoon Playbreak; Shown December 5, 1974 (ABC)

OUTSTANDING ACTRESS IN A DAYTIME DRAMA SERIES

★Susan Flannery, *Days Of Our Lives* (NBC)

Rachel Ames, *General Hospital* (ABC)

Susan Seaforth, *Days Of Our Lives* (NBC)

Ruth Warrick, *All My Children* (ABC)

OUTSTANDING ACTRESS IN A DAYTIME DRAMA SPECIAL

★Kay Lenz, *Heart In Hiding;* ABC Afternoon Playbreak; Shown November 14, 1974 (ABC)

Diane Baker, *Can I Save My Children?,* ABC Afternoon Playbreak; Shown October 17, 1974 (ABC)

Julie Kavner, *The Girl Who Couldn't Lose;* ABC Afternoon Playbreak; Shown February 13, 1975 (ABC)

Lois Nettleton, *The Last Bride Of Salem;* ABC Afternoon Playbreak; Shown May 8, 1974 (ABC)

OUTSTANDING HOST IN A GAME OR AUDIENCE PARTICIPATION SHOW

★Peter Marshall, *The Hollywood Squares* (NBC)

Monty Hall, *Let's Make A Deal* (ABC)

Gene Rayburn, *Match Game '75* (CBS)

OUTSTANDING HOST OR HOSTESS IN A TALK, SERVICE OR VARIETY SERIES

★Barbara Walters, *Today* (NBC)

Mike Douglas, *The Mike Douglas Show* (SYNDICATED)

Dinah Shore, *Dinah!* (SYNDICATED)

Jim Hartz, *Today* (NBC)

OUTSTANDING INDIVIDUAL DIRECTOR FOR A DAYTIME DRAMA SERIES (for a single episode)

★Richard Dunlap, *The Young and The Restless;* Shown November 25, 1974 (CBS)

Ira Cirker, *Another World;* Shown May 3, 1974 (NBC)

Joseph Behar, *Days Of Our Lives;* Shown November 20, 1974 (NBC)

OUTSTANDING INDIVIDUAL DIRECTOR FOR A DAYTIME SPECIAL PROGRAM

★Mort Lachman, *The Girl Who Couldn't Lose;* ABC Afternoon Playbreak; Shown February 13, 1975 (ABC)

Walter C. Miller, *Can I Save My Children?,* ABC Afternoon Playbreak; Shown October 17, 1974 (ABC)

OUTSTANDING INDIVIDUAL DIRECTOR FOR A GAME OR AUDIENCE PARTICIPATION SHOW (for a single episode)

★Jerome Shaw, *The Hollywood Squares;* Shown October 28, 1974 (NBC)

Joseph Behar, *Let's Make A Deal;* Shown March 6, 1975 (ABC)

OUTSTANDING INDIVIDUAL DIRECTOR FOR A DAYTIME VARIETY PROGRAM (for a single episode)

★Glen Swanson, *Dinah!;* Dinah Salutes Broadway (with Ethel Merman, Bobby Morse, Michelle Lee, Phil Silvers and Jack Cassidy) (SYNDICATED)

Dick Carson, *The Merv Griffin Show* (with Robert Goulet, Louis Prima and Shecky Greene) (SYNDICATED)

OUTSTANDING WRITING FOR A DAYTIME DRAMA SERIES (for a single episode of a series; or for the entire series)

★Harding Lemay, Tom King, Charles Kozloff, Jan Merlin and Douglas Marland, *Another World;* Series (NBC)

William J. Bell, *The Young and The Restless;* Shown October 22, 1974 (CBS)

William J. Bell, Pat Falken Smith and Bill Rega; *Days Of Our Lives;* Shown November 21, 1974 (NBC)

OUTSTANDING WRITING FOR A DAYTIME SPECIAL PROGRAM

★Audrey Davis Levin, *Heart In Hiding;* ABC Afternoon Playbreak; Shown November 14, 1974 (ABC)

Ruth Brooks Flippen, *Oh! Baby, Baby, Baby . . .;* ABC Afternoon Playbreak; Shown December 5, 1974 (ABC)

Lila Garrett and Sanford Krinski, *The Girl Who Couldn't Lose;* ABC Afternoon Playbreak; Shown February 13, 1975 (ABC)

THE DAYTIME AREAS

OUTSTANDING INDIVIDUAL ACHIEVEMENT IN DAYTIME PROGRAMMING (for a single episode of a series or for a special program)

Paul Lynde, Performer; *The Hollywood Squares* (NBC)

Jay Redack, Harry Friedman, Gary Johnson, Harold Schneider, Rick Kellard and Steve Levitch, Writers; *The Hollywood Squares;* Shown November 22, 1974 (NBC)

Stas Pyka, Graphic Design and Title Sequence; *How To Survive A Marriage;* Shown January 7, 1975 (NBC)

OUTSTANDING INDIVIDUAL ACHIEVEMENT IN CHILDREN'S PROGRAMMING (for a single episode of a series; or for a special program)

★Elinor Bunin, Graphic Design and Title Sequences; *Funshine Saturday & Sunday;* Umbrella Title Animations For Saturday & Sunday Morning Children's Programming; Shown January 24 & 25, 1975 (ABC)

Bob Keeshan, Performer; *Captain Kangaroo* (CBS)

Bill Cosby, Performer; *Highlights of Ringling Bros. Barnum & Bailey Circus;* Bell System Family Theatre; Shown February 16, 1975 (NBC)

Charles M. Schulz, Writer; *Be My Valentine, Charlie Brown;* Shown January 28, 1975 (CBS)

TV Programs 1974-1975

1 **ABC Afternoon Playbreak** ABC
Program Type Drama
90 minutes. Monthly. Series premiered in 1972. Season premiere: 10/17/74. Five films: "Can I Save My Children?" "The Girl Who Couldn't Lose," "Heart in Hiding," "The Last Bride of Salem," "Oh! Baby, Baby, Baby . . ." (*See* individual titles for cast and credits.)
Producer Various
Director Various
Writer Various

2 **ABC Afterschool Specials** ABC
Program Type Children's Show
60-minute specials. Premiere date: 10/72. Season premiere: 10/2/74. The Bank Street School of Education (New York City) serves as consultant for the series. 13 films: "The Bridge of Adam Rush," "The Crazy Comedy Concert," "Cyrano," "The Magical Mystery Trip Through Little Red's Head," "Pssst! Hammerman's After You!" "Rookie of the Year," "The Runaways," "Santiago's America," "Sara's Summer of the Swans," "The Secret Life of T. K. Dearing," "The Skating Rink," "The Toothpaste Millionaire," "Winning & Losing: Diary of a Campaign." (*See* individual titles for cast and credits.)
Producer Various
Director Various
Writer Various

3 **ABC Comedy Special** ABC
Program Type Comedy
Six 30-minute pilot films: "Guess Who's Coming to Dinner," "Home Cookin'," "How to Succeed in Business without Really Trying," "Mac," "The Orphan and the Dude," "Where's the Fire?" (*See* individual titles for cast and credits.)

4 **ABC Evening News with Howard K. Smith and Harry Reasoner** ABC
Program Type News
30 minutes. Monday-Friday. Continuous.
Executive Producer Av Westin
Production Company ABC News
Newscaster Howard K. Smith; Harry Reasoner

5 **ABC Evening News with Howard K. Smith and Harry Reasoner (Captioned for the Deaf)** PBS
Program Type News
30 minutes. Monday-Friday. ABC 7:00 p.m. news captioned at WGBH/Boston and fed to PBS stations at 11:p.m. (eastern time). Program funded by the U.S. Department of Health, Education and Welfare-Bureau of Education for the Handicapped.

6 **The ABC Monday Night Movie** ABC
Program Type Feature Film
Feature films of varying length presented irregularly: "The Boston Strangler" (1968) shown 1/27/75, "The Only Game in Town" (1970) shown 2/3/75, "Romance of a Horsethief" (1971) shown 8/1/75, "The Sterile Cuckoo" (1969) shown 1/13/75.

7 **ABC News Close-Up** ABC
Program Type Documentary/Special
60 minute monthly documentary specials. Premiere date: 10/18/73. Season premiere: 10/14/74. Programs shown during 1974-75: "ABC News Close-Up: Hoffa," "ABC News Close-Up on Autos: Spoiled by Success?" "ABC News Close-Up on Crashes: The Illusion of Safety," "ABC News Close-Up on Danger in Sports: Paying the Price," "ABC News Close-Up on Food: The Crisis of Price," "ABC News Close-Up on Illegal Aliens: The Gate Crashers," "ABC News Close-Up on IRS: A Question of Power," "ABC News Close-Up on Lawyers: Guilty as Charged?" "ABC News Close-Up on the Land Use Game: Who Controls Your Property?" "ABC News Close-Up on Washington Regulators: How They Cost You Money," "ABC News Close-Up: The CIA, "ABC News Close-Up: What's Happened Since." (*See* individual titles for credits.)
Executive Producer Av Westin
Producer Various
Production Company ABC News

8   ABC News Close-Up: Hoffa
ABC News Close-Up   ABC
Program Type Documentary/Special
Special. 60 minutes. Premiere date: 11/30/74.
Producer Stephen Fleischman
Production Company ABC News
Director Stephen Fleischman
Writer Richard Gerdau
Reporters Jim Kincaid; Brit Hume; Bill Gill

9   ABC News Close-Up on Autos: Spoiled by Success?
ABC News Close-Up   ABC
Program Type Documentary/Special
Special. 60 minutes. Premiere date: 8/15/75.
Producer James Benjamin
Production Company ABC News
Director James Benjamin
Writer Jules Bergman; Dan Cordtz; Debra Kram
Reporters Jules Bergman; Dan Cordtz

10   ABC News Close-Up on Crashes: The Illusion of Safety
ABC News Close-Up   ABC
Program Type Documentary/Special
Investigation of air and rail accidents. 60 minutes. Premiere date: 12/28/74.
Producer James Benjamin
Production Company ABC News
Writer James Benjamin; Jules Bergman
Reporter Jules Bergman

11   ABC News Close-Up on Danger in Sports: Paying the Price
ABC News Close-Up   ABC
Program Type Documentary/Special
Focus on high school football and tennis. 60 minutes. Premiere date: 10/14/74.
Producer Phil Lewis
Production Company ABC News
Director Phil Lewis
Reporter Jules Bergman

12   ABC News Close-Up on Food: The Crisis of Price
ABC News Close-Up   ABC
Program Type Documentary/Special
Special. The role of the United States in the world food shortage. 60 minutes. Premiere date: 6/27/75.
Producer Pamela Hill
Production Company ABC News
Director Pamela Hill
Writer Brit Hume; Pamela Hill
Reporter Brit Hume
Correspondent Peter Jennings

13   ABC News Close-Up on Illegal Aliens: The Gate Crashers
ABC News Close-Up   ABC
Program Type Documentary/Special
Special. 60 minutes. Premiere date: 1/3/75.
Producer Phil Lewis
Production Company ABC News
Director Phil Lewis
Writer Phil Lewis
Correspondent Ted Koppel
Reporters Frank Cruz; Bob Young

14   ABC News Close-Up on IRS: A Question of Power
ABC News Close-Up   ABC
Program Type Documentary/Special
The Internal Revenue Service potential for use as a political weapon. 60 minutes. Premiere date: 3/21/75.
Producer Paul Altmeyer
Production Company ABC News
Director Dick Roy
Writer Paul Altmeyer
Photographer Dick Roy
Narrator Tom Jarriel
Reporters Paul Altmeyer; Brit Hume

15   ABC News Close-Up on Lawyers: Guilty as Charged?
ABC News Close-Up   ABC
Program Type Documentary/Special
Special. 60 minutes. Premiere date: 4/19/75.
Producer Marlene Sanders
Production Company ABC News
Director Marlene Sanders
Writer Marlene Sanders
Correspondent Steve Bell

16   ABC News Close-Up on the Land Use Game: Who Controls Your Property?
ABC News Close-Up   ABC
Program Type Documentary/Special
Special. 60 minutes. Premiere date: 9/5/75.
Producer Richard Gerdau
Production Company ABC News
Writer Richard Gerdau
Correspondent Frank Reynolds
Reporter Brit Hume

17   ABC News Close-Up on Washington Regulators: How They Cost You Money
ABC News Close-Up   ABC
Program Type Documentary/Special
Special. Focus on the Interstate Commerce Commission and the Civil Aeronautics Board. 60 minutes. Premiere date: 2/1/75.
Producer Howard Enders; Sam Donaldson

Production Company ABC News
Writer Sam Donaldson
Reporter Sam Donaldson

18 ABC News Close-Up: The CIA

ABC News Close-Up   ABC
Program Type Documentary/Special
Special. 60 minutes. Premiere date: 5/30/75.
Producer Stephen Fleischman
Production Company ABC News
Reporter David Schoumacher

19 ABC News Close-Up: What's Happened Since

ABC News Close-Up   ABC
Program Type Documentary/Special
Special. Follow-up report on the investigations
for other "Close-Up" specials. 60 minutes. Pre-
miere date: 7/5/75.
Producer Marlene Sanders
Production Company ABC News
Director Marlene Sanders
Writer Marlene Sanders
Correspondent Ted Koppel

20 ABC News Special Events   ABC

Program Type Documentary/Special
Live and taped coverage of special events. *See*
"Elections '74," "Indochina - Savage Spring-
time," "Navidad Encantada: Enchanted Christ-
mas," "President Ford's State of the Union Mes-
sage to Congress," "The President in Asia,"
"Senate Rules Committee Hearings on the
Rockefeller Nomination for Vice-President,"
"Shark ... Terror, Death, Truth," "Union in
Space," "Union in Space (Preview)."
Production Company ABC News Special Events
  Unit
Producer Various

21 The ABC Saturday News with Ted Koppel   ABC

Program Type News
30 minutes. Saturday. Premiere date: 7/5/75.
Executive Producer Av Westin
Production Company ABC News
Newscaster Ted Koppel

22 The ABC Saturday Night Movie
                                                     ABC
Program Type TV Movie – Feature Film
Generally 120 minutes. Saturday. Season
premiere: 1/11/75. Primarily feature films commercially released with the exception of "The
Glass Menagerie," "Hustling," and "Thursday's
Game." (*See* individual titles for cast and credits.) The feature films are: "Battle of Britain"
(1969) shown 3/22/75, "Breakfast at Tiffany's"
(1961) shown 5/24/75, "The Carpetbaggers"
(1964) shown 7/5/75, "The Cowboys" (1972)
shown 1/11/75, "The Detective" (1968) shown
1/25/75, "Duel in the Sun" (1946) shown
5/17/75, "Electra Glide in Blue" (1973) shown
2/1/75, "Flap" (1970) shown 4/5/75, "Frenzy"
(1972) shown 2/8/75, "The Good, the Bad and
the Ugly" (1966) shown 5/3/75, "Ice Station
Zebra" (1968) shown 8/9/75, "Irma La Douce"
(1963) shown 7/19/75, "The Landlord" (1970)
shown 6/14/75, "The Molly Maguires" (1969)
shown 6/7/75, "Money from Home" (1954)
shown 6/15/75, "Nicholas and Alexandra"
(Part I) (1971) shown 5/10/75, "Norwood"
(1970) shown 4/19/75, "The Organization"
(1971) shown 3/15/75, "Rosemary's Baby"
(1968) shown 4/26/75, "Skullduggery" (1970)
shown 3/8/75, "Summer of '42" (1971) shown
2/15/75, "Sweet November" (1968) shown
4/12/75 and 7/12/75, "The Ten Commandments" (Part I) (1956) shown 3/29/75, "Walking Tall" (1973) shown 3/1/75, "WUSA" (1970)
shown 1/18/75.

23 The ABC Summer Movie   ABC

Program Type TV Movie – Feature Film
Combination of made-for-television films and
commercially released films. Times vary. Friday.
Premiere date: 7/11/75. Last show: 9/5/75. The
made-for-television films are: "Haunts of the
Very Rich," "The Mark of Zorro," "The Night
Strangler," "Roll, Freddy, Roll," "Search for the
Gods," "Trapped Beneath the Sea," "The
Tribe," "Trouble Comes to Town." (*See* individual titles for cast and credits.) The commercially
released motion pictures are "Born Free" (1966)
shown 8/15/75 and "The Cowboys" (1972)
shown 8/8/75.

24 The ABC Sunday Night Movie ABC

Program Type TV Movie – Feature Film
A combination of feature films and made-for-
television movies. Times vary. Sunday. Season
premiere: 9/15/74. The made-for-television films
are: "The Barbary Coast," "Friendly Persuasion," "Indict and Convict," "Judge Dee in the
Monastery Murders," "Man on the Outside,"
"My Father's House," "Reflections of Murder,"
"Search for the Gods," "The Story of Jacob and
Joseph," and "Strange New World." (*See* individual titles for cast and credits.) The feature
films are: "The Adventurers" (1970) shown
12/15/74, "Airport" (1970) shown 2/9/75,
"The Beguiled" (1971) shown 7/20/75, "The Big
Bounce" (1969) shown 4/13/75, "Charley"
(1968) shown 1/26/75, "Crazy Joe" (1974)
shown 2/2/75, "Dark of the Sun" (1968) shown
8/10/75, "Dr. No" (1962) shown 11/10/74,
"Fiddler on the Roof" (1971) shown 9/15/74,

The ABC Sunday Night Movie
Continued
"A Fistful of Dollars" (1967) shown 2/23/75, "Flap" (1971) shown 8/3/75, "For Love of Ivy" (1968) shown 12/1/74, "Funny Girl" (1968) shown 12/8/74, "The Heartbreak Kid" (1972) shown 1/19/75, "High Plains Drifter" (1973) shown 11/17/74, "The Honkers" (1972) shown 6/22/75, "The Hospital" (1971) shown 3/2/75, "How the West Was Won" (1962) shown 1/5/75, "Lady Liberty" (1971) shown 7/6/75, "The Last Picture Show" (1971) shown 10/6/74, "The Man" (1972) shown 4/27/75, "Man in the Wilderness" (1971) shown 4/6/75, "Midnight Cowboy" (1970) shown 11/3/74, "Money from Home" (1953) shown 8/2/75, "Nicholas and Alexandra" (Part II) (1971) shown 5/11/75, "The Odd Couple" (1968) shown 8/24/75, "Oliver!" (1968) shown 2/16/75, "The Poseidan Adventure" (1972) shown 10/27/74, "Rage" (1972) shown 10/20/74, "The Secret Life of an American Wife" (1968) shown 7/27/75, "Star!" (1968) shown 12/22/74, "The Ten Commandments" (Part II) (1956) shown 3/30/75, "Thunderball" (1965) shown 9/22/74, "The Valachi Papers" (1972) shown 9/29/74, "What's New, Pussycat?" (1965) shown 3/16/75, "Where It's At" (1969) shown 6/8/75, "You Can't Win 'Em All" (1970) shown 8/31/75.

25   **ABC Theatre**   ABC
Program Type Drama
Special presentations of varying lengths (120-180 minutes). Season premiere: 12/18/74. Seven plays: "Antony and Cleopatra," "Ceremonies in Dark Old Men," "I Will Fight No More Forever," "Judgment: The Court-Martial of Lt. William Calley," "Love Among the Ruins," "The Missiles of October," "A Moon for the Misbegotten." (*See* individual titles for cast and credits.)

26   **ABC's Championship Auto Racing**
                                                        ABC
Program Type Sports
Five races. 60-90 minutes. Tape and live coverage of events: 2/16/75 Daytona 500; 3/16/75 Phoenix 150; 3/22/75 Atlanta 500; 4/6/75 Trenton 200; 5/18/75 Indianapolis 500 time trials.
Executive Producer Roone Arledge
Production Company ABC Sports
Announcer Bill Flemming; Jim McKay; Keith Jackson; Jackie Stewart; Chris Economaki

27   **ABC's Wide World of Sports**   ABC
Program Type Sports
90-120 minutes. Saturday/Sunday. Premiere date: 4/29/61 (Saturday). Sunday "Wide World" premiered in January 1974. Saturdays continuous; sunday season premiere: 1/5/75.

Executive Producer Roone Arledge
Production Company ABC Sports
Director Various
Host Jim McKay
Announcer Jim McKay; Chris Schenkel; Bill Flemming; Howard Cosell; Keith Jackson; Frank Gifford

28   **The Abduction of Saint Anne**
Tuesday/Wednesday Movie of the Week ABC
Program Type TV Movie
90 minutes. Premiere date: 1/21/75. Based on the novel "The Issue of the Bishop's Blood" by Thomas Patrick McMahon.
Executive Producer Quinn Martin
Producer John Wilder
Production Company Quinn Martin Productions
Director Harry Falk
Writer Edward Hume
CAST
Dave Hatcher .... Robert Wagner
Bishop Francis Paul Logan .... E. G. Marshall
Carl Gentry .... Lloyd Nolan
Ann Benedict .... Kathleen Quinlan
Ted Morrissey .... William Windom
Pete Haggerty .... James Gregory
Angel Montoya .... A Martinez
Jose Montoya .... Rodolfo Hoyos
Sister Patrick .... Ruth McDevitt
Frank Benedict ....Alfred Ryder
Wayne Putnam .... George McCallister
Vanjack .... Tony Young
Mother Michael ....Martha Scott
Father Rubacava .... Vic Mohica
Sheriff Townsend .... Patrick Conway
Woody .... Roy Jenson

The Academy Awards *see* The Oscar Awards

29   **Accion Chicano**   PBS
Program Type Documentary/Special
Six-part series. 30 minutes. Weekly. Premiere date: 10/1/74. Chicano artists, musicians, poets and actors.
Executive Producer Jesus Trevino
Producer Various
Production Company KCET/Los Angeles

Action Biography *see* Rabin: Action Biography; Sadat: Action Biography

30   **Adam-12**   NBC
Program Type Crime Drama
Created by Robert A. Cinader; Jack Webb. 30 minutes. Tuesday. Premiere date: 9/12/68. Season premiere: 9/24/74. Last show: 8/26/75.
Producer Tom Williams

Production Company Mark VII Ltd. in association with Universal Television for NBC-TV
Director Various
Writer Various

CAST

Officer Jim Reed .... Kent McCord
Officer Pete Malloy .... Martin Milner
MacDonald .... William Boyett
Woods .... Fred Stromsoe

31 Adams of Eagle Lake ABC
Program Type TV Movie
Special. 60 minutes. Premiere date: 1/10/75. Repeat date: 8/23/75.
Executive Producer Richard O. Linke
Producer Walter Grauman; Charles Stewart
Production Company Andy Griffith Enterprises in association with MGM Television
Director Walter Grauman
Writer Charles Stewart; Jonathan Daly

CAST

Sam Adams .... Andy Griffith
Jerry Troy .... Nick Nolte
Kelly .... Abby Dalton
Jubal Hammond .... Iggie Wolfington
Ron Selleck .... Scott Marlowe
Jimmy Simpkins .... Peter Coffield
Doc Russell .... Jack Dodson
Grandma Simpkins .... Irene Tedrow
Cindy .... Lynne Marta
Debbie .... Brenda Scott

32 The Addams Family NBC
Program Type Animated Film
Based on cartoon characters created by Charles Addams and live-action television series "The Addams Family." 30 minutes. Saturday. Premiere date: 9/9/73. Reruns: 9/7/74. Last show: 8/30/75. Animated in England.
Executive Producer William Hanna; Joseph Barbera
Production Company Hanna-Barbera Productions
Musical Director Hoyt Curtin

VOICES

Gomez .... Len Weinrib
Morticia .... Janet Waldo
Fester .... Jackie Coogan
Lurch .... Ted Cassidy
Pugsley .... Jody Foster
Wednesday .... Cindy Henderson
Granny .... Janet Waldo

33 Adventure in America ABC
Program Type Documentary/Special
Projected as a series of specials; only the first aired. 60 minutes. Premiere date: 1/9/75. Two towns, Pine Valley and Julian, in the Cleveland National Forest, California prepare for fire. Judy Collins narrates and sings.
Producer Tom Bywaters
Production Company ABC News

Director Tom Bywaters
Writer Tom Bywaters

The Adventurers *see* The ABC Sunday Night Movie

34 Adventures of the Queen
The CBS Thursday/Friday Night Movies CBS
Program Type TV Movie
Some scenes filmed aboard the *Queen Mary* in Long Beach, California. 120 minutes. Premiere date: 2/14/75. Repeat date: 8/21/75.
Producer Irwin Allen
Production Company Irwin Allen Productions and 20th Century-Fox Television
Director David Lowell Rich
Writer John Gay

CAST

Capt. James Morgan .... Robert Stack
J. L. Dundeen .... Ralph Bellamy
Martin Reed .... Bradford Dillman
Dr. Peter Brooks .... David Hedison
Ted Trevor .... Burr De Benning
Ann Trevor .... Ellen Weston
Robert Dwight .... Sorrell Booke
John Howe .... John Randolph
Mathew Evans .... Linden Chiles
Claudine Lennart .... Sheila Matthews
Jim Geer .... Mills Watson
Phillips .... Frank Marth
Riley .... Richard X. Slattery
Betty Schuster .... Francine York
Bill Schuster .... Vito Scotti
Forbes .... Russell Johnson
Irene McKay .... Elizabeth Rogers
Barbara .... Lara Parker
Fletcher .... Paul Carr
Fedderson .... Than Wyenn

35 Aesop's Fables CBS
Program Type Children's Show
Special. Animation and live action. Based on "The Tortoise and the Hare." Songs arranged by Richard Delvy; Dave Roberts; lyrics by Earl Hamner. 30 minutes. Premiere date: 10/31/71. Repeat date: 12/23/74.
Executive Producer Lee Rich
Producer Lou Scheimer; Norm Prescott
Production Company A Lorimar Production in association with Filmation Associates, Inc.
Director Hal Sutherland; Bob Chenault
Writer Earl Hamner
Musical Director Richard Delvy; Dave Roberts
Choreographer Donald McKayle
Art Director Don Christensen

CAST

Aesop .... Bill Cosby
Joey .... Keith Hamilton
Marta .... Jerelyn Fields
Voices Larry Storch; Jane Webb; John Erwin; Dal McKennon; John Byner

36   AFC Championship

NBC Sports Special   NBC
Program Type Sports
American Football Conference championship.
Live coverage. 12/29/74. Pittsburgh Steelers
versus Oakland Raiders.
Production Company NBC Sports
Announcer Curt Gowdy; Al DeRogatis; Don
   Meredith

37   AFC-NFC Pro Bowl

ABC Sports Special   ABC
Program Type Sports
Fifth annual game. Live coverage from Orange
Bowl Stadium, Miami, Florida. 1/20/75.
Executive Producer Roone Arledge
Producer Don Ohlmeyer
Production Company ABC Sports
Director Chet Forte
Announcer Frank Gifford; Howard Cosell; Alex
   Karras

38   AFC Play-Offs (Game 1)

NBC Sports Special   NBC
Program Type Sports
American Football Conference play-off covered
live 12/21/74. Oakland Raiders versus Miami
Dolphins.
Executive Producer Scotty Connal
Production Company NBC Sports
Announcer Curt Gowdy; Al DeRogatis; Don
   Meredith

39   AFC Play-Offs (Game 2)

NBC Sports Special   NBC
Program Type Sports
American Football Conference play-off covered
live 12/22/74. Pittsburgh Steelers versus Buffalo
Bills.
Executive Producer Scotty Connal
Production Company NBC Sports
Announcer Jim Simpson; John Brody

The African Queen *see* NBC Nights at
   the Movies

40   After the Fall   NBC

Program Type Drama
Special. Adaptation of play by Arthur Miller.
150 minutes. Premiere date: 12/10/74.
Producer Gilbert Cates
Production Company Gilbert Cates Production
Director Gilbert Cates
Writer Arthur Miller
                     CAST
Maggie .... Faye Dunaway
Quentin ....Christopher Plummer
Holga .... Bibi Andersson

Louise .... Mariclare Costello
Mickey .... Murray Hamilton
Lou ....Lee Richardson
Mother .... Nancy Marchand
Father .... Addison Powell
Elsie .... Jennifer Warren

41   Agronsky and Company   PBS

Program Type Interview/Discussion
30 minutes. Weekly. Produced commercially by
WTOP-TV/Washington, D.C. Premiered in Oc-
tober 1969. Premiere date on PBS: 11/2/74.
Producer John Larkin
Production Company Eastern Educational Tele-
   vision Network
Host Martin Agronsky
Regular Peter Lisagor; Carl Rowan; Hugh
   Sidey; James J. Kilpatrick
Semi-regulars George Wills; Elizabeth Drew

42   AIAW National Swimming and Diving Championships

PBS Sports Special   PBS
Program Type Sports
90 minutes. 3/16/75. Coverage of events held
3/13/75–3/15/75 at Arizona State University,
Tempe, Arizona.
Producer John Repczynski
Production Company KAET/ Arizona State
   University, Tempe
Announcer Donna deVarona; Ralph Jon Fritz;
   Lenzi O'Connell

43   Ailey Celebrates Ellington

The CBS Festival of Lively Arts for Young
People   CBS
Program Type Children's Show
60 minutes. Premiere date: 11/28/74. Narration
written by Stanley Dance. Music by Duke Elling-
ton.
Executive Producer Herman Krawitz
Producer Robert Weiner
Production Company Jodav and Ring-Ting-A-
   Ling Productions
Director Joshua White
Writer Stanley Dance
Choreographer Alvin Ailey
Host Gladys Knight
Narrator Gladys Knight
Guest Artists Fred Benjamin; Marleane Furtick
Dancers Alvin Ailey American Dance Center
   Repertory Workshop Dancers

Airport *see* The ABC Sunday Night
   Movie

44 Alan King Tennis Classic
ABC Sports Special   ABC
Program Type Sports
Semifinal and final rounds of play taped in Las Vegas, Nevada. 90 minutes each. 5/17/75; 5/18/75.
Executive Producer Roone Arledge
Production Company ABC Sports

45 Alan Watts: A Conversation with Myself   PBS
Program Type Interview/Discussion
Special. Taped in 1973; Alan Watts in conversation. 30 minutes. Premiere date: 6/23/75. Program funded in part by the Corporation for Public Broadcasting.
Executive Producer Zev Putterman
Production Company KQED/San Francisco
Director David D. Grieve

Alexander Nevsky *see* Humanities Film Forum

Alfred the Great *see* The CBS Thursday/Friday Night Movies

46 All Creatures Great and Small
Hallmark Hall of Fame   NBC
Program Type TV Movie
Special. Adaptation of autobiography by James Herriot. 90 minutes. Premiere date: 2/4/75. Filmed in Yorkshire.
Producer David Susskind; Duane C. Bogie
Production Company Talent Associates-Norton Simon and Clarion Productions
Director Claude Whatham
Writer Hugh Whitemore
CAST
James Herriot .... Simon Ward
Siegfried Farnon .... Anthony Hopkins
Helen Alderson .... Lisa Harrow
Tristan Farnon .... Brian Stirner
Soames .... T. C. McKenna
Mr. Alderson .... John Collin
Mrs. Harbottle .... Brenda Bruce
Dean .... Burt Palmer
Connie ....Jane Collins

47 All-Disney Night   NBC
Program Type Feature Film
Two Disney films: "Mysteries of the Deep" documentary (20 minutes) and "The Parent Trap" (1961) (160 minutes). 10/26/74. Three hour show.
Production Company Walt Disney Productions

48 All for the Family?   PBS
Program Type Interview/Discussion
Special. The 1975 "family viewing hour" in discussion. 30 minutes. Premiere date: 5/29/75.
Production Company Mississippi Educational Television Network
Moderator Howard Latt

49 All in the Family   CBS
Program Type Comedy
Based on "Till Death Do Us Part" created for the BBC by Johnny Speight. Developed by Norman Lear. 30 minutes. Saturday. Premiere date: 1/12/71. Season premiere: 9/14/74. Opening theme by Lee Adams; Charles Strouse. Closing theme by Roger Kellaway; Carroll O'Connor. Show set in Queens, New York. January 1975 spin-off: "The Jeffersons."
Executive Producer Don Nicholl
Producer Michael Ross; Bernie West
Production Company Bud Yorkin-Norman Lear Tandem Productions, Inc.
Director Paul Bogart
Writer Various
CAST
Archie Bunker .... Carroll O'Connor
Edith Bunker ....Jean Stapleton
Mike Stivic .... Rob Reiner
Gloria Stivic .... Sally Struthers
Irene Lorenzo .... Betty Garrett
Frank Lorenzo .... Vincent Gardenia
George Jefferson ....Sherman Hemsley
Louise Jefferson ....Isabel Sanford
Lionel Jefferson .... Mike Evans

50 All My Children   ABC
Program Type Daytime Drama
30 minutes. Monday-Friday. Premiere date: 1/5/70. Continuous. Created by Agnes Nixon. Set in Pine Valley, U.S.A.
Producer Bud Kloss
Production Company Creative Horizens
Director Del Hughes; Henry Kaplan
Head Writer Wisner Washam
CAST
Ann Martin .... Judith Bancroft
Phillip Brent .... Nick Benedict
Mary Kennicott ....Susan Blanchard
Tara Martin Tyler .... Stephanie Braxton
Claudette Montgomery ....Paulette Breen
Kate Martin ....Kay Campbell
Dr. Frank Grant ....John Danelle
Ruth Martin ....Mary Fickett
Dr. Jeff Martin ....Charles Frank
Dr. Charles Tyler .... Hugh Franklin
Mona Kane .... Fran Heflin
Chuck Tyler .... Chris Hubbell
Kitty Shea Tyler .... Francesca James
Nick Davis ....Larry Keith
Margo Flax Martin .... Eileen Letchworth
Erica Kane Brent ....Susan Lucci
Dr. Joe Martin .... Ray MacDonnell
Paul Martin .... William Mooney

All My Children Continued

Phoebe Tyler	Ruth Warrick
Linc Tyler	Peter White
Nancy Grant	Lisa Wilkinson

51   All My Darling Daughters

Tuesday/Wednesday Movie of the Week ABC
Program Type TV Movie
90 minutes. Premiere date: 11/22/72. Repeat date: 10/16/74. Story by Robert Presnell, Jr.; Stan Dreban.
Executive Producer David Victor
Producer David J. O'Connell
Production Company Universal Television
Director David Lowell Rich
Writer John Gay

CAST

Charles Raleigh	Robert Young
Miss Freeling	Eve Arden
Matthew Cunningham	Raymond Massey
Susan Raleigh	Darleen Carr
Robin Raleigh	Judy Strangis
Jerry Greene	Jerry Fogel
Charlotte Raleigh	Fawne Harriman
Jennifer Raleigh	Sharon Gless
Bradley Coombs	Colby Chester
Andy O'Brien	Darrell Larson
Biff Brynner	Michael Richardson

52   All-Star Game

NBC Sports Special   NBC
Program Type Sports
46th All-Star Game. Live coverage from County Stadium, Milwaukee, Wisconsin. 7/15/75.
Executive Producer Scotty Connal
Producer Roy Hammerman
Production Company NBC Sports
Director Harry Coyle
Announcer Curt Gowdy; Joe Garagiola; Tony Kubek

53   All the Kind Strangers

Tuesday/Wednesday Movie of the Week ABC
Program Type TV Movie
90 minutes. Premiere date: 11/12/74. Filmed on location in Lebanon, Tennessee. Song "What Are You Living For?" written and sung by Regis Hall.
Executive Producer Jerry Gross
Producer Roger Lewis
Production Company A Jerry Gross Production for Cinemation Industries
Director Burt Kennedy
Writer Clyde Ware

CAST

Jimmy	Stacy Keach
Carol Ann	Samantha Eggar
Peter	John Savage
John	Robby Benson
Martha	Arlene Farber
Gilbert	Tim Parkison
Rita	Patti Parkison

James	Brent Campbell
Baby	John Connell

54   All Together Now

Tuesday/Wednesday Movie of the Week ABC
Program Type TV Movie
90 minutes. Premiere date: 2/5/75. Story by Rubin Carson; based on fact. Music by John Rubinstein; lyrics by Timothy McIntyre.
Executive Producer Deanne Barkley; Howard Rosenman
Producer Ron Bernstein
Production Company RSO Films
Director Randal Kleiser
Writer Jeff Andrus; Rubin Carson

CAST

Bill Lindsay	John Rubinstein
Carol Lindsay	Glynnis O'Connor
Andy Lindsay	Brad Savage
Susan Lindsay	Helen Hunt
Nicki	Dori Brenner
Charles Drummond	Bill Macy
Helen Drummond	Jane Withers
Mike	Larry Bishop
Jerry	Adam Arkin
Rafe	Moosie Drier
Joe	Tiger Williams

55   Almost Anything Goes   ABC

Program Type Game Show
Five-part show. 60 minutes. Thursday. Premiere date: 7/31/75. Last show: 8/28/75. Based on European show "It's a Knockout!"
Executive Producer Bob Banner; Beryl Vertue
Producer Jeff Harris; Bernie Kukoff
Production Company Bob Banner Associates, Inc. and the Robert Stigwood Organization, Inc.
Director Mac Hemion
Writer Jeff Harris; Bernie Kukoff
Play-By-Play Announcer Charles Jones
Color Reporter Lynn Shackelford
Field Announcer Dick Whittington

56   Aloha Means Goodbye

The CBS Thursday/Friday Night Movies CBS
Program Type TV Movie
Based on a novel by Naomi Hintze. 120 minutes. Premiere date: 10/11/74.
Executive Producer David Lowell Rich
Producer Sam Strangis
Production Company Universal Television
Director David Lowell Rich
Writer Dean Reisner; Joseph Stefano

CAST

Sara Moore	Sally Struthers
Pamela Crane	Joanna Miles
Dr. David Kalani	Henry Darrow
Dr. Lawrence Maddux	James Franciscus
Dr. DaCosta	Frank Marth
Torger Nilsson	Larry Gates
Dr. Franklin	Russell Johnson

Christian Nilsson .... Colin Losby
Mrs. Kalani .... Pat Li
Connie .... Tracy Reed

57 AM America   ABC
Program Type News Magazine
120 minutes. Monday-Friday. Continuous. Premiere date: 1/6/75. Stephanie Edwards replaced as co-host from New York by weekly guests as of 5/19/75. Ralph Story co-host on West Coast.
Producer Jules Power
Production Company ABC News
Host Bill Beutel; Stephanie Edwards; Peter Jennings
Regular Jack Anderson; Roger Caras; Thalassa Cruso; Sam Erwin; Dr. Sonya Friedman; Rev. Jesse Jackson; Dr. Timothy Johnson; John V. Lindsay; Bob Rosefsky; Ralph Story

58 The Ambassador
Benjamin Franklin   CBS
Program Type Drama
First of four-part series dealing with the life of Benjamin Franklin. 90 minutes. Premiere date: 11/21/74.
Executive Producer Lewis Freedman
Producer George Lefferts
Production Company CBS Television
Director Glenn Jordan
Writer Howard Fast
CAST
Benjamin Franklin .... Eddie Albert
Mme. Helvetius .... Alexis Smith
Count de Vergennes .... Gig Young
Gen. Lord Cornwallis ....James E. Brodhead
King Louis XVI .... Rene Auberjonois
King George III .... Victor Buono
Wentworth .... John Colicos
Lord North .... Robert Coote
Jacques ....John Heffernan
Dumont .... Frank Langella
Countess de Crecy .... Patricia Morison
Lord Stormont .... Edward Mulhare
Harry Pitkin .... Clive Revill
Additional Cast Michael Anderson, Jr; Nellie Bellflower; Anthony Costello; Ian Wolfe

59 America   PBS
Program Type Documentary/Special
First telecast on NBC as a 13-part series, 60 minutes each. Presented on PBS as a 26-part series, 30 minutes each with new introductions and closings. Premiere on PBS: 9/17/74. Series made possible by a grant from Xerox Corporation; presented by KCET/Los Angeles.
Producer Michael Gill
Production Company British Broadcasting Corporation in cooperation with Time/Life Films
Writer Alistair Cooke
Host Alistair Cooke
Narrator Alistair Cooke

60 America Abroad
NBC News Special   NBC
Program Type Documentary/Special
30 minutes. Premiere date: 4/10/75.
Producer Les Crystal
Production Company NBC News
Anchor John Chancellor

61 America in Transition
The Quarterly Report   PBS
Program Type Documentary/Special
Second in series. 130 minutes. Premiere date: 11/1/74. Panel discussion of President Ford's first 100 days in office.
Executive Producer Alvin H. Goldstein
Producer Linda Winslow
Production Company NPACT (National Public Affairs Center for Television)

62 American Airlines Tennis Games
PBS Sports Specials   PBS
Program Type Sports
Tape and live coverage of quarter-finals, semi-finals and finals from the Racquet Club and Tennis Ranch, Tucson, Arizona. 4/4/75; 4/5/75; 4/6/75.
Executive Producer Greg Harvey
Producer Marvin Smith
Production Company KUAT/University of Arizona
Announcer Bud Collins; Donald Dell

63 American Bandstand   ABC
Program Type Music/Dance
60 minutes. Saturday. Premiere date: 8/5/57. Continuous.
Executive Producer Dick Clark
Producer Judy Price
Production Company Dick Clark Productions in association with the ABC Television Network
Director Barry Glazer
Host Dick Clark

64 The American Film Institute Salute to Orson Welles   CBS
Program Type Awards Show
Special. Third presentation of A.F.I. Life Achievement Award. 90 minutes. Premiere date: 2/17/75.
Executive Producer George Stevens, Jr.
Producer Paul W. Keyes
Director Bill Foster
Head Writer Paul W. Keyes
Writer Paul W. Keyes; Marc London; Bob Howard
Musical Director Nelson Riddle
Host Frank Sinatra
Special Guest Orson Welles

American Football Conference *see* AFC

American Heritage *see* The Honorable Sam Houston

65   American Music Awards   ABC
Program Type Awards Show
Second annual presentation. 90 minutes. Live (in East). 2/18/75.
Executive Producer Dick Clark
Producer Bill Lee
Production Company dick clark teleshows, inc.
Director John Moffitt
Host Roy Clark; Helen Reddy; Sly Stone

66   The American Parade   CBS
Program Type Drama
A 13-part, hour-long, American history-oriented series presented over a three-year period for the Bicentennial. Four programs shown during 1974–75: "The Case Against Milligan," "F.D.R.: The Man Who Changed America," "The General," "Sojourner." (*See* individual titles for cast and credits.)
Executive Producer Joel Heller
Production Company CBS News for the CBS Television Network

67   The American Sportsman   ABC
Program Type Sports
45 minutes. Sunday. Show premiered in 1965. Season premiere: 2/9/75. Last show of season: 4/27/75.
Executive Producer Roone Arledge
Producer Neil Cunningham; Curt Gowdy; Pat Smith
Production Company ABC Sports
Director Neil Cunningham
Writer Curt Gowdy; Pat Smith

68   Americans All   ABC
Program Type Documentary/Special
30 minutes. Premiered in 1973–74 season. Season premiere: 11/17/74. Mini-documentaries highlighting the contributions of minorities to American life. Anna Bond replaced Melba Tolliver as host.
Executive Producer Av Westin
Producer Howard Enders
Production Company ABC News
Director Howard Enders
Writer Willie Suggs
Host Melba Tolliver; Anna Bond

69   America's Junior Miss Pageant   CBS
Program Type Awards Show
18th annual award. Live coverage (in East) from Mobile, Ala. 60 minutes. Premiere date: 5/5/75.
Executive Producer Saul Ilson; Ernie Chambers
Producer Harry Waterson
Director Art Fisher
Writer Brian Alison; J. Mendelson
Host Michael Landon
Special Guest Karen Morris

70   Amy Prentiss
NBC Sunday Mystery Movie   NBC
Program Type Crime Drama
Some episodes 90 minutes; others 120 minutes. Premiere date: 12/1/74. Last show: 7/6/75. Set in San Francisco.
Producer Cy Chermak
Production Company Universal Television and Francy Productions
CAST
Chief of Detectives Amy Prentiss .... Jessica Walter
Pena .... Art Metrano
Joan .... Gwenn Mitchell
Russell .... Steve Sandor

71   And Who Shall Feed This World?
NBC News Special   NBC
Program Type Documentary/Special
Special. 60 minutes. Premiere date: 11/24/74.
Executive Producer Robert Northshield
Producer Len Giovannitti
Production Company NBC News
Director Darold Murray
Writer Len Giovannitti
Narrator John Chancellor

The Andersonville Trial *see* Humanities Film Forum

72   The Andy Williams Christmas Show
          NBC
Program Type Music/Dance
Special. 60 minutes. Premiere date: 12/11/74. Christmas songs from the Williams family: Andy Williams; Claudine Longet; Danielle Longet; and nephews Andy and David.
Executive Producer Andy Williams
Producer Norman Campbell
Director Norman Campbell
Writer John McGreevey; Claudine Longet
Host Andy Williams

73   Animal World   Syndicated
Program Type Animal Documentary
Premiered on NBC in June 1968; in syndication since January 1973. 30 minutes. Weekly.
Executive Producer Charles Sutton

Production Company Bill Burrud Productions, Inc.
Distributor Trans-American Video Company
Writer Miriam Birch
Host Bill Burrud

74 Ann-Margret Olsson   NBC
Program Type Comedy/Variety
Special. 60 minutes. Premiere date: 1/23/75.
Stars Ann-Margret.
Executive Producer Roger Smith; Allan Carr
Producer Dwight Hemion; Gary Smith
Production Company ATV-ITC and RSVP Inc.
Director Dwight Hemion
Writer Marty Farrell
Choreographer Rob Iscove
Guests Tina Turner; The Osmonds; Rob Iscove
Dancers

75 Annie and the Hoods   ABC
Program Type Comedy/Variety
Special. 60 minutes. Premiere date: 11/27/74.
Executive Producer David J. Cogan
Producer Martin Charnin
Director Martin Charnin
Writer Gary Belkin; Martin Charnin; Bob Ellison; Thomas Meehan; Gail Parent; Bob Randall; Kenny Solms; Judith Viorst
Musical Director Elliot Lawrence
Choreographer Alan Johnson
Host Anne Bancroft
Costume Designer Bill Hargate
Guest Stars Alan Alda; Jack Benny; Mel Brooks; Tony Curtis; David Merrick; Robert Merrill; Carl Reiner; Gene Wilder

76 Another Part of the Forest
Hollywood Television Theatre   PBS
Program Type Drama
150 minutes. Premiere date: 10/2/72. Repeat date: 7/31/75.
Executive Producer Norman Lloyd
Producer Norman Lloyd
Production Company KCET/Los Angeles
Director Daniel Mann
Writer Lillian Hellman
CAST

Lavinia Hubbard	Dorothy McGuire
Marcus Hubbard	Barry Sullivan
Regina Hubbard	Tiffany Bolling
Oscar Hubbard	Andrew Prine
Benjamin	Robert Foxworth
John Bagtry	William Bassett
Birdie Bagtry	Patricia Sterling
Laurette Sincee	Lane Bradbury
Simon Isham	Kent Smith
Jacob	William Walker
Coralee	Maidie Norman
Harold Penniman	Jack Manning
Gilbert Jugger	Peter Brocco

77 Another World   NBC
Program Type Daytime Drama
First regularly scheduled 60 minute daytime serial on TV, as of 1/6/75. Monday-Friday. Continuous. Premiere date: 5/4/64. Set in Bay City, U.S.A. (Cast information as of 1/6/75.) Spin-off: "Somerset."
Executive Producer Paul Rauch
Producer Joseph Rothenberger; Mary S. Bonner
Production Company Procter & Gamble Productions
Director Ira Cirker; Melvin Bernhardt; Peter Levin; Art Wolff
Head Writer Harding LeMay
CAST

David Gilchrist	David Ackroyd
Zach Richards	Terry Alexander
Russ Matthews	David Bailey
Vic Hastings	John Considine, Jr.
Robert Delaney	Nicolas Coster
Alice Frame	Jacqueline Courtney
Liz Matthews	Irene Dailey
Jamie Frame	Bobby Doran
Mary Matthews	Virginia Dwyer
Willis Frame	John Fitzpatrick
Ada McGowan	Constance Ford
Neil Johnson	John Getz
Dennis Carrington	Michael Hammett
Carol Lamonte	Jeanne Lange
Wally Delaney	Dennis McKiernan
Iris Carrington	Beverlee McKinsey
Jim Matthews	Hugh Marlowe
Barbara Weaver	Roberta Maxwell
Louise Goddard	Anne Meacham
Linda Metcalf	Vera Moore
Marianne Randolph	Ariane Munker
Pat Randolph	Beverly Penberthy
Michael M. Ryan	John Randolph
Steven Frame	George Reinholt
Richard Gavin	William Roerick
Lenore Delaney	Susan Sullivan
Gil McGowan	Dolph Sweet
Mackenzie Corey	Douglass Watson
Rachel Frame	Victoria Wyndham

78 Antonio and the Mayor   CBS
Program Type Children's Show
Special. 90 minutes. Premiere date: 1/8/75.
Producer Howard Rodman; Jerry Thorpe
Production Company CBS Television Network Presentation
Director Jerry Thorpe
Writer Howard Rodman
CAST

Antonio	Diego Gonzales
Mayor Acambarros	Gregory Sierra
Federico Cervantes	Javier Marc
Mr. Camargo	Fernesio Bernal
Filipe Orpeza	Claudio Martinez
Mrs. Acambarros	Aurora Clavell
Father Montalvo	Julio Medina

79 Antony and Cleopatra
ABC Theatre   ABC
Program Type Drama
Special. "Antony and Cleopatra" by William
Shakespeare performed by the Royal Shake-
speare Company. 180 minutes. Premiere date:
1/4/75.
Executive Producer Cecil Clarke
Producer Trevor Nunn
Production Company Associated TeleVision
Corporation
Director Jon Scoffield
Writer William Shakespeare
CAST

Marc Antony	Richard Johnson
Cleopatra	Janet Suzman
Octavius Caesar	Corin Redgrave
Enobarbus	Patrick Stewart
Charmian	Rosemary McHale
Agrippa	Philip Locke
Octavia	Mary Rutherford
Lepidus	Raymond Westwall

80 Apollo-Soyuz: A Meeting in Space
CBS News Special   CBS
Program Type Documentary/Special
Live coverage of the U.S.-U.S.S.R. space linkup
from launch 7/15/75 through docking of the
spacecraft 7/17/75 to splashdown 7/24/75.
Walter Cronkite anchor with Wally Schirra, and
correspondents Nelson Benton in Texas; Richard
Roth and Steve Young in Moscow; and Morton
Dean in New York City.
Executive Producer Russ Bensley
Production Company CBS News

81 Apollo-Soyuz: A Meeting in Space Preview
CBS News Special   CBS
Program Type Documentary/Special
Walter Cronkite; Wally Schirra preview the mis-
sion. 30 minutes. 7/14/75.
Executive Producer Russ Bensley
Production Company CBS News

82 Apollo-Soyuz Joint Space Mission
NBC News Special   NBC
Program Type Children's Show
30 minutes. Program for young people. Preview
of space mission. 7/14/75. (*See also* "A Hand-
shake in Space"; "Joint U.S.-U.S.S.R. Mission.")
Producer James Kitchell
Production Company NBC News
Host Jim Hartz; Eugene Cernan

83 Apple's Way
CBS
Program Type Drama
Created by Earl Hamner. 60 minutes. Sunday.
Premiere date: 2/10/74. Season premiere:

9/15/74. Last show: 1/12/75. Show set in Ap-
pleton.
Executive Producer Lee Rich; Earl Hamner
Producer John Furia, Jr.
Production Company Lorimar Productions for
CBS-TV.
CAST

George Apple	Ronny Cox
Barbara Apple	Lee McCain
Grandpa	Malcolm Atterbury
Steven Apple	Eric Olson
Patricia Apple	Kristie McNichol
Paul Apple	Vincent Van Patten
Cathy	Patti Cohoon

84 Arabs and Israelis
PBS
Program Type Documentary/Special
Eight-part series. 30 minutes. Weekly. Premiere
date: 2/5/75. Repeat date: 4/21/75.
Producer Peter Cooke; Mohammed Salmawy;
Zvi Dor-Ner
Production Company WGBH/Boston

85 The Arbors
PBS
Program Type Music/Dance
Six-part series. Weekly. 30 minutes. Premiere
date: 8/7/75. The quartet consists of Ed Farran;
Fred Farran; Scott Herrick; Tom Herrick.
Producer Robert J. Chitester
Production Company WQLN/Erie, Pennsylva-
nia

86 Archer
NBC
Program Type Crime Drama
Based on the character created by Ross Mac-
Donald. 60 minutes. Thursday. Premiere date:
1/30/75. Last show: 3/13/75. (*See* "The Under-
ground Man" for cast and credits of pilot film.)
Executive Producer David Carp
Producer Jack Miller; Leonard B. Kaufman
Production Company Paramount Television and
Leda Productions
CAST

Lew Archer	Brian Keith
Lt. Barney Brighton	John P. Ryan

Around the World in Eighty Days *see*
The CBS Thursday/Friday Night
Movies

The Arrangement *see* NBC Nights at the
Movies

87 Art in Public Places
PBS
Program Type Documentary/Special
Special. Tour of outdoor art in New York City.
30 minutes. Premiere date: 10/28/74. Repeat
date: 4/28/75.

Producer Fred Barzyk
Production Company WGBH/Boston and the Metropolitan Museum of Art
Director Fred Barzyk
Narrator Russell Connor

88 Art Is ...   PBS
Program Type Documentary/Special
Special. The varieties of art forms such as music and ballet. 30 minutes. Premiere date: 6/25/74. Repeat date: 3/22/75. Program made possible by grants from the Associated Council of the Arts and The Sears Roebuck Foundation.
Producer Julian Krainin; DeWitt L. Sage
Production Company Krainin/Sage Productions, Inc.; WNET/New York
Guests Leonard Bernstein; Jerome Robbins; Edward Villella

89 Arthur Rubinstein in Great Performances
Great Performances   PBS
Program Type Music/Dance
Special. 90 minutes. Premiere date: 10/17/75. Arthur Rubinstein performs Bach and Beethoven. Presented in the United States by WNET-TV/New York. David Griffiths coordinating producer.
Executive Producer Fritz Buttenstedt
Producer Helmut Bauer
Production Company Unitel

90 As the World Turns   CBS
Program Type Daytime Drama
One of the many daytime dramas created by Irna Phillips. Set in Oakdale, U.S.A. 30 minutes. Monday-Friday. Premiere date: 4/2/56. Continuous. "As the World Turns" theme by Charles Paul. Helen Wagner, Santos Ortega and Don MacLaughlin are original cast members. (Cast list as of April 1975.) "As the World Turns" and "The Edge of Night" were the first two 30-minute daytime dramas.
Producer Joe Willmore
Production Company Procter & Gamble Productions
Director Leonard Valenta; Paul Lammers
Head Writer Robert Soderberg; Edith Sommer
Announcer Dan McCullough
CAST

John Dixon	Larry Bryggman
Julia Burke	Fran Carlon
Natalie Bannon	Judith Chapman
Tom Hughes	C. David Colson
Jay Stallings	Dennis Cooney
Betsy Stewart	Suzanne Davidson
Grant Colman	James Douglas
David Stewart	Henderson Forsythe
lisa Shea	Eileen Fulton
Emmy Stewart	Jenny Harris
Bob Hughes	Don Hastings
Kim Reynolds Dixon	Kathryn Hays
Mark Galloway	Anthony Herrera
Chris Hughes	Don MacLaughlin
Carol Hughes	Rita MacLaughlin
Susan Stewart	Marie Masters
Grandpa Hughes	Santos Ortega
Dan Stewart	John Reilly
Alma Miller	Ethel Remey
Joyce Colman	Barbara Rodell
Jennifer Ryan Hughes	Gillian Spencer
Nancy Hughes	Helen Wagner

91 The Ascent of Man   PBS
Program Type Documentary/Special
60 minutes. Weekly. Premiere date: 1/7/75. 13-part series presented by WGBH/Boston; made possible by a grant from the Arthur Vining Davis Foundation and the Mobil Oil Corporation. Theme, "The Ascent of Man" composed and conducted by Dudley Simpson. Introduction by Anthony Hopkins. Senior producer: Dick Gilling. Programs: "Lower Than the Angels," "The Harvest of the Seasons," "The Grain in the Stone," "The Hidden Structure," "Music of the Spheres," "The Starry Messenger," "The Majestic Clockwork," "The Drive for Power," "The Ladder of Creation," "World Within World," "Knowledge or Certainty?" "Generation Upon Generation," "The Long Childhood."
Story Editor Adrian Malone
Production Company British Broadcasting Corporation in cooperation with Time/Life Films
Writer Dr. Jacob Bronowski
Narrator Dr. Jacob Bronowski

92 Assignment America   PBS
Program Type Interview/Discussion
26-week series. Presented by WNET/New York. Weekly. Premiere date: 1/9/75. Hosts alternate. Profiles and interviews.
Executive Producer A. H. Perlmutter; Carey Winfrey
Producer Howard Weinberg; Carey Winfrey; Dick Siemanouski; Cynthia Kayan
Production Company WNET/New York
Host Studs Terkel; George F. Will; Maya Angelou; Doris Kearns

Association for Intercollegiate Athletics for Women National Swimming and Diving Championships *see* AIAW National Swimming and Diving Championships

93 Astro-Bluebonnet Bowl
ABC Sports Special   ABC
Program Type Sports
16th Astro-Bluebonnet Bowl from the As-

Astro-Bluebonnet Bowl *Continued*
trodome in Houston, Texas. Live coverage.
12/23/74. North Carolina State Wolfpack versus
Houston Cougars.
Executive Producer Roone Arledge
Production Company ABC Sports
Announcer Chris Schenkel; Darrell Royal

94   At the Top   PBS
Program Type Music/Dance
Four-part series of jazz specials. 60 minutes each.
Premiere date: 2/17/75. Artists: Thad Jones and
Mel Lewis; Buddy Greco; Modern Jazz Quartet;
Maynard Ferguson. Funded through the Station
Production Cooperative.
Executive Producer James A. DeVinney
Producer Jim Dauphinee
Production Company WXXI/Rochester
Director Jim Dauphinee

95   Atlanta Classic
ABC Sports Special   ABC
Program Type Sports
Live coverage of third and final round play from
the Atlanta Country Club. 5/31/75; 6/1/75.
Executive Producer Roone Arledge
Production Company ABC Sports
Announcer Jim McKay; Keith Jackson; Bill
Flemming; Dave Marr; Bob Rosburg

96   Austin City Limits   PBS
Program Type Music/Dance
Special. 60 minutes. Premiere date: 3/12/75.
Starring Willie Nelson with Jody Payne and Paul
English.
Producer Paul Bosner
Production Company KLRN/San Antonio-Austin
Director Bruce Scafe

**97   The Autobiography of Miss Jane
Pittman**   CBS
Program Type Drama
Special. Winner of nine Emmy Awards. Based on
novel by Ernest J. Gaines. Filmed near Baton
Rouge, La. Premiere date: 1/31/74. Repeat date:
11/3/74. 120 minutes.
Producer Robert W. Christiansen; Rick Rosenberg
Production Company Tomorrow Entertainment,
Inc.
Director John Korty
Writer Tracy Keenan Wynn
CAST
Jane .... Cicely Tyson
Big Laura .... Odetta
Mme. Gautier .... Josephine Premice
Sheriff Guidry .... Ted Airhart
Tee-Bob .... Sidney Arroyo

Jimmy (7 years old) .... Eric Brown
Freedom Investigator .... Woodrow Chambliss
Amma Dean .... Barbara Chaney
"Long-Haired Boy" .... Noel Cravenze
Master Bryant .... Richard Dysart
"Unc" Isom .... Joel Fluellen
Etienne .... Jerry Green
Mr. Clyde .... James Goodman
Elbert Cluveau .... Will Hare
Col. Dye .... David Hooks
Mary .... Elnora B. Johnson
Trooper Brown .... Dudley Knight
Little Ned (5 years old) .... Derrick Mills
Quentin Lerner .... Michael Murphy
Ticey (Jane at 10) .... Valerie O'Dell
Joe Pittman .... Rod Perry
Master Robert .... Roy Poole
Ned (42 years old) .... Thalmus Rasulala
Ned (15-18) .... Dan Smith
Vivian .... Carol Sutton
Timmy .... Tony Thomas
Mary Agnes .... Alana Villavaso
Elder Banks .... Bill Walker
Mistress Bryant .... Collin Wilcox-Horne
Jimmy .... Arnold Wilkerson
Lena .... Beatrice Winde

98   Aviation Weather   PBS
Program Type Educational
30 minutes. Weekly. Premiere date: 1/4/74.
Continuous. Produced in cooperation with the
Federal Aviation Authority and the National
Weather Service. Made possible in part by a
grant from the Aircraft Owners and Pilot Association's Air Safety Foundation. Jim English
became host May 1975.
Producer Lori Evans
Production Company Maryland Center for Public Broadcasting/Owings Mills, Maryland
Host Jan Allsman; Jim English

99   Avignon   CBS
Program Type Religious Program
CBS News religious special. A look at the city as
a religious center. 30 minutes. Premiere date:
3/30/74.
Executive Producer Pamela Ilott
Producer Ben Flynn
Production Company CBS News
Writer Ben Flynn
Narrator Alred Drake

100   Bach's Mass in B Minor
Great Performances   PBS
Program Type Music/Dance
Special. 150 minutes. Premiere date: 4/12/74.
Repeat date: 3/28/75. Presented in the United
States by WNET-TV/New York; David Griffiths coordinating producer. Dr. Karl Richter
conducting the Munich Bach Orchestra and
Choir.
Production Company Unitel

Director Arne Arnbom
Guest Artists Hermann Prey; Gundula Janowitz; Horst Laubenthal; Herta Topper

101 Bad Ronald
Tuesday/Wednesday Movie of the Week ABC
Program Type TV Movie
90 minutes. Premiere date: 10/23/74. Repeat date: 8/13/75. Based on a novel by John Holbrook Vance.
Executive Producer Lee Rich
Producer Philip Capice
Production Company Lorimar Productions
Director Buzz Kulik
Writer Andrew Peter Marin
CAST

Ronald Wilby	Scott Jacoby
Elaine Wilby	Kim Hunter
Mrs. Wood	Pippa Scott
Sgt. Lynch	John Larch
Duane Mathews	Ted Eccles
Mr. Wood	Dabney Coleman
Barbara Wood	Cindy Fisher
Althea Wood	Cindy Eilbacher
Ellen Wood	Lisa Eilbacher
Mrs. Schumacher	Linda Watkins
Mrs. Mathews	Aneta Corsaut
Laurie Mathews	Linda Purl
Carol Mathews	Angela Hoffman

102 Bailey's Comets   CBS
Program Type Animated Film
30 minutes. Sunday. Premiere date: 9/8/73. Reruns: 9/8/74. Last show: 8/31/75. Created for television by David H. DePatie and Friz Freleng in association with Ken Spears and Joe Ruby.
Producer David H DePatie; Friz Freleng
Production Company DePatie-Freleng Enterprises, Inc. in special arrangement with Viacom
Writer Dalton Sandifer; John W. Dunn; Larz Bourne
Musical Director Eric Rogers
Animation Director Bob McKimson; Sid Marcus
Voices Jim Begg; Daws Butler; Carl Esser; Kathy Gori; Bob Holt; Sarah Kennedy; Don Messick; Karen Smith; Frank Welker

103 The Bait
Tuesday/Wednesday Movie of the Week ABC
Program Type TV Movie
Based on the novel by Dorothy Uhnak. 90 minutes. Premiere date: 3/13/73. Repeat date: 4/16/75.
Producer Peter Nelson
Production Company Spelling/Goldberg Productions
Director Leonard Horn
Writer Don M. Mankiewicz; Gordon Cotler
CAST

Tracy	Donna Mills

Capt. Maryk	Michael Constantine
Earl Stokey	William Devane
Nora	June Lockhart
Solomon	Noam Pitlik
Nugent	Thalmus Rasulala
Ruggeri	Gianni Russo
Liz Fowler	Arlene Golonka
Mickey	Brad Savage
Denise	Xenia Gratsos

The Ballad of a Soldier *see* Humanities Film Forum

104 The Barbary Coast
The ABC Sunday Night Movie   ABC
Program Type TV Movie
120 minutes. Premiere date: 5/4/75. Pilot for series of the same name 1975–76 season; created by Douglas Heyes.
Producer Douglas Heyes
Production Company Paramount Television
Director Bill Bixby
Writer Douglas Heyes
Costume Designer Guy Verhille
CAST

Jeff Cable	William Shatner
Cash Conover	Dennis Cole
Clio DuBois	Lynda Day George
Lt. Tully	Charles Aidman
Diamond Jack Bassiter	Michael Ansara
Florrie Roscoe	Neville Brand
Flame	Bobbi Jordan
Moose Moran	Richard Kiel
Templar	John Vernon
Macdonald Keogh	Leo Gordon
Sgt. Hatch	Bob Hoy
Bret Hollister	Terry Lester
Brant Hollister	Simon Scott
Gibbon	Todd Martin
Mr. Speece	Byron Webster
Cheval	Erik Silju
Beaumont	Lucien Lanvin Martin
Mace	Michael Carr
Mame	Roberta McElroy
Jacques Fouchet	Louis de Farra
Marie	Lidia Kristen
Philippe Despard	Bill Bixby

Barefoot in the Park *see* NBC Nights at the Movies

105 Baretta   ABC
Program Type Crime Drama
60 minutes. Premiere date: 1/17/75. Moved from Fridays to Wednesdays. Created by Stephen J. Cannell. Baretta's pet cockatoo is named Fred.
Producer Jo Swerling, Jr.
Production Company A Public Arts/Roy Huggins Production in association with Universal Television
Director Various

Baretta *Continued*
Writer Various
CAST
Tony Baretta ....Robert Blake
Insp. Shiller .... Dana Elcar
Billy Truman .... Tom Ewell
Rooster .... Michael D. Roberts

106   **Barnaby Jones**   CBS
Program Type Crime Drama
60 minutes. Tuesday. Premiere date: 1/28/73.
Season premiere: 9/10/74.
Executive Producer Quinn Martin
Producer Philip Saltzman
Production Company Quinn Martin Productions
Director Various
Writer Various
CAST
Barnaby Jones ....Buddy Ebsen
Betty Jones .... Lee Meriwether

107   **Barney Miller**   ABC
Program Type Comedy
30 minutes. Thursday. Premiere date: 1/23/75.
Set in the 12th precinct detectives' squadroom in
New York City. Created by Danny Arnold;
Theodore J. Flicker.
Executive Producer Danny Arnold
Producer Chris Hayward
Production Company Four D Productions
Director Various
Writer Various
CAST
Capt. Barney Miller .... Hal Linden
Elizabeth Miller .... Barbara Barrie
Fish ....Abe Vigoda
Wojehowicz ....Max Gail
Chano .... Gregory Sierra
Nick Yemana .... Jack Soo
Ron Harris .... Ron Glass
Bernice Fish .... Florence Stanley

108   **Baseball Game of the Week**   NBC
Program Type Sports
40 regular season games. Saturdays and Mondays. Season premiere: 4/12/75. Play-offs began
10/5/75. (*See also* "World Series.") Jim Simpson
and Maury Wills announcers for extra games.
Production Company NBC Sports
Announcer Joe Garagiola; Curt Gowdy; Tony
Kubek; Jim Simpson; Maury Wills

109   **The Baseball World of Joe**
Garagiola   NBC
Program Type Sports
Precedes "NBC Monday Night Baseball," "Ma-
jor League Championship Playoffs" and "World
Series." 15 minutes. Premiere 1973. (*See also*
"Next Year Is Here," special show 4/6/75 at
start of 1975 baseball season.)

Executive Producer Joe Garagiola
Producer Don Ellis
Production Company NBC Sports and Joe
Garagiola Enterprises
Writer Frank Slocum
Host Joe Garagiola

Battle for the Planet of the Apes *see* The
CBS Thursday/Friday Night Movies

Battle of Britain *see* The ABC Saturday
Night Movie

The Battle of Culloden *see* Humanities
Film Forum

110   **Be My Valentine, Charlie Brown**
                                                CBS
Program Type Animated Film
Based on the comic strip created by Charles M.
Schulz. 30 minutes. Premiere date: 1/28/75. Mu-
sic by Vince Guaraldi.
Executive Producer Lee Mendelson
Producer Bill Melendez
Production Company Lee Mendelson-Bill Me-
lendez Production in cooperation with United
Features Syndicate, Inc. and Charles M.
Schulz Creative Associates
Director Phil Roman
Writer Charles M. Schulz
Music Supervisor John Scott Trotter
VOICES
Charlie Brown .... Duncan Watson
Linus ....Stephen Shea
Lucy ....Melanie Kohn
Schroeder .... Greg Felton
Violet .... Linda Ercoli
Sally .... Lynn Mortensen

111   **The Bear Who Slept Through**
Christmas   NBC
Program Type Animated Film
Special. Based on a story by John Barrett. 30
minutes. Premiere date: 12/17/73. Repeat date:
12/16/74. Music and lyrics by Doug Goodwin.
Executive Producer Norman Sedawie
Producer David H. DePatie; Friz Freleng
Production Company A DePatie-Freleng Sed-
Bar Production
Director Hawley Pratt; Gerry Chiniquy
Writer Larry Spiegel; John Barrett
VOICES
Bear .... Tommy Smothers
Patti Bear ....Barbara Feldon
Professor .... Arte Johnson
Santa Claus .... Robert Holt
Weather Bear .... Kelly Lange
Honey Bear .... Michael Bell
Additional Voices Casey Kasem; Caryn Paperny

112   **Beauty and the Beast**   PBS
Program Type Children's Show
Special. Fairy tale presented by the Zapletal Puppets. 30 minutes. Premiere date: 12/23/73. Repeat date: 12/25/74.
Producer Peter Zapletal
Production Company Mississippi Center for Educational Television
Puppeteers Peter Zapletal; Jarmila Zapletal

113   **Beavers of the North Country**
The Undersea World of Jacques Cousteau
                                              ABC
Program Type Animal Documentary
Special. Filmed in Saskatchewan, Canada. 60 minutes. Premiere date: 1/6/75. With Jacques Cousteau and the crew of the *Calypso.*
Executive Producer Jacques Cousteau; Marshall Flaum
Producer Andy White
Production Company A Marshall Flaum Production in association with The Cousteau Society and MPC Metromedia Producers Corporation and ABC News
Director Philippe Cousteau
Writer Andy White
Musical Director Walter Scharf
Host Jacques Cousteau
Photographer Philippe Cousteau
Underwater Camera Philippe Cousteau
Camera Francois Charlet
Narrator Joseph Campanella

The Beguiled *see* The ABC Sunday Night Movie

114   **Behind the Lines**   PBS
Program Type News Magazine
30 minutes. Weekly. Premiere date: 10/25/71. Season premiere: 10/31/74. Series made possible by a grant from the Martin Weiner Foundation and the Ford Foundation. Philip Curtis replaced Jeff Wheelwright as producer in February 1975.
Executive Producer Carey Winfrey
Producer Jeff Wheelwright; Philip Curtis
Production Company WNET/New York
Host Harrison E. Salisbury

115   **Bell System Family Theatre**   NBC
Program Type General
Specials of various types. Programs during the 1974–75 season: "The Canterville Ghost," "The Cay," "Christmas with the Bing Crosbys," "The Count of Monte Cristo," "Great Expectations," "Highlights of Ringling Bros. and Barnum & Bailey Circus." (*See* individual titles for credits.)

116   **The Belmont Stakes**
CBS Sports Special   CBS
Program Type Sports
107th Belmont Stakes. Live coverage from Belmont Park, Elmont, New York. 60 minutes. 6/7/75.
Production Company CBS Television Network Sports
Announcer Chic Anderson
Reporters Jack Whitaker; Heywood Hale Broun; Frank Wright

117   **Ben Vereen ... Comin' At Ya** NBC
Program Type Comedy/Variety
Four-part series. Thursday. 60 minutes. Premiere date: 8/7/75. Last show: 8/28/75. Special music by Ray Charles. Chorus members: KaRon Brown; Vicki Ally; Adele Yoshioka; Barbara Hancock.
Producer Jaime Rogers; Gene McAvoy
Production Company Hygene Productions, Inc.
Director Peter Calabrese
Head Writer Buz Kohan
Musical Director Jack Elliot; Allyn Ferguson
Choreographer Jerry Grimes
Host Ben Vereen
Regular Lola Falana; Liz Torres; Avery Schreiber

118   **Beneath the Frozen World**
The Undersea World of Jacques Cousteau
                                              ABC
Program Type Documentary/Special
Special. Filmed in the Antarctic. 60 minutes. Premiere date: 3/3/74. Repeat date: 6/9/75. With Jacques Cousteau and the crew of the *Calypso.*
Executive Producer Jacques Cousteau; Marshall Flaum
Producer Andy White
Production Company Metromedia Producers Corporation and Les Requins Associes in association with ABC News
Writer Andy White
Narrator Rod Serling

119   **Benjamin Franklin**   CBS
Program Type Drama
Four-part series dealing with the life of Benjamin Franklin. 90 minutes each. Premiere date: 11/21/74. Series consists of "The Ambassador," "The Rebel," "The Statesman," "The Whirlwind." (*See* individual titles for cast and credits.)
Executive Producer Lewis Freedman
Producer Glenn Jordan; George Lefferts
Production Company CBS Television
Director Glenn Jordan
Writer Various

120 Berlioz's Requiem   PBS
Program Type Music/Dance
Special. 90 minutes. Premiere date: 12/9/73. Repeat date: 12/24/74. "Grand Messe des Morts" by Hector Berlioz performed by the Music for Youth Symphony Orchestra; Concert Wind Ensemble in St. Josaphat's Basilica, Milwaukee, Wisconsin.
Producer Tom Frey
Production Company WMUS-WMVT/Milwaukee, Wisconsin
Director Tom Frey

121 Bernstein at Tanglewood
Great Performances   PBS
Program Type Music/Dance
Special. 60 minutes. Premiere date: 12/25/74. Leonard Bernstein conducting the Boston Symphony Orchestra. Produced in the United States by WNET-TV/New York; David Griffiths, producer.
Executive Producer Klaus Hallig; Harry Kraut
Production Company Unitel

122 Bess Myerson: In the Public Interest (Consumerism)   PBS
Program Type Interview/Discussion
Special. 60 minutes. Premiere date: 7/9/75. Bess Myerson talks with Ralph Nader.
Production Company WNET/New York

123 Bess Myerson: In the Public Interest (The Food Crisis)   PBS
Program Type Interview/Discussion
Special. The world food crisis and how to fight it. 60 minutes. Premiere date: 4/13/75.
Production Company WNET/New York
Host Bess Myerson
Guests Eugene Carson Blake; Lester P. Brown; Sen. Dick Clark; Dick Gregory; Frances Moore Lappe
Panelists Eileen Hots; Dr. Michael Jacobson; Rep. Benjamin Rosenthal

124 The Best Congress Money Can Buy
CBS Reports   CBS
Program Type Documentary/Special
Report on political campaigning. 60 minutes. Premiere date: 1/31/75.
Executive Producer Burton Benjamin
Producer John Sharnik
Production Company CBS News
Director Isaac Kleinerman; Joseph Zigman
Writer John Sharnik
Anchor Dan Rather

125 The Best of "All in the Family"
CBS
Program Type Comedy
Special. 60 minutes. Highlights of previous shows. Premiere date: 12/21/74. Repeat date: 8/9/75.
Executive Producer Don Nicholl
Producer Michael Ross; Bernie West
Production Company Bud Yorkin-Norman Lear Tandem Productions
Director H. Wesley Kenney
Host Henry Fonda
CAST
Archie Bunker .... Carroll O'Connor
Edith Bunker .... Jean Stapleton
Mike Stivic .... Rob Reiner
Gloria Stivic .... Sally Strothers

126 The Best of "Magazine"   CBS
Program Type News Magazine
Sample segments of "Magazine:" "Hysterrectomy" and "Sex After Sixty" produced by Irina Posner; "A Woman of the Cloth" produced by Mary Drayne, and an interview by Carole Taylor with Margaret Trudeau. 60 minutes. Premiere date: 6/11/75.
Executive Producer Perry Wolff
Production Company CBS News
Director Vern Diamond
Host Sylvia Chase; Hughes Rudd

127 Betrayal
Tuesday/Wednesday Movie of the Week   ABS
Program Type TV Movie
90 minutes. Premiere date: 12/3/74. Repeat date: 6/4/75. Based on the novel "Only Couples Need Apply" by Doris Miles Disney.
Executive Producer Charles Fries
Producer Gerald I. Isenberg
Production Company Metromedia Producers Corporation
Director Gordon Hessler
Writer James Miller
CAST
Helen Mercer .... Amanda Blake
Gretchen .... Tisha Sterling
Harold Porter .... Dick Haymes
Jay .... Sam Groom
Fred Hawkes .... Britt Leach
Roy .... Edward Marshall
Police Sergeant .... Ted Gehring
Highway Patrolman ....Dennis Cross
Mr. Hall .... Eric Brotherson
Savings Officer ....Vernon Weddle
Betty/Waitress .... Rene Bond
Eunice Russell .... Lucille Benson

128 Bicentennial Minutes   CBS
Program Type News Magazine
Daily narration of an incident of American history as it happened "200 years ago today." Pre-

miere date: 7/4/74. To conclude: 7/4/76. 60 seconds each. Different narrator daily.
Executive Producer Bob Markell; Lewis Freedman
Producer Gareth Davies; William Kayden
Production Company CBS News
Director Sam Sherman

129   **Big Band Cavalcade**   PBS
Program Type Music/Dance
Special. Music of the 1930's and 1940's recorded over three years. 60 minutes. Premiere date: 3/8/75. Singers with the Big Band Cavalcade: Freddy Martin; Margaret Whiting; Frankie Carle; Bob Crosby and the Bobcats.
Producer Larry Akin
Production Company Scene Three Productions
Director Mark W. Ball

130   **Big Blue Marble**   Syndicated
Program Type Children's Show
26 minutes. Weekly. Premiere: 9/74. Magazine format. Feature: "Dear Pen Pal." Show is a public service of I.T.T. Corporation. Created by Henry Fownes. Ron Campbell is animation producer.
Producer Henry Fownes
Production Company Alphaventure
Distributor Vitt Media International
Director Various
Writer Various
Musical Director Norman Paris
Animation Director Ron Campbell
Educational Consultant Clare Lynch O'Brien

The Big Bounce *see* The ABC Sunday Night Movie

A Big Hand for the Little Lady *see* NBC Nights at the Movies

131   **The Big Ripoff**
NBC World Premiere Movie   NBC
Program Type TV Movie
Pilot for "McCoy" series - 1975–76 season. Created by Roland Kibbee; Dean Hargrove. 90 minutes. Premiere date: 3/11/75. Repeat date: 8/26/75.
Producer Roland Kibbee; Dean Hargrove
Production Company Universal Television Production in association with NBC-TV
Director Dean Hargrove
Writer Roland Kibbee; Dean Hargrove
CAST
McCoy ....Tony Curtis
Silky .... Roscoe Lee Browne
Darnell .... Larry Hagman
Bishop ....John Dehner

Kelso .... Morgan Woodward
Brenda .... Brenda Vaccaro
Lt. Claypool .... Jay Varela

132   **The Big Showdown**   ABC
Program Type Game Show
30 minutes. Monday-Friday. Continuous. Premiere date: 12/23/74. Last show: 7/4/75.
Executive Producer Don Lipp; Ron Greenberg
Producer Shelley Dobbins
Production Company A Don Lipp-Ron Greenberg Production in association with ABC Television Network
Host Jim Peck

133   **The Bikinians**   PBS
Program Type Documentary/Special
Special. 30 minutes. Premiere date: 2/17/75.
Executive Producer William H. Hale
Producer Hill Bermont
Production Company WGTV-University of Georgia/Athens-Atlanta
Director Hill Bermont
Writer Hill Bermont

134   **Bill Moyer's Journal: International Report**   PBS
Program Type News Magazine
20 week series. 60 minutes. Premiere date: 1/16/75. Series made possible by a grant from the German Marshall Fund of the United States, the Corporation for Public Broadcasting, the Ford Foundation, IBM, and the Inter-American Foundation.
Executive Producer Jack Sameth
Production Company WNET/New York
Host Bill Moyers

135   **Billy Graham Anniversary Celebration**   Syndicated
Program Type Religious Program
Three programs from the Hollywood Bowl, Hollywood, California. 60 minutes each. Premiere dates: 12/2/74; 12/3/74; 12/4/74. Dr. Billy Graham; with singers Manuel Bonilla; Myrtle Hall; The Hawaiians; Joyous Celebration Youth Chorus; George Beverly Shea; Kim Wickes; Norma Zimmer; organist John Innes; pianist Tedd Smith; and the Crusade Choir directed by Cliff Barrows.
Executive Producer Walter F. Bennett; Fred Dienert
Producer Cliff Barrows

136   **Billy Graham Crusade: Mississippi**
          Syndicated
Program Type Religious Program
Three programs from Jackson, Mississippi. 60

Billy Graham Crusade: Mississippi
Continued
minutes each. Premiere: 9/75. Dr. Billy Graham
with vocalists Myrtle Hall; Bob Henley; Jane
Henley; George Beverly Shea; organist John
Innes; pianist Tedd Smith; the Crusade Choir
directed by Cliff Barrows; and guests Johnny
Cash; June Carter; Ethel Waters.
Executive Producer Walter F. Bennett; Fred
   Dienert
Producer Cliff Barrows
Director Tom Ivy

137   Billy Graham Crusade: New Mexico
Syndicated
Program Type Religious Program
Three programs from Albuquerque, New Mexico. 60 minutes each. Premiere: 6/75. Dr. Billy
Graham with Bonnie Barrows; vocalists Myrtle
Hall; Bob Henley; Jane Henley; George Beverly
Shea; organist Don Hustad; pianist Tedd Smith
and the Crusade Choir directed by Cliff Barrows.
Executive Producer Walter F. Bennett; Fred
   Dienert
Producer Cliff Barrows
Director Tom Ivy

**138   Billy Graham Crusade: Tidewater
Virginia**   Syndicated
Program Type Religious Program
Three programs from Norfolk, Virginia. 60
minutes each. Premiere: 3/75. Dr. Billy Graham
with vocalists Myrtle Hall; The Hawaiians; Bob
Henley; Jane Henley; Kim Wickes; organist John
Innes; pianist Tedd Smith; the Crusade Choir
directed by Cliff Barrows and guests Johnny
Cash; June Carter; Robert Hale; Dean Wilder;
Carrie ten Boom; Jeanette Clift.
Executive Producer Walter F. Bennett: Fred
   Dienert
Producer Cliff Barrows
Director Marshall Diskia

139   Bing Crosby and His Friends   CBS
Program Type Comedy/Variety
Special. 60 minutes. Premiere date: 10/9/74.
Taped at the Hollywood Palace Theatre. Musical
material written by Ken Welch; Mitzi Welch.
Producer Bob Finkel
Production Company Bob Finkel-Teram Productions
Director Marty Pasetta
Writer Harry Crane; George Bloom; Ken Welch
   and Mitzi Welch
Musical Director Peter Matz
Choreographer Buddy Schwab
Host Bing Crosby
Guests Bob Hope; Pearl Bailey; Sandy Duncan

140   Bing Crosby Pro-Am Tournament
ABC Sports Special   ABC
Program Type Sports
34th tournament from Pebble Beach, California.
Live coverage 1/25/75; 1/26/75.
Executive Producer Roone Arledge
Production Company ABC Sports
Host Bing Crosby

141   Black Bart
Comedy Special   CBS
Program Type Comedy
30 minutes. Pilot film. Based on Mel Brooks motion picture "Blazing Saddles." Premiere date:
4/4/75.
Executive Producer Mark Tuttle
Producer Michael Elias; Frank Shaw; Robert
   Butler
Production Company Warner Brothers Television
Director Robert Butler
Writer Michael Elias; Frank Shaw
CAST
Black Bart .... Lou Gossett
Reb Jordan .... Steve Landesberg
Belle Buzzer .... Millie Slavin
Mayor Malaga .... Noble Willingham
Moonwolf .... Ruben Moreno
Mr. Swenson .... Ted Lehmann
Curley .... Gerrit Graham
Jennifer .... Brooke Adams
Porter .... Rand Bridges
O'Brien ....Jock Livingston
Mrs. Swenson ....Tamar Cooper
Hughie .... Poindexter

142   Black Is a Beautiful Woman   PBS
Program Type Documentary/Special
Special. 60 minutes. Premiere date: 6/18/74. Repeat date: 8/25/75. One-woman show by Margo
Barnett dramatizing the prose and poetry of
Richard Wright; Langston Hughes; Nikki Giovanni.
Executive Producer Sam Johnson
Production Company WETA/Washington

143   Black Journal   PBS
Program Type News Magazine
13-part series. 60 minutes. Weekly. Premiere
date: 6/12/68. Season premiere: 1/9/75.
Executive Producer Tony Brown
Production Company WNET/New York
Host Tony Brown

144   Blank Check   NBC
Program Type Game Show
25 minutes. Monday-Friday. Continuous. Premiere date: 1/6/75. Last show: 7/4/75.
Executive Producer Jack Barry
Producer Mike Metzger

Production Company Jack Barry Productions
Director Richard S. Kline
Host Art James
Announcer Johnny Jacobs

145 Blankety Blanks   ABC
Program Type Game Show
30 minutes. Monday-Friday. Continuous. Premiere date: 4/21/75. Last show: 6/27/75.
Executive Producer Bob Stewart
Producer Donald K. Epstein
Production Company A Bob Stewart Production
Director Mike Gargiulo
Host Bill Cullen

146 The Blue Knight
The CBS Thursday/Friday Night Movies CBS
Program Type TV Movie
Sequel to 1973–74 pilot film. Based on the character created by Joseph Wambaugh. 90 minutes. Premiere date: 5/9/75. Repeat date: 8/15/75.
Executive Producer Lee Rich
Producer John Furia, Jr.
Production Company Lorimar Productions
Director J. Lee Thompson
Writer Albert Ruben
CAST
Bumper Morgan ....George Kennedy
Det. Bronski .... Alex Rocco
Edwin Beall .... Glynn Turman
Moody Larkin ....Verna Bloom
Zugarelli ....Michael Margotta
Piskor .... Seth Allen
Wimpey .... John Steadman
Det. Hartman ....Richard Hurst
Randy .... Bart Burns
Tank Whittier ....Ji-Tu Cumbuke
Personnel Officer .... Walter Barnes

147 The Blue Knight (miniseries)
NBC Nights at the Movies   NBC
Program Type Drama
Special. Adapted from the novel by Joseph Wambaugh. Originally shown as four-part miniseries 11/13/73-11/16/73. Repeat dates: 4/30/75; 5/1/75. 120 minutes each.
Executive Producer Lee Rich
Producer Walter Coblenz
Production Company Lorimar Productions
Director Robert Butler
Writer E. Jack Neuman
CAST
Bumper Morgan .... William Holden
Cassie Walters ....Lee Remick
Sgt. Cruz Segovia .... Joe Santos
Charlie Bronski .... Sam Elliott
Marvin .... David Moody
Yasser Hafiz ....Jamie Farr
Officer Grogan .... Vic Tayback
Zoot .... George Dicenzo
Hilliard ....Raymond Guth
Cites .... Stanley Clay

Hughes .... Kenneth Smedberg
Rudy ....Ernest Esparza, III
Ruthie .... Gloria Leroy

148 The Boarding House   PBS
Program Type Music/Dance
Six-part series. 30 minutes. Premiere date: 8/7/74. Repeat date: 7/21/75. Taped at The Boarding House club in San Francisco.
Executive Producer Zev Putterman
Production Company KQED/San Fransisco
Director Robert Zagove
Guests Mary McCreary; Esther Phillips; The Pointer Sisters; Leo Sayer; Taj Mahal; Wendy Waldman

149 The Bob Crane Show   NBC
Program Type Comedy
30 minutes. Thursday. Premiere date: 3/6/75. Last show: 6/19/75.
Producer Norman S. Powell; Martin Cohan
Production Company MTM Enterprises, Inc.
Director Various
Writer Various
CAST
Bob Wilcox ....Bob Crane
Ellie Wilcox ....Trisha Hart
Marvin .... Todd Susman
Lyle Ingersoll .... Jack Fletcher
Mr. Busso ....Ronny Graham
Jerry Mallory .... James Sutorius

150 Bob Hope Desert Classic
NBC Sports Special   NBC
Program Type Sports
Live coverage of third and final rounds from Palm Springs, California. 2/8/75; 2/9/75.
Producer Don Ellis
Production Company NBC Sports
Announcer Jim Simpson; Cary Middlecoff; Jay Randolph; John Brodie; Pat Hernon; Charlie Jones; Bob Hope

151 Bob Hope on Campus   NBC
Program Type Comedy/Variety
60 minutes. Premiere date: 4/17/75. On campus at the University of California at Los Angeles.
Executive Producer Bob Hope
Producer Mort Lachman
Production Company Bob Hope Enterprises
Director Dick McDonough
Writer Charles Lee and Gig Henry; Mort Lachman; Lester White and Mel Tolkin; Steve White
Musical Director Les Brown
Choreographer Jack Baker
Host Bob Hope
Guests John Wayne; Flip Wilson; Aretha Franklin; America

152   The Bob Hope Special   NBC
Program Type Comedy/Variety
First show of the season. Celebrating Bob Hope's silver anniversary on television. 60 minutes. Premiere date: 9/25/74.
Executive Producer Bob Hope
Producer Mort Lachman
Production Company Bob Hope Enterprises
Director Sid Smith
Writer Mort Lachman; Lester White and Mel Tolkin; Charles Lee and Gig Henry; Steve White
Musical Director Les Brown
Host Bob Hope
Guests Glen Campbell; Carol Channing; Jackie Gleason; Shirley Cothran; Rufus with Chaka Khan

153   The Bob Hope Special   NBC
Program Type Comedy/Variety
Second show. 60 minutes. Premiere date: 12/15/74.
Executive Producer Bob Hope
Producer Mort Lachman
Production Company Bob Hope Enterprises
Musical Director Les Brown
Host Bob Hope
Guests Dean Martin; Dyan Cannon; Olivia Newton-John

154   The Bob Hope Special   NBC
Program Type Comedy/Variety
Third show. Taped in Las Vegas. Introducing 10 "Hollywood Stars of Tomorrow." 60 minutes. Premiere date: 3/5/75.
Executive Producer Bob Hope
Producer Mort Lachman
Production Company Bob Hope Enterprises
Host Bob Hope

155   The Bob Newhart Show   CBS
Program Type Comedy
30 minutes. Saturday. Premiere date: 9/16/72. Season premiere: 9/14/74. Show set in Chicago.
Executive Producer David Davis; Lorenzo Music
Producer Tom Patchett; Jay Tarses
Production Company MTM Enterprises, Inc.
Director Various
Writer Various

CAST
Bob Hartley .... Bob Newhart
Emily Hartley .... Suzanne Pleshette
Jerry Robinson .... Peter Bonerz
Howard Borden .... Bill Daily
Carol Kester .... Marcia Wallace

156   The Bobby Goldsboro Show
Syndicated
Program Type Comedy/Variety
30 minutes. Country variety show. Weekly.
Executive Producer Bill Graham
Producer Bill Hobin; Jane Dowden; Reginald Dunlap
Production Company Show Biz, Inc.
Director Bill Hobin
Writer Ed Hider
Musical Director Timothy Tappan
Host Bobby Goldsoro
VOICES
Jonathan Rebel .... Peter Culler

157   The Bolero   PBS
Program Type Music/Dance
Special. 30 minutes. 1973 Oscar winner for "Best Short Subject." Premiere: 2/73. Repeat date: 5/28/75. Zubin Mehta conducts the Los Angeles Philharmonic Orchestra. Program made possible by grants from the National Endowment for the Arts, the Corporation for Public Broadcasting, and the Musicians Performance Trust Funds.
Producer Allan Miller

Bonnie and Clyde *see* The CBS
    Thursday/Friday Night Movies

158   Bonnie Raitt and Paul Butterfield
PBS
Program Type Music/Dance
Special. 60 minutes. Premiere date: 12/31/74. Repeat date: 7/26/75. Bonnie Raitt; Paul Butterfield; and Butterfield's Better Days Band.
Producer Taylor Hackford
Production Company KCET/Los Angeles

159   Book Beat   PBS
Program Type Interview/Discussion
30 minutes. Weekly. Premiered in 1965. Interviews with authors.
Producer Patricia Barey
Production Company WTTW/Chicago
Host Robert Cromie

160   Born Free   NBC
Program Type Drama
Filmed in Africa. Created by Carl Forman. Based on the books by Joy Adamson. 60 minutes. Monday. Premiere date: 9/9/74. Last show: 12/30/74.
Executive Producer David Gerber
Producer Paul Radin
Production Company David Gerber Productions in association with Columbia Pictures Television

CAST

George Adamson .... Gary Collins
Joy Adamson .... Diana Muldaur
Makedde .... Hal Frederick

Born Free (feature film) *see* The ABC
Summer Movie

161 **Born Innocent**
NBC World Premiere Movie   NBC
Program Type TV Movie
120 minutes. Premiere date: 9/10/74. Season
premiere of series.
Executive Producer Rick Rosenberg; Bob Chris-
tiansen
Producer Bruce Cohn Curtis
Production Company Tomorrow Entertainment
Production
Director Donald Wrye
Writer Gerald Di Pego

CAST

Christine Parker .... Linda Blair
Barbara Clark ....Joanna Miles
Mrs. Parker .... Kim Hunter
Mr. Parker .... Richard Jaeckel
Moco ....Nora Heflin
Denny .... Janit Baldwin
Miss Lasko .... Allyn Ann McLerie
Additional Cast Tina Andrews; Sandra Ego; Mitch Vo-
gel

162 **The Borrowers**
Hallmark Hall of Fame   NBC
Program Type Children's Show
Special. Based on the story by Mary Norton.
Music by Rod McKuen; sung by Rod McKuen
and Shelby Flint. Special effects by Doug Trum-
bull. 90 minutes. Premiere date: 12/14/73. Re-
peat date: 12/13/74.
Executive Producer Duane C. Bogie
Producer Walt DeFaria; Warren L. Lockhart
Production Company Walt DeFaria Productions
in association with 20th Century-Fox, Charles
Schulz Creative Associates and Foote-Cone-
Belding Productions
Director Walter C. Miller
Writer Jay Presson Allen

CAST

Pod Clock .... Eddie Albert
Homily Clock ....Tammy Grimes
Aunt Sophy ....Judith Anderson
Arrietty Clock .... Karen Pearson
The Boy .... Dennis Larson
Mrs. Crampfurl .... Beatrice Straight
Crampfurl .... Barnard Hughes

The Boston Strangler *see* The ABC
Monday Night Movie

Boy *see* The Japanese Film

The Boy Friend *see* The CBS
Thursday/Friday Night Movies

163 **The Boys**
Comedy Special   CBS
Program Type Comedy
30 minutes. Pilot film. Premiere date: 5/16/74.
Repeat date: 5/23/75.
Producer Bill Persky; Sam Denoff
Director Bill Persky
Writer Bill Persky; Sam Denoff

CAST

Eddie Ryan .... Tim Conway
Harry Rufkin ....Herb Edelman
Cassie ....Esther Sutherland
Alice .... Gwynne Gilford
Dr. Ferguson .... Richard Stahl
Vicki ....Elizabeth Davis

164 **The Brady Bunch**   ABC
Program Type Comedy
30 minutes. Monday-Friday. Daytime reruns of
evening series originally seen between September
1969 and August 1974. Created by Sherwood
Schwartz. Season premiere: 9/9/74. Last show:
4/18/75. Return date: 6/30/75. Last show:
8/29/75.
Executive Producer Sherwood Schwartz
Producer Howard Leeds; Lloyd J. Schwartz
Production Company Paramount Television

CAST

Mike Brady .... Robert Reed
Carol Brady .... Florence Henderson
Alice .... Ann B. Davis
Marcia Brady .... Maureen McCormick
Jan Brady .... Eve Plumb
Cindy Brady ....Susan Olsen
Gred Brady .... Barry Williams
Peter .... Christopher Knight
Bobby Brady .... Michael Lookinland

Breakfast at Tiffany's *see* The ABC
Saturday Night Movie

165 **Brian's Song**
Special Movie Presentation   ABC
Program Type TV Movie
True-life drama; filmed partly on location at the
Chicago Bears training camp in Rensselaer, Indi-
ana. 90 minutes. Premiere date: 11/30/71. Re-
peat date: 11/9/74.
Producer Paul Junger Witt
Production Company Screen Gems
Director Buzz Kulik
Writer William Blinn

CAST

Brian Piccolo ....James Caan

Brian's Song *Continued*

George Halas	Jack Warden
Gale Sayers	Billy Dee Williams
Joy Piccolo	Shelley Fabares
Linda Sayers	Judy Pace
Ed McCaskey	David Huddleston
J. C. Caroline	Bernie Casey
Doug Atkins	Ron Feinberg
Abe Gibron	Abe Gibron
Jack Concannon	Jack Concannon
Ed O'Bradovich	Ed O'Bradovich
Dick Butkus	Dick Butkus
Reporter No. 1	Mario Machado
Reporter No. 2	Bud Furillo
Speaker	Stu Nahan

The Bridge at Remagen *see* NBC Nights at the Movies

166   The Bridge of Adam Rush
ABC Afterschool Specials   ABC
Program Type Children's Show
Special. 60 minutes. Premiere date: 10/23/74. Filmed at Morristown National Historic Park, Morristown, New Jersey.
Producer Daniel Wilson
Production Company Bayberry Productions, Inc.
Director Larry Elikann
Writer Lee Kalcheim
CAST

Adam Rush	Lance Kerwin
Tom Rush	James Pritchett
Rebecca Rush	Barbara Andres
Elizabeth	Karen Sedore
Jody	Ray Belleran
Matt Price	Ed Crowley
The Drover	Brendon Fey

167   Brief Encounter
Hallmark Hall of Fame   NBC
Program Type TV Movie
Special. Adaptation of the 1936 drama "Still Life" by Noel Coward. 90 minutes. Premiere date: 11/12/74.
Executive Producer Duane C. Bogie
Producer Cecil Clarke
Production Company Carlo Ponti-Cecil Clarke Productions by arrangement with the Rank Organization in association with NBC and FCB
Director Alan Bridges
Writer John Bowen
CAST

Alec Harvey	Richard Burton
Anna Jesson	Sophia Loren
Graham	Jack Hedley
Mrs. Gaines	Rosemary Leach
Melanie	Ann Firbank
Dolly	Gwen Cherrell

Additional Cast Benjamin Edney; John Lemesurier; Jumoke Debayo; Madeline Hinde; Marco Orlandini; Patricia Franklin; Ernest C. Jennings; Jacki Harding; Maggie Walker; Christopher Hammond; Norman Mitchell

168   British Open
ABC Sports Special   ABC
Program Type Sports
Taped coverage of closing play from the 104th British Open at Carnoustie Golf Links, Scotland. 120 minutes. 7/12/75.
Executive Producer Roone Arledge
Production Company ABC Sports
Announcer Jim McKay; Chris Schenkel; Dave Marr

169   Broken Treaty at Battle Mountain
PBS
Program Type Documentary/Special
Special. 1974 prize-winning film. The case of the Shoshone Indians against the U.S. government. 60 minutes. Premiere date: 7/7/75.
Producer Joel L. Freedman
Production Company WLIW/Garden City, New York
Writer Tom Schachtman
Narrator Robert Redford

170   Broken Treaty at Battle Mountain: A Discussion   PBS
Program Type Interview/Discussion
Special. Follow-up discussion to film "Broken Treaty at Battle Mountain." 30 minutes. Premiere date: 7/7/75.
Producer Robert J. Aviello
Production Company WLIW/Garden City, New York
Moderator Hugh Downs
Panelists John Vance; Martin Seneca; Glenn V. Holley, Sr.; Kathy Collard; Vine De Loria

171   The Bronx Is Burning
Window on the World   Syndicated
Program Type Documentary/Special
60 minute special. With Dennis Smith and Engine Company 82 in the Bronx, New York. Premiere: 6/75.
Production Company BBC-TV and Time-Life Television
Narrators Burgess Meredith; Jeremy James

172   Brother to Dragons
Theater in America   PBS
Program Type Drama
Play by Robert Penn Warren performed by the Trinity Square Repertory Company. 90 minutes. Premiere date: 2/19/75. Series funded by Exxon Corporation and the Corporation for Public Broadcasting. (Cast in order of appearance.)
Executive Producer Jac Venza

Production Company WNET/New York
Director Adrian Hall
Writer Robert Penn Warren; Adrian Hall
Host Hal Holbrook
CAST

The Writer	Richard Kneeland
Thomas Jefferson	James Eichelberger
Lucy Lewis	Marguerite Lenert
Dr. Charles Lewis	George Martin
Lilburn Lewis	David Kennett
Isham Lewis	Robert Black
Aunt Cat	Barbara Meek
John	Ben Powers
Laetitia Lewis	Pamela Payton-Wright
Billy Rutter	T. Richard Mason
Sheriff	Richard K. Jenkins
Sudie Persley	Mina Manente
Head Man	George Collins
Clerk	Howard London
Family Slaves	Rick Wiley; Rose Weaver; Kim Delgado
Rednecks	Timothy Crowe; William Damkoehler
Little Lilburn	Ted Orson
Little Isham	John Case
Writer's Father	Robert Penn Warren

173 **Brunswick Red Crown Classic**
CBS Sports Special   CBS
Program Type Sports
Final round live coverage of the Professional Women's Bowling Association tournament. 1/4/75.
Producer Howard Reifsnyder
Production Company CBS Television Network Sports
Announcer Frank Glieber; Jane Chastain; Shirley Garms

Buck and the Preacher *see* NBC Nights at the Movies

174 **The Bugs Bunny Show**   ABC
Program Type Animated Film
30 minutes. Saturday. Reruns of old "Bugs Bunny" cartoons. Season reruns: 9/7/74. Last show: 8/30/75.
Producer Jacquelyn Smith
Production Company Warner Brothers Television

Bullitt *see* The CBS Thursday/Friday Night Movies

175 **Burglar Proofing**   PBS
Program Type Educational
Six-part series. 30 minutes. Weekly. Premiere date: 10/1/74.
Producer Everett Marshburn
Production Company Maryland Center for Public Broadcasting
Host Kene Holliday

Butterflies Are Free *see* NBC Nights at the Movies

176 **Byron Nelson Golf Classic**
ABC Sports Special   ABC
Program Type Sports
Live coverage of third and final round play from the Preston Trail Golf Club, Dallas, Texas. 5/10/75; 5/11/75.
Executive Producer Roone Arledge
Production Company ABC Sports
Announcer Chris Schenkel; Keith Jackson; Dave Marr

Cactus Flower *see* NBC Nights at the Movies

177 **Cage without a Key**
The CBS Thursday/Friday Night Movies CBS
Program Type TV Movie
Filmed in part at the Las Palmas School for Girls, City of Commerce, California. 120 minutes. Premiere date: 3/14/75.
Executive Producer Douglas S. Cramer
Producer Buzz Kulik
Production Company Douglas S. Cramer Company in association with Columbia Pictures Television
Director Buzz Kulik
Writer Joanna Lee
CAST

Valerie Smith	Susan Dey
Tommy	Jonelle Allen
Buddy Goleta	Sam Bottoms
Joleen	Anne Bloom
Betty Holian	Karen Carlson
Angel Perez	Edith Diaz
Suzy	Suesie Elene
Ben Holian	Michael Brandon
Sarah	Dawn Frame
Mrs. Little	Katherine Helmond
Jamie	Vicky Huxtable
Mrs. Turner	Karen Morrow
Noreen	Lani O'Grady
Wanda Polsky	Margaret Willock

178 **The California Kid**
Tuesday/Wednesday Movie of the Week ABC
Program Type TV Movie
90 minutes. Premiere date: 9/25/74. Repeat date: 5/6/75. Filmed in the Piru, Saugus and Soledad Canyon area of California.
Executive Producer Paul Mason
Producer Howie Horwitz
Production Company Universal Television
Director Richard Heffron
Writer Richard Compton

The California Kid Continued

CAST

Michael McCord	Martin Sheen
Sheriff Roy Childress	Vic Morrow
Maggie	Michelle Phillips
The Deputy	Stuart Margolin
Buzz Stafford	Nick Nolte
Sissy	Janit Baldwin
Lyle Stafford	Gary Morgan
Judge Hooker	Frederic Downs
Jack	Donald Mantooth
Don McCord	Joseph Estevez
Johnny	Britt Leach
Howard	Norman Bartold
Edith	Barbara Collentine
Charley	Michael Richardson
Tom	Gavan O'Herlihy
Pete	Jack McCulloch
Harlie	Ken Johnson
Leona	Sandy Brown Wyeth
Stranger	Trent Dolan
Gerry	Monika Henreid

179 Call It Macaroni   Syndicated
Program Type Children's Show
Real-life adventure specials. 30 minutes. Monthly. Premiere: 1/75. Theme "Anything Is Possible": music by David Lucas; lyrics by Gail Frank; Stephanie Meagher; sung by chorus with Ralph Carter. Each special co-produced by local Westinghouse station. Eight programs shown during 1974–75 season: "Exploring Yesterday," "Fly Like a Bird," "Give the Circus a Tumble," "It's a Long Way Up," "Once Upon a Horse," "Sail on the Wind's Time," "A Seaful of Adventure," "Texas Tenderfoot." (*See* individual titles for credits.)
Executive Producer George Moynihan
Producer Gail Frank; Stephanie Meagher
Production Company Group W Productions
Distributor Westinghouse Broadcasting Company
Director Gail Frank; Stephanie Meagher

Call Me Bwana *see* NBC Nights at the Movies

180 Cambodia: An American Dilemma
CBS News Special   CBS
Program Type Documentary/Special
30 minutes. Premiere date: 3/5/75.
Executive Producer Leslie Midgley
Producer Hal Haley; Bernard Birnbaum
Production Company CBS News
Anchor Charles Collingwood
Reporters Bruce Dunning; Marvin Kalb; Ike Pappas

181 Camera Three   CBS
Program Type Experimental Program
Experimental series dealing with "people, ideas, performances and new directions in the arts and sciences." 30 minutes. Sunday. Local premiere date: 5/16/53 (WCBS-TV, New York); national premiere: 1/22/56 (CBS Television Network). Season premiere: 9/8/74.
Executive Producer Merrill Brockway
Producer Various
Production Company WCBS-TV, CBS owned station in New York, in cooperation with the New York State Education Department
Director Various
Writer Various

182 Can I Save My Children?
ABC Afternoon Playbreak   ABC
Program Type TV Movie
Special. Filmed in Los Angeles County. 90 minutes. Premiere date: 10/17/74. (Season premiere of series.) Repeat date: 4/10/75.
Executive Producer Stanley L. Colbert
Producer Lee Miller
Production Company Stanley L. Colbert Co-Production Associations, Inc. and 20th Century-Fox Television
Director Walter Miller
Writer A. Roy Moore; Jonah Royston; Norman Hudis

CAST

Diana Hansen	Diane Baker
Clay Hollinger	David Hedison
Melanie Hansen	Tammi Bula
Harry Hansen	Jack Ging
Braddock	Jack Riley
Peter	Todd Gross
Doug	Ken Tobey
Bert	Mike McHenry
Matthew	Pat Cranshaw
George	Billy Bowles
Ambulance Attendant	Paul Van
David	Stuart Nisbet

183 Canada: Not for Sale   PBS
Program Type Documentary/Special
Special. 60 minutes. Premiere date: 1/9/75. Program made possible by a grant from the Financial Post.
Executive Producer Don Dixon
Producer Richard McCutchen
Production Company WNET/New York

184 Canada Week at Chautauqua   PBS
Program Type Music/Dance
Three-part series of concerts taped in 1973 at the Chautauqua Institution in New York State. Series made possible by a grant from the Zurn Corporation. 60 minutes each. Premiere date: 10/6/74. Repeat date: 8/26/75.

Producer Robert J. Chitester
Production Company WQLN/Educational Television of Northwest Pennsylvania, Inc./Erie, Pa.
Director Robert J. Chitester
Host Arnold Edinborough
Conductor Boris Brott
Guest Artists Joseph Macerello; Louis Quilico; Steven Staryk

185 The Canadian Open
CBS Sports Special   CBS
Program Type Sports
Third and final round play of the 66th Candian Open. Live coverage from the Royal Montreal Golf Club, Ile Bizard, Quebec 7/26/75; 7/27/75.
Production Company CBS Television Network Sports
Announcer Pat Summerall; Jack Whitaker; Frank Glieber; Ben Wright; Ken Venturi

The Candidate *see* NBC Nights at the Movies

186 Cannon   CBS
Program Type Crime Drama
60 minutes. Wednesday. Premiere date: 9/14/71. Season premiere: 9/11/74.
Executive Producer Quinn Martin
Supervising Producer Russell Stoneham
Producer Anthony Spinner
Production Company Quinn Martin Productions
Director Various
Writer Various
CAST
Frank Cannon .... William Conrad

187 The Canterville Ghost
Bell System Family Theatre   NBC
Program Type TV Movie
Special. Filmed at Berkeley Castle and in Bristol, Lacock and Bath, England. Adapted from story by Oscar Wilde. 60 minutes. Premiere date: 3/10/75.
Executive Producer Joseph Cates
Producer Timothy Burrill
Production Company Timothy Burrill in association with HTV Ltd. and Studio Hamburg/ Gyula Trebitsch, Polytel International Ltd., Cinecoord, International, Ltd.
Director Walter Miller
Writer Robin Miller
CAST
Sir Simon de Canterville .... David Niven
Hiram Otis .... James Whitmore
Lucretia Otis .... Audra Lindley
Mrs. Umney .... Flora Robson
Virginia Otis .... Lynne Frederick
Jefferson Otis .... Bobby Doran
Lincoln Otis .... Christopher Morris

Lord Canterville .... Maurice Evans
Charles, Duke of Cheshire .... Nicholas Jones

188 Captain Kangaroo   CBS
Program Type Children's Show
Created by Bob Keeshan. 60 minutes. Monday-Friday. Premiere date: 10/3/55. Continuous. Set in the Captain's Place. Cosmo Allegretti is the voice of many characters: Dancing Bear, Mr. Moose, Bunny Rabbit, Homer the Dog, Grandfather Clock, Miss Frog, Magic Drawing Board, etc. Hugh "Lumpy" Brannum plays Mr. Bainter, the Painter, Percy, The Professor, etc.
Producer Jimmy Hirshfeld
Production Company Robert Keeshan Associates, Inc.
Director Peter Birch
Head Writer Bob Colleary
Puppeteer Cosmo Allegretti
CAST
Captain Kangaroo .... Bob Keeshan
Mr. Green Jeans .... Hugh "Lumpy" Brannum
Dennis, the Apprentice .... Cosmo Allegretti

Captain Nemo and the Underwater City *see* The CBS Thursday/Friday Night Movies

The Caretakers *see* NBC Nights at the Movies

The Carey Treatment *see* The CBS Thursday/Friday Night Movies

189 Caribe   ABC
Program Type Crime Drama
60 minutes. Monday. Premiere date: 2/17/75. Last show: 8/11/75. Two-man Caribbean Force attached to the Miami Police Department. Filmed in Miami, Florida and in the West Indies.
Executive Producer Quinn Martin
Producer Anthony Spinner
Production Company Quinn Martin Productions
Director Various
Writer Various
CAST
Lt. Ben Hogan .... Stacy Keach
Sgt. Mark Walters .... Carl Franklin
Sgt. Ed Rawlings .... Robert Mandan

190 Carmen: The Dream and the Destiny   PBS
Program Type Music/Dance
Special. Rehearsals for Georges Bizet's "Carmen" as directed by Regina Resnik at the Hamburg State Opera in Germany. 90 minutes. Premiere date: 3/3/75. Program made possible by a grant from the Xerox Corporation.

Carmen: The Dream and the Destiny
Continued
Producer Christopher Nupen
Production Company WNET/New York
Editor Peter Heelas
Camera David Findlay
CAST
Carmen ....Hugette Tourangeau
Don Jose .... Placido Domingo

191 Carnival of Animals   PBS
Program Type Children's Show
Special. Filmed in Pennsylvania parks and zoos.
Hans Conreid reads Ogden Nash poetry written
for the "Carnival of Animals" by Charles Ca-
mille Saint-Saens. Pianists Veri and Jamanis per-
form. 60 minutes. Premiere date: 10/27/74. Pro-
gram made possible by a grant from the
Pennsylvania Public Television Network.
Producer Harold Plant
Production Company WITF/Hershey, Pennsyl-
vania
Director Harold Plant

192 The Carol Burnett Show   CBS
Program Type Comedy/Variety
60 minutes. Saturday. Premiere date: 9/11/67.
Season premiere: 9/14/74.
Executive Producer Joe Hamilton
Producer Ed Simmons
Production Company Punkin Productions, Inc.
Director Dave Powers
Head Writer Ed Simmons
Host Carol Burnett
Regular Harvey Korman; Vicki Lawrence; the
Ernest Flatt Dancers; Peter Matz Orchestra

The Carpetbaggers see The ABC
Saturday Night Movie

193 Carrascolendas   PBS
Program Type Children's Show
30 minutes. Weekly. Premiere: 10/72. Season
premiere: 10/2/74. Bilingual show: Spanish and
English. Series made possible by ESAA funds
from the U.S. Office of Education.
Executive Producer Aida Barrera
Production Company KLRN-TV (Southwest
Texas Public Broadcasting Council)/San An-
tonio-Austin, Texas
Story Editor Raoul Gonzales
CAST
Agapito, The Lion .... Harry Frank Porter
Campamocha, the Fix-It Shop Owner ..Mike Gomez
Caracoles, the Restaurant Owner .... Agapito Leal
Dyana, a Live Doll .... Dyana Elizondo
Pepper, the Detective ....Lizanne Brazell
Uncle Andy, the Shoemaker .... Joe Bill Hogan
Berta, a Live Doll .... Berta Cruz
Tio Cheo .... Armando Roblan

Senorita Hernandez .... Camille Carrion
Mabel the Magician .... Chequita Jackson

194 The Case Against Milligan
The American Parade   CBS
Program Type Drama
Part five of series. 60 minutes. Premiere date:
1/26/75. Program based on actual case.
Executive Producer Joel Heller
Producer Jack Willis
Production Company CBS News for the CBS
Television Network
Director Jan Kadar
Writer Loring Mandel
Narrator Joel Fabiani
CAST
Lambdin P. Milligan .... Richard Basehart
Sarah Milligan .... Alice Drummond
Moses Milligan .... Tim Kirkpatrick
Lou Milligan .... Glenn Zachar
Coffroth ....David Rounds
Bowles .... Henderson Forsythe
Humphrey .... Robert Gerringer
Horsey ....Jack Bittner
Heffren .... Don Moore
Pres. Lincoln .... Fred Stuthman
Pres. Johnson .... Walter Klavun
Secy. Stanton ....Ralph Bell
Justice Davis .... Brooks Rogers
Gov. Morton .... John Wardwell
Gov. Hovey .... Fred Scollay
Capt. Case .... David Gale
Col. Warner .... Frank Latimore

195 A Case of Rape
NBC Nights at the Movies   NBC
Program Type TV Movie
120 minutes. Premiere date: 2/20/74. Repeat
date: 2/17/75.
Producer David Levinson
Production Company Universal Television
Director Boris Sagal
Writer Robert E. Thompson
CAST
Ellen Harrod ....Elizabeth Montgomery
David Harrod .... Ronny Cox
Leonard Alexander .... William Daniels
Larry .... Cliff Potts
Defense Attorney .... Rosemary Murphy

196 The Case of the Plastic Peril
CBS Reports   CBS
Program Type Documentary/Special
Investigation into the hazards of vinyl chloride.
60 minutes. Premiere date: 10/19/74.
Executive Producer Burton Benjamin
Producer Eugene DePoris
Production Company CBS News
Director Eugene DePoris
Correspondent Morton Dean

197   **Castro, Cuba and the U.S.A.**
CBS Reports   CBS
Program Type Documentary/Special
Premier Fidel Castro interviewed. 60 minutes.
Premiere: 10/22/74.
Executive Producer Leslie Midgley
Producer Gordon Manning
Production Company CBS News
Interviewers Dan Rather; Frank Mankiewicz;
   Kirby Jones

198   **Catholics**   CBS
Program Type TV Movie
Special. Adaptation by Brian Moore from his
novel. 90 minutes. Premiere date: 11/29/73. Re-
peat date: 8/1/75.
Executive Producer Sidney Glazier
Supervising Producer Lewis Freedman
Producer Barry Levinson
Production Company Sidney Glazier Production
Director Jack Gold
Writer Brian Moore
                    CAST
Abbot .... Trevor Howard
Father Kinsella .... Martin Sheen
Father Manus .... Cyril Cusack
Father Matthew .... Andrew Keir
Brother Kevin .... Michael Gambon
Brother Donald .... Leon Vitale
Father Terrence .... Tom Jordan
Father Walter .... Godfrey Quigley
Brother Paul .... John Kelly
Brother Alphonsus .... Richard Oliver
Brother Sean .... Patrick Long
Brother John .... Gilbert McIntyre
Brother Michael .... Conor Evans
Brother Pius .... Seamus Healy
Brother Martin .... John Franklin
Brother Malachy .... Cecil Sheridan
Brother Daniel .... Liam Burk
Father Colum .... Frank Howard
Brother Benedict .... John Pine
Dirty Monk .... Derry Power
Boatman .... Joe Pilkington

Catlow *see* The CBS Thursday/Friday
   Night Movies

199   **Caught in the Act**   PBS
Program Type Music/Dance
Seven-part series. 30 minutes. Weekly. Premiere
date: 9/29/74. Repeat date: 7/7/75.
Executive Producer Peter Anderson
Production Company WNJT-TV/Trenton (New
   Jersey Public Broadcasting Authority)
Director Various
Guest Artists The Bottle Hill Boys; Boys of the
   Lough; Jonathan Edwards; Raun MacKinnon
   and Jeremiah Burnheim; Murphy and Salt;
   The Persuasions; Arthur Prysock

200   **Caution: Water May Be Dangerous
to Your Health**
CBS Reports   CBS
Program Type Documentary/Special
The dangers of water. 60 minutes. Premiere:
12/5/74.
Executive Producer Perry Wolff
Producer Judy Crichton
Production Company CBS News
Director Judy Crichton
Writer Perry Wolff; Judy Crichton
Reporters Sylvia Chase; Dan Rather

201   **Cavalcade of Champions Awards**
                                          NBC
Program Type Awards Show
Special. Awards in 11 categories of sports. 90
minutes. Premiere date: 4/8/75.
Executive Producer Bob Hope
Producer Mort Lachman
Production Company Bob Hope Enterprises
Host Bob Hope; Barbara Walters

202   **The Cay**
Bell System Family Theatre   NBC
Program Type TV Movie
Special. Adapted from the book by Theodore
Taylor. Filmed on Grand Caye Isle and Belize
City, Belize, British Honduras. 60 minutes. Pre-
miere date: 10/21/74.
Executive Producer Frank O'Connor
Producer Walter Seltzer; Russell Thacher
Production Company Russell Thacher-Walter
   Seltzer Productions in association with Uni-
   versal Television
Director Patrick Garland
                    CAST
Timothy .... James Earl Jones
Phillip .... Arthur Lutter III
Phillip's Mother .... Gretchen Corbett

203   **CBS All-American Thanksgiving
Day Parade**   CBS
Program Type Documentary/Special
Special. 180 minutes. Live coverage of five pa-
rades: 48th annual New York City Macy's Pa-
rade; 55th annual Philadelphia Gimbels' Parade;
70th annual Toronto Eaton's Santa Claus Pa-
rade; 48th annual Detroit J.L. Hudson Parade;
2nd annual Hawaii Aloha Floral Parade.
11/18/74.
Executive Producer Mike Gargiulo
Producer Vern Diamond; Clarence Schimmel;
   John Polorski; Wilf Fielding; Mike Gargiulo;
   Malachy Wienges
Production Company CBS Television
Writer Beverly Schanzer; Janet Hirschfeld;
   Carolyn Miller; Rene Alkoff
Host William Conrad

CBS All-American Thanksgiving Day Parade *Continued*
Commentators Rob Reiner; Lee Meriwether; John Amos; Esther Rolle; The Hudson Brothers; Michael Learned; Jack Lord; Lori Matsukawa

204 CBS Children's Film Festival CBS
Program Type Children's Show
Films for children from around the world hosted by Kukla, Fran and Ollie with Fran Allison; Burr Tillstrom, puppeteer. 60 minutes. Saturday.
Producer Various
Production Company CBS Television Network Presentation

205 CBS Evening News with Walter Cronkite CBS
Program Type News
First 30-minute nightly news program as of 9/2/63. Monday-Friday. Burton Benjamin replaced Paul Greenberg as executive producer in January 1975. "On the Road," a weekly feature with Charles Kuralt, became "On the Road to '76" on 7/4/75 with bicentennial history themes.
Executive Producer Paul Greenberg; Burton Benjamin
Production Company CBS News
Newscaster Walter Cronkite
Commentator Eric Sevareid
Substitute Roger Mudd

206 The CBS Festival of Lively Arts for Young People CBS
Program Type Children's Show
Five specials. 60 minutes each. Season premiere: 11/28/74. Programs aired during the 1974–75 season: "Ailey Celebrates Ellington," "A Child's Christmas in Wales," "Danny Kaye's Look-In at the Metropolitan Opera," "Harlequin," "Today Is Ours." (*See* individual titles for cast and credits.)

The CBS Friday Night Movies *see* The CBS Thursday/Friday Night Movies

207 CBS Midday News With Douglas Edwards CBS
Program Type News
5 minutes. Monday-Friday.
Production Company CBS News
Newscaster Douglas Edwards

208 CBS Morning News with Hughes Rudd and Bruce Morton CBS
Program Type News
60 minutes. Monday-Friday. Hughes Rudd in New York; Bruce Morton in Washington. William Rusher guest contributor as of 8/11/75.
Executive Producer Joseph T. Dembo
Producer Ed Turner
Production Company CBS News
Newscaster Hughes Rudd; Bruce Morton
Guest contributors Kingman Brewster, Jr.; Milton Friedman; William J. Fulbright; Prof. Eric F. Goldman; Dr. C. Jackson Grayson; Martha Griffiths; Dr. S. I. Hayakawa; Father Theodore Hesburgh; Rep. Barbara Jordan; William Rusher

209 CBS News Special CBS
Program Type Documentary/Special
Live and taped coverage of special events. 1974–75 programs: "Apollo-Soyuz: A Meeting in Space," "Apollo-Soyuz: A Meeting in Space Preview," "Cambodia: An American Dilemma," "Chavez and the Teamsters: An Update," "A Conversation with the President," "Conversations with Eric Sevareid," "Death of a King: What Changes for the Arab World?" "The Economic Summit: Concluding Remarks," "The Economic Summit: Summary and Analysis," "Election '74," "Haldeman: The Nixon Years," "Indochina: 1975 - The End of the Road?" "Is the Recession Finally Ending?" "Mr. Rooney Goes to Dinner," "Mr. Rooney Goes to Washington," "1974: A Television Album," "On the Road with Charles Kuralt," "President Ford's Address on Amnesty and Pardon," "President Ford's Address on the Economy Before Congress," "President Ford's Address to Sigma Delta Chi Convention," "President Ford's Address to the Future Farmers of America," "President Ford's Address to the United Nations," "President Ford's Appearance Before the House Judiciary Committee's Subcommittee on Criminal Justice," "President Ford's Economic Address to the Nation," "President Ford's State of the Union Message to Congress," "Senate Rules Committee Hearings on the Rockefeller Nomination for Vice-President," "A Tribute to Jack Benny," "The Ups and Downs of Henry Kissinger," "Vietnam: A War That Is Finished," "What's Going On Here? The Troubled American Economy." (*See* individual titles for credits.)
Production Company CBS News
Producer Various

CBS News Specials for Young People *see* What's It All About?

210 **CBS Pilot Film**   CBS
Program Type Drama
30-minute pilot films. *See* "Mr. and Mrs. Cop,"
"Stat!" and "Supercops" for individual cast and
credits.

211 **CBS Reports**   CBS
Program Type Documentary/Special
Documentary specials. Generally 60 minutes
each. Season premiere: 10/19/74. Programs
shown during the 1974–75 season: "The Best
Congress Money Can Buy," "The Case of the
Plastic Peril," "Castro, Cuba and the U.S.A.,"
"Caution: Water May Be Dangerous to Your
Health," "The District Attorney," "The Guns of
Autumn," "The IQ Myth," "Prescription: Take
with Caution," "A Tale of Two Irelands."
(*See* individual titles for credits.)
Production Company CBS News
Producer Various

212 **CBS Sports Spectacular**   CBS
Program Type Sports
A composite of various athletic events filmed
around the world. Times vary (60 minutes-120
minutes). Saturday. Season premiere: 9/14/74.
Sunday. Winter-spring premiere: 1/5/75. Pat
Summerall became anchor as of 1/5/75. Joan
Richman became executive producer 7/14/75.
Executive Producer Joan Richman
Production Company CBS Television Network
Sports
Director Various
Anchor Pat Summerall

213 **CBS Tennis Classic/Pressure Point**
CBS
Program Type Sports
60 minutes. Sunday. Season premiere: 6/1/75.
Final games: 8/24/75. Fourth annual "Tennis
Classic" plus "Pressure Point": 13-point sudden-
death play-offs between top women players.
Games played at Palmas Del Mar, Puerto Rico.
Producer Bill Fitts
Production Company CBS Television Network
Sports
Director Bob Dailey
Announcer Vin Scully; Tony Trabert

214 **The CBS Thursday/Friday Night
Movies**   CBS
Program Type TV Movie – Feature Film
A series of 17 made-for-television movies and 59
films made for commercial distribution before
being seen on television. The 17 made-for-televi-
sion movies are: "Adventures of the Queen,"
"Aloha Means Goodbye," "The Blue Knight,"
"Cage without a Key," "The Crime Club," "Da-

vid Copperfield," "Dracula," "The Family Kovack," "The FBI Story: The FBI Versus Alvin
Karpis, Public Enemy Number One," "The FBI
Story: The FBI Versus the Ku Klux Klan,"
"Fer-De-Lance," "Force Five," "Kate
McShane," "Nightmare," "Shell Game," "Sunshine," "Switch." (*See* individual titles for cast
and credits.) The 59 films commercially distrib-
uted before being seen on television are: "Alfred
the Great" (1969) shown 7/4/75, "Around the
World in Eighty Days" (1956) shown 7/11/75,
"Battle for the Planet of the Apes" (1973) shown
1/17/75, "Bonnie and Clyde" (1967) shown
9/27/74, "The Boy Friend" (1971) shown
6/20/75, "Bullitt" (1968) shown 10/4/74, "Captain Nemo and the Underwater City" (1970)
shown 6/27/75, "The Carey Treatment" (1972)
shown 12/6/74, "Catlow" (1971) shown
12/19/74 and 7/3/75, "C.C. and Company"
(1970) shown 11/22/74, "The Cheyenne Social
Club" (1970) shown 10/24/74, "Chitty Chitty
Bang Bang" (1968) shown 1/3/75, "Cold Turkey" (1971) shown 10/31/74, "Conquest of the
Planet of the Apes" (1972) shown 11/14/74,
"Dillinger" (1973) shown 2/6/75, "Dirty Dingus McGee" (1970) shown 2/7/75, "Don't
Drink the Water" (1969) shown 5/16/75, "The
Family" (1970) shown 1/30/75, "The Games"
(1970) shown 6/6/75 and 8/15/75, "Generation" (1969) shown 5/8/75 and 8/7/75, "Going
Home" (1971) shown 5/16/75, "Golden Nee-
dles" (1974) shown 2/28/75, "The Good Guys
and the Bad Guys" (1969) shown 10/10/74 and
4/24/75, "The Graduate" (1967) shown
11/1/74, "The Great White Hope" (1970)
shown 5/29/75 and 8/14/75, "Hawaii" (1966)
shown 5/1/75, "The Hawaiians" (1970) shown
10/3/74, "The Hot Rock" (1972) shown
4/10/75, "How Sweet It Is!" (1969) shown
11/7/74, "Kansas City Bomber" (1972) shown
12/20/74, "Kelly's Heroes" (1970) shown
1/24/75, "The Last Run" (1971) shown
12/27/74 and 7/18/75, "Lawmen" (1971)
shown 3/13/75, "MacKenna's Gold" (1968)
shown 1/23/75, "M*A*S*H" (1970) shown
9/13/74, "The McKenzie Break" (1970) shown
6/26/75, "The Mephisto Waltz" (1971) shown
1/16/75, "Mrs. Pollifax - Spy" (1971) shown
6/20/75, "One Is a Lonely Number" (1972)
shown 6/19/75, "One More Time" (1970)
shown 6/13/75 and 8/22/75, "The Other"
(1972) shown 4/4/75, "The People Next Door"
(1970) shown 6/13/75 and 8/22/75, "Planet of
the Apes" (1968) shown 4/25/75, "The Professionals" (1966) shown 12/12/74, "Shaft" (1971)
shown 1/17/75 and 6/27/75, "Skin Game"
(1971) shown 9/26/74, "Soylent Green" (1973)
shown 3/7/75, "The Stalking Moon" (1969)
shown 11/15/74, "Support Your Local Gunfighter" (1971) shown 9/19/74, "They Call Me
Trinity" (1972) shown 6/12/75 and 8/8/75,

The CBS Thursday/Friday Night Movies
Continued
"They Only Kill Their Masters" (1972) shown 10/25/74, "Who's Afraid of Virginia Woolf?" (1966) shown 7/24/75, "The Wicked Dreams of Paula Schultz" (1968) shown 7/18/75, "The Wild Bunch" (1969) shown 1/2/75, "Wild Rovers" (1971) shown 12/26/74, "Willard" (1971) shown 9/20/74, "The Wrecking Crew" (1968) shown 5/2/75, "The Yellow Submarine" (1968) shown 7/4/75, "Zigzag" (1970) shown 6/6/75 and 8/8/75.

215   CBS Weekend News with Dan Rather   CBS
Program Type News
Saturday (early evening): 30 minutes; Sunday (late night): 15 minutes. Dan Rather became anchor on 8/31/74.
Production Company CBS News
Newscaster Dan Rather

C.C. and Company *see* The CBS Thursday/Friday Night Movies

216   Celebrity Bowling   Syndicated
Program Type Game Show
Preceded by "The Celebrity Bowling Classic" in 1969. In syndication since January 1971. 30 minutes.
Producer Joe Siegman; Don Gregory
Production Company 7-10 Productions
Distributor Syndicast Services, Inc.
Director Don Buccola
Host Jed Allan

217   Celebrity Sweepstakes   NBC
Program Type Game Show
25 minutes. Monday-Friday. Six guest celebrities; 2 contestants. Premiere date: 4/1/74. Continuous.
Executive Producer Ralph Andrews
Producer Tom Cole
Production Company Ralph Andrews Productions in association with NBC-TV
Director Dick McDonough
Host Jim McKrell
Announcer Bill Armstrong
Regular Carol Wayne

218   Celebrity Sweepstakes   Syndicated
Program Type Game Show
Evening version of daytime show. 30 minutes. Weekly. Premiere date: 9/74. Six guest celebrities; two contestants.
Executive Producer Ralph Andrews
Producer Tom Cole

Production Company Ralph Andrews Productions in association with Burt Sugarman
Distributor Carbie Distribution, Inc.
Director Dick McDonough
Host Jim McKrell
Announcer Bill Armstrong
Regular Carol Wayne

219   Ceremonies in Dark Old Men
ABC Theatre   ABC
Program Type Drama
Special. From the play by Lonne Elder III. Performed by the members of the Negro Ensemble Company, New York. 120 minutes. Premiere date: 1/6/75.
Executive Producer Gerald S. Krone
Producer Jacqueline Babbin
Director Michael S. Schultz; Kirk Browning
Writer Lonne Elder III
CAST
Russell B. Parker .... Douglas Turner Ward
Theo Parker .... Glynn Turman
Bobby Parker .... J. Eric Bell
Mr. Jenkins .... Godfrey Cambridge
Blue Haven .... Robert Hooks
Adele Parker .... Rosalind Cash

220   The Ceremony of Innocence
Theater in America   PBS
Program Type Drama
Play by Ronald Ribman. 90 minutes. Repeat date: 8/13/75.
Executive Producer Jac Venza
Producer Bob Mackell
Production Company WNET/New York
Director Arthur A. Seidelman
CAST
King Ethelred .... Richard Kiley
Earl of Sussex .... James Broderick
Queen Mother Alfreda ....Jesse Royce Landis
Earl of Kent .... Larry Gates
Queen Emma .... Elizabeth Hubbard
Prince Edmund .... John Horn
Princess Thulja .... Gilmer McCormick
Bishop Aelfhun .... Bob Gerringer
Abbot .... William Hickey
King Sweyn .... Ernest Graves
Thorkill .... Howard Green

Championship Auto Racing *see* ABC's Championship Auto Racing

221   Changing Seasons   PBS
Program Type Documentary/Special
Special. 30 minutes. Repeat date: 8/7/75. A tour of Boston's Arnold Arboretum.
Production Company WGBH/Boston
Host Thalassa Cruso

222 **Charles Ives - An American Original**
Special of the Week   PBS
Program Type Music/Dance
Special. "Concord Sonata" by Charles Ives performed by pianist Harvey Hinshaw and flutist Laura Larson. 60 minutes. Premiere date: 7/28/75.
Executive Producer Shep Morgan
Producer Jeanne Wolf
Production Company WPBT/Miami
Director Richard Carpenter

Charley *see* The ABC Sunday Night Movie

Charley Varrick *see* NBC Nights at the Movies

223 **A Charlie Brown Christmas**   CBS
Program Type Animated Film
30 minute special. Created by Charles M. Schulz. Music by Vince Guaraldi. Premiere date: 12/9/65. Repeat date: 12/17/74.
Executive Producer Lee Mendelson
Producer Lee Mendelson; Bill Melendez
Production Company Lee Mendelson-Bill Melendez Production in cooperation with United Features Syndicate, Inc.
Director Bill Melendez
Writer Charles M. Schulz
Musical Director Vince Guaraldi
Music supervisor John Scott Trotter
VOICES
Charlie Brown .... Peter Robbins
Lucy .... Tracy Stratford
Linus .... Christopher Shea

224 **A Charlie Brown Thanksgiving** CBS
Program Type Animated Film
Special. 30 minutes. Created by Charles M. Schulz. Music composed by Vince Guaraldi. Premiere date: 11/20/73. Repeat date: 11/21/74.
Producer Lee Mendelson; Bill Melendez
Production Company A Lee Mendelson-Bill Melendez Production
Director Bill Melendez; Phil Roman
Writer Charles M. Schulz
Musical Director Vince Guaraldi
Music supervisor John Scott Trotter
VOICES
Charlie Brown .... Todd Barbee
Linus .... Stephen Shea
Peppermint Patty .... Christopher Defaria
Lucy .... Robin Kohn
Sally .... Hilary Momberger
Marcie .... Jimmy Ahrens
Franklin .... Robin Reed

225 **Chavez and the Teamsters: An Update**
CBS News Special   CBS
Program Type Documentary/Special
Follow-up to a two-part "Lamp Unto My Feet." 30 minutes. Premiere: 10/20/74.
Producer Walter Lister
Production Company CBS News
Reporter Terry Drinkwater

226 **Cher**   CBS
Program Type Comedy/Variety
60 minutes. Sunday. Premiere date: 2/16/75. Preceded by special 2/12/75 (*see* next entry).
Executive Producer George Schlatter
Production Executive Lee Miller
Producer Lee Miller; Allan Katz; Don Reo
Production Company Apis Productions, Inc., in association with George Schlatter Productions
Director Art Fisher
Choreographer Tony Charmoli
Host Cher
Costume Designer Bob Mackie

227 **Cher Special**   CBS
Program Type Comedy/Variety
60 minute special. Preview of "Cher" series. Premiere date: 2/12/75. Repeat date: 8/25/75.
Producer George Schlatter
Production Executive Lee Miller
Production Company George Schlatter Productions in association with Apis Productions, Inc.
Director Art Fisher
Head Writer Digby Wolfe
Writer Digby Wolfe; Reo Don and Allan Katz; Iris Rainer; Pat Proft and Bo Kaprall; David Panich; Ron Pearlman; Nick Arnold; John Boni; Ray Taylor; Billy Barnes and Earl Brown
Choreographer Tony Charmoli
Host Cher
Guests Elton John; Bette Midler; Flip Wilson

The Cheyenne Social Club *see* The CBS Thursday/Friday Night Movies

228 **The Chicago Conspiracy Trial**
Hollywood Television Theatre   PBS
Program Type Drama
Edited from the 23,000-page court transcript by Christopher Burstall; Stuart Hood. Presented in the U.S. by KCET/Los Angeles. 150 minutes. Premiere date: 7/10/75.
Producer Christopher Burstall
Production Company British Broadcasting Corporation; Bavarian Television
Director Christopher Burstall

The Chicago Conspiracy Trial *Continued*
Narrator Tony Church
CAST

Judge Julius Hoffman	Morris Carnovsky
Jerry Rubin	Ronny Cox
Bobby Seale	Al Freeman, Jr.
William Kunstler	James Patterson
Richard Schultz	Neil McCallum
Abbie Hoffman	Cliff Gorman
David Dellinger	Barton Heyman
Rennie Davis	Peter Jobin
Tom Hayden	Douglas Lambert
Leonard Weinglass	Robert Loggia
Thomas Foran	Shane Rimmer
John Froines	Paul Arlington

229   **Chico and the Man**   NBC
Program Type Comedy
30 minutes. Friday. Premiere date: 9/13/74. Set in the barrio of East Los Angeles.
Executive Producer James Komack
Producer Alan Sacks
Production Company The Wolper Organization Ltd. in association with The Komack Company
Director Peter Baldwin; James Komack
Writer Various
CAST

Ed Brown	Jack Albertson
Chico	Freddie Prinze
Louie	Scat Man Crothers
Ramon	Isaac Ruiz
Rudy	Rodolfo Hoyos

Children's Film Festival *see* CBS Children's Film Festival

230   **A Child's Christmas in Wales**
The CBS Festival of Lively Arts for Young People   CBS
Program Type Children's Show
The Dylan Thomas story read by Michael Redgrave and acted out by the National Theatre of the Deaf. Translator: Bernard Bragg. 60 minutes. Premiere date: 12/16/73. Repeat date: 12/25/74.
Executive Producer Herman Krawitz
Producer Robert Weiner
Director David Hays
Costume Designer Fred Voelpel

231   **The Chinese Prime Minister**
Hollywood Television Theatre   PBS
Program Type Drama
90 minutes. Premiere date: 10/23/74. Repeat date: 8/20/75.
Executive Producer Norman Lloyd
Producer George Turpin
Production Company KCET-TV/Los Angeles
Director Brian Murray; George Turpin

Writer Enid Bagnold
CAST

She	Judith Anderson
Sir Gregory	Stephen Elliott
Alice	Elayne Heilveil
Tarver	Richard Clarke
Oliver	Peter Coffield
Roxane	Kathleen Miller
Bent	Don McHenry

Chisum *see* NBC Nights at the Movies

Chitty Chitty Bang Bang *see* The CBS Thursday/Friday Night Movies

232   **Christmas at Pops**   PBS
Program Type Music/Dance
Special. 60 minutes. Premiere date: 12/23/74. Repeat date: 12/24/74. Arthur Fiedler conducts the Boston Pops Orchestra and the Tanglewood Festival Chorus. Program funded by the Martin Marietta Corporation.
Producer Bill Cosel
Production Company WGBH/Boston

233   **A Christmas Carol**   ABC
Program Type Animated Film
Special. Animated with drawings done in the style of the 1840s. 30 minutes. Premiere date: 12/21/71. Repeat date: 12/7/74.
Executive Producer Chuck Jones
Producer Richard Williams
Director Richard Williams
Writer Charles Dickens
Musical Director Tristram Cary
Narrator Michael Redgrave
VOICES

Scrooge	Alastair Sim
Marley's Ghost	Michael Hordern
Bob Cratchit	Melvyn Hayes
Mrs. Cratchit	Joan Sims
Ragpicker/Fezziwig	Paul Whitsun-Jones
Scrooge's Nephew/Charity Man	David Tate
Ghost of Christmas Past	Diana Quick
Ghost of Christmas Present	Felix Felton
Ghost of Christmas Yet to Come	Annie West
Mrs. Dilber	Mary Ellen Ray
Tiny Tim	Alexander Williams

234   **The Christmas Day Service**   NBC
Program Type Religious Program
60 minutes. Premiere date: 12/25/74. From the Washington Cathedral. Episcopal service; sermon by the Very Reverend Francis B. Sayre.
Executive Producer Doris Ann
Production Company The NBC Television Religious Programs Unit
Director Richard Cox

235 **A Christmas Eve Celebration** CBS
Program Type Religious Program
CBS News religious special. The Third Baptist
Church in St. Louis at midnight. 60 minutes.
Premiere date: 12/25/75.
Executive Producer Pamela Ilott
Producer Alan Harper

236 **Christmas Is** Syndicated
Program Type Animated Film
30 minutes. Premiere: 12/70. Shown each year.
Music composed by Jimmy Haskell.
Executive Producer Dr. Martin J. Neeb, Jr.
Producer Rev. Ardon D. Albrecht
Production Company Lutheran Television
Director Leonard Gray
Writer Don Hall
Principal Voices Hans Conreid

237 **Christmas with Oral Roberts**
Syndicated
Program Type Religious Program
Musical special. 60 minutes. Premiere: 12/74.
Producer Dick Ross
Production Company Production Associates,
Inc.
Director Dick Ross
Musical Director Ralph Carmichael
Choreographer Andrae Tayir
Host Oral Roberts
Regular Richard Roberts; Patti Roberts; World
Action Singers
Guests Florence Henderson; Charley Pride

238 **Christmas with the Bing Crosbys**
Bell System Family Theatre NBC
Program Type Comedy/Variety
Special. With Bing Crosby; Kathryn Crosby and
children Harry, Nathaniel and Mary Frances. 60
minutes. Premiere date: 12/15/74.
Executive Producer Bob Finkel
Producer Bill Angelos; Buz Kohan
Production Company Teram Productions
Director Marty Pasetta
Writer Bill Angelos; Buz Kohan
Musical Director Peter Matz
Choreographer Robert Sidney
Guests Karen Valentine; Mac Davis

239 **Christopher Closeup** Syndicated
Program Type Religious Program
30 minutes. Premiere date: 10/52. Produced by
the founder of the Christophers, Father James
Keller, M.M. Weekly. Interpreter for the deaf:
Carol Tipton.
Executive Producer Rev. Richard Armstrong
Producer Jeanne Glynn
Production Company A Christopher Production

Director Raymond Hoesten
Host Rev. Richard Armstrong; Jeanne Glynn

240 **The Chrome Plated Nightmare** PBS
Program Type Documentary/Special
Special. 60 minutes. Premiere date: 5/27/74. Re-
peat date: 9/9/74. The automobile in American
society.
Producer Bill Stewart
Production Company NPACT (National Public
Affairs Center for Television)
Writer Bill Stewart
Host John Jerome
Narrator Bill Stewart

241 **Cities for People** PBS
Program Type Documentary/Special
Special. Urban space from an aesthetic point of
view; filmed in Italy and the United States. 60
minutes. Premiere date: 1/2/75. Music by John
Lewis.
Executive Producer Paul Marshall
Producer Amanda C. Pope; John Louis Field
Production Company KPBS/California State
University, San Diego
Director Amanda C. Pope; John Louis Field
Narrator Cloris Leachman

242 **The Cities: Uncle Sam, Can You
Spare a Dime?** PBS
Program Type Documentary/Special
Special. 60 minutes. Premiere date: 7/16/75.
Producer Christopher Gaul
Production Company NPACT (National Public
Affairs Center for Television)
Correspondents Carolyn Lewis; Paul Duke;
Christopher Gaul

243 **The City That Forgot About
Christmas** Syndicated
Program Type Animated Film
30 minutes. Premiere: 12/74.
Executive Producer Mr. Martin J. Neeb, Jr.
Producer Rev. Ardon D. Albrecht
Production Company Lutheran Television
Director Leonard Gray
Writer Mary Warren
Principal Voices Charles Nelson Reilly; Sebastian
Cabot.

Clarence Darrow Starring Henry Fonda
see Henry Fonda as Clarence Darrow

244 **Clerow Wilson's Great Escape** NBC
Program Type Animated Film
Special. 30 minutes. Repeat date: 12/16/74.

Clerow Wilson's Great Escape *Continued*
Executive Producer David H. DePatie; Friz Freleng
Production Company DePatie-Freleng and Clerow Productions in association with NBC
Director Corny Cole
Voices Flip Wilson

245   Coaches All-American Football Game
ABC Sports Special   ABC
Program Type Sports
15th annual game from Lubbock, Texas. Live coverage. 6/21/75.
Executive Producer Roone Arledge
Production Company ABC Sports
Announcer Chris Schenkel; Frank Broyles

Cold Sweat *see* NBC Nights at the Movies

Cold Turkey *see* The CBS Thursday/Friday Night Movies

246   Colgate-Dinah Shore Winners Circle
ABC Sports Special   ABC
Program Type Sports
Live coverage from the Mission Hills Golf and Country Club, Palm Springs, California. 4/19/75; 4/20/75.
Executive Producer Roone Arledge
Production Company ABC Sports
Producer Chuck Howard
Host Dinah Shore
Announcer Jim McKay; Chris Schenkel; Dave Marr; Cathy Duggan

A Colgate Women's Sports Special *see* The Lady Is a Champ . . . A Colgate Women's Sports Special

247   College All-Star Football Game
ABC Sports Special   ABC
Program Type Sports
42nd annual game between college all-stars and Super Bowl champions. 8/1/75. Live coverage from Soldier Field, Chicago.
Executive Producer Roone Arledge
Production Company ABC Sports
Announcer Keith Jackson; Howard Cosell; Bud Wilkinson

248   College Football Bowl Preview
ABC Sports Special   ABC
Program Type Sports
30 minutes. Premiere date: 12/15/74.
Executive Producer Roone Arledge
Producer Terry Jastrow
Production Company ABC Sports
Host Bud Wilkinson; Duffy Daugherty

249   College Football '74   ABC
Program Type Sports
Highlights of college football games. 60 minutes. Sunday. Season premiere: 9/15/74. Last show of season: 12/8/74.
Executive Producer Roone Arledge
Production Company ABC Sports
Host Bill Flemming

250   Columbo
NBC Sunday Mystery Movie   NBC
Program Type Crime Drama
Some episodes 90 minutes; others 120 minutes. Sundays on irregular basis. Based on "NBC World Premiere 'Prescription: Murder'" (2/20/68) and "NBC World Premiere 'Ransom for a Dead Man'" (3/1/71) by Richard Levinson; William Link. Premiere date: 9/15/71. Season premiere: 9/15/74.
Executive Producer Dean Hargrove; Roland Kibbee
Producer Everett Chambers
Production Company Universal Television in association with the NBC Television Network
Director Various
Writer Various
CAST
Lt. Columbo .... Peter Falk

251   The Comedy Awards   ABC
Program Type Awards Show
Special. The first American Academy of Humor awards to entertainers, writers, programs and films. 90 minutes. Premiere date: 1/29/75.
Executive Producer Alan King; Rupert Hitzig; John Gilroy
Producer Herb Sargent; Bill Foster
Production Company King-Hitzig Productions
Director Bill Foster
Writer Steve Allen; George Bloom; Alan King; George Ricker; Harry Crane
Musical Director Nick Perito
Host Alan King

252   Comedy Special   CBS
Program Type Comedy
30-minute pilot films. *See* "Black Bart," "The Boys," "Grandpa Max," "Harry and Maggie," "Love Nest," "Popi," "Rosenthal and Jones,"

"Salt and Pepe," "Wives" for individual cast and credits.

253 Commercial Union Grand Prix Masters Tennis Tournament
PBS Sports Special   PBS
Program Type Sports
Early-round, semifinals, and finals from Kooyong Stadium, Melbourne, Australia. 12/14/74; 12/21/74; 12/22/74. Four hours each day. Repeat date: 3/16/75 (final day play). Program made possible by grants from Fieldcrest Mills, Inc., Volvo of America Corporation, Volvo Distributing, Inc., and American Airlines.
Production Company WGBH/Boston
Announcer Bud Collins; Donald Dell

254 Como Country ... Perry and His Nashville Friends   CBS
Program Type Comedy/Variety
Special. 60 minutes. From the Grand Old Opry House, Nashville, Tenn. Premiere date: 2/17/75.
Producer Joseph Cates
Production Company Roncom Productions
Director Walter Miller
Writer Marty Farrell
Host Perry Como
Choral Director Ray Charles
Guests Chet Atkins with Floyd Cramer and Boots Randolph; Donna Fargo; Loretta Lynn; Charley Pride; Charlie Rich; Danny Davis and The Nashville Brass.

255 Concentration   Syndicated
Program Type Game Show
Syndicated two ways: Monday-Friday (daytime) and once a week (evenings). 30 minutes. In syndication since 9/73.
Executive Producer Howard Felcher
Production Company Goodson-Todman Productions
Distributor Jim Victory Television, Inc.
Director Ira Skutch
Host Jack Narz
Announcer Johnny Olson

256 The Confessions of Dick Van Dyke   ABC
Program Type Comedy/Variety
Special. 60 minutes. Premiere date: 4/10/75.
Executive Producer Byron Paul
Producer Bill Persky; Sam Denoff
Production Company Van Perden Productions
Director Marc Breaux
Writer Norman Barasch; Carroll Moore; Bill Persky; Sam Denoff
Host Dick Van Dyke
Guests Michele Lee; Stacy Van Dyke

Featured Guests David Doyle; Cliff Pellow; Moosie Drier; Iris Edwards; Dee Dee Wood Dancers

Conquest of the Planet of the Apes *see* The CBS Thursday/Friday Night Movies

257 Consumer Reports   Syndicated
Program Type Educational
One-two minute consumer information reports for use with local news shows and local consumer reporter narrating. Premiere: 6/74. Twice weekly.
Producer David Burke; Ellen Levine
Production Company Consumers Union

258 Consumer Survival Kit   PBS
Program Type Educational
26 programs. 30 minutes. Premiere date: 1/9/75. Repeat date: 7/8/75. Series made possible by grants from the Corporation for Public Broadcasting, the Ford Foundation, and Public Television Stations.
Executive Producer Vince Clews
Production Company Maryland Center for Public Broadcasting
Host Lary Lewman

259 Contemporary Dimensions   PBS
Program Type Music/Dance
Special. 30 minutes. Premiere date: 10/20/73. Repeat date: 1/15/75. Contemporary Dimensions perform two original compositions. Taped at Virginia Union University.
Production Company WCVE/Richmond, Virginia
Director Richard Hall
Musical Director Odell Hobbs

260 The Contractor
Theater in America   PBS
Program Type Drama
Play by David Storey performed by the Chelsea Theater Center, Brooklyn, New York. Taped live at Longue Vue Gardens, New Orleans. 150 minutes. Premiere date: 4/10/74. Repeat dates: 5/7/75; 6/16/75. Series made possible by grants from Exxon Corporation and the Corporation for Public Broadcasting.
Executive Producer Jac Venza
Producer Ken Campbell
Production Company WNET/New York
Director Barry Davis
Host Hal Holbrook
CAST
Ewbank .... John Wardell
Fitzpatrick .... Joseph Maher

The Contractor *Continued*
Glendenning .... Kevin O'Connor
Marshall .... Michael Finn
Kay .... Reid Shelton
Bennett ....George Taylor
Paul .... John Roddick

261   A Conversation with Dr. Margaret Mead   NBC
Program Type Interview/Discussion
Special. 60 minutes. Premiere date: 6/22/75.
Producer Doris Ann
Production Company NBC Television Religious
  Programs Unit
Director Robert Priaulx
Interviewer Edwin Newman
Guest Margaret Mead

262   A Conversation with Dr. Philip A. Potter   NBC
Program Type Interview/Discussion
Special. 60 minutes. Premiere date: 5/25/75.
Producer Doris Ann
Production Company NBC Television Religious
  Programs Unit
Director Richard Cox
Guest Dr. Philip A. Potter

263   A Conversation with Dr. Robert Gordis
The Eternal Light   NBC
Program Type Religious Program
Special. 30 minutes. Premiere date: 12/8/74.
Produced for the Jewish Seminary of America by
Milton E. Krents.
Executive Producer Doris Ann
Producer Martin Hoade
Production Company NBC Television Religious
  Program Unit
Director Martin Hoade
Interviewer Rabbi Edward Sandrow
Guest Dr. Robert Gordis

264   A Conversation with Leo Rosten
The Eternal Light   NBC
Program Type Interview/Discussion
Special presented by the Jewish Theological Sem-
inary of America; executive producer: Milton E.
Krents. 60 minutes. Premiere date: 2/2/75.
Executive Producer Doris Ann
Production Company The NBC Television Reli-
  gious Program Unit
Interviewer Martin Bookspan
Guest Leo Rosten

265   A Conversation with President Ford
NBC News Special   NBC
Program Type Interview/Discussion
60 minutes. Premiere date: 1/23/75. Live cover-
age (Eastern time) of conversation with Pres.
Gerald Ford.
Executive Producer Frank Jordan
Producer Robert Asman
Production Company NBC News
Correspondents John Chancellor; Tom Brokaw

266   A Conversation with Rabbi Jules Harlow
The Eternal Light   NBC
Program Type Religious Program
Special. 30 minutes. Premiere date: 9/22/74.
Discussion of the Jewish High Holy Days. Pro-
duced for the Jewish Theological Seminary of
America by Milton E. Krents.
Executive Producer Doris Ann
Producer Martin Hoade
Production Company NBC Television Religious
  Programs Unit
Director Martin Hoade
Moderator Rabbi Wolfe Kelman
Guest Rabbi Jules Harlow

267   A Conversation with the President
CBS News Special   CBS
Program Type Interview/Discussion
Live. 60 minutes. Premiere: 4/21/75. Interview
with Pres. Gerald R. Ford.
Producer Sanford Socolow
Production Company CBS News
Interviewers Walter Cronkite; Eric Sevareid; Bob
  Schieffer

268   Conversations with Eric Sevareid
CBS News Special   CBS
Program Type Interview/Discussion
Seven-part summer series. 60 minutes. Sunday.
Premiere date: 7/13/75. Last show: 9/7/75. In-
terviewees: Willy Brandt; Robert Hutchins;
George Kennan; John J. McCloy; Leo Rosten;
and Marietta Tree; Mary Peabody; Frances Fitz-
gerald.
Executive Producer Perry Wolff
Producer Various
Production Company CBS News Presentation
Interviewer Eric Sevareid

Cool Hand Luke *see* NBC Nights at the
  Movies

269   Cops   PBS
Program Type Documentary/Special
Special. Originally shown on WNET/New York

as segment of "The 51st State." Premiere date on PBS: 6/19/75. 30 minutes.
Producer Dick Kotuk
Production Company WNET/New York

270   The Coral Divers of Corsica
The Undersea World of Jacques Cousteau
ABC
Program Type Documentary/Special
Special. 60 minutes. Premiere date: 2/21/75. With Jacques Cousteau and the crew of the *Calypso.*
Executive Producer Jacques Cousteau; Marshall Flaum
Producer Andy White
Production Company A Marshall Flaum Production in association with The Cousteau Society and MPC Metromedia Producers Corporation and ABC News
Director Jacques Renoir
Writer Andy White
Musical Director Walter Scharf
Host Jacques Cousteau
Underwater Camera Yves Omer
Camera Jacques Renoir
Chief Diver Alberta Falco
Narrator Joseph Campanella

271   Cotton Bowl
CBS Sports Special   CBS
Program Type Sports
Live coverage of the 39th Cotton Bowl in Dallas, Texas. 1/1/75. Penn State Nittany Lions versus Baylor Bears.
Production Company CBS Television Network Sports
Announcer Lindsey Nelson; John Sauer; Jane Chastain

272   The Cotton Bowl Festival Parade
CBS
Program Type Documentary/Special
Special. 60 minutes. Live coverage of the 19th annual parade from Dallas. 1/1/75.
Producer Mike Gargiulo
Production Company CBS Television
Director Mike Gargiulo
Writer Beverly Schanzer
Host William Conrad; Sandy Duncan

273   Cotton Club '75   NBC
Program Type Comedy/Variety
Special. Revue recreating the Cotton Club. 90 minutes. Premiere date: 11/23/74.
Executive Producer Burt Reynolds; Henry Jaffe
Producer Bob Booker; George Foster
Production Company Booker-Foster Produc-

tions and Burt Reynolds-Henry Jaffe Productions
Director Mark Warren
Writer Bob Booker; George Foster
Musical Director Phil Moore
Stars Franklyn Ajaye; Jonelle Allen; Ray Charles; Billy Daniels; Johnny Dankworth; Clifton Davis; Redd Foxx; Goldfinger and Dove; Rosey Grier; Cleo Laine; The Lockers; Nicholas Brothers; Buddy Rich; Jimmie Walker

Cotton Comes to Harlem *see* NBC Nights at the Movies

274   The Count of Monte Cristo
Bell System Family Theatre   NBC
Program Type Drama
Special. Adapted from the novel by Alexandre Dumas. Filmed in France (at the Chateau D'If) and in Italy. 120 minutes. Premiere date: 1/10/75.
Producer Norman Rosemont
Production Company A Norman Rosemont Production in association with ITC and ATV Company
Director David Greene
Writer Sidney Carroll
CAST
Edmund Dantes .... Richard Chamberlain
De Villefort .... Louis Jourdan
Abbe Faria .... Trevor Howard
Danglars .... Donald Pleasance
Gen. Mondego .... Tony Curtis
Mercedes .... Kate Nelligan
Albert Mondego .... Dominic Guard
Valentine De Villefort .... Taryn Power

275   A Country Called Watts
NBC News Special   NBC
Program Type Documentary/Special
Special. 60 minutes. Premiere date: 6/29/75.
Producer Thomas Tomizawa
Production Company NBC News
Director Robert Priaulx
Writer Patricia Creaghan; Thomas Tomizawa
Reporters Tom Pettit; Gail Christian

276   Country Matters
Masterpiece Theatre   PBS
Program Type Drama
Four-part series. 60 minutes. Weekly. Premiere date: 2/2/75. Series made possible by a grant from the Mobil Oil Corporation. Produced in U.S. by WGBH-TV/Boston. "The Higgler," "The Black Dog," and "The Watercress Girl" written by A. E. Coppard; "The Mill" written by H. E. Bates.
Executive Producer Derek Granger

Country Matters *Continued*
Production Company Granada Television, England.
Host Alistair Cooke

The Black Dog
Writer James Saunders
CAST
Orianda Crabbe .... Jane Lapotaire
The Hon. Gerald Loughlin .... Stephen Chase
Crabbe .... Glyn Houston
Lizzie .... June Watson
Porter .... Herbert Ramskill

The Higgler
CAST
Harvey Whitlow .... Keith Drinkel
Sophy Daws .... Jane Carr
Mrs. Sadgrove .... Sheila Ruskin
Mary .... Rosalie Crutchley

The Mill
Writer James Saunders
CAST
Alice Hartop .... Rosalind Ayers
Albert Holland .... Tom Chadborn
Holland .... Ray Smith
Mrs. Holland .... Brenda Bruce
Hartop .... Robert Keegan
Mrs. Hartop .... Maria Charles

The Watercress Girl
Writer Hugh Leonard
CAST
Mary MacDowall .... Susan Fleetwood
Elizabeth Plantney .... Susan Tebbs
Frank Oppidan .... Gareth Thomas
Father .... John Welsh

277 Country Music Association Awards
CBS
Program Type Awards Show
Special. 60 minutes. 8th annual awards presentation from The New Grand Old Opry House, Nashville, Tenn. 10/14/74. Live coverage.
Executive Producer Joseph Cates
Coordinating Producer Chet Hagan
Producer Walter Miller
Director Walter Miller
Writer Chet Hagan
Musical Director Milton Delugg
Host Johnny Cash
Performers Bill Anderson; Roy Clark; Rita Coolidge; Little Sammy Dickens; Waylon Jennings; Kris Kristofferson; Dolly Parton; Charlie Rich; Johnny Rodriguez; Hank Snow; Tanya Tucker; Kitty Wells

The Cowboys *see* The ABC Saturday Night Movie; The ABC Summer Movie

The Cranes Are Flying *see* Humanities Film Forum

278 The Crazy Comedy Concert
ABC Afterschool Specials   ABC
Program Type Children's Show
Special. Live and animation. Live action sequence filmed in the Hollywood Bowl. 60 minutes. Premiere date: 6/5/74. Repeat date: 5/28/75.
Executive Producer Joseph Barbera; William Hanna
Producer Alan Handley; Bill Schwartz; Iwao Takamoto
Production Company Hanna-Barbera Productions
Director Alan Handley
Writer Duane E. Poole
CAST
Janitor .... Tim Conway
Cleaning Woman .... Ruth Buzzi

Crazy Joe *see* The ABC Sunday Night Movie

279 The Cricket in Times Square   ABC
Program Type Animated Film
Special. Based on book by George Selden. 30 minutes. Premiere date: 4/24/73. Repeat date: 11/9/74.
Producer Chuck Jones
Director Chuck Jones
Writer Chuck Jones
Violinist Israel Baker
VOICES
Chester C. Cricket/Harry the Cat/Father/Music
    Teacher .... Les Tremayne
Tucker the Mouse .... Mel Blanc
Mother .... June Foray
Mario .... Kerry MacLane

280 The Crime Club
The CBS Thursday/Friday Night Movies CBS
Program Type TV Movie
90 minutes. Premiere date: 4/3/75. Repeat date: 7/25/75.
Executive Producer Matthew Rapf
Producer James McAdams
Production Company Universal Television
Director Jeannot Szwarc
Writer Gene R. Kearney
CAST
Alex Norton .... Robert Lansing
Daniel Lawrence .... Eugene Roche
John "Jake" Keesey .... Scott Thomas
Byron Craine .... Biff McGuire
Angela Swoboda .... Barbara Rhoades
Frank Swoboda .... Michael Cristofer
Peter Karpf .... David Clennon
Dr. Schroeder .... Martine Beswick

Lt. Doyle	M. Emmet Walsh
Pam Agostino	Kathy Beller
Mary Jo	Jennifer Shaw
Gamos	Carl Gottlieb
Jack Dowd	Regis Cordic

281 Crossfire
NBC Nights at the Movies   NBC
Program Type TV Movie
90 minutes. Premiere date: 3/24/75. Repeat date: 7/5/75.
Executive Producer Quinn Martin
Producer Philip Saltzman
Production Company Quinn Martin Productions
Director William Hale
Writer Philip Saltzman
CAST

Vince Rossi	James Farentino
Capt. McCardle	Ramon Bieri
Dave Ambrose	John Saxon
Lane Fielding	Patrick O'Neal
Sheila Fielding	Pamela Franklin
Bert Ganz	Herb Edelman
Albert Ambrose	Frank de Kova
Arthur Peabody	Lou Frizzell
Jimmy	Joseph Hindy

282 Cry For Help
Tuesday/Wednesday Movie of the Week ABC
Program Type TV Movie
90 minutes. Premiere date: 2/12/75. Repeat date: 7/1/75.
Executive Producer Richard Levinson; William Link
Producer Howie Horwitz
Production Company Universal Television
Director Daryl Duke
Writer Peter S. Fischer
CAST

Harry Freeman	Robert Culp
Ingrid Brunner	Elayne Heilveil
Paul Church	Ken Swofford
Buddy Marino	Chuck McCann
Arthur Schullman	Donald Mantooth
Tony Garafolas	Ralph Manza
Sgt. Shirley	Lee De Broux
Philip Conover	Michael Lerner

283 A Cry in the Wilderness
Tuesday/Wednesday Movie of the Week ABC
Program Type TV Movie
90 minutes. Premiere date: 3/26/74. Repeat date: 5/20/75. Based on a story by Gilbert Wright.
Producer Lou Morheim
Production Company Universal Television
Director Gordon Hessler
Writer Stephen Karpf; Elinor Karpf
CAST

Sam Hadley	George Kennedy
Delda Hadley	Joanna Pettet
Gus Hadley	Lee H. Montgomery
Bess Millard	Collin Wilcox-Horne
Rex Millard	Roy Poole
Mr. Hainie	Liam Dunn
Mr. Griffey	Bing Russell
Old Woman	Irene Tedrow
Sam's Grandmother	Anne Seymour
First Man	Bob Roy
Doctor	Robert Brubaker
Sam's Father	Paul Sorensen
Second Man	Troy Melton

284 Cuba: The People   PBS
Program Type Documentary/Special
Special. Taped in Cuba in spring, 1974. 60 minutes. Premiere date: 12/2/74. Program made possible by grants from the Ford Foundation and the Corporation for Public Broadcasting.
Producer Jon Alpert; Keiko Tsuno; Yoko Maruyama; Patricia Sides
Production Company WNET/New York in cooperation with Downtown Community Television Center
Director Jon Alpert; Keiko Tsuno
Writer Jon Alpert
Host Harrison E. Salisbury
Narrator Jon Alpert

285 Cyrano
ABC Afterschool Specials   ABC
Program Type Animated Film
Special. Based on "Cyrano de Bergerac" by Edmond Rostand. Translator: Leonard Spigelgass. 60 minutes. Premiere date: 3/6/74. Repeat date: 4/9/75.
Executive Producer Joseph Barbera; William Hanna
Producer Iwao Takamoto
Production Company Hanna-Barbera Productions
Director Charles A. Nichols
Writer Harvey Bullock
VOICES

Cyrano	Jose Ferrer
Roxane	Joan Van Ark
Ragueneau	Kurt Kasznar
Comte de Guiche	Martyn Green
Christian	Victor Garber
Duenna	Joan Connell
First Cadet/de Brigny	Alan Oppenheimer
Richelieu	John Stephenson

286 Cyrano de Bergerac
Theater in America   PBS
Program Type Drama
Play by Edmond Rostand performed by the American Conservatory Theater, San Francisco. 150 minutes. Premiere date: 2/6/74. Repeat date: 2/26/75. Program funded by Exxon Corporation and the Corporation for Public Broadcasting.
Executive Producer Jac Venza
Producer Matthew N. Herman; Dennis Powers

Cyrano de Bergerac *Continued*
Production Company WNET/New York
Director William Ball; Bruce Franchini
Host Hal Holbrook
CAST

Cyrano	Peter Donat
Roxane	Marsha Mason
Christian	Marc Singer
Rageuneau	Robert Mooney
De Guiche	Paul Shenar
Duenna	Elizabeth Huddle
Le Bret	Earl Boen
Bellerose	Roger Aaron Brown
Capuchin	Andy Backer
Orange Girl	Janie Atkin

287   Dan August   CBS
Program Type Crime Drama
Created by Quinn Martin. Originally on ABC
1970–1971; series on CBS 5/23/73–10/17/73.
Reruns for summer 1975 premiered 4/16/75. 60
minutes. Wednesday.
Executive Producer Quinn Martin
Supervising Producer Adrian Samish
Producer Anthony Spinner
Production Company Quinn Martin Productions
CAST

Dan August	Burt Reynolds
Sgt. Wilentz	Norman Fell
Chief Untermeyer	Richard Anderson
Sgt. Rivera	Ned Romero
Katy Grant	Eva Hartman

288   Danny Kaye's Look-In at the Metropolitan Opera
The CBS Festival of Lively Arts for Young
People   CBS
Program Type Children's Show
Special. 60 minutes. Premiere date: 4/27/75.
James Levine conducting the Metropolitan Op-
era Orchestra.
Executive Producer Sylvia Fine
Producer Bernard Rothman; Jack Wohl; Herb
Boni
Production Company Dena Pictures, Inc. and the
Metropolitan Opera Association
Director Robert Scheerer
Writer Herbert Baker; Sylvia Fine
Musical Director James Levine
Host Danny Kaye
Guest Stars Beverly Sills; Robert Merrill
Guests Judith Blegen; Adriana Maliponte; Rosa-
lind Elias; Cynthia Munzer; Charles Anthony;
Jose Carreras; Enrico di Giuseppe; Robert
Goodloe; Richard Best; Edmond Karlsrud;
James Morris

Dark of the Sun *see* The ABC Sunday
Night Movie

289   The Daughters of Joshua Cabe
Tuesday/Wednesday Movie of the Week ABC
Program Type TV Movie
90 minutes. Premiere date: 9/13/72. Repeat
date: 8/5/75. *See* sequel "The Daughters of
Joshua Cabe Return."
Executive Producer Aaron Spelling; Leonard
Goldberg
Producer Richard Lyons
Production Company Spelling/Goldberg Pro-
ductions
Director Philip Leacock
Writer Paul Savage
CAST

Joshua Cabe	Buddy Ebsen
Charity	Karen Valentine
Mae	Lesley Warren
Ada	Sandra Dee
Bitterroot	Jack Elam
Blue	Don Stroud
Codge Collier	Henry Jones
Amos Wetherall	Leif Erickson
Cole Wetherall	Michael Anderson, Jr.
Deke Wetherall	Paul Koslo
Sister Mary Robert	Julie Mannix
Arnie	Ron Soble
Billy Jack	Bill Katt
Warden Tippet	Claudia Bryar

290   The Daughters of Joshua Cabe Return
Tuesday/Wednesday Movie of the Week ABC
Program Type TV Movie
90 minutes. Premiere date: 1/28/75. *See also*
"The Daughters of Joshua Cabe."
Executive Producer Aaron Spelling; Leonard
Goldberg
Producer Richard E. Lyons
Production Company A Spelling-Goldberg Pro-
duction
Director David Lowell Rich
Writer Kathleen Hite
CAST

Joshua Cabe	Dan Dailey
Bitterroot	Dub Taylor
Ada	Ronne Troup
Charity	Christina Hart
Mae	Brooke Adams
Essie	Kathleen Freeman
Will	Carl Betz
Miner	Arthur Hunnicutt
Sgt. Maxwell	Terry Wilson
Jim Finch	Randall Carver
Jenny Finch	Jane Alice Brandon
Claver	Robert Burton
Vickers	Greg Leydig

291   David Castle in Concert   PBS
Program Type Music/Dance
Special. 30 minutes. Premiere date: 11/6/74. Pianist David Castle sings and plays his own compositions.

Production Company WCVE/Richmond, Virginia

292 David Copperfield

CBS Thursday/Friday Night Movies   CBS
Program Type TV Movie
Filmed in England. 120 minutes. Based on the novel by Charles Dickens. Premiere date: 3/15/70. Repeat date: 7/10/75.
Producer Frederick H. Brogger
Production Company Omnibus Productions in association with NBC-TV
Director Delbert Mann
Writer Jack Pulman; Frederick H. Brogger
CAST

David Copperfield	Robin Phillips
Agnes Wickfield	Susan Hampshire
Aunt Betsey Trotwood	Edith Evans
Mr. Peggotty	Michael Redgrave
Mr. Micawber	Ralph Richardson
Mrs. Micawber	Wendy Hiller
Steerforth	Corin Redgrave
Dora	Pamela Franklin
Uriah Heep	Ron Moody
Mr. Creakle	Laurence Olivier
Young David Copperfield	Alistair Mackenzie
Dick	Emlyn Williams
Mr. Tungay	Richard Attenborough
Barkis	Cyril Cusack
Murdstone	James Donald
Clara Peggotty	Megs Jenkins
Jane Murdstone	Anna Massey

293 Davis Cup American Interzone Elimination Matches

CBS Sports Special   CBS
Program Type Sports
Live coverage of matches from the Racquet Club, Palm Springs, California. 2/1/75; 2/2/75.
Producer Frank Chirkinian
Production Company CBS Television Network Sports
Announcer Jack Kramer; Tom Kelly

294 Day at Night   PBS

Program Type Interview/Discussion
30 minutes. Monday-Friday. Premiere date: 1/7/74. Continuous.
Executive Producer Winter Horton
Producer Jack Sameth
Distributor Publivision, Inc.
Director Jack Sameth
Host James Day

295 The Day the Earth Moved

Tuesday/Wednesday Movie of the Week   ABC
Program Type TV Movie
90 minutes. Premiere date: 9/18/74. Repeat date: 7/9/75. Story by Jack Turley. Filmed partly on location at Dry Lake, Nevada.

Producer Bobby Sherman; Ward Sylvester
Production Company ABC Circle Films
Director Robert Michael Lewis
Writer Jack Turley; Max Jack
CAST

Steve Barker	Jackie Cooper
Harley Copeland	Cleavon Little
Judge Backsler	William Windom
Helen Backsler	Beverly Garland
Officer Pat Ferguson	Kelly Thordsen
Miss Porter	Lucille Benson
Evelyn Ferguson	Ellen Blake
Henry Butler	E. J. Andre
Chief	Sid Melton
Angela	Tammy Harrington
Kate Barker	Stella Stevens

296 Days of Our Lives   NBC

Program Type Daytime Drama
Second regularly scheduled 60-minute daytime drama as of 4/21/75. Premiere date: 11/8/65. Monday-Friday. Continuous. Created by Ted Corday; Irna Phillips; Allan Chase. Set in "Salem, U.S.A." (Cast as of 4/21/75.)
Executive Producer Betty Corday
Producer Jack Herzberg; Al Rabin
Production Company Corday Productions, Inc., and Columbia Pictures Television in association with NBC-TV
Director Joe Behar; Frank Pacelli; Richard Sandwick; Alan Pultz
Head Writer William J. Bell
Writer Patricia Falken Smith; Bill Rega; Margaret Stewart
CAST

Atty. Don Craig	Jed Allen
Dr. Greg Peters	Peter Brown
Dr. Tom Horton	Macdonald Carey
Mickey Horton	John Clarke
Phyllis Anderson	Corinne Conley
Jack Clayton	Jack Denbo
Ben	Ben Di Tosti
Sam Monroe	Burt Douglas
Michael Horton	Wesley Eure
Dr. Laura Horton	Susan Flannery
Amanda Howard	Mary Frann
Dr. Neil Curtis	Joseph Gallison
Susan Peters	Bennye Gatteys
Doug Williams	Bill Hayes
Atty. Jim Phillips	Victor Holchak
Helen Cantrell	Jan Jordan
Eric Peters	Stanley Kamel
Bill Horton	Edward Mallory
Linda Patterson	Margaret Mason
Alice Horton	Frances Reid
Max	Hal Riddle
Maggie Hanson	Suzanne Rogers
Julie Horton	Susan Seaforth
Mary Anderson	Nancy Stephens
Bob Anderson	Bob Tapscott
Trish Clayton	Patty Weaver

297 The Dead Don't Die

NBC World Premiere Movie   NBC
Program Type TV Movie
90 minutes. Premiere date: 1/14/75. Repeat
date: 6/17/75.
Executive Producer Douglas S. Cramer
Producer Henry Colman
Production Company Douglas Cramer Productions
Director Curtis Harrington
Writer Robert Bloch
CAST

Don	George Hamilton
Moss	Ray Milland
Levenia	Joan Blondell
Vera	Linda Cristal
Lt. Reardon	Ralph Meeker
Specht	James McEachin
Perdido	Reggie Nalder
Ralph Drake	Jerry Douglas

298 Dead Man on the Run

Tuesday/Wednesday Movie of the Week ABC
Program Type TV Movie
90 minutes. Premiere date: 4/2/75. Filmed on
location in New Orleans, Louisiana.
Executive Producer Bob Sweeney
Producer William Finnegan
Production Company A Sweeney/Finnegan Production
Director Bruce Bilson
Writer Ken Pettus
CAST

Jim Gideon	Peter Graves
Libby Stockton	Katherine Justice
Brock Dillon	Pernell Roberts
Jason Monroe	John Anderson
Meg	Diana Douglas
Father Sebastian	Mills Watson
Fletcher	Tom Rosqui
"Rocky" Flanagan	Jack Knight
DiMosco	Joe E. Tata
Stockton	Hank Brandt
Hollander	Stocker Fontelieu
Sam Daggett	Donald Hood
Antoine LeClerc	Eugene Autry

299 Dealer's Choice   Syndicated

Program Type Game Show
Created by Ed Fishman; Randall Freer, 30
minutes. Monday-Friday. Premiere date:
1/21/74. Continuous.
Producer Ed Fishman; Randall Freer
Production Company Fishman-Freer Productions, Inc. in association with Columbia Pictures Television
Director Dan Smith
Host Jack Clark

300 Dean Martin Celebrity Roast   NBC

Program Type Comedy
Series of specials honoring different celebrities.
60 minutes each. Celebrities: Lucille Ball
(2/7/75); Sammy Davis, Jr. (4/24/75); Jackie
Gleason (2/27/75); Bob Hope (10/31/74); Michael Landon (5/15/75); Telly Savalas
(11/15/74).
Producer Greg Garrison
Director Greg Garrison
Host Dean Martin

301 Dean Martin Tucson Open

NBC Sports Special   NBC
Program Type Sports
Third and final rounds of the Dean Martin Tucson Open from the National Golf Club, Tucson,
Arizona. 1/18/75; 1/19/75.
Production Company NBC Sports
Announcer Jim Simpson; Jay Randolph; Pat
Hernon; Charlie Jones; Cary Middlecoff

302 Dean's Place   NBC

Program Type Comedy/Variety
Special. 60 minutes. Premiere date: 9/6/75.
Filmed at Cave des Roys, a private club in Beverly Hills, California.
Producer Greg Garrison
Production Company A Sasha Production in association with Greg Garrison Productions and
NBC-TV
Director Greg Garrison
Writer Mike Marmer; Stan Burns
Musical Director Lee Hale
Choreographer Ed Kerrigan
Host Dean Martin
Costume Designer Robert Fletcher
Guests Robert Mitchum; Angie Dickinson; Ronald Reagan; Nancy Reagan; Sherman Hemsley; Isabel Sanford; Georgia Engel; Jessi
Colter; Kelly Monteith; The Goldiggers; The
Untouchables
CAST

Dean	Dean Martin
Maitre D'	Jack Cassidy
Drunk	Foster Brooks
Italian Chef	Vincent Gardenia
Bartender	Guy Marks

303 Death Among Friends

NBC World Premiere Movie   NBC
Program Type TV Movie
90 minutes. Premiere date: 5/20/75. Repeat
date: 8/12/75.
Executive Producer Douglas S. Cramer
Producer Alex Beaton
Production Company Warner Brothers Television and Douglas S. Cramer Productions
Director Paul Wendkos
Writer Stanley Ralph Ross

CAST
Lt. Shirley Ridgeway .... Kate Reid
Buckner .... Martin Balsam
Chico Donovan .... Jack Cassidy
Otto Schiller ....Paul Henreid
Lisa Manning ....Lynda Day George
Capt. Lewis .... John Anderson
Off. Manny Reyes .... A Martinez

304 Death Be Not Proud
Tuesday/Wednesday Movie of the Week;
Special Tuesday Movie of the Week   ABC
Program Type TV Movie
120 minutes. Premiere date: 2/4/75. Based on
the memoir "Death Be Not Proud" by John
Gunther.
Executive Producer Charles G. Mortimer, Jr.
Producer Donald Wrye
Production Company A Good Housekeeping
Presentation in association with Westfall Pro-
ductions, Inc.
Director Donald Wrye
Writer Donald Wrye
CAST
John Gunther .... Arthur Hill
Frances Gunther ....Jane Alexander
Johnny Gunther ....Robby Benson
Dr. Tracy Putnam .... Linden Chiles
Frank Boyden .... Ralph Clanton
Mary Wilson .... Wendy Phillips

305 Death Cruise
Tuesday/Wednesday Movie of the Week ABC
Program Type TV Movie
90 minutes. Premiere date: 10/30/74. Repeat
date: 5/21/75.
Producer Aaron Spelling; Leonard Goldberg
Production Company Spelling/Goldberg Pro-
ductions
Director Ralph Senensky
Writer Jack B. Sowards
CAST
Dr. Burke ....Michael Constantine
Jerry Carter .... Richard Long
Sylvia Carter .... Polly Bergen
Mary Frances Radney .... Kate Jackson
James Radney .... Edward Albert
Elizabeth Mason .... Celeste Holm
David Mason ....Tom Bosley
Capt. Vettori .... Cesare Danova
Barrere .... Alain Patrick
Lynn .... Amzie Strickland
Room Steward .... Maurice Sherbanee

306 The Death Goddess   PBS
Program Type Music/Dance
Special. Japanese opera on theater art of
"rakugo." 60 minutes. Premiere date: 1/22/73
on "WNET Opera Theater." Repeat dates:
9/9/74; 8/5/75. Adapted from the work of Shin-
Ichiro Ikebe; featuring the Japan Broadcasting

Corporation Symphony and the Tokyo Broad-
casting Chorus conducted by Hiroshi Wakasugi.
Executive Producer Peter Herman Adler
Producer Kametaro Aramaki
Production Company WNET/New York
Director Norikazu Sugi
Writer Shohei Imamura
CAST
The Death Goddess .... Masako Saito
Undertaker ....Yoshiharu Nakamura
Wife .... Echiko Narita

307 Death of a King: What Changes for the Arab World?
CBS News Special   CBS
Program Type Documentary/Special
Implications on the death of King Faisal of Saudi
Arabia. 30 minutes. Premiere: 3/25/75.
Executive Producer Leslie Midgley
Producer Bernard Birnbaum; Hal Haley
Production Company CBS News
Anchor Charles Collingwood
Reporter Bill McLaughlin

308 Death Sentence
Tuesday/Wednesday Movie of the Week ABC
Program Type TV Movie
90 minutes. Premiere date: 10/2/74. Repeat
date: 7/30/75. Based on the novel "After the
Trial" by Eric Roman.
Producer Aaron Spelling; Leonard Goldberg
Production Company Spelling/Goldberg Pro-
ductions
Director E. W. Swackhamer
Writer John Neufeld
CAST
Susan Davies ....Cloris Leachman
Don Davies .... Laurence Luckinbill
John Healy .... Nick Nolte
Lubell .... Alan Oppenheimer
Tanner .... William Schallert
Judge .... Peter Hobbs
Martin Gorman .... Murray MacLeod
Mae Sinclair ....Meg Wyllie
Marilyn Healy .... C. J. Hincks
Mrs. Cottard ....Doreen Lang
Elaine Croft .... Yvonne Wilder
Lowell Hayes ....Herb Voland
Emily Boylan .... Hope Summers
Trooper .... Bing Russell
Mr. Bowman .... Lew Brown

309 Death Stalk
NBC World Premiere Movie   NBC
Program Type TV Movie
Based on a novel by Thomas Chastain. 90
minutes. Premiere date: 1/21/75. Repeat date:
7/8/75.
Executive Producer Herman Rush; Ted Berg-
mann
Producer Richard Caffey

Death Stalk *Continued*
Production Company Herman Rush Associates
Production in association with Wolper Pictures and NBC-TV
Director Robert Day
Writer Steven Kandel; John W. Bloch
CAST

Brunner	Vic Morrow
Jack	Vince Edwards
Cody	Norman Fell
Fourth Convict	Larry Wilcox
Shepherd	Neville Brand
Pat	Anjanette Comer
Hugh	Robert Webber
Cathy	Carol Lynley

The Defiant Ones *see* NBC Nights at the Movies

310 Delancey Street: The Crisis Within
NBC Nights at the Movies   NBC
Program Type TV Movie
Based on the work of John Maher, founder of the Delancey Street Foundation. 90 minutes. Premiere date: 4/19/75. Repeat date: 7/30/75.
Executive Producer Emmet G. Lavery, Jr.
Producer Anthony Wilson
Production Company Paramount Pictures Corporation in association with Emmet G. Lavery, Jr. Productions, Inc. and The Culzean Corporation in association with NBC-TV
Director James Frawley
Writer Robert Foster
CAST

John McCann	Walter McGinn
Joe	Carmine Caridi
Robert Holtzman	Michael Conrad
Otis James	Lou Gossett
Philip Donaldson	Mark Hamill
Mrs. Donaldson	Barbara Babcock
Ms. Somerville	Barbara Cason
Tony	Anthony Charnota
Rudolfo	Hector Elias
Richard Copell	John Karlen
Suzie Franklin	Jeri Woods
Mr. Donaldson	John Ragin
George Miles	Joseph X. Flaherty
Ruby James	Sylvia Soares
Mary	Leigh French
Dixon	Bart Cardinelli
Slim Jim	David Moody
T. D.	Bill Toliver
Detective	M. P. Murphy
Guard No. 2	James Jeter

311 The Desperate Miles
Tuesday/Wednesday Movie of the Week ABC
Program Type TV Movie
Based on the true-life experiences of Jim Mayo. Story by Arthur Ross. 90 minutes. Premiere date: 3/5/75.
Executive Producer Joel Rogosin

Producer Robert Greenwald; Frank von Zerneck
Production Company Universal Television Production
Director Daniel Haller
Writer Joel Rogosin; Arthur Ross
CAST

Joe Larkin	Tony Musante
Ruth Merrick	Joanna Pettet
Mrs. Larkin	Jeanette Nolan
Al	Richard Reicheg
Jason	Purvis Atkins
Ruiz	Pepe Serna
Lou	Shelly Novack
Dr. Bryson	John Larch
Jill	Lynn Loring

The Detective *see* The ABC Saturday Night Movie

312 Devlin   ABC
Program Type Animated Film
30 minutes. Saturday. Premiere date: 9/7/74.
Executive Producer William Hanna; Joseph Barbera
Producer Iwao Takamoto
Production Company A Hanna-Barbera Production
Director Charles A. Nichols
Story Editor Norm Katkov
Writer Willie Gilbert; Locke Sam and Paul Roberts; Maurice Tombragel; Rik Vollaerts; Carey Wilber; Shimon Wincelberg
Musical Director Hoyt Curtin
Executive Story Consultant Myles Wilder
VOICES

Ernie	Mike Bell
Tod	Mickey Dolenz
Sandy	Michele Robinson
Hank	Norm Alden

313 The Diamond Head Game   NBC
Program Type Game Show
Filmed at the Kuilima Hotel, Oahu, Hawaii. 30 minutes. Monday-Friday. Premiere date: 1/6/75. Continuous.
Producer Ed Fishman; Randall Freer
Production Company Fishman-Freer Productions, Inc. in association with Columbia Pictures Television
Director Terry Kyne
Host Bob Eubanks
Announcer Jim Thompson
Hostess Jane Nelson

314 The Diamond Head Game Syndicated
Program Type Game Show
Filmed at the Kuilima Hotel, Oahu, Hawaii. 30 minutes. Weekly. Evening version of daytime show. Premiere date: 1/11/75.
Producer Ed Fishman; Randall Freer

Production Company Fishman-Freer Productions, Inc. in association with Columbia Pictures Television
Director Terry Kyne
Host Bob Eubanks
Announcer Jim Thompson
Hostess Jane Nelson

315 The Dick Cavett Show   CBS
Program Type Comedy/Variety
Four-part summer series. 60 minutes. Saturday. Premiere date: 8/16/75. Through 9/6/75.
Producer Carole Hart; Bruce Hart
Director Alan Meyerson; Clark Jones
Writer Dick Cavett; Carole Hart and Bruce Hart; Christopher Porterfield; Marshall Efron; Alfa-Betty Olsen; Tom Meehan; Tony Geis; Clark Gessner
Musical Director Steven Lawrence
Host Dick Cavett
Regular Marshall Efron; Leigh French

316 Died Young   PBS
Program Type Documentary/Special
Special. The rise and decline of the Union Terminal Railroad Station in Cincinnati. 30 minutes. Premiere date: 4/14/75.
Executive Producer Charles Vaughan
Producer Gene Walz
Production Company WCET/Cincinnati
Director Gene Walz
Writer Jack Gwyn
Narrator Cecil Hale

317 Dig It   PBS
Program Type Educational
15 programs. Gardening and landscaping. Premiere date: 9/24/74. Weekly. From the Public Television Library.
Producer Ev O'Hare
Production Company WMVS-TV/Milwaukee
Director Ev O'Hare
Host Tom Lied

Dillinger *see* The CBS Thursday/Friday Night Movies

318 Dinah!   Syndicated
Program Type Variety/Talk Show
Successor to "Dinah's Place." 90 minutes. Monday-Friday. Premiere date: 10/21/74. Continuous.
Executive Producer Henry Jaffe; Carolyn Raskin
Producer Fred Tatashore
Production Company Produced by the CBS Television Stations
Distributor Twentieth Century-Fox Television
Director Glen Swanson

Writer Bill Walker; Bob Shayne; Donald Ross; Norman Martin
Musical Director John Rodby
Host Dinah Shore
Announcer Johnny Gilbert

319 The Dipsy Doodle Show   Syndicated
Program Type Children's Show
Live action/animation special. 60 minutes. Premiere: 12/74. Host is animated character Dipsy Doodle; also seven live actors: Karen League Barrett; Sandy Faison; Jon Freeman; Michael McGee; Harry Gold; Emil Herrera; Helene Leonard. Music composed and produced by Nitondo, Inc.
Executive Producer Bob Huber
Producer Jerry Leonard; Tony Lolli
Production Company WJW-TV/Cleveland
Animator Rick Reinert Productions
VOICES
Dipsy Doodle .... Leslie Sawyer

320 Directions   ABC
Program Type Religious Program
30 minutes. Sunday. Premiere date: 11/13/60. Season premiere: 9/22/74.
Executive Producer Sid Darion
Producer Various
Production Company ABC News Public Affairs
Director Various
Writer Various

Dirty Dingus McGee *see* The CBS Thursday/Friday Night Movies

321 The Disappearance of Flight 412
NBC World Premiere Movie   NBC
Program Type TV Movie
Executive Producer Gerald L. Adler
Production Company Cinemobile Productions in association with NBC-TV
Director Jud Taylor
Writer George Simpson; Neal Burger
Narrator Herb Ellis
CAST
Col. Pete Moore .... Glenn Ford
Maj. Dunning .... Bradford Dillman
Col. Trottman .... Guy Stockwell
Capt. Roy Bishop .... David Soul
Capt. Cliff Riggs .... Robert F. Lyons
Capt. Tony Podryski .... Greg Mullavey
Ferguson .... Stanley Clay
Additional Cast Kent Smith; Jonathan Lippe; Jack Ging

322 Discovery   NBC
Program Type Religious Program
Special. Tour of the Holy Land. 60 minutes. Premiere date: 1/17/74. Repeat date: 7/27/75. Music by David Amram.

Discovery *Continued*
Producer Doris Ann
Production Company NBC Television Religious Programs Unit
Director Joseph Vadala
Host Alexander Scourby
Camera Joseph Vadala

323 The District Attorney
CBS Reports   CBS
Program Type Documentary/Special
A "Justice in America" look inside the office of F. Emmett Fitzpatrick, District Attorney of Philadelphia. 60 minutes. Premiere date: 5/25/75.
Executive Producer Perry Wolff
Producer Jay McMullen
Production Company CBS News
Director Jay McMullen
Writer Jay McMullen
Narrator Jay McMullen

324 Doc   CBS
Program Type Comedy
30 minutes. Pilot film for CBS series 1975–76 season. Premiere date: 8/16/75. Created by Ed. Weinberger; Stan Daniels.
Producer Ed. Weinberger; Stan Daniels
Production Company MTM Enterprises, Inc.
Director Robert Moore
Writer David Lloyd
CAST
"Doc" Joe Bogert .... Barnard Hughes
Annie Bogert ....Elizabeth Wilson
Nurse Tully .... Florida Friebus
"Happy" Miller .... Irwin Corey
Gwen Bogert ....Linda Kelsey
John Russell .... Derek Stroud
Mrs. Russell .... Masla Gibbs
Mr. Albright ....Robert Moore
Young Lady .... Judith Hanson
Patient ....Roma Alvarez

325 Doc Severinsen's Rose Parade Preview   NBC
Program Type Documentary/Special
45 minutes. 1/1/75. Preview of the parade with highlights of previous year.
Producer Dick Schneider
Production Company NBC Television Network
Host Doc Severinsen

326 The Doctors   NBC
Program Type Daytime Drama
30 minutes. Monday-Friday. Continuous. Premiere date: 4/1/63.
Producer Joseph Stuart
Production Company Channelex, Inc.

Director Hugh McPhillips; Norman Hall; Joseph Stuart
Head Writer Eileen Pollock; Robert Mason Pollock
CAST
Erich Aldrich .... Keith Blanchard
Dr. Maggie Powers .... Lydia Bruce
Carolee Aldrich .... Carolee Campbell
Dr. Ann Larimer .... Geraldine Court
Dr. Hank Iverson .... Palmer Deane
Margo Stewart .... Mary Denham
Penny Davis .... Julia Duffy
Dr. Alan Stewart .... Gil Gerard
Dr. Nick Bellini .... Gerald Gordon
Martha Allen .... Sally Gracie
Dr. Althea Davis .... Elizabeth Hubbard
Alvin Ing .... Alan Koss
Dr. Karen Werner .... Laryssa Lauret
Dr. Steve Aldrich ....David O'Brien
Dr. Matt Powers ....James Pritchett
Dr. Gil Lawford .... Dale Robinette
Luke McAllister .... Alex Sheafe
Sgt. Cadman .... George Smith
Toni Ferra .... Anna Stuart
Lauri James .... Marie Thomas

Doctors' Wives *see* NBC Nights at the Movies

327 Don Kirshner's Rock Concert
                                         Syndicated
Program Type Music/Dance
90 minutes. Weekly. Guest host each week. Premiere: 9/73.
Executive Producer Don Kirshner
Producer David Yarnell
Production Company Don Kirshner Productions in association with Viacom
Distributor Viacom

328 The Don Rickles Show   CBS
Program Type Comedy/Variety
Special. 60 minutes. Premiere date: 1/19/75.
Executive Producer Joseph Scandore; Herbert Solow
Producer Paul W. Keyes
Production Company Warmth Productions
Director Bill Foster
Writer Paul W. Keyes; Marc London; Bob Howard; Bob O'Brien; Terry Hart
Musical Director Nelson Riddle
Host Don Rickles
Guests Jack Klugman; Dean Martin; Bob Newhart; Helen Reddy; Frank Sinatra; Loretta Swit; John Wayne
Other Guests: Charlie Callas; Jim Connell; Steve Landesberg; Marcia Lewis; Jaye P. Morgan; Billy Seluga; Rip Taylor

Don't Drink the Water *see* The CBS Thursday/Friday Night Movies

329   **Doors of Mystery**   PBS
Program Type Children's Show
Special. Tongue-in-cheek salute to Halloween performed by members of the Long Wharf Theatre, New Haven, Conn. 60 minutes. Premiere date: 10/27/74. Music and lyrics by Terrence Sherman; set by Peter Gould.
Producer Patterson Denny
Production Company Connecticut Educational Television Corporation in cooperation with WEDH/Hartford
Director Patterson Denny
Writer Craig Anderson
Cast January Eckert; Jerry Fischer; Jack Hoffman; Jennifer Jestin; Antonino Pandolfo; Terrence Sherman; Christie Virtue

330   **Doris Day Today**   CBS
Program Type Comedy/Variety
Special. 60 minutes. Premiere date: 2/19/75.
Producer George Schlatter
Director Tony Charmoli
Writer Digby Wolfe; George Schlatter
Musical Director Tommy Oliver
Choreographer Tony Charmoli
Host Doris Day
Guests Tim Conway; Rich Little; The Lockers
Special Guest John Denver

331   **Double Reed**   PBS
Program Type Music/Dance
Special. Profile of the chamber music players of the Boston Symphony Orchestra and their instruments. (*See also* "Violin.") 30 minutes. Premiere date: 8/7/72. Repeat date: 6/11/75.
Executive Producer Syrl A. Silberman
Producer Bill Cosel
Production Company WGBH/Boston and the Massachusetts Council for the Humanities, Inc. with the cooperation of the Boston Symphony Orchestra
Director Boyd Estus

332   **Double Solitaire**
Hollywood Television Theatre   PBS
Program Type Drama
90 minutes. Premiere date: 1/16/74. Repeat dates: 10/30/74; 3/11/75.
Executive Producer Norman Lloyd
Producer Martin Manulis
Production Company KCET/Los Angeles
Director Paul Bogart
Writer Robert Anderson
                          CAST
Charley Potter .... Richard Crenna
Barbara Potter ....Susan Clark
Peter Potter .... Nicholas Hammond
Ernest Potter .... Norman Foster
Irene Potter .... Irene Tedrow

George .... Harold Gould
Sylvia .... Norma Crane

Double Suicide *see* The Japanese Film

Dr. No *see* The ABC Sunday Night Movie

333   **Dr. Seuss' Horton Hears a Who**
                                                CBS
Program Type Animated Film
Special. 30 minutes. Created by Theodor Seuss Geisel. Music by Eugene Poddany; lyrics by Theodor Seuss Geisel. Premiere date: 3/19/70. Repeat date: 3/24/75.
Producer Theodor Seuss Geisel; Chuck Jones
Director Chuck Jones
Writer Theodor Seuss Geisel
Narrator Hans Conreid

334   **Dr. Seuss' How the Grinch Stole Christmas**   CBS
Program Type Animated Film
Special. 30 minutes. Based on the book by Theodor Seuss Geisel. Premiere date: 12/18/66. Repeat date: 12/13/74. Music composed by Albert Hague; lyrics by Theodor Seuss Geisel.
Producer Chuck Jones; Theodor Seuss Geisel
Production Company MGM Television
Director Chuck Jones
Writer Theodor Seuss Geisel
Narrator Boris Karloff
                        VOICES
Christmas Spoiler ....Boris Karloff

335   **Dr. Seuss on the Loose**   CBS
Program Type Animated Film
Special. 30 minutes. Three stories created by Theodor Seuss Geisel: "Green Eggs and Ham," "The Zax," "The Sneetches." Music by Dean Elliott; lyrics by Theodor Seuss Geisel. Premiere date: 10/15/73. Repeat date: 10/28/74.
Executive Producer David H. DePatie
Producer Theodor Seuss Geisel; Friz Freleng
Production Company A DePatie-Freleng Production in association with the CBS Television Network
Director Hawley Pratt
Writer Theodor Seuss Geisel
Narrator Hans Conreid
                        VOICES
Cat in the Hat .... Allan Sherman
Joe/Sam .... Paul Winchell
Zax/Sylvester/McMonkey McBean .... Bob Holt

336   **Dr. Seuss' The Cat in the Hat**   CBS
Program Type Animated Film
Special. 30 minutes. Based on "The Cat in the

Dr. Seuss' The Cat in the Hat *Continued*
Hat" by Theodor Seuss Geisel. Premiere date:
3/10/71. Repeat date: 1/31/75. Music composed
by Dean Elliott; lyrics by Theodor Seuss Geisel
Executive Producer David H. DePatie; Friz Fre-
leng
Producer Chuck Jones; Theodor Seuss Geisel
Production Company A DePatie-Freleng Pro-
duction
Director Hawley Pratt
Musical Director Eric Rogers
Narrator Allan Sherman
VOICES
The Cat in the Hat .... Allan Sherman
Additional Voices Gloria Camacho; Daws Butler; Pam
Ferdin; Tony Frazier

**337 Dr. Seuss' The Hoober-Bloob
Highway**   CBS
Program Type Animated Film
Special. 30 minutes. Premiere date: 2/19/75.
First "Dr. Seuss" story created for television.
Music by Dean Elliott; lyrics by Theodor Seuss
Geisel.
Executive Producer David H. DePatie
Producer Friz Freleng; Theodor Seuss Geisel
Production Company DePatie-Freleng Produc-
tion
Director Alan Zaslov
Writer Theodor Seuss Geisel
Voices Bob Holt

338 Dr. Who   PBS
Program Type Science Fiction
13 stories; 72 episodes. 30 minutes. Weekly. Pre-
miere date: 7/1/75. "Dr. Who and the Silurians"
(in seven parts): premiere date: 7/1/75. "Ambas-
sadors of Death" (in seven parts): premiere date:
8/19/75.
Producer Barry Letts
Production Company British Broadcasting Cor-
poration
Distributor Time-Life Films
Director Various
Writer Various
CAST
Dr. Who (the Time Lord) ....Jon Pertwee
Liz Shaw .... Caroline John
Brig. Lethbridge-Stewart .... Nicholas Courtney

339 Dracula
The CBS Thursday/Friday Night Movies CBS
Program Type TV Movie
Based on the novel by Bram Stoker. 120 minutes.
Premiere date: 2/8/74. Repeat date: 5/30/75.
Producer Dan Curtis
Production Company Dan Curtis Productions
Director Dan Curtis
Writer Richard Matheson

CAST
Count Dracula .... Jack Palance
Mrs. Westenra .... Pamela Brown
Van Helsing .... Nigel Davenport
Arthur Holmwood .... Simon Ward
Lucy Westenra .... Fiona Lewis
Mina Murray .... Penelope Horner
Jonathan Harker .... Murray Brown

340 A Dream for Christmas
Special Movie Presentation   ABC
Program Type TV Movie
Based on characters created by Earl Hamner, Jr.
120 minutes. Premiere date: 12/24/73. Repeat
date: 12/21/74.
Executive Producer Lee Rich
Producer Walter Coblenz
Production Company Lorimar Productions
Director Ralph Senensky
Writer John McGreevey
CAST
Rev. Will Douglas .... Hari Rhodes
Grandma Bessie .... Beah Richards
Sarah Douglas .... Lynn Hamilton
Joey Douglas .... George Spell
Bradley .... Marlin Adams
George Briggs .... Robert DoQui
Arthur Rogers .... Joel Fluellen
Fannie Mitchell .... Juanita Moore
Donald Freeland .... Clarence Muse
Emmarine .... TaRonce Allen

341 The Dream Makers
NBC World Premiere Movie   NBC
Program Type TV Movie
90 minutes. Premiere date: 1/7/75. Kenny Rog-
ers and Mickey Jones of the First Edition are in
the cast.
Executive Producer Charles Robert McLain
Producer Boris Sagal
Production Company MGM Television Produc-
tion in association with NBC-TV
Director Boris Sagal
Writer Bill Svanoe
CAST
Sammy Stone .... James Franciscus
Mary Stone .... Diane Baker
Manny Wheeler .... John Astin
Sally .... Jamie Donnelly
Mike .... Michael Lerner
Dave .... Ron Thompson
Earl .... Kenny Rogers
Jesse .... Mickey Jones
Additional Cast Devon Ericson; Steven Keats; Ron Rif-
kin; Erica Yohn; Regis J. Cordic; John Lupton; Lois
Walden; David Mann

**342 The Dreamer That Remains: Harry
Partch**   PBS
Program Type Music/Dance
Special. Award-winning film on the life and work
of composer Harry Partch. 30 minutes. Premiere
date: 3/31/75.

Executive Producer Saul Rubin; Elaine Attias
Producer Betty Freeman
Production Company Tantalus-Whitelight Productions
Director Stephen Pouliot

343 Drink, Drank, Drunk PBS
Program Type Documentary/Special
Special. 60 minutes. Premiere date: 10/21/74. Repeat dates: 1/1/75; 7/3/75. Program made possible by a grant from the 3M Company.
Executive Producer Tom Skinner
Producer Charlie Hauck
Production Company WQED/Pittsburgh
Director Jack Kuney; Joe Hamilton
Writer Joseph Bologna; Renee Taylor; John Boni; Charlie Hauck; Jack B. Weiner
Host Carol Burnett
Guests Larry Blyden; Joseph Bologna; Ron Carey; Morgan Freeman; Stanley Grover; Linda Hopkins; Ellen Madison; E. G. Marshall; Maeve McGuire; Renee Taylor

Duel in the Sun see The ABC Saturday Night Movie

344 The Dyn-O-Mite Saturday Preview Special CBS
Program Type Children's Show
30-minute preview of 1975–76 children's programs: "Far Out Space Nuts," "Shazam!," "Isis," "Ghost Busters." 9/4/75.
Executive Producer Virginia Carter
Producer Allan Manings
Production Company T.A.T. Communications Company
Director Gordon Wiles
Writer Allan Manings
Musical Director Jeff Barry
Host Jimmie Walker; Ralph Carter; Bern-Nadette Stanis
Costume Designer Rita Riggs
CAST
Junior .... Bob Denver
Barney .... Chuck McCann
The Honk .... Patty Maloney
World's Mightiest Mortal .... John Davey
Andrea/Isis .... JoAnna Cameron
Spenser .... Larry Storch
Kong .... Forrest Tucker
Tracy the Gorilla .... Bob Burns

345 An Eames Celebration PBS
Program Type Documentary/Special
Special. Profile of Charles Eames; Ray Eames. 90 minutes. Premiere date: 2/3/75. Program funded by IBM and the National Science Foundation.
Producer Perry Miller Adato

Production Company WNET/New York
Director Perry Miller Adato

Early Summer see The Japanese Film

346 East-West Shrine Game
NBC Sports Special NBC
Program Type Sports
50th Shrine Game. Live coverage from Stanford, California. 1/28/75.
Producer George Finkel
Production Company NBC Sports
Announcer Jim Simpson; John Brodie; Charlie Jones

347 Easter Is Syndicated
Program Type Animated Film
Religious special. 30 minutes. Premiere: 3/74. Repeat: 3/75. Music composed by Jimmy Haskell; sung by Leslie Uggams.
Executive Producer Dr. Martin J. Neeb, Jr.
Producer Rev. Ardon D. Albrecht
Production Company Lutheran Television
Director Leonard Gray
Writer Rev. Donald Hinchey
Principal Voices Leslie Uggams; Hans Conreid

348 The Easter Promise CBS
Program Type Drama
Based on a story by Gail Rock; Alan Shayne. Continuing the saga of the Mills family. (*See also* "The House without a Christmas Tree" and "The Thanksgiving Treasure.") 90 minutes. Premiere date: 3/26/75.
Producer Alan Shayne
Production Company CBS Television
Director Paul Bogart
Writer Gail Rock
CAST
Constance Payne .... Jean Simmons
James Mills .... Jason Robards, Jr.
Grandmother Mills .... Mildred Natwick
Addie Mills .... Lisa Lucas
Mrs. Coyne .... Elizabeth Wilson
Cora Sue .... Franny Michel
Terry .... Vicki Schrech
Linda .... Lori Ann Rutherford

349 Easter Service CBS
Program Type Religious Program
CBS News religious special. Easter service from Mother Bethel African Methodist Episcopal Church in Philadelphia. 60 minutes. Premiere date: 3/30/75. Sermon by Bishop Hubert Nelson Robinson.
Executive Producer Pamela Ilott
Producer Bernard Seabrooks
Production Company CBS News
Director Alvin Thaler

350   **Easter Sunday Service**   NBC
Program Type Religious Program
Special. 60 minutes. From University Baptist
Church, Fort Worth, Texas. Service conducted
by Dr. James G. Harris. Sermon, "Not by Bread
Alone." Premiere date: 3/30/75.
Executive Producer Doris Ann
Production Company NBC Television Religious
   Programs Unit
Director Richard Cox

Eat Art *see* Faces of the City/Eat Art

351   **The Economic Summit: Concluding
Remarks**
CBS News Special   CBS
Program Type Documentary/Special
Live coverage. Washington, D.C. 9/28/74.
Executive Producer Leslie Midgley
Production Company CBS News

352   **The Economic Summit: Summary
and Analysis**
CBS News Special   CBS
Program Type Documentary/Special
60 minutes. 9/29/74.
Executive Producer Leslie Midgley
Producer Hal Haley; Bernard Birnbaum
Production Company CBS News
Anchor John Hart
Correspondents Mitchell Krauss; Bob Schieffer

353   **The Edge of Night**   CBS
Program Type Daytime Drama
30 minutes. Monday-Friday. Premiere date:
4/2/56. Continuous. (Cast information as of
April 1975.) Set in "Monticello, U.S.A." Theme
"The Edge of Night" by Paul Taubman. "The
Edge of Night" and "As the World Turns" were
the first two 30-minute daytime dramas.
Producer Erwin Nicholson
Director Allen Fristoe; John Sedwick
Head Writer Henry Slesar
Announcer Hal Simms
                      CAST
Brandy Henderson .... Dixie Carter
Mike Karr .... Forrest Compton
Tracy Dallas .... Pat Conwell
Laurie Dallas .... Linda Cook
Danny Micelli .... Lou Criscuolo
Lt. Luke Chandler .... Herb Davis
Kevin Jamison .... John Driver
Nancy Karr .... Ann Flood
John (Whitney butler) .... George Hall
Trudy (Whitney maid) .... Mary Hayden
Rose Pollock .... Virginia Kaye
Martha Marceau .... Teri Keane
Geraldine Whitney .... Lois Kibbee
Bill Marceau .... Mandel Kramer
Johnny Dallas .... John LaGioia

Noel Douglas .... Dick Latessa
Phoebe Smith ....Johanna Leister
Tiffany Douglas .... Lucy Marten
Adam Drake .... Donald May
Joe Pollock .... Allen Nourse
Dr. Henderson .... Michael Stroka

354   **Edward S. Curtis: The Shadow
Catcher**   PBS
Program Type Documentary/Special
Special. 90 minutes. Premiere date: 7/2/75. The
photographer, Edward S. Curtis, and his struggle
to capture American Indian traditions. Excerpts
from Curtis's journals are read by Donald Suth-
erland. Program made possible by grants from
the National Endowment for the Arts, the Lilly
Endowment, Inc., the Irwin-Sweeney-Miller
Foundation, and the Corporation for Public
Broadcasting.
Producer T. C. McLuhan
Production Company South Carolina Educa-
   tional Television Network
Director T. C. McLuhan

355   **The Elders**   PBS
Program Type Documentary/Special
Special. 60 minutes. Originally telecast on the
Iowa Educational Broadcasting Network 10/73.
Premiere date: 11/13/74. Repeat date: 4/19/75.
Program funded by the National Endowment for
the Humanities.
Producer John Beyer
Production Company Iowa Educational Broad-
   casting Network/Des Moines
Director John Beyer
Writer John Beyer
Cinematographer Ron Burnell
Narrator Matthew Faison

356   **Election '74**
CBS News Special   CBS
Program Type Documentary/Special
Live coverage of election results. Correspon-
dents: Lesley Stahl (the West); Mike Wallace
(East); Dan Rather (Midwest); Roger Mudd
(South); John Hart (at large). 11/5/74.
Executive Producer Russ Bensley
Production Company CBS News
Executive-in-Charge Bill Leonard
Anchor Walter Cronkite
Analyst Eric Sevareid

357   **Elections in Great Britain**   PBS
Program Type Documentary/Special
Special. Live coverage via satellite through the
Canadian Broadcasting Corporation. 30
minutes. 10/10/74.
Production Company Canadian Broadcasting
   Corporation

Host Lloyd Robertson
Reporter David Halton

358   **Elections '74**
ABC News Special Events   ABC
Program Type Documentary/Special
Seven hours of live coverage. 11/5/74.
Executive Producer Walter J. Pfister, Jr.
Producer Robert Siegenthaler
Production Company ABC News Special Events Unit
Director Marvin Schlenker
Anchors Howard K. Smith; Harry Reasoner
Correspondents Steve Bell; Bob Clark; Sam Donaldson; Stephen Geer; Bill Gill; Tom Jarriel; Herbert Kaplow; Ted Koppel; Frank Reynolds; David Schoumacher

Electra Glide in Blue *see* The ABC
Saturday Night Movie

359   **The Electric Company**   PBS
Program Type Children's Show
30 minutes. Monday-Friday. Premiere: 10/25/71. Season premiere: 10/22/74. Program made possible by grants from the U.S. Office of Education-Department of Health, Education and Welfare, Public Television Stations, the Ford Foundation, the Corporation for Public Broadcasting, the Carnegie Corporation of New York.
Executive Producer Samuel Y. Gibbon
Producer Andrew Ferguson
Production Company Children's Television Workshop
Regular Luis Avalos; Jim Boyd; Morgan Freeman; Judy Graubart; Skip Hinnant; Rita Moreno; Danny Seagren; Hattie Winston

360   **Ellery Queen**
NBC Sunday Mystery Movie   NBC
Program Type TV Movie
Special. Based on a novel by Ellery Queen. Pilot for "Ellery Queen" series-1975–76 season. 120 minutes. Premiere date: 3/23/75. Repeat date: 9/7/75.
Producer Richard Levinson; William Link
Production Company Universal Television
Director David Greene
Writer Richard Levinson; William Link
CAST
Ellery Queen .... Jim Hutton
Insp. Richard Queen .... David Wayne
Carson McKell .... Ray Milland
Marion McKell .... Kim Hunter
Tom McKell .... Monte Markham
Simon Brimmer ....John Hillerman
Waterson .... Tim O'Connor
Monica Grey .... Nancy Mehta

Sgt. Velie .... Tom Reese
Gail Stevens .... Gail Strickland
Additional Cast John Larch; Warren Berlinger; Vic Mohica; Dwan Smith

Elvis—That's the Way It Is *see* NBC
Nights at the Movies

361   **Emergency!**   NBC
Program Type Drama
Paramedic Services of Squad 51. 60 minutes. Saturday. Premiere date: 1/22/72. Season premiere: 9/14/74.
Executive Producer Robert A. Cinader
Producer Ed Self
Production Company Mark VII Ltd. in association with Universal Television
Director Various
Writer Various
CAST
Dr. Kelly Brackett .... Robert Fuller
Nurse Dixie McCall ....Julie London
Dr. Joe Early ....Bobby Troup
Gage ....Randolph Mantooth
DeSoto .... Kevin Tighe

362   **Emergency Plus 4**   NBC
Program Type Animated Film
Based upon the paramedics of "Emergency!" 30 minutes. Saturday. Premiere date: 9/8/73. Season premiere: 9/7/74.
Producer Fred Calvert
Production Company Fred Calvert Productions in association with Universal Television and NBC-TV
VOICES
Roy DeSoto .... Kevin Tighe
John Gage ....Randolph Mantooth
Matt ....Matthew Harper
Jason .... Jason Phillips
Carol .... Carol Harper
Randy .... Randy Alrich

363   **The Emmy Awards**   CBS
Program Type Awards Show
Live coverage from Hollywood of the 27th annual Emmy Awards for prime-time entertainment shows on television. 120 minutes. 5/19/75.
Producer Paul W. Keyes
Director Tim Kiley
Writer Paul W. Keyes; Marc London; Bob Howard
Host Beatrice Arthur; Lucille Ball; Carol Burnett; Cher; Teresa Graves; Michael Learned; Mary Tyler Moore; Susan Saint James; Jean Stapleton; Karen Valentine
Announcer Johnny Gilbert

364   Emmy Awards for Daytime Programming   ABC
Program Type Awards Show
Second annual awards show seen live in the east. 90 minutes. 5/15/75. Show held aboard an excursion boat cruising the Hudson River near New York. 24 daytime television celebrities presented awards.
Producer Bill Carruthers; Joel Stein
Director Bill Carruthers
Writer Marty Farrell
Musical Director Milton DeLugg
Host Monty Hall; Stephanie Edwards

365   The End of the Ho Chi Minh Trail   PBS
Program Type Interview/Discussion
Special. 90 minutes. Premiere date: 6/5/75. Includes film from the Vietnam War.
Production Company NPACT (National Public Affairs Center for Television); British Broadcasting Corporation
Journalists Jim Lehrer; Julian Pettifer; Olivier Todd

366   Enemies
Theater in America   PBS
Program Type Drama
Play by Maxim Gorky; translated by Jeremy Brooks; Kitty Hunter-Blair. Performed by the Repertory Theatre of Lincoln Center, New York City. 120 minutes. Premiere date: 1/23/74. Repeat date: 3/5/75. Series made possible by grants from Exxon Corporation and the Corporation for Public Broadcasting.
Executive Producer Jac Venza
Producer Bob Goldman
Production Company WNET/New York
Director Ellis Rabb; Kirk Browning
Host Hal Holbrook
CAST
Zakhar Bardin .... Peter Donat
Paulina Bardin .... Frances Sternhagen
Yakov Bardin .... Ellis Rabb
Tatiana Bardin .... Carrie Nye
Kleopatra Skrobotov .... Kate Reid
Madya ....Susan Sharkey
Gen. Pechenegov .... Rick Woods
Kon .... Will Lee
Michail Skrobotov ....Stefan Gierasch
Nikolai Skrobotov .... Josef Sommer
Agrafena .... Jane Rose
Pologgy .... George Pentecost
Sinstove .... Dan Sullivan

367   Entertainer of the Year Awards   CBS
Program Type Awards Show
Special. 90 minutes. Fifth annual presentation by the American Guild of Variety Artists (AGVA) to its top performers. Taped 12/15/74 at Caesars Palace, Las Vegas. Premiere date: 1/18/74. 90 minutes.
Executive Producer Robert H. Precht
Producer Robert Arthur; Joe Bigelow
Production Company Sullivan Productions
Director Russ Petranto
Writer Joe Bigelow; Robert Arthur; Robert H. Precht
Musical Director Ray Bloch
Host Jackie Gleason
Winners Appearing Carol Burnett; Chicago; Peggy Fleming; Joel Grey; Gladys Knight and The Pips; Rich Little; Olivia Newton-John; Helen Reddy; Charlie Rich

368   Entertainment Hall of Fame Awards   NBC
Program Type Awards Show
Special. Second annual award chosen by newspaper entertainment editors. 120 minutes. 2/22/75. Keynoter: George C. Scott.
Executive Producer John Green
Producer Jack Wohl; Bernard Rothman
Production Company A Rothman-Wohl Production
Writer John Green
Musical Director Nelson Riddle
Choreographer Ron Field
Host Gene Kelly
Cast George Burns; Richard Chamberlain; Bette Davis; Sandy Duncan; Peter Falk; Ralph Grierson; Marvin Hamlisch; Florence Henderson; Danny Kaye; Jack Lemmon; Hal Linden; Fred MacMurray; Anthony Newley; Jack Paar; Gregor Piatigorsky; Freddie Prinze; Don Rickles; Ginger Rogers; Rosalind Russell; George C. Scott; Isaac Stern; Ben Vereen; Edward Villella; Flip Wilson; Joanne Woodward

369   Essene   PBS
Program Type Documentary/Special
Special. 1972 cinema-verite film shot in an Anglican monastery in Michigan. 90 minutes. Repeat date: 8/12/75.
Producer Frederick Wiseman
Production Company WNET/New York
Director Frederick Wiseman

370   The Eternal Light   NBC
Program Type Religious Program
Specials produced for the Jewish Seminary of America by Milton E. Krents and the NBC Television Religious Programs Unit. 1974–75 programs: "A Conversation with Dr. Robert Gordis," "A Conversation with Leo Rosten," "A Conversation with Rabbi Jules Harlow," "A Family Odyssey," "A Peculiar Treasure," "The

Tender Grass." (*See* individual titles for casts and credits.)
Executive Producer Doris Ann
Production Company NBC Television Religious Programs Unit

371 Evel Knievel—Portrait of a Daredevil   ABC
Program Type Documentary/Special
Special. 60 minutes. Premiere date: 9/4/75. Report on Evel Knievel with Frank Gifford.
Executive Producer Roone Arledge
Producer Doug Wilson
Production Company ABC Sports
Director Doug Wilson

372 Evening at Pops   PBS
Program Type Music/Dance
13-part series reprising best shows of past seasons. 60 minutes. Weekly. Premiere date: 7/6/75. Series made possible by a grant from the Martin Marietta Corporation. Shows reprised star Leroy Anderson; Chet Atkins; Eubie Blake; Carmen de Lavallade; Ferrante & Teicher; Benny Goodman; Richard Hayman; Peggy Lee; Jose Molina; Bobby Short; Richard Tucker and Robert Merrill; Ilana Vered; Roger Williams.
Production Company WGBH/Boston
Host Arthur Fiedler; the Boston Pops Orchestra

373 Evening at Symphony   PBS
Program Type Music/Dance
12-part series. 60 minutes. Weekly. Premiere date: 10/6/74. Repeat date: 4/15/75. Features the Boston Symphony Orchestra with Seiji Ozawa, music director; guest conductors and soloists. Programs made possible by grants from the Corporation for Public Broadcasting, the Ford Foundation, Public Television Stations, Raytheon Company.
Producer Jordan Whitelaw
Production Company WGBH-TV/Boston
Musical Director Seiji Ozawa
Guests Colin Davis; Beverly Sills; Joseph Silverstein; William Steinberg; Michael Tilson Thomas

374 An Evening of Championship Skating
PBS Sports Special   PBS
Program Type Sports
60 minutes. Premiere date: 12/15/74. Repeat date: 4/7/75. Annual skating exhibition for the "Jimmy Fund." Program made possible by grants from the Champion Spark Plug Company and Pepsi Cola Company.
Production Company WGBH/Boston
Host John Misha Petkevich

375 An Evening with John Denver   ABC
Program Type Comedy/Variety
Special. 60 minutes. Premiere date: 3/10/75. Cousteau sequence edited by George Folsey, Jr.; Aspen sequence by Mark Stouffer; Marty Stouffer.
Executive Producer Jerry Weintraub
Producer Rich Eustis; Al Rogers
Director Bill Davis
Writer Ray Jessel; Tom Tenowich; Ed Scharlach; Rich Eustis and Al Rogers
Musical Director Milt Okum
Choreographer Danny Daniels
Host John Denver
Guest Star Danny Kaye
Special Appearance Jacques Cousteau

376 An Evening with Mabel Mercer, Bobby Short and Friends   PBS
Program Type Music/Dance
Special. 60 minutes. Premiere date: 1/1/73 (midnight New Year's Day). Repeat date: 1/1/75 (midnight New Year's Day). Stars Mabel Mercer; Bobby Short.
Producer Tony Grosbell
Production Company South Carolina Educational Television Network
Director Tony Crosbell
Host George Frazier

377 Every Man Needs One
Tuesday/Wednesday Movie of the Week ABC
Program Type TV Movie
90 minutes. Premiere date: 12/13/72. Repeat date: 8/19/75.
Producer Jerry Paris
Production Company Spelling-Goldberg Production for ABC-TV
Director Jerry Paris
Writer Carl Kleinschmitt
CAST
Beth Walden	Connie Stevens
David Chase	Ken Berry
Pauline Kramer	Gail Fisher
Rasmussen	Steve Franken
Walt	Henry Gibson
Marty Ranier	Jerry Paris
Louise Lathrop	Louise Sorel
David's Mother	Nancy Walker
Nancy	Carol Wayne
Bus Driver	Stanley Adams
Desk Clerk	Ogden Talbot

378 The Execution of Private Slovik
NBC Nights at the Movies   NBC
Program Type TV Movie
Based on a true story; book by William Bradford Huie. 150 minutes. Premiere date: 3/13/74. Repeat date: 5/13/75.

The Execution of Private Slovik
Continued
Executive Producer Richard Levinson; William Link
Producer Richard Dubelman
Production Company Universal Television
Director Lamont Johnson
Writer Richard Levinson; William Link
CAST
Eddie Slovik .... Martin Sheen
Antoinette .... Mariclare Costello
Father Stafford .... Ned Beatty
Jimmy Feedek .... Gary Busey
Margaret ....Kathryn Grody

379   Exploring Yesterday
Call It Macaroni   Syndicated
Program Type Children's Show
Real-life adventure of Pittsburgh youngsters in Minnesota wilderness. 30 minutes. Premiere: 8/75.
Executive Producer George Moynihan
Production Company Group W Productions
Distributor Westinghouse Broadcasting Company

380   Face the Nation   CBS
Program Type Interview/Discussion
30 minute interview show. Premiered in 1954. Continuous. Sunday. George Herman and two guest journalists interview people in the news. Herman has been moderator since 1969. Broadcast originates live from Washington.
Producer Mary O. Yates
Production Company CBS News
Director Robert Vitarelli
Moderator George Herman

381   Faces of the City/Eat Art   PBS
Program Type Documentary/Special
Special. Two short films. 20 minutes. Premiere date: 6/11/75. Producers of "Faces of the City:" Jean Walkenshaw; Jesse Haas. Producer of "Eat Art:" Steve Welch in cooperation with the Henry Art Gallery of the University of Washington.
Production Company KCTS/Seattle

The Family *see* The CBS
Thursday/Friday Night Movies

382   A Family at War   PBS
Program Type Drama
60 minutes. Weekly. Premiere date: 10/10/74. The Ashtons of Liverpool from 1938–1945.
Executive Producer Richard Doubleday
Production Company Granada Television
Distributor Eastern Educational Network

CAST
Margaret Ashton .... Lesley Nunnerly
Freda Ashton ....Barbara Flynn
Mr. Ashton ....Colin Douglas
Mrs. Ashton .... Shelagh Fraser
Philip Ashton .... Keith Drinkel
David Ashton ....Colin Campbell
Additional Cast Coral Atkins; Trevor Bowen; John McKelvey

383   Family Circle Cup
NBC Sports Special   NBC
Program Type Sports
Taped coverage of semifinal and final matches from Amelia Plantation near Jacksonville, Florida. 5/17/75 (60 minutes); 5/18/75 (90 minutes).
Production Company NBC Sports
Announcer Jim Simpson; Bobby Riggs; Julie Heldman

384   The Family Kovack
The CBS Thursday/Friday Night Movies CBS
Program Type TV Movie
90 minutes. Premiere date: 3/22/74. Repeat date: 8/1/75.
Producer Ron Roth
Production Company Playboy Productions
Director Ralph Senensky
Writer Adrian Spies
CAST
Vinnie Kovack ....James Sloyan
Ma Kovack ....Sarah Cunningham
Butch Kovack ....Andy Robinson
Karen Kovack .... Tammi Bula
Lennie Kovack .... Richard Gilliland
Jill .... Renne Jarrett
Mrs. Linsen .... Mary La Roche
Jo-Jo Linsen ....Phil Bruns

385   The Family Nobody Wanted
Tuesday/Wednesday Movie of the Week   ABC
Program Type TV Movie
Story by Helen Doss; based on her book. 90 minutes. Premiere date: 2/19/75.
Executive Producer David Victor
Producer William Kayden
Production Company Groverton Productions, Ltd. in association with Universal Television
Director Ralph Senensky
Writer Suzanne Clauser
CAST
Helen Doss ....Shirley Jones
Carl Doss .... James Olson
Mrs. Bittner .... Katherine Helmond
Elmer Franklin .... Woodrow Parfrey
James Collins .... Beeson Carroll
Eunice Franklin .... Claudia Bryar
Mrs. Kimberly .... Ann Doran
Donny .... Willie Aames
Rick .... Ernest Esparza III
Tina .... Dawn Biglay
Tony .... Guillermo San Juan

Lynette .... Jina Tan
Pam .... Tina Toyota
Aram .... Haig Movsesian
Angela ....Knar Keshishian
Ton .... Tim Kim
Debby .... Sherry Lynn Kupahu
Andy .... Michael Stadnik; Robert Stadnik

386 A Family Odyssey
The Eternal Light   NBC
Program Type Interview/Discussion
Special. Conductor Michael Tilson Thomas and screenwriter father Theodor Herzl Thomas interviewed. 60 minutes. Premiere date: 6/8/75.
Producer Doris Ann
Production Company NBC Television Religious Programs Unit
Director Robert Priaulx
Interviewer Martin Bookspan

387 The Fashion Awards   ABC
Program Type Awards Show
Special. 1975 awards honoring the winning costumes of America's top designers. 90 minutes. Premiere date: 3/19/75.
Producer David Lawrence; Ray Aghayan
Production Company David Lawrence & Ray Aghayan Productions
Director John Moffitt
Writer Bill Richmond
Musical Director Jack Elliott
Choreographer Carl Jablonski
Host Diahann Carroll; John Davidson
Special Guest Star Juliet Prowse
Guest Star Ken Berry

388 Fat Albert and the Cosby Kids   CBS
Program Type Animated Film
Reruns. Cartoon characters created by Bill Cosby. 30 minutes. Saturday. Premiere date: 9/9/72. Season reruns: 9/7/74.
Executive Producer William H. Cosby, Jr.
Producer Norm Prescott; Lou Scheimer
Production Company Bill Cosby-Filmation Associates
Director Hal Sutherland
Writer Jim Ryan; Bill Danch; Chuck Menville; Len Janson
Animation Director Don Towsley; Lou Zukor
Art Director Don Christensen
VOICES
Fat Albert/Rudy/Mushmouth/Dumb Donald/Weird Harold .... Bill Cosby
Additional Voices Keith Allen; Pepe Brown; Erika Carroll; Jan Crawford; Gerald Edwards; Lane Vaux

389 The FBI Story: The FBI Versus Alvin Karpis, Public Enemy Number One
The CBS Thursday/Friday Night Movies   CBS
Program Type TV Movie
Special. 120 minutes. Premiere date: 11/8/74. Repeat date: 7/31/75. Film produced in cooperation with the FBI and its director, Clarence M. Kelley. First of the FBI landmark case series.
Executive Producer Quinn Martin
Producer Philip Saltzman
Production Company Quinn Martin Productions in association with Warner Brothers Television
Director Marvin Chomsky
Writer Calvin Clements
CAST
Alvis Karpis .... Robert Foxworth
Maynard Richards .... David Wayne
Shirley .... Kay Lenz
Fred Barker .... Gary Lockwood
Colette .... Anne Francis
Earl Anderson ....Chris Robinson
J. Edgar Hoover .... Harris Yulin
Ma Barker .... Eileen Heckart
Alex Denton .... James Gammon
Dr. Williams .... Robert Emhardt
Vicky Clinton .... Alexandra Hay
Bernice Griffiths ....Janice Lynde
Arthur (Doc) Barker .... Charles Cyphers
Smith .... Gerald McRaney
Frank .... Fred Sadoff
Chief of Detectives ....Kelly Thorsden
Rita ....Lenore Kasdorf
Aide No. 1 ....Charles Bateman
Aide No. 2 .... Mark Roberts
West .... Byron Mabe
Mary ....Betty Anne Rees
Sen. McKellar .... Whit Bissel

390 The FBI Story: The FBI Versus the Ku Klux Klan
The CBS Thursday/Friday Night Movie   CBS
Program Type TV Movie
Second of the FBI landmark case series produced in cooperation with the FBI and its director, Clarence M. Kelley. Presented in two parts: 2/20/75 and 2/21/75. 120 minutes each.
Executive Producer Quinn Martin
Producer Philip Saltzman
Production Company Quinn Martin Productions in association with Warner Brothers Television
Director Marvin Chomsky
Writer Calvin Clements
CAST
Deputy Sheriff Ollie Thompson .... Ned Beatty
George Greg ....John Beck
Dave Keene .... Billy Green Bush
Paul Mathison .... Dabney Coleman
Insp. Ryder .... Andrew Duggan
Atty. Ralph Paine .... Ed Flanders
Atty. Clay .... George Grizzard
Roy Ralston .... L. Q. Jones

The FBI Story: The FBI Versus the Ku Klux Klan *Continued*

Sheriff Ed Duncan .... Geoffrey Lewis
Jean Foster .... Marilyn Mason
Dan Foster ....Wayne Rogers
Ben Jacobs .... Peter Strauss
Glen Tuttle ....Rip Torn
Dee Malcom .... Mills Watson
Harry Dudley .... James Hampton
Linn Jacobs .... Sheila Larken
Steve Bronson ....Andrew Parks
Charles Gilmore .... Hilly Hicks
Aaron Cord .... Luke Askew
Jailer Sutton .... John McLiam
Bea Sutton .... Martine Bartlett
Logan Ramsey ....Thurston Carson

391   F.D.R.: The Man who Changed America

The American Parade   CBS
Program Type Documentary/Special
Seventh show of series. 60 minutes. Premiere date: 9/3/75. The first two terms of President Franklin D. Roosevelt, using film footage and tape recordings.
Executive Producer Joel Heller
Producer Joel Heller
Production Company CBS News for the CBS Television Network
Director Vern Diamond
Writer Andrew A. Rooney
Narrator Henry Fonda

392   Feasting with Panthers

Theater in America   PBS
Program Type Drama
Play performed by the Trinity Square Repertory Company of Providence, Rhode Island. Based on the life and work of Oscar Wilde. Music by Richard Cumming. 60 minutes. Premiere date: 3/27/74. Repeat date: 1/22/75. Series funded by Exxon Corporation and the Corporation for Public Broadcasting.
Executive Producer Jac Venza
Producer Ken Campbell
Production Company WNET/New York
Director Adrian Hall; Rick Hauser
Writer Adrian Hall; Richard Cumming
Host Hal Holbrook
CAST
Oscar Wilde .... Richard Kneeland
Isaacson .... George Martin
Sir Edward Clarke .... David Kennett
The Warden .... Richard K. Jenkins
A Prisoner ....Robert Black
Marquis of Queensberry .... Robert J. Colonna
A Prisoner ....James Eichelberger
Justice Wills .... David C. Jones
Dorian Gray .... Richard Kavanaugh
Lord Alfred Douglas .... T. Richard Mason
Wooldridge ....Daniel Von Bargen
Constance Wilde .... Jobeth Williams
Frank Harris ....Timothy Crowe

Robert Ross .... William Damkoehler
Lady Wilde .... Marguerite Lenert
Ada Leverson .... Barbara Orson

393   Feeling Good   PBS

Program Type Educational
60 minutes. Weekly. Premiere date: 11/20/74. Last show: 1/29/75. (*See* "Feeling Good" in 30 minute format for new show.) Program made possible by grants from the Corporation for Public Broadcasting, the Robert Wood Johnson Foundation, Exxon Corporation and the Aetna Life and Casualty Company. Action set at Mac's Place.
Executive Producer William Kobin
Production Company Children's Television Workshop
Director Don Mischer; Stan Lathan; David Wilson
Head Writer Tony Geiss
CAST
Mac ....Tex Everhart
Rita .... Priscilla Lopez
Mrs. Stebbins .... Ethel Shutta
Melba .... Marjorie Barnes
Jason .... Joe Morton
Hank .... Ben Slack

394   Feeling Good (new format)   PBS

Program Type Educational
30 minutes. Weekly. Premiere date: 4/1/75. Repeat date: 7/8/75. Show captioned for the deaf on 30 stations in April; on all PBS stations in July. The 30-minute version deals with one topic per week, the 60-minute version (see "Feeling Good" 60 minutes) deals with a variety of topics.
Production Company Children's Television Workshop
Host Dick Cavett

395   Fer-De-Lance

The CBS Thursday/Friday Night Movies CBS
Program Type TV Movie
90 minutes. Premiere date: 10/18/74. Repeat date: 7/25/75.
Executive Producer Leslie Stevens
Producer Dominic Frontiere
Production Company Leslie Stevens Productions in association with MGM Television
Director Russ Mayberry
Writer Leslie Stevens
CAST
Russ Bogan ....David Janssen
Elaine Wedell .... Hope Lange
Joe Voit .... Ivan Dixon
Cmdr. Kirk ....Jason Evers
Lt. Nicholson .... Charles Robinson
Lt. Whitehead .... Ben Piazza
Torquale .... George Pan
Liz McCord ....Sherry Boucher
Masai Ikeda .... Robert Ito
Wayne Bradley .... Bill Mims

Suan Kuroda .... Shizuko Hoshi
Lt. Scott .... Robert Burr

396 Ferrill, Etc.   PBS
Program Type Drama
Special. A dramatization of the works of Thomas
Hornsby Ferrill by the Third Eye Theatre in
Denver.
Production Company KRMA/Denver

Fiddler on the Roof *see* The ABC
   Sunday Night Movie

397 Fiesta Bowl
CBS Sports Special   CBS
Program Type Sports
Fourth Fiesta Bowl in Tempe, Arizona. Okla-
homa State Cowboys versus Brigham Young
Cougars. Live coverage. 12/28/74.
Production Company CBS Television Network
   Sports
Announcer Ray Scott; Wayne Walker; Phyllis
   George

398 The Finest Hours   PBS
Program Type Documentary/Special
Special. 1964 English documentary honoring the
100th anniversary of the birth of Winston
Churchill. 120 minutes. Shown on PBS:
11/28/74.

399 Firing Line   PBS
Program Type Interview/Discussion
60 minutes. Weekly. Continuous. Show pre-
miered in 1966.
Producer Warren Steibel
Production Company Southern Educational
   Communications Association
Director Warren Steibel
Host William F. Buckley

**400 First Ladies' Diaries: Rachel
Jackson**   NBC
Program Type TV Movie
Special. First of three daytime dramas focusing
on the first ladies. 90 minutes. Premiere date:
4/18/75.
Producer Paul Rauch
Director Ira Cirker
Writer Jerome Alden
                     CAST
Rachel D. Jackson .... Fran Brill
Andrew Jackson .... Gerald Gordon
John Overton ....David O'Brien
Jane .... Dolores Sutton
Robards .... Armand Assante
Mrs. Donelson .... Tresa Hughes
Mrs. Robards .... Lenka Peterson

Moll .... Juanita Bethea
George .... Bill Cobbs
Norma Livingston .... Martha Greenhouse
Livingston .... Ed Herlihy
Dickinson .... Rod Loomis
Severn .... Sam Schacht
Millard .... William Shust
Rachel's Doctor .... Philip Sterling

401 The First 36 Hours of Dr. Durant
Tuesday/Wednesday Movie of the Week ABC
Program Type TV Movie
90 minutes. Premiere date: 5/13/75.
Executive Producer Stirling Silliphant
Producer James H. Brown
Production Company Edling Productions, Inc. in
   association with Columbia Pictures Television
Director Alexander Singer
Writer Stirling Silliphant
                     CAST
Dr. Chris Durant .... Scott Hylands
Dr. Konrad Zane .... Lawrence Pressman
Nurse Katherine Gunther .... Katherine Helmond
Nurse Clive Olin .... Karen Carlson
Dr. Lynn Peterson .... Renne Jarrett
Dr. Alex Keefer .... Alex Henteloff
Mr. Graham .... Michael Conrad
Dr. Bryce .... Peter Donat
Dr. Atkinson .... David Doyle
Dr. Baxter ....James Naughton
Mr. Wesco .... Dennis Patrick
Dr. Hutchins .... Dana Andrews
Mrs. Graham .... Joyce Jameson
Surgical Secretary .... Janet Brandt
Dr. Dorsett .... Davis Roberts

A Fistful of Dollars *see* The ABC
   Sunday Night Movie

Flap *see* The ABC Saturday Night
   Movie; The ABC Sunday Night
   Movie

Flight from Ashiya *see* NBC Nights at
   the Movies

402 Flight: The Sky's the Limit
A Smithsonian Institution Special   CBS
Program Type Documentary/Special
Second of three Smithsonian specials. 60
minutes. Premiere date: 1/31/75. Documentary
focuses on four boys: Byron Cooke; Leroy Ellis;
David Muse; Tyrone Segears.
Executive Producer George Lefferts
Producer Mel Stuart
Production Company Wolper Productions in co-
   operation with The Smithsonian Institution
Director Robert Young
Writer Paul Boorstin
Narrator Barry Sullivan

403 Flip Wilson ... Of Course   NBC
Program Type Comedy/Variety
First of four specials of the 1974–75 season. 60 minutes. Premiere date: 10/18/74.
Executive Producer Monte Kay
Producer Lorne Michaels
Production Company Clerow Productions
Director Tim Kiley
Writer John Boni; Jack Burns; John Donley; Carl Gottlieb; John Head; Don Hinkley; Ray Jessel; Lorne Michaels; Thad Mumford; Earl Pomerantz; Kurt Taylor; Flip Wilson
Musical Director George Wyle
Host Flip Wilson
Guests Peter Sellers; Lily Tomlin; Richard Pryor; Martha Reeves

404 The Flip Wilson Special   NBC
Program Type Comedy/Variety
Second show. 60 minutes. Premiere date: 12/11/74.
Executive Producer Monte Kay
Producer Jack Burns
Production Company Clerow Productions
Director Bill Foster
Writer Carl Gottlieb; John Boni; Ann Elder; Charlie Hauck; Thad Mumford; Alan Thicke; Jerry Winnick; Flip Wilson
Host Flip Wilson
Guests Freddie Prinze; Paul Williams; Diahann Carroll

405 The Flip Wilson Special   NBC
Program Type Comedy/Variety
Third show. 60 minutes. Premiere date: 2/27/75.
Executive Producer Monte Kay
Producer Jack Burns
Production Company Clerow Productions
Director Bill Davis
Writer Jim Cranna; Ann Elder; Carl Gottlieb; John Head; Thad Mumford; Alan Thicke; Jerry Winnick; George Yanok; Flip Wilson
Musical Director George Wyle
Host Flip Wilson
Guests Sammy Davis, Jr.; William Conrad; Helen Reddy

406 The Flip Wilson Special   NBC
Program Type Comedy/Variety
Fourth and final show of season. 60 minutes. Premiere date: 5/7/75.
Executive Producer Monte Kay
Producer Jack Burns
Production Company A Clerow Production
Director Bill Hobin
Writer Jim Cranna; Ann Elder; Carl Gottlieb; John Head; Thad Mumford; Alan Thicke; Jerry Winnick; George Yanok; Flip Wilson
Musical Director George Wyle

Host Flip Wilson
Guests Cher; Richard Pryor; Kenny Rankin; McLean Stevenson

407 Florida Citrus Open Golf Tournament
CBS Sports Special   CBS
Program Type Sports
Live coverage of finals at Orlando, Florida Rio Pinar Country Club. 3/8/75–3/9/75.
Producer Frank Chirkinian
Production Company CBS Television Network Sports
Announcer Pat Summerall; Ken Venturi; Jack Whitaker

408 Fly Like a Bird
Call It Macaroni   Syndicated
Program Type Children's Show
Real-life aerial adventures of two San Francisco youngsters in New England. 30 minutes. Premiere: 3/75. Co-produced by WBZ-TV Boston.
Executive Producer George Moynihan
Producer Gail Frank
Production Company Group W Productions
Distributor Westinghouse Broadcasting Company
Director Gail Frank
Cinematographer Dick Roy

409 Food: The Crisis and the Churches
    NBC
Program Type Religious Program
Special. Discussion with the Rev. Theodore Hesburgh; and the Rev. J. Bryan Hehir. 60 minutes. Premiere date: 1/26/75.
Producer Doris Ann
Production Company NBC Television Religious Programs Unit
Director Robert Priaulx
Moderator Philip Scharper

For a Few Dollars More *see* Special Movie Presentation

For Love of Ivy *see* The ABC Sunday Night Movie

410 For the Use of the Hall
Hollywood Television Theatre   PBS
Program Type Comedy
90 minutes. Premiere date: 1/2/75. Repeat date: 8/7/75.
Executive Producer Norman Lloyd
Producer George Turpin
Production Company KCET/Los Angeles

Director Lee Grant; Rick Bennewitz
Writer Oliver Hailey
CAST
Charlotte .... Barbara Barrie
Alice .... Joyce Van Patten
Terry .... Susan Anspach
Allen .... David Hedison
Bess .... Aline MacMahon
Martin .... George Furth

411 Force Five
The CBS Thursday/Friday Night Movies CBS
Program Type TV Movie
90 minutes. Premiere date: 3/28/75. Repeat date: 9/5/75.
Producer Michael Gleason; David Levinson
Production Company Universal Television
Director Walter Grauman
Writer Michael Gleason; David Levinson
CAST
Lt. Roy Kessler .... Gerald Gordon
James T. O'Neill .... Nick Pryor
Vic Bauer .... William Lucking
Lester White .... James Hampton
Arnie Kogan .... Roy Jenson
Norman Ellsworth .... David Spielberg
Carl Newkirk .... Leif Erickson
Arthur Haberman .... Normann Burton
Michael Dominick .... Bradford Dillman
Frankie Hatcher ....Victor Argo
Steve Ritchie .... Lee Paul
Ginger ....Belinda Balaski
Reggie Brinkle .... Rod Haase
Patty ....Nancy Fuller
Det. Felcher .... George Loros

412 Fore!   PBS
Program Type Sports
Five-part series on golf from the Congressional Golf Club, Bethesda, Maryland. First shown in 1973. Presented through the Eastern Educational Television Network. Repeat date: 5/1/75.
Production Company New Jersey Public Broadcasting Company
Host Bob Benning

413 Forget-Me-Not Lane
Theater in America   PBS
Program Type Comedy
Play by Peter Nichols performed by the Long Wharf Theatre, New Haven, Conn. 100 minutes. Premiere date: 3/12/75. Series made possible by grants from Exxon Corporation and the Corporation for Public Broadcasting.
Executive Producer Jac Venza
Producer Jac Venza; Lindsay Law
Production Company WNET/ New York and Connecticut Public Television
Director Arvin Brown; John Desmond
Host Hal Holbrook
CAST
Frank Bisley .... Joseph Maher

Amy Bisley ....Geraldine Fitzgerald
Ursula Bisley ....Joyce Ebert
Charles Bisley .... Donald Moffat
Young Frank .... Tom Hulce
Young Ursula .... Betsy Slade
Ivor .... Bruce Kimmel
Mr. Magic ....George Taylor
Miss 1940 ....Astrid Ronning

414 The Forgotten War   PBS
Program Type Documentary/Special
Special. 1918 attempt to remove the Bolsheviks from power in Russia. 60 minutes. Premiere date: 6/17/74. Repeat date: 4/21/75.
Producer Julian Jaccott
Production Company British Broadcasting Corporation and WNET/New York
Narrator Robert MacNeil

415 Frank Sinatra - The Main Event - Madison Square Garden   ABC
Program Type Music/Dance
Special. Live concert (Eastern time). Starring Frank Sinatra; at ringside: Howard Cosell. Woody Herman Orchestra. 60 minutes. Premiere date: 10/13/74.
Executive Producer Jerry Weintraub
Producer Roone Arledge
Production Company Management III
Director Bill Carruthers
Musical Director Bill Miller

416 Frankenstein: The True Story
NBC Nights at the Movies   NBC
Program Type TV Movie
Based on the novel by Mary Shelley. Presented in two parts 120 minutes each. Premiere dates: 11/30/73; 12/1/73. Repeat dates: 12/30/74; 12/31/74.
Producer Hunt Stromberg, Jr.
Production Company Universal Television
Director Jack Smight
Writer Christopher Isherwood; Don Bachardy
CAST
Dr. Victor Frankenstein .... Leonard Whiting
Dr. Polidori .... James Mason
Creature ....Michael Sarrazin
Dr. Henry Clervel .... David McCallum
Prima .... Jane Seymour
Elizabeth .... Nicola Pagett
Landlady ....Agnes Moorehead
Additional Cast Michael Wilding; John Gielgud; Ralph Richardson; Tom Baker; Margaret Leighton; Clarissa Kaye

Frenzy *see* The ABC Saturday Night Movie

417   Friendly Persuasion
The ABC Sunday Night Movie; Special Movie
Presentation   ABC
Program Type TV Movie
120 minutes. Premiere date: 5/18/75. Based on
"Friendly Persuasion" and "Except for Me and
Thee" by Jessamyn West. Filmed in Jackson
County, Missouri and Chattanooga, Tennessee.
Executive Producer Emanuel L. Wolf
Producer Herbert B. Leonard; Joseph Sargent
Production Company International Television
   Productions
Director Joseph Sargent
Writer William P. Woods
                      CAST
Jess Birdwell .... Richard Kiley
Eliza Birdwell .... Shirley Knight
Sam Jordan .... Clifton James
Josh Birdwell .... Michael O'Keefe
Laban Birdwell .... Kevin O'Keefe
Mattie Birdwell .... Tracie Savage
Little Jess .... Sparky Marcus
Enoch .... Eric Holland
Swan Stebeney .... Paul Benjamin
Lily Truscott .... Maria Grimm
Burk .... Bob Minor

Friends and Lovers *see* Paul Sand in
   Friends and Lovers

418   Friends of Man   Syndicated
Program Type Animal Documentary
30 minutes. Weekly. Premiere: January 1975.
Executive Producer John Must
Producer Tony Bond; Henning Jacobsen; Rupert
   McNee
Production Company Mediavision
Writer Brian Shaw
Host Glenn Ford

419   From Sea to Shining Sea   Syndicated
Program Type Drama
Seven-part miniseries on American history for
the bicentennial. Three programs shown during
the 1974–75 season: "Give Me Liberty," "Land
of the Free," "The Unwanted." (*See* individual
titles for cast and credits.)
Producer John H. Secondari; Helen Jean Sec-
   ondari
Production Company John H. Secondari Produc-
   tions, Ltd.
Distributor The Hughes Television Network
Director Various
Writer Various

420   Frosty the Snowman   CBS
Program Type Animated Film
Special. 30 minutes. Premiere date: 12/7/69. Re-
peat date: 12/8/74. Based on the song by Jack

Rollins. Music and lyrics by Jules Bass; Maury
Laws.
Producer Arthur Rankin, Jr.; Jules Bass
Director Arthur Rankin, Jr.; Jules Bass
Writer Romeo Muller
Narrator Jimmy Durante
                  VOICES
Frosty .... Jackie Vernon
Prof. Hindle .... Billy De Wolfe

Funny Girl *see* The ABC Sunday Night
   Movie

421   Funny Girl to Funny Lady
The Sentry Collection Presents   ABC
Program Type Comedy/Variety
Special. Live broadcast of Barbra Streisand in
concert (in Eastern time zone) from the Kennedy
Center, Washington, D.C. 60 minutes. Premiere
date: 3/9/75.
Executive Producer Ray Stark
Producer Gary Smith
Production Company Raystar Productions, Inc.
Director Dwight Hemion
Writer Herb Sargent
Musical Director Peter Matz
Host Dick Cavett
Guests Muhammad Ali; James Caan; Frank Gif-
ford; Eunice Shriver

422   Funshine Saturday Sneak Peek ABC
Program Type Children's Show
Preview of 1975–76 Saturday morning children's
programs. 30 minutes. 9/5/75.
Producer Sid Krofft; Marty Krofft
Production Company Sid and Marty Krofft Pro-
   duction for the ABC Television Network
Host Jim Nabors; Ruth Buzzi

423   Gambit   CBS
Program Type Game Show
30 minutes. Monday-Friday. Continous. Pre-
miere date: 9/4/72.
Executive Producer Merrill Heatter; Bob Quigley
Producer Robert Nash
Production Company Heatter-Quigley Produc-
   tions
Director Jerome Shaw
Host Wink Martindale
Hostess/Dealer Elaine Stewart

The Games *see* The CBS
   Thursday/Friday Night Movies

424 The Garden Party
Special of the Week   PBS
Program Type Drama
Special. 30 minutes. Premiere date: 10/7/74. Repeat date: 2/12/75. Adapted from the story by Katherine Mansfield.
Producer Paul Gurian
Production Company Gurian-Sholder Productions and WNET/New York
Director Jack Sholder
Writer Jack Sholder
CAST
Laura Sheridan .... Maia Danziger
Mrs. Sheridan .... Beatrice Straight
Ted .... Mark Metcalf
Peggy ....Jessica Harper

Gate of Hell *see* The Japanese Film

425 A Gathering of One   NBC
Program Type Religious Program
Special. 60 minutes. Premiere date: 2/16/75. Dramatic profile of 18th century theologian Jonathan Edwards.
Executive Producer Doris Ann
Producer Martin Hoade
Production Company NBC Television Religious Programs Unit
Director Martin Hoade
Writer Jerome Olden
CAST
Jonathan Edwards ....Lee Richards
Sarah .... Rita Gam
McKenzie .... Roy Poole
Joseph Hawley ....Clarence Felder
Mayor Seth Pomeroy ....Addison Powell

426 The Gathering Storm
Hallmark Hall of Fame   NBC
Program Type TV Movie
Special. Based on Winston Churchill memoirs of World War II. 90 minutes. Premiere date: 11/29/74.
Executive Producer Duane C. Bogie
Producer Jack Le Vien; Andrew Osborn
Production Company BBC Production in association with Clarion and Le Vien Productions
Director Herbert Wise
Writer Colin Morris
CAST
Winston Churchill ....Richard Burton
Clemmie Churchill .... Virginia McKenna
Lord Beaverbrook .... Robert Beatty
Hitler .... Ian Bannen
Von Ribbentrop .... Robert Hardy
Neville Chamberlain .... Robin Bailey
King Edward VII .... Ian Ogilvy
Randolph Churchill ....Clive Francis

427 Gator Bowl
ABC Sports Special   ABC
Program Type Sports
31st Gator Bowl at Jacksonville, Florida. Live coverage. 12/30/74. Texas Longhorns versus Auburn Tigers.
Executive Producer Roone Arledge
Production Company ABC Sports
Announcer Chris Schenkel; Frank Broyles

GE Theater *see* General Electric Theater

428 The General
The American Parade   CBS
Program Type Documentary/Special
Fourth show of series. 60 minutes. Premiere date: 12/5/74. Portrait of Gen. George C. Marshall, seen primarily through newsreel footage.
Executive Producer Joel Heller
Producer James B. Faichney
Production Company CBS News for the CBS Television Network
Director James B. Faichney
Writer Richard F. Hanser
Narrator Ben Gazzara

429 General Electric Theater   CBS
Program Type Drama
Premiered as 30-minute series 2/1/53. Returned after decade 12/18/73. Season premiere: 11/27/74. Six programs: "I Heard the Owl Call My Name," "In This House of Brede," "It's Good to Be Alive," "Larry," "Miles to Go Before I Sleep," "Things in Their Season." (*See* individual titles for cast and credits.)

430 General Hospital   ABC
Program Type Daytime Drama
30 minutes. Monday-Friday. Premiere date: 4/1/63. Continuous. Created by Frank Hursley; Doris Hursley. John Beradino and Emily McLaughlin are original cast members; Peter Hansen and Lucille Wall joined the show during the first year.
Producer James Young
Production Company Oxbow Productions
Writer Jerome Dobson; Bridget Dobson
CAST
Dr. Leslie Williams .... Denise Alexander
Audrey Hobart ....Rachel Ames
Samantha Livingstone .... Kimberly Beck
Dr. Steve Hardy ....John Beradino
Chase Murdock .... Ivan Bonar
Beth Maynard .... Michele Conaway
Caroline Chandler .... Augusta Dabney
Bobby Chandler ....Ted Eccles
Lee Baldwin .... Peter Hansen
Jane Dawson .... Shelby Hiatt
Dr. Peter Taylor .... Craig Huebing
Dr. Henry Pinkham .... Peter Kilman

General Hospital *Continued*

Cameron Faulkner	Don Matheson
Dr. Joel Stratton	Rod McCary
Augusta McLeod	Judith McConnell
Jessie Brewer	Emily McLaughlin
Martha Taylor	Jennifer Peters
Margaret Caulson	Betty Anne Rees
Kira Faulkner	Victoria Shaw
Dr. James Hobart	James Sikking
Diana Taylor	Valerie Starrett
Felix Buchanon	Mark Travis
Lucille Weeks	Lucille Wall

Generation *see* The CBS Thursday/Friday Night Movies

431 The George Segal Show   NBC
Program Type Comedy/Variety
Special. 90 minutes. Premiere date: 10/26/74.
Executive Producer Alan D. Courtney
Producer Herb Sargent
Production Company Alan Courtney Productions
Director John Moffitt
Writer Herb Sargent
Host George Segal
Guests Teresa Brewer; Maxine Weldon; Kathe Green; David Steinberg; Buck Henry; Victor Fink; Hank Jones; ILGWU Senior Citizen's Mandolin Society

432 Gerald Ford's America   PBS
Program Type Documentary/Special
Four-part series. 30 minutes each. Premiere date: 12/29/74. Experiment by TVTV (Top Value Television) and WNET/New York on the potential of half-inch video tape technology. Produced with grants from the Ford Foundation and the Rockefeller Foundation and assistance from WGBH-TV New Television Workshop.
Producer David Loxton
Production Company TVTV (Top Value Television) and the Television Workshop, WNET/-New York

Geronimo *see* NBC Nights at the Movies

433 Get Christie Love!   ABC
Program Type Crime Drama
60 minutes. Premiere date: 9/11/74. Last show: 7/18/75. Moved from Wednesday to Friday. Based on the novel by Dorothy Uhnak. Pilot aired on "Tuesday Movie of the Week" 1/22/74. Set in the Special Investigations Division of the Los Angeles Police Department. Paul Mason replaced as producer by Glen A. Larson and Ron Satlof.
Producer Paul Mason; Glen A. Larson; Ron Satlof

Production Company Wolper Productions in association with Universal Television.
Director Various
Writer Various
Executive Story Consultant Gerald Sanford
CAST
Christie Love	Teresa Graves
Lt. Matt Reardon	Charles Cioffi
Joe Caruso	Andy Romano
Steve Belmont	Dennis Rucker
Valencia	Scott Peters

434 The Girl in My Life   ABC
Program Type Audience Participation
30 minutes. Monday-Friday. Last show: 12/20/74.
Executive Producer William Carruthers
Producer Brad Lachman
Production Company Tom Naud Productions in association with Metromedia Producers Corporation
Host Fred Holliday

435 The Girl Most Likely To ...
Tuesday/Wednesday Movie of the Week ABC
Program Type TV Movie
90 minutes. Premiere date: 11/6/73. Repeat date: 3/26/75. Based on a story by Joan Rivers.
Producer Everett Chambers
Production Company ABC Circle Films
Director Lee Philips
Writer Agnes Gallin; Joan Rivers
CAST
Miriam Knight	Stockard Channing
Det. Ralph Varrone	Edward Asner
Prof. Tilson	Jim Backus
Dr. Green	Joe Flynn
The Coach	Chuck McCann
Dr. Hankin	Carl Ballantine
The Chaplain	Cyril Delevanti
Dr. Ted Gates	Fred Grandy
The Housemother	Ruth McDevitt
Heidi	Suzanne Zenor
Herman	Warren Berlinger
Moose Myers	Larry Wilcox
Fred	Daniel Spelling

436 A Girl Named Sooner
IBM Presents   NBC
Program Type TV Movie
Special. Based on the book by Suzanne Clauser. 120 minutes. Premiere date: 6/18/75.
Executive Producer Frederick Brogger
Producer Fred Hamilton
Production Company 20th Century-Fox Television in association with Frederick Brogger and Associates
Director Delbert Mann
Writer Suzanne Clauser
CAST
Elizabeth McHenry	Lee Remick
Mac McHenry	Dick Crenna

Old Mam ....Cloris Leachman
Sheriff Phil Rotteman .... Don Murray
Selma Goss .... Anne Francis
Sooner .... Susan Deer
Jim Seevey ....Michael Gross
Teacher .... Nancy Bell
Harvey .... Ken Harden
Judith Ann Drumond .... Tonia Scotti

437 The Girl Who Came Gift Wrapped
Tuesday/Wednesday Movie of the Week ABC
Program Type TV Movie
90 minutes. Premiere date: 1/29/74. Repeat date: 1/1/75.
Producer Aaron Spelling; Leonard Goldberg
Production Company Spelling/Goldberg Productions
Director Bruce Bilson
Writer Susan Silver
CAST
Sandy .... Karen Valentine
Michael .... Richard Long
Sylvia .... Louise Sorel
Miss Markin ....Reta Shaw
Stanley .... Dave Madden
Cindy .... Patti Cubbison
Harold ....Tom Bosley
Louise .... Shelley Morrison
Larry .... Michael Haynes
Patty .... Farrah Fawcett Majors

438 The Girl Who Couldn't Lose
ABC Afternoon Playbreak   ABC
Program Type TV Movie
Special. 90 minutes. Premiere date: 2/13/75. Repeat date: 7/10/75.
Executive Producer Ira Barmak
Producer Lila Garrett
Production Company Filmways, Inc.
Director Mort Lachman
Writer Lila Garrett; Sanford Krinski
CAST
Jane Darwin .... Julie Kavner
Jackie Leroy .... Jack Carter
Mark Linden .... Frank Stell
Florence Darwin .... Fritzi Burr
Charlie Darwin .... Milton Selzer
Susan Miller .... Beverly Sanders
Walter Mersh .... Edward Marshall
Judd More .... Oliver Clark
Rosalie ....Candy Azzara
Sonny Miller .... Milt Kogan
Andy Martin ....Dennis Dugan

439 Give Me Liberty
From Sea to Shining Sea   Syndicated
Program Type Drama
First of a seven-part miniseries on American history for the bicentennial. 90 minutes. Premiere date: 9/74. Filmed in Georgia. Music by Michel Legrand; lyrics by Hal David.
Producer John H. Secondari; Helen Jean Secondari

Production Company John H. Secondari Productions, Ltd.
Distributor The Hughes Television Network
Director Buzz Kulik
Writer Ernest Kinoy
CAST
John Freeborn .... Robert Culp
James Robertson ....Richard Kiley
Col. George Washington ....Fritz Weaver
Sarah .... Sheila Sullivan
Fairfax .... Stephen Neuman
Sam Adams ....Richard Venture
John Hancock .... Phil Pleasants
Printer.. Kenneth Tigar

440 Give the Circus a Tumble
Call It Macaroni   Syndicated
Program Type Children's Show
Real-life adventure. Three Pittsburgh 11-year olds at the Circus Vargas, in Colorado. 30 minutes. Premiere: 2/75.
Executive Producer George Moynihan
Producer Gail Frank
Production Company Group W Productions
Distributor Westinghouse Broadcasting Company
Director Gail Frank

441 Gladys Knight and the Pips   NBC
Program Type Comedy/Variety
Four-part series. 60 minutes. Premiere date: 7/10/75. Last show: 7/31/75. The Pips: William Guest; Edward Patten; Merald "Bubba" Knight, Jr.
Producer Bob Henry
Production Company Perfection in Performance, Inc. and Bob Henry Productions
Director Tony Charmoli
Writer Herbert Baker; George Yanok; Peter Gallay
Musical Director George Wyle
Host Gladys Knight; The Pips

442 The Glass Menagerie
The ABC Saturday Night Movie   ABC
Program Type TV Movie
135 minutes. Premiere date: 12/16/73. Repeat date: 6/28/75. The 1944 prize-winning play by Tennessee Williams.
Producer David Susskind
Production Company Talent Associates - Norton Simon, Inc.
Director Anthony Harvey
Writer Tennessee Williams
Costume Designer Patricia Zipprodt
CAST
Amanda Wingfield .... Katherine Hepburn
Tom Wingfield .... Sam Waterston
Jim O'Connor .... Michael Moriarty
Laura Wingfield ....Joanna Miles

443   Glen Campbell Los Angeles Open
ABC Sports Special   ABC
Program Type Sports
Live coverage of third and final round play from the Riviera Country Club, Los Angeles. 2/22/75; 2/23/75.
Executive Producer Roone Arledge
Production Company ABC Sports
Announcer Jim McKay; Frank Gifford

444   Go   NBC
Program Type Children's Show
Informational series. First person experiences in varied locales. 30 minutes. Sunday. Premiere date: 9/8/73. Season premiere: 9/8/74.
Executive Producer George A. Heinemann
Producer Various
Production Company NBC-TV
Director Various

445   The Godchild
Tuesday/Wednesday Movie of the Week ABC
Program Type TV Movie
90 minutes. Premiere date: 11/26/74. Repeat date: 6/18/75. Based on "The Three Godfathers" (1910) by Peter B. Kyne. Special effects by Harold P. Elmendorf.
Executive Producer Charles Robert McLain
Producer Richard Collins
Production Company A Mor-Film Fare - Alan Neuman Production in association with MGM Television
Director John Badham
Writer Ron Bishop
CAST
Rourke .... Jack Palance
Dobbs .... Jack Warden
Lt. Louis .... Keith Carradine
Crees .... Ed Lauter
Sanchez .... Jose Perez
Crawley .... Bill McKinney
Loftus .... Jesse Vint
Denton .... John Quade
William .... Simon Deckard
Shaw .... Ed Bakey
Mony .... Kermit Murdock
Virginia .... Fionnuala Flanagan

The Godfather *see* NBC Nights at the Movies

446   God's Country with Marshall Efron   CBS
Program Type Children's Show
Religious special. 30 minutes. Premiere date: 12/1/74. How the first Protestants, Catholics and Jews came to America in the early 17th century.
Executive Producer Pamela Ilott
Producer Ted Holmes

Production Company CBS News
Director Alvin Thaler
Writer Marshall Efron; Alfa-Betty Olsen
Host Marshall Efron

Godspell *see* Special Movie Presentation

447   Godspell Goes to Plimouth Plantation for Thanksgiving with Henry Steele Commager   PBS
Program Type Music/Dance
Special. 30 minutes. Boston cast of musical "Godspell" and historian Henry Steele Commager. Premiere date: 11/18/73. Repeat date: 11/28/74 (captioned for the deaf).
Producer Rick Hauser
Production Company WGBH/Boston

Going Home *see* The CBS Thursday/Friday Night Movies

448   The Golden Globe Awards
                                               Syndicated
Program Type Awards Show
32nd annual awards presented by the Hollywood Foreign Press Association to motion picture industry. 90 minutes. Premiere: 1/25/75.
Executive Producer Stephen Jahn
Producer Richard Dunlap; Kjell F. Rasten
Production Company FunCo Corporation in association with Metromedia Television
Director Richard Dunlap
Writer Arnie Kogen
Musical Director Nelson Riddle
Host John Davidson

Golden Needles *see* The CBS Thursday/Friday Night Movies

449   Golden Spring   NBC
Program Type Religious Program
Special. 60 minutes. Premiere date: 1/5/75. Filmed in Venice, Florence and Rome.
Producer Doris Ann
Production Company NBC Television Religious Programs Unit
Director Joseph Vadala
Writer Philip Scharper
Host Alexander Scourby
Camera Joseph Vadala

450   Golf Highlights
ABC Sports Special   ABC
Program Type Sports
Highlights of the U.S. Open, U.S. Men's Ama-

teur and U.S. Women's Open. 30 minutes. Premiere date: 12/15/74.
Executive Producer Roone Arledge
Production Company ABC Sports
Host Chris Schenkel

451 Goober and the Ghost Chasers ABC
Program Type Animated Film
30 minutes. Sunday. Premiere date: 9/8/73. Reruns: 9/8/74. Last show: 8/31/75.
Executive Producer William Hanna; Joseph Barbera
Producer Iwao Takamoto
Production Company Hanna-Barbera Productions, Inc.
Director Charles A. Nichols
Story Editor Tom Dagenais
Writer Dick Robbins; Barry Blitzer; Tom Dagenais; Jack Kaplan; Warren Murray; Marty Roth; Dick Wesson; Steve White
Musical Director Hoyt Curtin
VOICES
Goober .... Paul Winchell
Gilly .... Ronnie Schell
Ted .... Jerry Dexter
Tina ....Jo Ann Harris
Laurie .... Susan Dey
Chris .... Brian Forster
Tracy .... Suzanne Crough
Danny .... Danny Bonaduce

The Good Guys and the Bad Guys *see* The CBS Thursday/Friday Night Movies

The Good, the Bad and the Ugly *see* The ABC Saturday Night Movie

452 Good Times CBS
Program Type Comedy
Derived from "Maude." 30 minutes. Tuesday. Premiere date: 2/8/74. Season premiere: 9/10/74. Created by Eric Monte; Mike Evans. Set in a Chicago ghetto.
Executive Producer Norman Lear
Producer Allan Manings
Production Company Tandem Productions, Inc.
Director Herbert Kenwith
Writer Various
CAST
Florida Evans .... Esther Rolle
James Evans .... John Amos
Willona ....Ja'net DuBois
James "J. J." Evans, Jr. .... Jimmie Walker
Thelma Evans ....BernNadette Stanis

453 The Good Times Are Killing Me
PBS
Program Type Documentary/Special
Special. 60 minutes. Premiere date: 6/25/75. The Cajuns in southern Louisiana. Program made possible by grants from the Ford Foundation and the Rockefeller Foundation.
Production Company TVTV and the Television Laboratory of WNET/New York
Director David Loxton

454 Gorilla CBS
Program Type Animal Documentary
Special. Filmed in Zaire. 60 minutes. Premiere date: 3/7/75. Featuring Adrien Deschryver, warden of the game park.
Producer Aubrey Buxton
Production Company Survival Anglia Ltd. in association with the World Wildlife Fund
Writer Colin Willock
Camera Dieter Plage
Narrator David Niven

The Graduate *see* The CBS Thursday/Friday Night Movies

455 The Grammy Awards CBS
Program Type Awards Show
17th annual Grammy Awards for "outstanding achievement in the recording industry." 100 minutes. 3/1/75. With numerous presenters and musical numbers.
Executive Producer Pierre Cossette
Producer Marty Pasetta
Director Marty Pasetta
Writer Marty Farrell
Musical Director Jack Elliott
Host Andy Williams

The Grand Illusion *see* Humanities Film Forum

456 Grand Prix Tennis: Summer Tour
PBS Sports Special   PBS
Program Type Sports
Live and tape coverage of seven tournaments: Washington Star News International Championship 7/27/75, 7/28/75; First National Tennis Classic, Louisville, Kentucky 8/3/75, 8/4/75; U.S. Clay Court Championship, Indianapolis 8/10/75, 8/11/75; Canadian Open, Toronto 8/16/75, 8/17/75; City National Buckeye Classic, Columbus, Ohio 8/18/75; Medi-Quick Women's Classic, Harrison, New York 8/24/75; U.S. Professional Championship, Chestnut Hills, Massachusetts 8/25/75. Programs made possible

Grand Prix Tennis: Summer Tour
Continued
by grants from Fieldcrest Mills, Inc., American Airlines, and Aetna Life and Casualty.
Production Company PBS
Announcer Bud Collins; Donald Dell

457   Grandpa Max
Comedy Special   CBS
Program Type Comedy
30 minutes. Pilot film. Premiere date: 3/28/75. Repeat date: 7/17/75.
Producer Aaron Ruben; John Rich
Production Company Aaron Ruben-John Rich Enterprises
Director John Rich
Writer Aaron Ruben
CAST
Grandpa Max .... Larry Best
Paul Sherman .... Michael Lerner
Liz Sherman .... Suzanne Astor
Michael Sherman .... Brad Savage
Louie Yates .... Shimen Ruskin
Betty .... Susan Alpern
Mr. Unger .... Dick Van Patten

458   Great Decisions   PBS
Program Type Interview/Discussion
Eight-part series sponsored by the Foreign Policy Association. 30 minutes. Weekly. Season premiere: 1/31/75. Discussions cover the world food problem, the Soviet Union today, Brazil, the changing world economy, controlling nuclear weapons, Japan, the oil states of the Persian Gulf, and the oceans and the seabed.
Production Company WGTV/Georgia Center for Continuing Education, University of Georgia
Host Reg Murphy

The Great Escape *see* NBC Nights at the Movies

459   Great Expectations
Bell System Family Theatre   NBC
Program Type Drama
Special. Based on the novel by Charles Dickens. 120 minutes. Premiere date: 11/22/74.
Producer Robert Fryer
Production Company A Robert Fryer-James Cresson Production for Bell Systems Family Theatre in association with NBC and ATV-ITC
Director Joseph Hardy
Writer Sherman Yellin
CAST
Pip .... Michael York
Estella .... Sarah Miles
Miss Havisham .... Margaret Leighton
Magwitch .... James Mason

Pumblechook .... Robert Morley
Jaggers .... Anthony Quayle
Biddy .... Heather Sears
Joe Gargery ....Joss Ackland
Young Pip .... Simon Gipps-Kent
Herbert .... Andrew Ray
Drummie ....James Faulkner
Mrs. Joe Gargery .... Rachel Roberts

460   The Great Ice Rip-Off
Tuesday/Wednesday Movie of the Week ABC
Program Type TV Movie
90 minutes. Premiere date: 11/6/74. Repeat date: 8/12/75.
Producer Dan Curtis
Production Company An ABC Circle Film
Director Dan Curtis
Writer Andrew Peter Marin
CAST
Willy ....Lee J. Cobb
Harkey .... Gig Young
Helen .... Grayson Hall
Checker .... Robert Walden
Georgie .... Matt Clark
Archie .... Geoffrey Lewis
Sam .... Hank Garrett
Cab Driver .... Bill Smillie
Boat Proprietor ....Orin Cannon
Bus Driver .... Norman A. Honath

461   The Great Migration: Year of the Wildebeeste   CBS
Program Type Animal Documentary
Special. Filmed in the Serengeti Plain, in East Africa. 60 minutes. Premiere date: 5/5/75.
Executive Producer Aubrey Buxton
Producer Alan Root
Production Company Survival Anglia Ltd. in association with the World Wildlife Fund
Writer John Lloyd
Photographer Alan Root
Narrator Richard Widmark

462   The Great Niagara
Tuesday/Wednesday Movie of the Week ABC
Program Type TV Movie
90 minutes. Premiere date: 9/24/74. Repeat date: 7/2/75. Filmed at Niagara Falls, Ontario, Canada.
Producer Ron Roth
Production Company Playboy Productions, Inc.
Director William Hale
Writer Robert E. Thompson
CAST
Aaron Grant .... Richard Boone
Lonnie Grant ....Michael Sacks
Carl Grant ....Randy Quaid
Lois Grant .... Jennifer Salt
Ace Tully ....Burt Young
Smitty .... Les Rubie
Young Mountie ....David Schurmann

Doctor .... Jack Von Evera
Driver ....Jonathan White

463   Great Performances   PBS
Program Type Music/Dance
Series of special programs of varying lengths. Features guest artists in the fields of opera, ballet, music. Season premiere: 10/17/74. Series produced in the United States by WNET/New York; Jac Venza executive producer. Programs made possible by a grant from the Exxon Corporation. Seven programs: "Arthur Rubinstein in Great Performances," "Bach's Mass in B Minor," "Bernstein at Tanglewood," "Herbert von Karajan and the Berlin Philharmonic Orchestra," "Karl Bohm Conducts the Vienna Symphony Orchestra," "Pagliacci," "Three By Balanchine with the New York City Ballet." (*See* individual titles for credits.)

The Great White Hope *see* The CBS Thursday/Friday Night Movies

464   The Greatest Gift
NBC Nights at the Movies   NBC
Program Type TV Movie
Pilot for "The Family Holvak" series - 1975–76 season. Based on the novel "Ramey" by Jack Farris. 120 minutes. Premiere date: 11/4/74. Repeat date: 7/24/75.
Producer Dean Hargrove
Production Company Universal Television Production in association with NBC-TV
Director Boris Sagal
Writer Ben Goodman
CAST
The Rev. Holvak .... Glenn Ford
Elizabeth Holvak .... Julie Harris
Ramey Holvak .... Lance Kerwin
Julie Mae Holvak .... Cari Anne Warder
Hog Yancy .... Harris Yulin
Jim ....J. Don Ferguson
Eli Wiggins ....Albert Smith
Willis Graham .... Furman Walters
Amos Goodlie .... Charles Tyner
Deacon Hurd .... Dabbs Greer
Tincy Bell .... Leslie Thorsen
Additional Cast Elsie Travis; Bob Hannah

Greatest Sports Legends *see* Paul Hornung's Greatest Sports Legends

The Greatest Story Ever Told *see* NBC Nights at the Movies

465   The Grover Monster/Jean Marsh Cartoon Special   PBS
Program Type Animated Film
Special. The best animated films from "Seasame Street" and "The Electric Company." 60 minutes. Premiere date: 3/10/75. Dave Connell is producer for the Children's Television Workshop. The Grover Monster is cohost of the special with Jean Marsh.
Executive Producer Zev Putterman
Producer Dave Connell
Production Company KQED/San Francisco
Director Jim Scalem
Writer Jim Thurman; Norman Stiles
Host Jean Marsh

466   Growing Up Female   PBS
Program Type Documentary/Special
Special. 1970 film "Growing Up Female" produced at Antioch College, plus discussion of film by panel. 90 minutes. Repeat date: 6/19/75.
Producer Joan Sullivan
Production Company WGBH/Boston

467   Guess Who's Coming to Dinner
ABC Comedy Special   ABC
Program Type Comedy
Special based on motion picture of the same name. "The Glory of Love," motion picture score retained. 30 minutes. Premiere date: 7/4/75.
Producer Stanley Kramer
Production Company Stanley Kramer, Ltd. Production in association with Columbia Pictures Television
Director Stanley Kramer
Writer Bill Idelson
CAST
Joanna Prentiss .... Leslie Charleson
John Prentiss .... Bill Overton
Matt Drayton .... Richard Dysart
Christine Drayton .... Eleanor Parker
Sarah Prentiss .... Madge Sinclair
Ralph Prentiss ....Lee Weaver
Tillie .... Rosetta Le Noir
Joe Delaney .... William Callaway

468   Guess Who's Sleeping in My Bed?
Tuesday/Wednesday Movie of the Week ABC
Program Type TV Movie
90 minutes. Premiere date: 10/31/73. Repeat date: 4/8/75.
Producer Mark Carliner
Production Company An ABC Circle Film
Director Theodore J. Flicker
Writer Pamela Herbert Chais
CAST
Francine Gregory .... Barbara Eden
George Gregory .... Dean Jones
Mitchell Bernard ....Kenneth Mars
Chloe Gregory .... Susanne Benton

Guess Who's Sleeping in My Bed?
Continued

Mrs. Guzmando	Reta Shaw
Adam	Todd Lookinland
Delores	Diana Herbert
Waiter	Walter Beakel

469 The Guiding Light   CBS
Program Type Daytime Drama
Prior to its television debut on 6/30/52 "The Guiding Light" was on radio for 15 years. Set in "Springfield, U.S.A." Theme "La Lumiere," by Charles Paul. 30 minutes. Monday-Friday. Continuous. Cast information as of April 1975. Charita Bauer has been with the show since its start. Show created by Irna Phillips.
Producer Charlotte Ciraulo
Production Company Procter & Gamble Productions
Director Harry Eggart; John Litvak
Head Writer James Lipton
Story Editor Lucy Rittenberg
Announcer Alan Burns
CAST

Leslie Bauer	Lynne Adams
Dr. Sara McIntyre Werner	Millette Alexander
Bertha (Bert) Bauer	Charita Bauer
Barbara Morris Thorpe	Barbara Berjer
Dr. Joe Werner	Anthony Call
Dr. Tim Ryan	Jordan Clarke
Holly Norris Bauer	Lynn Deerfield
T. J.	T. J. Hargrave
Dr. Ed Bauer	Mart Hulswit
Janet Norris	Caroline McWilliams
Adam Thorpe	Robert Milli
Peggy Fletcher	Fran Myers
Ken Norris	Roger Newman
Dr. Stephen Jackson	Stephan Schnabel
Pam Chandler	Maureen Silliman
Michael Bauer	Don Stewart
Roger Thorpe	Michael Zaslow

470 The Gun
Tuesday/Wednesday Movie of the Week ABC
Program Type TV Movie
90 minutes. Premiere date: 11/13/74. Repeat date: 7/8/75. Based on a story by Jay Benson; Richard Levinson; William Link.
Producer Richard Levinson; William Link
Production Company Fairmont/Foxcroft Production in association with Universal Television
Director John Badham
Writer Richard Levinson; William Link
CAST

Art Hilliard	Stephen Elliott
Fran	Jean Le Bouvier
Howie	Wallace Rooney
Wayne	David Huffman
Natcho	Pepe Serna
Gloria	Edith Diaz
Senor Peralta	Felipe Turich
Frank	Van Devargas

Walt Kelsy	Ramon Bieri
Wilke	Michael McGuire
Tom	Ron Thompson
Braverman	John Sylvester White
Gil Strauss	Richard Bright
Beryl	Mariclare Costello
Kenny	Randy Gray

471 The Guns of Autumn
CBS Reports   CBS
Program Type Documentary/Special
Hunting in the U.S. as recreation. 90 minutes. Premiere date: 9/5/75.
Executive Producer Perry Wolff
Producer Irv Drasnin
Production Company CBS News
Director Irv Drasnin
Writer Irv Drasnin
Narrator Dan Rather

The Guns of Navarone *see* Special Movie Presentation

472 Gunsmoke   CBS
Program Type Western
Prior to its 9/10/55 premiere on television, "Gunsmoke" was heard on the CBS Radio Network for three years. 60 minutes. Monday. Season premiere: 9/9/74. Last show: 9/1/75.
Executive Producer John Mantley
Producer Leonard Katzman
Production Company CBS Television Network
CAST

Marshall Matt Dillon	James Arness
Doc	Milburn Stone
Festus	Ken Curtis
Newly	Buck Taylor
Burke	Ted Jordan

473 Haldeman: The Nixon Years
CBS News Special   CBS
Program Type Interview/Discussion
H. R. Haldeman interviewed by Mike Wallace. Two programs. 60 minutes each. 3/23/75; 3/30/75.
Executive Producer Perry Wolff
Producer Gordon Manning; Marion Goldin
Production Company CBS News

474 Hallmark Hall of Fame   NBC
Program Type TV Movie
Specials. Generally 90 minutes. Season premiere: 11/12/74. Five programs: "All Creatures Great and Small," "The Borrowers," "Brief Encounter," "The Gathering Storm," "The Small Miracle." (*See* individual titles for cast and credits.)

475 The Hambletonian Stake
CBS Sports Special   CBS
Program Type Sports
50th anniversary running of the Habletonian Stake; first time on national television. Live coverage from DuQuoin, Illinois. 30 minutes. 8/30/75.
Production Company CBS Television Network Sports
Host Jack Whitaker

Hamlet *see* Humanities Film Forum

476 A Handshake in Space
NBC News Special   NBC
Program Type Documentary/Special
Special. Coverage of the Apollo-Soyuz meeting from liftoff to docking to splashdown. 7/15/75–7/22/75. (For previews, *see* "Apollo-Soyuz Joint Space Mission," "Joint U.S.-U.S.S.R. Space Mission.")
Production Company NBC News
Reporters John Chancellor; Jim Hartz; John Dancy; Roy Neal; Alan B. Shepard, Jr..

Hang 'Em High *see* Special Move Presentation

477 Hanukkah   PBS
Program Type Religious Program
Special. 30 minutes. Premiere date: 12/2/74.
Producer Henry Kline II; Edward Cohen
Production Company Mississippi Authority for Educational Television
Director Henry Kline II
Writer Edward Cohen
Host Edward Asner
Narrator Edward Asner

478 Happy Anniversay and Goodbye   CBS
Program Type Comedy
Special. 60 minutes. Premiere date: 11/19/74.
Producer Gary Morton
Production Company Lucille Ball Productions
Director Jack Donohue
Writer Arnie Rosen; Arthur Julian
Musical Director Nelson Riddle
CAST
Norma Michaels .... Lucille Ball
Malcolm Michaels .... Art Carney
Fay Lucas .... Nanette Fabray
Greg Carter .... Peter Marshall
Ed Murphy .... Don Porter
Rico .... Arnold Schwarzenegger
Doug .... Rhodes Reason
Linda .... Doria Cook
Terry .... Louisa Moritz

479 Happy Days   ABC
Program Type Comedy
30 minutes. Tuesday. Premiere date: 1/15/74. Season premiere: 9/10/74. Set in the 1950's; much of it at Jefferson High.
Executive Producer Thomas L. Miller; Edward K. Milkis; Garry Marshall
Producer William S. Bickley
Production Company Miller-Milkis Productions in association with Paramount Studios
Director Various
Writer Various
CAST
Richie Cunningham .... Ron Howard
Howard Cunningham .... Tom Bosley
Marion Cunningham .... Marion Ross
Potsie Weber .... Anson Williams
Fonzie .... Henry Winkler
Ralph Malph .... Donny Most
Joanie Cunningham .... Erin Moran
Chuck .... Gavan O'Herlihy
Wendy .... Misty Rowe
Marsha .... Beatrice Colen

480 Happy Endings   ABC
Program Type Comedy
Special. Four original plays. 60 minutes. Premiere date: 4/10/75. Additional material written by Herb Sargent; Alan King.
Executive Producer Alan King; Rupert Hitzig; John Gilroy
Producer Herb Sargent
Production Company King-Hitzig Productions
Director Robert Moore

Big Joe and Kansas
Writer Neil Simon
CAST
Big Joe .... James Earl Jones
Kansas .... Alan King

A Commercial Break
Writer Peter Stone
CAST
Catherine .... Lauren Bacall
Harry .... Robert Preston

I'm with Ya, Duke
Writer Herb Gardner
CAST
Sam Margolis .... Alan King
Dr. MacIntyre .... John Cunningham
Nurse Carswell .... Nancy Andrews

Kidnapped
Writer Jules Feiffer
CAST
Al .... Art Carney
Edna .... Elizabeth Wilson
Penny .... Lisa Rochelle
Buddy .... Jimmy Fields

Harakiri *see* The Japanese Film

481   The Harlem Globetrotters Popcorn Machine   CBS
Program Type Children's Show
30 minutes. Saturday. Premiere date: 9/7/74. The Harlem Globetrotters are Geese Ausbie; Nate Branch; Tex Harrison; Marques Haynes; Theodis Lee; Meadowlark Lemon; Bobby Joe Mason; Curley Neal; John Smith.
Executive Producer Frank Peppiatt; John Aylesworth
Producer Norman Baer
Production Company Funhouse Productions, Inc.
Director Tony Mordente
Writer Frank Peppiatt; John Aylesworth; Jack Burns
Regular Rodney Allen Rippy; Avery Schreiber

482   Harlem Voices, Faces   PBS
Program Type Documentary/Special
Special. 1973 film for Swedish television. Presented by WNET/New York and produced by Anthony Mahn. 90 minutes. Premiere date: 5/19/75.
Producer Lars Ulvenstam; Thomas Dillen
Production Company Swedish Broadcasting Corporation
Director Lars Ulvenstam; Thomas Dillen
Camera Anders Ribbsjo
Editor Tord Paag

483   Harlem: Voices, Faces: A Consideration   PBS
Program Type Interview/Discussion
Special. Follow-up to the documentary. 30 minutes. Premiere date: 5/19/75.
Producer Anthony Mahn
Production Company WNET/New York
Moderator Roger Wilkins

484   Harlequin
The CBS Festival of Lively Arts for Young People   CBS
Program Type Children's Show
60 minutes. Premiere date: 4/10/74. Repeat date: 3/28/75. Original ballet choreographed and performed by Edward Villella; commissioned by CBS. Sculptures by Yasuhide Kobashi. Fantasy creatures by Michael Dennison.
Executive Producer Edward Villella
Producer Gardner Compton
Production Company CBS Television
Director Gardner Compton
Musical Director Gordon Harrell
Choreographer Edward Villella
Costume Designer Lare Schultz
CAST
Harlequin ....Edward Villella
Columbine .... Rebecca Wright

Scaramouche ....Dermot Burke
Additional Cast National Ballet School of Canada

Harp of Burma *see* The Japanese Film

485   Harry and Maggie
Comedy Special   CBS
Program Type Comedy
30 minutes. Pilot film. Premiere date: 4/25/75. Repeat date: 7/17/75.
Producer James Parker; Arnold Margolin
Production Company Parker-Margolin Productions in association with MGM Television
Director Jay Sandrich
Writer James Parker; Arnold Margolin
CAST
Harry Kellogg ....Don Knotts
Maggie Sturvidant ....Eve Arden
Arlo Wilson .... Tom Poston
Thelma .... Lucille Benson
Clovis Kellogg .... Kathy Davis
Max Lovechild .... Eddie Quillan

486   Harry O   ABC
Program Type Crime Drama
60 minutes. Thursday. Premiere date: 9/12/74. Originally set in San Diego, moved midseason to Los Angeles. Henry Darrow as Det. Lt. Manuel Quinlan, San Diego Police Department, replaced by Anthony Zerbe as Lt. K. C. Trench, Los Angeles Police Department. Pilots shown on "The ABC Sunday Night Movie:" "Harry O" (60 minutes) seen 3/11/73; "Smile, Jenny, You're Dead" (90 minutes) seen 2/3/74 (repeat date 7/31/75 - *see* title for cast and credits).
Executive Producer Jerry Thorpe
Producer Robert E. Thompson
Production Company Warner Brothers Television
Director Various
Writer Various
CAST
Harry Orwell .... David Janssen
Det. Lt. Manuel Quinlan .... Henry Darrow
Lt. K. C. Trench .... Anthony Zerbe

Hatari *see* Special Movie Presentation

487   The Hatfields and the McCoys
Tuesday/Wednesday Movie of the Week   ABC
Program Type TV Movie
90 minutes. Premiere date: 1/15/75. Repeat date: 6/3/75.
Executive Producer Charles Fries
Producer George Edwards
Production Company A Charles Fries Production
Director Clyde Ware
Writer Clyde Ware

CAST

Devil Anse Hatfield	Jack Palance
Randall McCoy	Steve Forrest
Johnse Hatfield	Richard Hatch
Rose Ann McCoy	Karen Lamm
Jim McCoy	James Keach
Cotton Top	John Calvin
Bob Hatfield	Robert Carradine
Calvin McCoy	Gerrit Graham
Ellison Hatfield	Morgan Woodward
Cap Hatfield	Jim Bohan
Troy Hatfield	Joe Estevez
Sarah McCoy	Joan Caulfield
Mary Hatfield	Brooke Palance
Levicy Hatfield	Virginia Baker
Allifair McCoy	Charley Young
Tolbert McCoy	Darrell Fetty

488 Haunts of the Very Rich
The ABC Summer Movie   ABC
Program Type TV Movie
90 minutes. Premiere date: 9/20/72. Repeat
date: 7/11/75. Story by T. K. Brown. Filmed at
Biscayne Bay, Florida.
Producer Lillian Gallo
Director Paul Wendkos
Writer William Wood
CAST

Ellen Blunt	Cloris Leachman
Dave Woodbrough	Lloyd Bridges
Al Hunsicker	Edward Asner
Annette Larrier	Anne Francis
Lyle	Tony Bill
Laurie	Donna Mills
The Rev. Mr. Fellows	Robert Reed
Seacrist	Moses Gunn
Miss Vick	Beverly Gill
Reta	Phyllis Hill

Hawaii *see* The CBS Thursday/Friday
Night Movies

489 Hawaii Five-O   CBS
Program Type Crime Drama
Created by Leonard Freeman. Set in Hawaii. Bill
Finnegan (in Hawaii) and Bob Sweeney (in Hol-
lywood) replaced midseason by Richard Newton
and Philip Leacock, respectively. 60 minutes.
Tuesday. Premiere date: 9/26/68. Season
premiere: 9/10/74.
Supervising Producer Bob Sweeney; Philip Lea-
cock
Producer Bill Finnegan; Richard Newton
Production Company Leonard Freeman Produc-
tions for the CBS Television Network
Director Various
Writer Various
CAST

Steve McGarrett	Jack Lord
Danny Williams	James MacArthur
Chin Ho	Kam Fong
Che Fong	Harry Endo
Governor	Richard Denning

Doc	Al Eben
Duke	Herman Wedemeyer
Jenny	Peggy Ryan
Dr. Judith Patrick	Linda Ryan
Ben Kokua	Al Harrington

490 Hawaiian Open Golf Championship
ABC Sports Special   ABC
Program Type Sports
Third and final round play in the Hawaiian Open
from Waialae Country Club, Honolulu. 2/1/75;
2/2/75. Live coverage.
Executive Producer Roone Arledge
Producer Chuck Howard
Production Company ABC Sports
Announcer Chris Schenkel; Frank Gifford; Dave
Marr

The Hawaiians *see* The CBS
Thursday/Friday Night Movies

491 Heart in Hiding
ABC Afternoon Playbreak   ABC
Program Type TV Movie
Special. 90 minutes. Premiere date: 11/14/74.
Repeat date: 3/13/75.
Producer Peter Levin
Production Company Filmways, Inc.
Director Peter Levin
Writer Audrey Davis Levin
CAST

Clancy Jesson	Kay Lenz
Ford Lanier	Clu Gulager
Adam	Jordan Christopher
Jascha	Manu Tupou
Sally	Carol Corbett

Additional Cast Lois Markle; Stephen Macht; Kate Wilkinson

492 Heartbeat for Bangladesh   NBC
Program Type Religious Program
Discussion. 30 minutes. Premiere date: 4/27/75.
Producer Doris Ann
Production Company NBC Television Religious
Programs Unit
Director Robert Priaulx
Moderator Dr. Wendell W. Kempton
Panel Rev. David Jay Walsh; Dr. Donn W.
Ketcham

The Heartbreak Kid *see* The ABC
Sunday Night Movie

493 Heatwave
Tuesday/Wednesday Movie of the Week ABC
Program Type TV Movie
90 minutes. Premiere date: 1/26/74. Repeat

Heatwave *Continued*
date: 6/10/75. Based on a story by Herbert F. Solow.
Executive Producer Harve Bennett
Producer Herbert F. Solow
Production Company Universal Television
Director Jerry Jameson
Writer Peter Allan Fields; Mark Weingart
CAST
Frank Taylor .... Ben Murphy
Laura Taylor .... Bonnie Bedelia
Dr. Grayson ....Lew Ayres
Mr. Toler .... John Anderson
Mr. Brady .... David Huddleston
Powers ....Robert Hogan
Prescott .... Dana Elcar
Terry .... Lionel Johnston

494   Hee Haw   Syndicated
Program Type Comedy/Variety
Country variety show originally on CBS in 1969. Went into syndication in 1971. 60 minutes. Weekly.
Executive Producer Frank Peppiatt; John Aylesworth
Producer Sam Lovullo
Production Company Yongestreet Productions
Director Bob Boatman
Writer Gordie Tapp; Don Harron; Archie Campbell; Bud Wingard
Musical Director George Richey
Host Roy Clark; Buck Owens
Regular Cathy Baker; Barbi Benton; Archie Campbell; Harry Cole; Marianne Gordon; Don Harron; Gunilla Hutton; "Grandpa" Jones; George Lindsey; Minnie Pearl; Lulu Roman; Misty Rowe; Junior Samples; Gailard Sartain; Roni Stoneham; Gordie Tapp; Lisa Todd

495   The Heimaey Eruption   PBS
Program Type Documentary/Special
Special. 30 minutes. Premiere date: 3/9/75. Repeat date: 5/1/75. A town in five months of volcanic eruption.
Producer Dr. Alan V. Morgan
Director Dr. Alan V. Morgan
Writer Dr. Alan V. Morgan
Editor Ralph Brunjes
Narrator Cy Strange

496   Hello, Dali   PBS
Program Type Documentary/Special
Special. 50 minutes. Premiere date: 3/10/75. Repeat date: 5/6/75. A portrait of Salvador Dali and wife Gala. English subtitles under Dali's speech.
Producer Russell Harty
Production Company London Weekend Television, England

497   Helsinki Summit: The Price of Detente
NBC News Special   NBC
Program Type Documentary/Special
Special. 30 minutes. Premiere date: 8/2/75.
Producer Gordon Manning; Ray Lockhart
Production Company NBC News
Anchor Edwin Newman
Correspondents Garrick Utley; Tom Brokaw; Richard Valeriani; Douglas Kiker

498   Henry Fonda as Clarence Darrow
                                           PBS
Program Type Drama
Special. Based on "Clarence Darrow for the Defense" by Irving Stone. Originally broadcast on NBC as "IBM Presents Clarence Darrow Starring Henry Fonda." Premiere date on PBS: 3/17/75. Repeat date: 7/21/75. 90 minutes. Program made possible by a special grant from the IBM Corporation.
Producer Mike Merrick; Don Gregory
Production Company Dome Productions
Director John Rich
Writer David W. Rintels
Artistic Adviser John Houseman
CAST
Clarence Darrow .... Henry Fonda

499   Herb Alpert & The TJB
The Sentry Collection Presents   ABC
Program Type Music/Dance
Special. 60 minutes. Premiere date: 10/13/74. The Tijuana Brass: Lani Hall, vocalist; Vince Charles, steel drum; Papito, bass; Bomb Edmondson, trombone; John Pisano, guitar; Bob Findley, trumpet; Dave Frishberg, piano; Steve Schaeffer, drums; Julius Wechter, vibes. Guests: the Muppets created by Jim Henson.
Executive Producer Gary Smith; Dwight Hemion
Producer Gary Smith
Production Company ATV
Director Dwight Hemion
Host Herb Alpert; The Tijuana Brass

500   Herbert von Karajan and the Berlin Philharmonic Orchestra
Great Performances   PBS
Program Type Music/Dance
Special. 60 minutes. Premiere date: 11/13/74. Presented in the United States by WNET/New York; David Griffiths, coordinating producer. Herbert von Karajan conducts the Berlin Philharmonic Orchestra.
Executive Producer Fritz Buttenstedt
Producer Horant H. Hohlfeld
Production Company Unitel

501 The High Cost of Healing   PBS
Program Type Documentary/Special
Special. 60 minutes. Premiere date: 12/19/74.
Program made possible by a grant from the National Economists Club Educational Fund.
Executive Producer David Prowitt
Producer Kathy Cade
Production Company Science Program Group, Inc. in cooperation with WCET/Cincinnati
Host David Prowitt

High Plains Drifter *see* The ABC
Sunday Night Movie

502 High Rollers   NBC
Program Type Game Show
30 minutes. Monday-Friday. Premiere date: 7/1/74. Continuous.
Executive Producer Merrill Heatter; Bob Quigley
Producer Bob Noah
Production Company Merrill Heatter-Bob Quigley Productions
Director Jerry Shaw
Host Alex Trebek
Announcer Ken Williams
Hostess Ruta Lee

503 Highlights of Ringling Bros. and Barnum & Bailey Circus
Bell System Family Theatre   NBC
Program Type Comedy/Variety
Special. 60 minutes. Premiere date: 2/16/75.
With stars of the 105th edition of the circus.
Executive Producer Irwin Feld; Kenneth Feld
Producer Walter C. Miller
Production Company Mattel-Ringling Productions
Director Walter C. Miller
Writer Lou Solomon
Host Bill Cosby

504 Hit Lady
Tuesday/Wednesday Movie of the Week ABC
Program Type TV Movie
90 minutes. Premiere date: 10/8/74. Repeat date: 6/17/75.
Producer Aaron Spelling; Leonard Goldberg
Production Company Spelling-Goldberg Production
Director Tracy Keenan Wynn
Writer Yvette Mimieux
CAST
Angela de Vries .... Yvette Mimieux
Jeffrey Baine .... Joseph Campanella
Roarke .... Clu Gulager
Doug Reynolds .... Dack Rambo
Buddy McCormack .... Keenan Wynn
Eddie .... Roy Jenson
Webb .... Paul Genge

Hansen .... Del Monroe
Woman at Airport .... Mitzi Hoag

505 Hocking Valley Bluegrass   PBS
Program Type Music/Dance
Special. The Eagle Mountain Boys in concert, taped live at the Ohio University Forum Theater in Athens, Ohio. 30 minutes. Premiere date: 9/3/75. Program funded in part by a grant from the Central Educational Television Network.
Executive Producer David B. Liroff
Producer John Harnack
Production Company WOUB/Athens, Ohio
Director John Harnack

506 The Hollywood Squares   NBC
Program Type Game Show
30 minutes. Monday-Friday. Premiere: 10/66. Continuous. Nine celebrity panelists in tic-tac-toe board (three are regulars).
Executive Producer Merrill Heatter; Bob Quigley
Producer Jay Redack
Production Company Heatter-Quigley Productions
Director Jerome Shaw
Writer Gary Johnson; Harold Schneider; Rick Keller; Steve Levitch
Host Peter Marshall
Announcer Ken Williams
Regular Rose Marie; George Gobel; Paul Lynde

507 The Hollywood Squares   Syndicated
Program Type Game Show
Evening version of daytime game. 30 minutes. Twice a week. With nine guest celebrities (three are regulars).
Executive Producer Merrill Heatter; Bob Quigley
Producer Jay Redack
Production Company Heatter-Quigley Productions
Distributor Rhodes Productions
Director Jerome Shaw
Writer Gary Johnson; Harold Schneider; Rick Keller; Steve Levitch
Host Peter Marshall
Announcer Ken Williams
Regular Rose Marie; George Gobel; Paul Lynde

508 Hollywood Television Theatre   PBS
Program Type Drama
Series of plays of varying lengths presented throughout the year. Premiere date: 5/17/70. Season premiere: 10/23/74. Two films, "Shakespeare Wallah" (1965) and "Wanda" (1970) were shown 7/24/75 and 8/28/75 respectively. 15 plays: "Another Part of the Forest," "The Chicago Conspiracy Trial," "The Chinese Prime Minister," "Double Solitaire," "For the Use of the Hall," "Incident at Vichy," "Knuckle," "La-

Hollywood Television Theatre *Continued*
dies of the Corridor," "The Lady's Not for Burning," "The Man of Destiny," "Nourish the Beast," "Requiem for a Nun," "Steambath," "Two Plays," "Winesburg, Ohio." (*See* individual titles for cast and credits.)
Executive Producer Norman Lloyd
Producer Various
Production Company KCET/Los Angeles
Director Various
Writer Various

509   Holy Year 1975   NBC
Program Type Religious Program
Special. 105 minutes. 12/24/74. Christmas service from the Vatican.
Executive Producer Doris Ann
Producer Martin Hoade
Production Company NBC Television Religious Programs Unit
Director Martin Hoade

510   Home Cookin'
ABC Comedy Special   ABC
Program Type Comedy
Special. 30 minutes. Premiere date: 7/11/75.
Executive Producer Lawrence Gordon
Producer Don Van Atta
Production Company Lawrence Gordon Production
Director Herb Kenwith
Writer Tom Rickman; Ron Friedman
CAST
Adelle	Fannie Flagg
Ernie	Wynn Erwin
Dinette	Nancy Fox
Mouse	Roy Applegate
Jammer	Burton Gilliam
Bevo	Frank McRay
Trooper	Walker Edmiston
Shorty	Bill McLean

511   The Homecoming - A Christmas Story   CBS
Program Type Drama
Special. 120 minutes. Premiere date: 12/19/71. Repeat date: 12/8/74. Based on the novel by Earl Hamner, Jr. Led to series "The Waltons."
Executive Producer Lee Rich
Producer Robert L. Jacks
Production Company CBS Television Network Production
Director Fielder Cook
Writer Earl Hamner, Jr.
Costume Designers Betsy Cox; Bob Harris
CAST
Olivia Walton	Patricia Neal
Grandpa	Edgar Bergen
Grandma	Ellen Corby
John Walton	Andrew Duggan
Miss Mamie Baldwin	Josephine Hutchinson

Hawthorne Dooley	Cleavon Little
Miss Emily Baldwin	Dorothy Stickney
John-Boy Walton	Richard Thomas
Charlie Sneed	William Windom
Jason Walton	Jon Walmsley
Mary Ellen Walton	Judy Norton
Erin Walton	Mary Elizabeth McDonough
Ben Walton	Eric Scott
Jim-Bob Walton	David S. Harper
Elizabeth Walton	Kami Cotler
Sheriff Bridges	David Huddleston
Ike Godsey	Woodrow Parfrey
City Lady	Sally Chamberlain
Claudie Dooley	Donald Livingston

512   The Homely Place   CBS
Program Type Religious Program
CBS News religious special. A history of the synagogue. 30 minutes. Premiere date: 4/15/73. Repeat date: 4/6/75.
Executive Producer Pamela Ilott
Production Company CBS News
Writer Jan Hartman
Narrator Michael Dunn

513   Hong Kong Phooey   ABC
Program Type Animated Film
30 minutes. Saturday. Premiere date: 9/7/74.
Executive Producer William Hanna; Joseph Barbera
Producer Iwao Takamoto
Production Company A Hanna-Barbera Production
Director Charles A. Nichols
Writer Fred Fox and Seaman Jacobs; Len Janson and Chuck Menville; Larz Bourne; Jack Mendelsohn
Musical Director Hoyt Curtin
Executive Story Consultant Myles Wilder
VOICES
Hong Kong Phooey	Scat Man Crothers
Rosemary	Kathy Gori
Spot	Don Messick
Sarge	Joe E. Ross

The Honkers *see* The ABC Sunday Night Movie

514   The Honorable Sam Houston
American Heritage   ABC
Program Type Drama
Special. 60 minutes. Premiere date: 1/22/75.
Producer Stan Margulies
Production Company A David L. Wolper Production
Director Richard T. Heffron
Writer Jean Holloway
Musical Director Al DeLory
Historical Consultant Dr. Ralph A. Wooster
CAST
Gov. Sam Houston	Robert Stack

Margaret Houston	Lynn Carlin
Wilson	Charles Aidman
Sam Houston, Jr.	Ted Eccles
Nancy Houston	Jewel Blanch
George Chiltan	Jim Antonio
Farley, Sr.	Walter Brooke
Justice Roberts	Robert Symonds
Brown	Norm Alden
Richard Farley	Chris Nelson
Martin	Myron Healey
Harrison	Jack Manning
Netty Houston	Shelly Hines
Mary Houston	Shannon Terhune
Peters	Donald Elson
Jamison	William Wintersole

The Hospital *see* The ABC Sunday Night Movie

515 Hot l Baltimore   ABC
Program Type Comedy
30 minutes. Friday. Premiere date: 1/24/75. Last show: 6/6/75. Based on the play by Lanford Wilson.
Executive Producer Rod Parker
Producer Ron Clark; Gene Marcione
Production Company T.A.T. Communications Company
CAST

April Green	Conchata Ferrell
Bill Lewis	James Cromwell
Charles Bingham	Al Freeman, Jr.
Clifford Ainsley	Richard Masur
Suzy Marta Rocket	Jeannie Linero
Mr. Morse	Stan Gottlieb
Jackie	Robin Wilson
Millie	Gloria Le Roy
George	Lee Bergere
Gordon	Henry Calvert
Mrs. Bellotti	Charlotte Rae

The Hot Rock *see* The CBS Thursday/Friday Night Movies

Hotel *see* NBC Nights at the Movies

516 Hour of Power   Syndicated
Program Type Religious Program
60 minutes. Premiere: 2/70. Continuous. Produced from campus of the Garden Grove Community Church, Garden Grove, California. Ministers: Dr. Robert H. Schuller; Dr. Raymond Beckering; Rev. Kenneth Van Wyk; Rev. Calvin Rynbrandt.
Executive Producer Stuart Ehrlich
Producer Michael C. Nason
Production Company Mascom Advertising
Director Michael Conley
Musical Director Don G. Fontana
Organist Richard Unfreid

517 The House without a Christmas Tree   CBS
Program Type Drama
Special. Adapted from a story by Gail Rock. First in a series about the Mills family. Set in Nebraska in 1946. (*See also* "The Thanksgiving Treasure," "The Easter Promise.") 90 minutes. Premiere date: 12/3/72. Repeat date: 12/13/74.
Producer Alan Shayne
Production Company CBS Television Network
Director Paul Bogart
Writer Eleanor Perry
CAST

James Mills	Jason Robards
Grandmother	Mildred Natwick
Addie Mills	Lisa Lucas
Carla Mae	Alexa Kenin
Miss Thompson	Kathryn Walker
Billy Wild	Brady MacNamara
Mrs. Cott	Maya Kenin Ryan
Gloria Cott	Gail Dusome
Mr. Brady	Murray Westgate

How Sweet It Is! *see* The CBS Thursday/Friday Night Movies

How the West Was Lost *see* The Mickey Finns Finally Present … How the West Was Lost

How the West Was Won *see* The ABC Sunday Night Movie

518 How to Succeed in Business without Really Trying
ABC Comedy Special   ABC
Program Type Comedy
Special. Based on the musical drawn from the book by Shepherd Mead. 30 minutes. Premiere date: 6/27/75.
Producer Abe Burrows
Director Burt Brinckerhoff
Writer Abe Burrows
CAST

J. Pierpont "Ponty" Finch	Alan Bursky
Rosemary	Susan Blanchard
Bratt	Larry Haines
Frump	Jim Jansen
Smitty	Marcella Lowery
Gatch	Steve Roland
J. B. Biggley	Max Showalter
Miss Jones	Polly Rowles
Twimble	Sam Smith
Peterson	Alan Resin
Matthews	George Coe
Tackaberry	Thomas Batten

519 How to Survive a Marriage NBC
Program Type Daytime Drama
Created by Anne Howard Bailey. 30 minutes.
Premiere date: 1/7/74. (90-minute special).
Monday-Friday. Continuous. Last show:
4/17/75. Set in Lakeview, a fictitious suburb of
Chicago. Cast information as of 1/20/75.
Executive Producer Peter Engel
Producer Peter Andrews
Production Company MCA Theatricals, Inc.
Director Richard McCue; Robert Myhrum
Head Writer Rick Edelstein
CAST
Joshua T. Browne .... F. Murray Abraham
Johnny McGhee ....Armand Assante
Fran Bachman .... Fran Brill
Robert Monday .... Gene Bua
Monica Courtland .... Joan Copeland
Susan Pritchett .... Veleka Gray
Lori Kirby .... Cathy Greene
Chris Kirby ....Jennifer Harmon
Peter Willis ....Berkeley Harris
Larry Kirby .... Ken Kercheval
Rachel Bachman .... Elissa Leeds
Sandra Henderson .... Lynn Lowry
Joan Willis ....Tricia O'Neil
Moe Bachman .... Albert Ottenheimer
Dr. Maxwell Cooper .... James Shannon
Maria McGhee .... Lauren White

520 Howard Cosell Sports Magazine
ABC
Program Type Sports
15 minutes. Sunday. Premiere date: 1/7/72. Sea-
son premiere: 1/19/75. Last show of season:
4/27/75.
Executive Producer Roone Arledge
Producer Bob Kelly
Production Company ABC Sports
Director Joe Aceti
Host Howard Cosell

521 Huckleberry Finn ABC
Program Type Drama
Special. Based on the novel by Mark Twain. 90
minutes. Premiere date: 3/25/75. Theme song
sung by Roy Clark.
Producer Steven North
Production Company ABC Circle Films
Director Robert Totten
Writer Jean Holloway
CAST
Huckleberry Finn ....Ron Howard
Jim ....Antonio Fargas
Tom Sawyer .... Donny Most
Mark Twain ....Royal Dano
The King .... Jack Elam
The Duke .... Merle Haggard
Pap Finn .... Rance Howard
Widow Douglas ....Jean Howard
Arch .... Clint Howard
Old Doc ....Shug Fisher
Aunt Polly .... Sarah Selby

522 The Hudson Brothers Razzle Dazzle Show CBS
Program Type Children's Show
30 minutes. Saturday. Stars Bill Hudson; Mark
Hudson; Brett Hudson. Premiere date: 9/7/74.
Executive Producer Alan Blye; Chris Bearde
Producer Bob Arnott; Coslough Johnson; Stan
Jacobson
Production Company Blye-Beard Productions
Director Art Fisher
Writer George Burditt; Bob Einstein; David Pa-
nich; Ronny Graham; Chris Bearde; Alan
Blye
Musical Director Jack Eskew
Choreographer Jaime Rogers
Regular Ronny Graham; Stephanie Edwards;
Gary Owens; Katie McClure

523 Hula Bowl
ABC Sports Special ABC
Program Type Sports
29th Hula Bowl in Honolulu, Hawaii. Live cov-
erage. 1/4/75.
Executive Producer Roone Arledge
Production Company ABC Sports
Announcer Keith Jackson; O. J. Simpson

524 Human Rights ... Human Reality
PBS
Program Type Interview/Discussion
Special. Highlights of 1973 conference celebrat-
ing the 25th anniversary of the United Nations'
Declaration of Human Rights. 60 minutes. Pre-
miere date: 12/28/74.
Producer Robert Cozens
Production Company KUHT/Houston
Director Jack Veres
Writer Peter Wood

525 Humanities Film Forum PBS
Program Type Feature Film
10 film classics in this expanded version of series.
Premiere date: 1/23/75. Times vary. Weekly. Se-
ries made possible by a grant from the National
Endowment for the Humanities. Films shown:
"Alexander Nevsky" (1936), "The Anderson-
ville Trial" (1970), "The Ballad of a Soldier"
(1960), "The Battle of Culloden" (1964), "The
Cranes Are Flying" (1957), "The Grand Illu-
sion" (1937), "Hamlet" (1969), "Potemkin"
(1925), "The Rise of Louis XIV" (1966), "Um-
berto D" (1952).
Executive Producer Mark Waxman
Production Company KCET/Los Angeles
Host Dr. James Billington

526 Hurricane
Tuesday/Wednesday Movie of the Week ABC
Program Type TV Movie
90 minutes. Premiere date: 9/10/74. Repeat
date: 3/25/75. Based on the novel "Hurricane
Hunters" by William C. Anderson.
Executive Producer Charles Fries
Producer Edward J. Montagne
Production Company Montagne Productions in
association with Metromedia Producers Cor-
poration
Director Jerry Jameson
Writer Jack Turley
CAST

Paul Damon	Larry Hagman
Major Stoddard	Martin Milner
Louise Damon	Jessica Walter
Hank Stoddard	Barry Sullivan
Lee Jackson	Michael Learned
Bert Pearson	Frank Sutton
Dr. McCutcheon	Will Geer
Pappy	Lonny Chapman
Suzanne	Ayn Ruymen
Richie Damon	Barry Livingston
Capt. Mackey	Jim Antonio, Jr.
Barker	Ric Carrott
The Newscaster	Jack Colvin
Weyburn	Alan Landers
Wyn Stokey	Charles Lampkin
Amelia	Maggie Malooly
Highway Patrolman	Read Morgan
The Woman	Jessica Rains
Tarkinson	Paul Tulley

527 Hustling
Special World Premiere ABC Saturday Night
Movie; The ABC Saturday Night Movie ABC
Program Type TV Movie
120 minutes. Premiere date: 2/22/75. Based on
the book by Gail Sheehy.
Producer Lillian Gallo
Production Company A Lillian Gallo Production
in association with Filmways
Director Joseph Sargent
Writer Fay Kanin
CAST

Fran Morrison	Lee Remick
Orin Dietrich	Monte Markham
Wanda	Jill Clayburgh
Swifty	Alex Rocco
Dee Dee	Melanie Mayron
Gizelle	Beverly Hope Atkinson
Keogh	Dick O'Neill
Gustavino	Burt Young
Lester Traube	Paul Benedict
Geist	John Sylvester White
Harold Levine	Allan Miller

528 The Hyena Story
Jane Goodall and the World of Animal
Behavior ABC
Program Type Animal Documentary
Special. Jane Goodall studying the hyena.
Filmed at Ngorongoro Crater, East Africa. 60
minutes. Premiere date: 3/19/75.
Executive Producer Marshall Flaum
Producer Bill Travers; Hugo Van Lawick
Production Company Swan Productions, Ltd. in
association with Marshall Flaum, Metromedia
Producers Corporation and ABC News
Director Hugo Van Lawick
Writer Kenneth M. Rosen
Musical Director John Scott
Photographers Hugo Van Lawick; Charles W.
Feil
Narrator Hal Holbrook

529 I Believe in Miracles   Syndicated
Program Type Religious Program
In syndication since 1966. 30 minutes. Religious
show featuring Kathryn Kuhlman; with soloist
Jimmy McDonald; pianist Dino.
Producer Dick Ross
Production Company Productions Associates,
Inc.
Director Dick Ross

530 I Heard the Owl Call My Name
General Electric Theater   CBS
Program Type Drama
Special. 90 minutes. Premiere date: 12/18/73.
Repeat date: 12/23/74. Based on the novel by
Margaret Craven.
Executive Producer Roger Gimbel
Producer Daryl Duke
Production Company Tomorrow Entertainment,
Inc.
Director Daryl Duke
Writer Gerald Di Pego
Musical Director Peter Matz
CAST

Father Mark Brian	Tom Courtenay
Bishop	Dean Jagger
Jim Wallace	Paul Stanley
Keetah	Marianne Jones
George P. Hudson	George Clutesi
Alan Spencer	Keith Pepper
Marta Stevens	Margaret Atleo

I Want to Live! *see* NBC Nights at the
Movies

531 I Will Fight No More Forever
ABC Theatre   ABC
Program Type Drama
Special. Dramatization of the saga of the Nez
Perce tribe. Filmed in central Mexico. 120
minutes. Premiere date: 4/14/75.
Executive Producer David L. Wolper
Producer Stan Margulies
Production Company Wolper Productions, Inc.
Director Richard T. Heffron

I Will Fight No More Forever *Continued*
Writer Jeb Rosebrook; Theodore Strauss
Costume Designer Jack Martell
CAST

Gen. Oliver O. Howard	James Whitmore
Chief Joseph	Ned Romero
Capt. Wood	Sam Elliott
Wahlitits	John Kauffman
Olloket	Emilio Delgado
Rainbow	Nick Ramus
Toma	Linda Redfearn
White Bird	Frank Salsedo
Looking Glass	Vincent St. Cyr
Col. Gibbon	Delroy White

IBM Presents A Girl Named Sooner *see* A Girl Named Sooner

IBM Presents Clarence Darrow Starring Henry Fonda *see* Henry Fonda as Clarence Darrow

Ice Station Zebra *see* The ABC Saturday Night Movie

If It's Tuesday, This Must Be Belgium *see* NBC Nights at the Movies

532   If You Think It Was Tough to Make Ends Meet in 1974, Wait 'Til You Hear About 1975
NBC News Special   NBC
Program Type Documentary/Special
Special. 60 minutes. Premiere date: 1/1/75.
Producer Ron Steinman
Production Company NBC News
Director Walter Kravetz
Host Edwin Newman

Ikiru *see* The Japanese Film

Impasse *see* NBC Nights at the Movies

533   The Imperial Grand Band   ABC
Program Type Children's Show
Special. Filmed in Toronto, Canada. 60 minutes. Premiere date: 2/22/75.
Executive Producer Dick Clark
Producer Seymour Berns
Production Company Dick Clark Productions
Director Seymour Berns
Writer Charles Isaacs
CAST

Sue Barton	Libby Stephens
Gary Barton	Jaro Dick
Skip Jenkins	Shimmy Plener
Marvin Baxter	Martin Short

Albert Flynn	Jack Creley
Margaret Flynn	Kay Hawtrey
Additional Cast DeFranco Family	

534   The Imposter
NBC World Premiere Movie   NBC
Program Type TV Movie
90 minutes. Premiere date: 3/18/75. Repeat date: 7/29/75.
Executive Producer Richard Bluel
Producer Robert Stambler
Production Company Warner Brothers Television
Director Edward M. Abroms
Writer Ken August; Jon Sevorg
CAST

Joe Tyler	Paul Hecht
Victoria Kent	Nancy Kelly
Julie	Meredith Baxter
Rennick	Jack Ging
Margaret Elliott	Barbara Baxley
Sheriff Turner	John Vernon
Barney West	Edward Asner
Teddy	Paul Jenkins
Elliott	Joseph Gallison
Additional Cast Bruce Glover; Sherwood Price; Victor Campos; Suzanne Zenor; Ronnie Schell; George Murdock	

535   In Fashion
Theater in America   PBS
Program Type Comedy
Based on the play "Tailleur Pour Dames" by Georges Feydeau. Music by Jerry Blatt; lyrics by Lonnie Burstein. Performed by the Actors Theatre of Louisville. 90 minutes. Premiere date: 3/13/74. Repeat date: 8/6/75. Series made possible by grants from Exxon Corporation and the Corporation for Public Broadcasting.
Executive Producer Jac Venza
Producer Matthew N. Herman
Production Company WNET/New York
Writer Jon Jory
Choreographer Donald Saddler
Host Hal Holbrook
CAST

Etienne	Max Wright
Yvonne Moulineaux	Susan Kaslow
Mme. Aigreville	Charlotte Rae
Aubin	Ken Jenkins
Dr. Moulineaux	Daniel Davis
Suzanne Aubin	Pamela Hall
Bassinet	Patrick Tovatt
Rosa	Donna Curtis

536   In Performance at Wolf Trap   PBS
Program Type Music/Dance
Seven specials in music and dance from the Wolf Trap Center for the Performing Arts, Washington, D.C. Premiere date: 10/14/74. Biweekly. Times vary. Series made possible by a grant from the Atlantic Richfield Company. Guest artists:

Eliot Feld Ballet with Eliot Feld; Andre Kostela-netz; Yehudi Menuhin; National Folk Festival; Preservation Hall Jazz Band; Beverly Sills (in Donizetti's "The Daughter of the Regiment"); Sarah Vaughan and Buddy Rich.
Executive Producer David Prowitt
Production Company WETA/Arlington, Va.
Host David Prowitt

537 In Recital PBS
Program Type Music/Dance
Four specials presented weekly. 30 minutes each. Premiere date: 11/27/74.
Producer Don Pash
Production Company WKAR (Michigan State University Television)/East Lansing, Michigan
Director Bob Page
Guest Artists: Murray Perahia; Christopher Parkening; Ralph Votapek; Albertine Votapek

538 In the Beginning PBS
Program Type Documentary/Special
Special. 60 minutes. Premiere date: 6/2/75. Special made possible by a grant from Mrs. Paul's Kitchens, Inc. Commissioned for public television by The Reader's Digest Association. Filmed in Egypt.
Producer Colin Clark
Production Company KCET/Los Angeles
Director Michael Gill
Writer Kenneth Clark
Narrator Kenneth Clark

539 In the News CBS
Program Type Children's Show
2 1/2-minute topical news broadcasts for school-age children. 10 topics on Saturdays; two on Sundays. Premiere date: 9/11/71. Continuous.
Executive Producer Joel Heller
Producer Judy Reemtsma
Production Company CBS News
Reporter/Narrator Christopher Glenn

In the Public Interest *see* Bess Myerson: In the Public Interest

540 In This House of Brede
General Electric Theater CBS
Program Type Drama
Special based on novel by Rumer Godden. 120 minutes. Premiere date: 2/27/75. Filmed at St. Mary's Abbey, England; Drishane Convent, County Cork, Ireland; and in London, England.
Executive Producer Philip Barry, Jr.
Producer George Schaefer
Production Company Tomorrow Entertainment, Inc.

Director George Schaefer
Writer James Costigan
CAST
Philippa Talbot	Diana Rigg
Joanna	Judi Bowker
Catherine	Gwen Watford
Dame Agnes	Pamela Brown
Richard	Dennis Quidley
David	Nicholas Clay
Emily	Gladys Spencer
Penny	Julia Blalock
Miss Bowen	Frances Rowe
Diana	Charlotte Mitchell
Jeremy	Peter Sproule
Cynthia	Margaret Heery
Margaret	Elizabeth Bradley
Beatrice	Dervla Molloy
Jane	Ann Rye
Ellen/Renata	Catherine Willmer
Maura	Valerie Lush
Barbara	Janette Legge
Louise	Stacey Tendetter
Mr. Scanlon	Peter Geddis
Mrs. Scanlon	Janet Davies
Mariko	Yasuko Nagazumi
Sumi	Michi Takeda
Louise	Frances Kearney
Kasiko	Sanae Fukua
Yoko	Michiko Sukomoro
Yuri	Jun Majima
Bishop	Brian Hawkesley
Abbot	Hugh Morton
Headwaiter	Gerald Cox
Matsuki	N. K. Sonoda

541 Incident at Vichy
Hollywood Television Theatre PBS
Program Type Drama
90 minutes. Premiere date: 12/5/73. Repeat date: 10/16/74 as part of 1973–74 season. Repeat date: 9/18/75 as part of 1974–75 season. Adapted by Arthur Miller from his play.
Executive Producer Norman Lloyd
Producer George Turpin
Production Company KCET/Los Angeles
Director Stacy Keach
Writer Arthur Miller
CAST
Lebeau	Allen Garfield
Leduc	Harris Yulin
Von Berg	Richard Jordan
Bayard	Barry Primus
Monceau	Rene Auberjonois
Marchand	Bert Freed
Major	Andy Robinson
Ferrand	Ed Bakey
Boy	Sean Kelly
Old Jew	William Hansen

542 The Indianapolis 500
ABC Sports Special ABC
Program Type Sports
59th Indianapolis 500 from the Indianapolis Motor Speedway. 120 minutes. 5/25/75.
Executive Producer Roone Arledge

The Indianapolis 500 *Continued*
Production Company ABC Sports
Announcer Sam Posey; Jackie Stewart; Chris Schenkel; Chris Economaki; Keith Jackson

543   Indianapolis 500 Festival Parade
ABC
Program Type Documentary/Special
19th annual parade. 120 minutes. 5/24/75. Peter DePaolo is Grand Marshal of the parade.
Production Company ABC Sports
Host Bob Barker; Josephine Hauck

544   Indict and Convict
The ABC Sunday Night Movie   ABC
Program Type TV Movie
120 minutes. Premiere date: 1/6/74. Repeat date: 8/17/75. Based on the book by Bill Davidson.
Executive Producer David Victor
Producer Winston Miller
Production Company Universal Television in association with Groverton Associates
Director Boris Sagal
Writer Winston Miller
CAST
Bob Mathews ....George Grizzard
Mike Bellano .... Reni Santoni
Joanna Garrett .... Susan Howard
Timothy Fitzgerald .... Ed Flanders
DeWitt Foster .... Eli Wallach
Sam Belden .... William Shatner
Judge Taylor .... Myrna Loy
Mel Thomas .... Harry Guardino
Norman Hastings .... Kip Niven
Phyllis Dorfman .... Ruta Lee
Frank Rogers ....Del Russel
Barbara Mathews ....Marie Cheatham
Muriel Fitzgerald ....Eunice Christopher

545   Indochina: 1975-The End of the Road?
CBS News Special   CBS
Program Type Documentary/Special
Special. 60 minutes. Premiere: 4/8/75.
Executive Producer Leslie Midgley
Producer Bernard Birnbaum; Hal Haley
Production Company CBS News
Host Charles Collingwood
Field Producer James Clevenger

546   Indochina-Savage Springtime
ABC News Special Events   ABC
Program Type Documentary/Special
Special. 60 minutes. Premiere date: 4/5/75.
Executive Producer Robert Siegenthaler
Producer Bob Rogow
Production Company ABC News
Director Charles Hienz
Host Frank Reynolds

Reporters Jim Bennett; Irv Chapman; Jim Giggans; Ken Kashiwahara; Frank Mariano

547   Inflation: A Few Answers Syndicated
Program Type Documentary/Special
Special. 180 minutes. Premiere: 12/74. A "survival course for consumers" featuring experts in the field.
Producer Al Korn
Production Company RKO in association with Business Week Magazine
Distributor Allied Artists Television
Host Sander Vanocur

548   Inflation: The Money Merry-Go-Round
Special of the Week   PBS
Program Type Documentary/Special
Special. 60 minutes. Premiere date: 10/7/74. Program sponsored by the National Economists Club Educational Fund.
Executive Producer David Prowitt
Production Company WCET/Cincinnati
Host David Prowitt
Guests Milton Friedman; John Kenneth Galbraith; Walter Heller

549   Inflation: Winners and Losers NBC
Program Type Documentary/Special
Special. 60 minutes. Premiere date: 3/30/75.
Producer Ephraim Katz
Production Company WNBC-TV
Writer Ephraim Katz
Host Betty Furness

550   Inheritance
Special of the Week   PBS
Program Type Documentary/Special
Special. Focuses on America's vanishing craftspeople. 60 minutes. Premiere date: 11/4/74. Program funded by the National Endowment for the Humanities and the New York State Council on the Arts.
Producer Jack Ofield
Production Company WMHT-TV/Schenectady, New York
Director Jack Ofield

551   Insight   Syndicated
Program Type Religious Program
In 14th year. 30 minutes. Weekly dramatic show. Continuous.
Executive Producer Rev. Ellwood E. Kieser
Producer John Meredyth Lucas
Production Company Paulist Productions
Director Various
Writer Various

552 Interface PBS
Program Type News Magazine
13-week series. 30 minutes. Premiere date:
10/14/69. Return date: 3/4/75. Repeat date:
7/18/75. Series made possible by a grant from
the Corporation for Public Broadcasting.
Executive Producer Tony Batten
Production Company WETA/Washington, D.C.
Host Tony Batten

**553 The International Animation
Festival** PBS
Program Type Animated Film
13-part series of animated films for adults. Premiere date: 4/8/75. Repeat date: 7/15/75. Series
made possible by grants from the Corporation
for Public Broadcasting, the Ford Foundation,
and Public Television Stations.
Producer Various
Production Company KQED/San Francisco
Host Jean March

**554 International Drum and Bugle
Corps Championship** PBS
Program Type Documentary/Special
Live coverage of finals of the championship held
at Franklin Field, Philadelphia. Four hours. Pre-
miere date: 8/16/75.

555 International Gymnastics
PBS Sports Special PBS
Program Type Sports
U.S. and West German national teams. 120
minutes. Premiere date: 2/9/75. Taped at Recre-
ation Hall, Pennsylvania State University, Uni-
versity Park, Pennsylvania.
Executive Producer James W. Burkett
Producer Frank Fisher
Production Company Pennsylvania State Univer-
sity Division of Broadcasting
Announcer Fran Fisher

International Track Association Classic
see ITA Classic

556 The Invisible Man
NBC World Premiere Movie NBC
Program Type TV Movie
Based on the novel by H. G. Wells; story by
Harve Bennett; Steven Bochco. 90 minutes. Pre-
miere date: 5/6/75. Repeat date: 9/2/75. Pilot
for "The Invisible Man" series, 1975–76 season.
Executive Producer Harve Bennett
Producer Steven Bochco
Production Company Silverton Productions Inc.
in association with Universal Television and
NBC-TV

Director Robert Michael Lewis
Writer Steven Bochco
CAST
Dr. Daniel Weston .... David McCallum
Kate Weston .... Melinda Fee
Walter Carlson .... Jackie Cooper
Dr. Nick Maggio .... Henry Darrow
Rick Steiner .... Alex Henteloff
Gen. Turner .... Arch Johnson
Blind Man .... John McLiam
Gate Guard .... Ted Gehring

557 The IQ Myth
CBS Reports CBS
Program Type Documentary/Special
Examines the significance and accuracy of intel-
ligence tests. 60 minutes. Premiere date:
4/22/75. Repeat date: 7/7/75.
Executive Producer John Sharnik
Producer Peter Poor
Production Company CBS News
Anchor Dan Rather

Irma La Douce *see* The ABC Saturday
Night Movie

558 Ironside NBC
Program Type Crime Drama
Based on pilot of the same name produced in
1967. 60 minutes. Thursday. Premiere date:
9/14/67. Season premiere: 9/12/74. Last show:
1/16/75.
Executive Producer Joel Rogosin
Producer Albert Aley; Norman Jolley
Production Company Harbour Productions and
Universal Television in association with NBC-
TV
CAST
Chief of Detectives
Robert T. Ironside .... Raymond Burr
Sgt. Ed Brown .... Don Galloway
Fran Belding .... Elizabeth Baur
Mark Sanger .... Don Mitchell
Diana Sanger .... Joan Pringle

559 Is the Recession Finally Ending?
CBS News Special CBS
Program Type Documentary/Special
30 minutes. Premiere: 6/24/75.
Executive Producer Leslie Midgley
Producer Sanford Socolow
Production Company CBS News
Anchor George Herman
Reporters David Culhane; Randy Daniels; David
Dick; Richard Threlkeld

560 Isn't It Shocking?
Tuesday/Wednesday Movie of the Week ABC
Program Type TV Movie
90 minutes. Premiere date: 10/2/73. Repeat

Isn't It Shocking? *Continued*
date: 7/29/75. Filmed on location in Mount Angel, Oregon and other small towns near Salem, Oregon.
Producer Ron Bernstein; Howard Rosenman
Production Company An ABC Circle Film
Director John Badham
Writer Lane Slate
CAST
Sheriff Dan .... Alan Alda
Blanche .... Louise Lasser
Justin Oates ....Edmond O'Brien
Jesse Chapin .... Lloyd Nolan
Dr. Lemuel Lovell .... Will Geer
Marge Savage .... Ruth Gordon
Doc Lovell .... Dorothy Tristan
Ma Tate .... Pat Quinn
Myron Flagg .... Liam Dunn
Michael ....Michael Powell
Hattie .... Jacqueline Allan McClure

561 Issues and Answers   ABC
Program Type Interview/Discussion
30 minutes. Sunday. Premiere date: 10/60. Continuous. Interviews usually conducted live from Washington by ABC News correspondents. Bob Clark named chief correspondent and first permanent panelist in March 1975.
Producer Peggy Whedon
Production Company ABC News Public Affairs
Director Richard Armstrong; W. P. Fowler; Robert Delaney
Chief Correspondent Bob Clark

562 It Couldn't Happen to a Nicer Guy
Tuesday/Wednesday Movie of the Week ABC
Program Type TV Movie
90 minutes. Premiere date: 11/19/74. Repeat date: 6/11/75.
Executive Producer Gerald I. Isenberg
Producer Arne Sultan
Production Company The Jozak Company
Director Cy Howard
Writer Arne Sultan; Earl Barret
CAST
Harry Walters .... Paul Sorvino
Janet Walters ....Michael Learned
Ken Walters .... Adam Arkin
Sgt. Riggs .... Ed Barth
Ed Huxley ....Bob Dishy
Stu Detney .... Roger Bowen
Wanda .... JoAnna Cameron
The Judge .... Barbara Cason
Sgt. Rose Templeton .... Elaine Shore
Warren Morgan .... G. Wood
Alan Ronston .... Graham Jarvis
Mrs. Carter .... Sandra Deel
Wineberger .... Dick Yarmy
Carl Gallagher .... Edward Marshall
Mrs. Gibbs .... Lorna Thayer
Mrs. Kellog .... Ruth Warshawsky
Hovey .... Carl Franklin

563 ITA Classic
NBC Sports Special   NBC
Program Type Sports
Taped highlights of the International Track Association Classic from Los Angeles. 3/22/75.
Production Company NBC Sports

564 Italian Open
NBC Sports Special   NBC
Program Type Sports
Taped coverage of the Italian Open from the Foro Italico in Rome. 5/31/75; 6/1/75.
Production Company NBC Sports
Announcer Jim Simpson; Bud Collins

565 It's a Long Way Up
Call It Macaroni   Syndicated
Program Type Children's Show
Real-life adventure special. 30 minutes. Premiere: 1/75. Philadelphia children mountain climbing. Co-produced by Neil Bobrick, KYW-TV/Philadelphia.
Executive Producer George Moynihan
Producer Stephanie Meagher
Production Company KYW-TV/Philadelphia and Group W Productions
Distributor Westinghouse Broadcasting Company
Director Stephanie Meagher
Cinematographer Dick Roy
Editor David E. Roland

566 It's A Mystery, Charlie Brown CBS
Program Type Animated Film
Special. Created by Charles M. Schulz. Music by Vince Guaraldi. 30 minutes. Premiere date: 2/18/74. Repeat date: 2/17/75.
Executive Producer Lee Mendelson
Producer Bill Melendez
Production Company A Lee Mendelson-Bill Mendez Production
Director Phil Roman
Writer Charles M. Schulz
Musical Director Vince Guaraldi
Music Supervisor John Scott Trotter
VOICES
Charlie Brown .... Todd Barbee
Lucy ....Melanie Kohn
Linus ....Stephen Shea
Sally .... Lynn Mortensen
Peppermint Patty .... Donna Forman
Marcie .... James Ahrens
Pigpen .... Thomas A. Muller

567 It's Good to Be Alive
General Electric Theater   CBS
Program Type Drama
Special based on autobiography "It's Good to Be Alive" by Roy Campanella. 120 minutes. Pre-

miere date: 2/22/74. Repeat date: 5/22/75. Campanella family appears in introduction and epilogue.
Executive Producer Larry Harmon; Charles Fries
Producer Gerald I. Isenberg
Production Company Larry Harmon Pictures Corporation in association with Metromedia Producers Corproation
Director Michael Landon
Writer Steven Gethers
CAST
Roy Campanella .... Paul Winfield
Mrs. Ruthe Campanella .... Ruby Dee
Sam Brockington .... Lou Gossett
Walter O'Malley .... Ramon Bieri
Campanella's Father .... Joe De Santis
David Campanella .... Ty Henderson
Campanella's Mother .... Ketty Lester
Dr. Rusk .... Julian Burton

568   **It's the Easter Beagle, Charlie Brown**   CBS
Program Type Animated Film
30 minute special. Created by Charles M. Schulz. Music composed by Vince Guaraldi. Premiere date: 4/9/74. Repeat date: 3/26/75.
Executive Producer Lee Mendelson
Producer Bill Melendez
Production Company Lee Mendelson-Bill Melendez Production in cooperation with United Features Syndicate, Inc. and Charles M. Schulz Creative Associates
Director Phil Roman
Writer Charles M. Schulz
Musical Director Vince Guaraldi
Music Supervisor John Scott Trotter
VOICES
Charlie Brown .... Todd Barbee
Lucy .... Melanie Kohn
Linus .... Stephen Shea
Peppermint Patty .... Linda Ercoli
Sally .... Lynn Mortensen
Marcie .... James Ahrens

569   **It's the Great Pumplin, Charlie Brown**   CBS
Program Type Animated Film
Special. 30 minutes. Created by Charles M. Schulz. Music composed by Vince Guaraldi. Premiere date: 10/27/66. Repeat date: 10/28/74. Seventh showing.
Executive Producer Lee Mendelson
Producer Lee Mendelson
Production Company A Lee Mendelson-Bill Melendez Production
Director Bill Melendez
Writer Charles M. Schulz
Musical Director Vince Guaraldi
Music Supervisor John Scott Trotter
VOICES
Charlie Brown .... Peter Robbins

Lucy .... Sally Dryer
Linus .... Chris Shea
Sally .... Cathy Steinberg

570   **Jack Benny: We Remember**
NBC News Special   NBC
Program Type Documentary/Special
Tribute to the comedian. Premiere date: 12/27/74.
Producer Joseph Angotti; Gene Farinet; William B. Hill
Production Company NBC News

571   **Jackpot!**   NBC
Program Type Game Show
25 minutes. Monday-Friday. Premiere date: 1/7/74. Continuous.
Executive Producer Bob Stewart
Producer Bruce Burmester
Production Company Bob Stewart Productions
Director Mike Gargiulo
Host Geoff Edwards
Announcer Don Pardo

572   **James Whitmore: The Man Who's Giving 'em Hell**   PBS
Program Type Interview/Discussion
Special. Interview with James Whitmore. 30 minutes. Premiere date: 4/30/75. Taped at March 21st premiere of play "Give 'Em Hell, Harry!" in Hershey, Pennsylvania.
Production Company WITF/Hershey, Pennsylvania
Interviewer Bill Varney

Jane Goodall and the World of Animal Behavior *see* The Hyena Story

573   **The Japanese Film**   PBS
Program Type Feature Film
13 programs of Japanese feature films. Weekly. Times vary. Premiere date: 1/13/75. Series made possible by a grant from the National Endowment for the Humanities. Additional underwriting support from the Bank of America. Production assistance from Japan Air Lines. The films are: "Boy" (1969); "Double Suicide" (1969); "Early Summer" (1951); "Gate of Hell" (1953); "Harakiri" (1962); "Harp of Burma" (1956); "Ikiru" (1952); "Night Drum" (1958); "Sanjuro" (1962); "Sansho the Bailiff" (1954); "Twenty Four Eyes" (1954); "Ugetsu" (1953); "When a Woman Ascends the Stairs" (1960).
Executive Producer Sheldon Renan
Producer Rick Wise
Production Company KQED/San Francisco in association with the Pacific Film Archive of the University of California at Berkeley

The Japanese Film *Continued*
Director Rick Wise
Host Edwin O. Reischauer

574   Jean Shepherd's America   PBS
Program Type News Magazine
13-part series of "sensual essays." Originally shown in 1971. Repeat date: 7/8/75. Created by Jean Shepherd. Essays: "One Man's Version of Heaven Is a Howard Johnsons with 28 Flavors," "The Phantom of the Open Hearth Lives - Somewhere in Indiana," "Riding the City of Los Angeles," "A Bunch of the Boys Were Whooping It Up at the Malamute Saloon," "There's a Lot More to Life Than a Hostess Twinkie," "And the Bad Guys Are Back on Shore and Shaking Their Fists," "The Perpetual Swish of the Windshield Wipers Is the Soundtrack for Our Lives," "It Won't Always Be This Way," "From Its Golden, Ice-Cool Depths Come the Echos of Lost Battles, the Sound of Ancient Victories, the Noise of a Million Ball Games," "I Might Even Snag One for Old Ahab Himself," "When There's No Place to Go But Up," "Like All Great Inner-Tube Specialists, He Finally Made the Classic Mistake," "Make School or Die."
Producer Fred Barzyk
Production Company WGBH/Boston
Director Fred Barzyk
Writer Jean Shepherd
Host Jean Shepherd

575   Jeanne Wolf With ...   PBS
Program Type Interview/Discussion
30 minutes. Weekly. Second season premiere: 7/16/75. Program made possible by a grant from the Ben Tobin Foundation.
Executive Producer Shep Morgan
Producer Jeanne Wolf
Production Company WPBT/Miami
Director Tom Donaldson
Host Jeanne Wolf

576   Jeannie   CBS
Program Type Animated Film
Reruns. 30 munutes. Saturday. Premiere date: 9/8/73. Last show: 8/30/75.
Executive Producer Joseph Barbera; William Hanna
Producer Iwao Takamoto
Production Company Hanna-Barbera Productions
Director Charles A. Nichols
Writer Sid Morse; Bill Canning; Marion Hargrove; Irma Kalish and Austin Kalish; Dave Ketchum; Bruce Shelly; Arlene Stadd and Leonard Stadd; Frank Waldman; Phyllis White and Robert White
Musical Director Hoyt Curtin

Voices Gay Autterson; Julie Bennett; Joe Besser; Tommy Cook; Indira Danks; Mark Hamill; Bob Hastings; Tina Holland; Sherry Jackson; Julie McWhirter; Don Messick; Hal Smith; John Stephenson; Judy Strangis; Ginny Tyler; Vincent Van Patten

577   The Jeffersons   CBS
Program Type Comedy
Spin-off from "All in the Family." Created by Don Nicholl, Michael Ross and Bernie West. Developed by Norman Lear. Theme song, "Movin' on Up" by Jeff Barry; Ja'net DuBois. Premiere date: 1/18/75. 30 minutes. Saturday. Set in Manhattan.
Executive Producer Norman Lear
Producer Don Nicholl; Michael Ross; Bernie West
Production Company A T.A.T. Communications Company Production in association with NRW Productions
Director Jack Shea
Writer Don Nicholl; Michael Ross; Bernie West
CAST
Louise Jefferson .... Isabel Sanford
George Jefferson .... Sherman Hemsley
Lionel Jefferson .... Mike Evans
Helen Willis .... Roxie Roker
Tom Willis .... Franklin Cover
Harry Bentley .... Paul Benedict
Jenny Willis .... Berlinda Tolbert
Mother Jefferson ....Zara Cully

578   Jeopardy!   NBC
Program Type Game Show
30 minutes. Monday-Friday. Premiered in 1964. Last show: 1/3/75.
Executive Producer Robert H. Rubin
Producer Lynette Williams
Production Company Griffin Productions
Director Jeffrey Goldstein
Host Art Fleming
Announcer Don Pardo

579   Jeopardy!   Syndicated
Program Type Game Show
Evening version of daytime game. 30 minutes. Weekly. Premiere: 9/74.
Executive Producer Robert H. Rubin
Producer Lynette Williams
Production Company Griffin Productions in association with Metromedia Producers Corporation
Director Jeffrey Goldstein
Host Art Fleming
Announcer Don Pardo

580 Jerry Lewis Labor Day Telethon Against Muscular Dystrophy Syndicated
Program Type Documentary/Special
10th annual national telethon. 21 1/2 hours. Live and tape. 8/31/75–9/1/75. Jerry Lewis with Ed McMahon host show from Las Vegas; Julius La Rosa from New York.
Producer Arthur Forrest
Production Company Muscular Dystrophy Association
Director Arthur Forrest

581 The Jetsons NBC
Program Type Animated Film
Set in the 21st century. 30 minutes. Sunday. Premiere date: 9/11/71. Reruns: 9/8/74. Last show: 8/31/75.
Executive Producer William Hanna; Joseph Barbera
Production Company Hanna-Barbera Productions for Screen Gems
Director William Hanna; Joseph Barbera
Writer Warren Foster; Mike Maltese; Harvey Bullock; Larry Markes; Tony Benedict
Musical Director Hoyt Curtin
VOICES
Jan Jetson .... Penny Singleton
George Jetson .... George O'Hanlon
Judy Jetson .... Janet Waldo
Elroy Jetson .... Daws Butler

582 The Jim Stafford Show ABC
Program Type Comedy/Variety
Six-part series. 60 minutes. Wednesday. Premiere date: 7/30/75. Last show: 9/3/75.
Executive Producer Phil Gernhard; Tony Scotti
Producer Rich Eustis; Al Rogers
Production Company Stafford Entertainment, Inc./Fours Company Production
Director Lee Bernhardi
Writer Rich Eustis; Al Rogers and Jim Stafford; with Rod Warren; April Kelly; Bo Kaprall; Pat Proft; George Ticker; Stuart Birnbaum; Matt Neuman
Musical Director Eddie Karam
Choreographer Carl Jablonski
Host Jim Stafford
Regular Valerie Curtin; Richard Stahl; Phil MacKenzie; Deborah Allen; Cyndi Wood; Jeanne Sheffield; Tom Biener; Gallagher

583 Joan Baez PBS
Program Type Music/Dance
Special. 60 minutes. Premiere date: 12/14/74. Joan Baez in concert.
Producer Jim Scalem; Leslie Miner
Production Company KQED/San Francisco
Director Jim Scalem; Leslie Miner

Joe Kidd *see* NBC Nights at the Movies

584 Joey & Dad CBS
Program Type Comedy/Variety
Four-part summer series. 60 minutes. Sunday. Premiere date: 7/6/75. Last show: 7/27/75. Featured Henny Youngman conducting the Henny Youngman orchestra.
Executive Producer Alan Blye; Bob Einstein
Producer Bob Arnott; Coslough Johnson; Stan Jacobson
Production Company Blye-Einstein Productions
Director Mark Warren
Writer George Burditt; Robert Illes; Jim Stein; Harvey Weitzman; Alan Blye; Bob Einstein
Host Joey Heatherton; Ray Heatherton
Regular Pat Paulsen; Pat Proft

585 John Bassette ... This Time Around PBS
Program Type Music/Dance
Special. Concert taped in a Cleveland coffeehouse. 30 minutes. Premiere date: 10/9/74.
Producer John Harnack
Production Company WOUB/WOUC-TV/ Athens, Ohio
Director John Harnack
Star John Bassette

586 The John Denver Show; A Family Event ABC
Program Type Comedy/Variety
Special. Magic created by Mark Wilson. 60 minutes. Premiere date: 12/1/74.
Executive Producer Jerry Weintraub
Producer Rich Eustis; Al Rogers
Production Company John-Jer Productions, Inc.
Director Bill Davis
Writer Ray Jessel; Harry Lee Scott; Rich Eustis; Al Rogers
Musical Director Milt Okum
Choreographer Danny Daniels
Host John Denver
Costume Designer Bill Belew
Guests Doris Day; Dick Van Dyke; George Gobel; Robbie Rist

587 Johnny Cash Ridin' the Rails - The Great American Train Story ABC
Program Type Comedy/Variety
Special. Filmed throughout the country. 60 minutes. Premiere date: 11/22/74.
Producer Nicholas Webster; Dyann Rivkin
Production Company Webster/Rivkin Productions
Director Nicholas Webster
Host Johnny Cash

588   Joint U.S.-U.S.S.R. Space Mission Preview

NBC News Special   NBC
Program Type Documentary/Special
Special. 30 minutes. Preview of space mission.
7/14/75. (*See also* "Handshake in Space.")
Production Company NBC News
Host John Chancellor

589   The Joker's Wild   CBS

Program Type Game Show
30 minutes. Monday-Friday. Continuous. Premiere date: 9/4/72. Last show: 6/13/75.
Executive Producer Daniel Enright
Producer Justin Edgerton
Production Company Jack Barry Productions
Director Richard S. Kline
Host Jack Barry

590   Journey From Darkness

NBC World Premiere Movie   NBC
Program Type TV Movie
Story by Stephen Pouliot based on fact. 120 minutes. Premiere date: 2/25/75. Repeat date: 8/5/75.
Executive Producer Bob Banner
Producer Tom Egan; Stephen Pouliot
Production Company Bob Banner Associates
Director James Goldstone
Writer Peggy Chantler Dick
CAST

David Hartman	Marc Singer
Cheri Hartman	Kay Lenz
Mike	Wendell Burton
Dr. Cavaliere	William Windom
Dr. Schroeder	Joseph Campanella
Fred Hartman	Jack Warden
Bill	Dirk Benedict
Bobbi Hartman	Nancy Wolfe
Mrs. Hartman	Dorothy Tristan

591   Judge Dee in the Monastery Murders

The ABC Sunday Night Movie   ABC
Program Type TV Movie
120 minutes. Premiere date: 12/29/74. Based on the novel "Judge Dee at the Haunted Monastery" by Robert Van Gulick.
Producer Gerald I. Isenberg
Production Company An ABC Circle Film
Director Jeremy Kagan
Writer Nicholas Meyer
CAST

Judge Dee	Khigh Alx Dhiegh
Tao Gan	Mako
Kang I-Te	Soon-Taik Oh
Jade Mirror	Miiko Taka
Celestial Image	Irene Tsu
Lord Sun Ming	Keye Luke
Miss Ting	Suesie Elene
Prior	James Hong

Bright Flower	Beverly Kushida
White Rose	Ching Hocson
Pure Faith	Yuki Shimoda
Tsung Lee	Robert Sadang
Mrs. Pao	Frances Fong
True Wisdom	Tommy Lee
Driver No. 1	Richard Lee-Sung
Motai	Tadashi Yamashita

592   Judgment: The Court-Martial of Lt. William Calley

ABC Theatre   ABC
Program Type Drama
Special. Dramatization of the court-martial of Lt. William Calley. 120 minutes. Premiere date: 1/12/75.
Producer Stanley Kramer
Production Company Stanley Kramer Productions, Ltd. in association with Wolper Productions
Director Stanley Kramer
Writer Henry Denker
CAST

Lt. William Calley	Tony Musante
George Latimer	Richard Basehart
Capt. Aubrey Daniel	Bo Hopkins
Military Judge	G. D. Spradlin
The Captain	Bill Lucking
Frank Crowder	Harrison Ford
Calley's Girl	Linda Haynes
Capt. Briggs	Jan Merlin
Mr. Alston	Elven Havard
Mr. Josephs	Lee Weaver
Westover	Jim Lough
Sgt. Crutch	James Jeter
Mr. Stover	Oliver Clark
Air Force Lt. Kent	Ben Piazza
Mr. Peters	Geoffrey Horne
Maj. David	Darrell Zwerling
Mr. Driscoll	Leon Russom
Mr. Langham	Frank McRae
Mr. Kingston	R. Chadwick Harper
Father Randall	Ted Gehring
Capt. Vorst	Marty Berman
Sgt. Jackson	W. T. Zacha
Mr. Judd	Roland "Bob" Harris
Newsman	Jim Warring
Asst. Counsel	Fredd Wayne
Chaplain	Jamie Reidy

593   Julie - My Favorite Things   ABC

Program Type Comedy/Variety
Special. Muppet material by Marshall Brickman. 60 minutes. Premiere date: 4/18/75.
Producer Bob Wells
Production Company Independent Television Corporation (ITC)
Director Blake Edwards
Writer Frank Waldman; Bob Wells; Blake Edwards
Musical Director Ian Fraser
Choreographer Paddy Stone
Host Julie Andrews
Conductor Jack Parnell

Guest Star Peter Sellers
Muppeteers Frank Oz; Jerry Nelson; John Lovelady; David Goelz; Jim Henson

594   June Moon
Theater in America   PBS
Program Type Comedy
Play by George S. Kaufman; Ring Lardner. 90
minutes. Premiere date: 1/30/74. Repeat date:
7/30/75. Series made possible by grants from
Exxon Corporation and the Corporation for
Public Broadcasting.
Executive Producer Jac Venza
Producer Bo Goldman
Production Company WNET/New York
Director Burt Shevelove; Kirk Browning
Host Hal Holbrook
CAST
Paul Sears .... Jack Cassidy
Lucille Sears .... Estelle Parsons
Mr. Hart ....Kevin McCarthy
Fred Stevens ....Tom Fitzsimmons
Maxie Schwartz .... Stephen Sondheim
Eileen .... Susan Sarandon
Bennie Fox .... Austin Pendleton
Edna Baker .... Barbara Dana
Miss Rixley .... Lee Meredith
Window Cleaner .... Marshall Efron
Goldie .... Beatrice Colen

595   Junior Davis Cup Matches
PBS Sports Special   PBS
Program Type Sports
17th annual tournament taped in Miami Beach.
Four hours. 12/28/75. Program sponsored by
the Miami Beach Tourist Development Author-
ity.
Production Company WPBT/Miami
Announcer Bill Talbert; Donna Fales

596   Junior Orange Bowl Parade   NBC
Program Type Documentary/Special
26th annual parade. 45 minutes. 1/1/75.
Producer Elmer Gorry
Production Company NBC Television Network
Host Joe Garagiola; Lisa Donavan

Kansas City Bomber *see* The CBS
   Thursday/Friday Night Movies

597   Karen   ABC
Program Type Comedy
30 minutes. Friday. Premiere date: 1/30/75. Last
show: 6/19/75. Series set in Washington, D.C.
citizens' action group, Open America. Denver
Pyle was replaced by Charles Lane in the second
episode.
Executive Producer Gene Reynolds; Larry Gelbart

Producer Carl Kleinschmitt
Production Company 20th Century-Fox Televi-
sion
Director Various
Writer Various
CAST
Karen Angelo .... Karen Valentine
Dale Busch .... Denver Pyle; Charles Lane
Dena Madison .... Dena Dietrich
Cissy Peterson .... Aldine King
Ernie Stone .... Joseph Stern
Adam Cooperman .... Will Seltzer

598   Karl Bohm Conducts the Vienna Symphony Orchestra
Great Performances   PBS
Program Type Music/Dance
Special. 90 minutes. Premiere date: 2/12/75.
Presented in the United States by WNET/New
York; David Griffiths, coordinating producer.
Karl Bohm conducts the Vienna Symphony Or-
chestra.
Executive Producer Fritz Buttenstedt
Producer Horant H. Hohlfeld
Production Company Unitel

599   Kate McShane
The CBS Thursday/Friday Night Movies   CBS
Program Type TV Movie
Pilot for series. Created by E. Jack Neuman. 90
minutes. Premiere date: 4/11/75. Repeat date:
8/29/75.
Producer E. Jack Neuman
Production Company P. A. Productions, Inc. in
association with Paramount Television
Director Marvin Chomsky
Writer E. Jack Neuman
CAST
Kate McShane .... Anne Meara
Pat McShane .... Sean McClory
Ed Shane ....Charles Haid
Angelo Romero .... Cal Bellini
Charlotte .... Christine Belford
Harold Cutler .... Charles Cioffi
Judge Platte ....Larry Gates
Dr. Tishman ....Stefan Gierasch
Additional Cast Marian Collier; Richard Erdman; Alan
Fudge

600   Keep on Truckin'   ABC
Program Type Comedy/Variety
Four-part series. 60 minutes. Saturday. Premiere
date: 7/12/75. Last show: 8/2/75.
Producer Frank Peppiatt; John Aylesworth
Production Company Funhouse Production
Director Tony Mordente
Regular Franklyn Ajaye; Rhonda Bates; Kath-
rine Baumann; Jeannine Burnier; Didi Conn;
Charles Fleischer; Wayland Flowers; Larry
Ragland; Marion Ramsey; Rhilo; Jack Riley;

Keep on Truckin' *Continued*
Fred Travalena; Gailard Sartain; Richard Lee
Sung
Puppeteer Wayland Flowers

Kelly's Heroes *see* The CBS
Thursday/Friday Night Movies

601 Kemper Open Golf Tournament
CBS Sports Special   CBS
Program Type Sports
Live coverage of third and final round of tournament from Quail Hollow Country Club, Charlotte, North Carolina. 6/7/75; 6/8/75.
Producer Frank Chirkinian
Production Company CBS Television Network
Sports
Announcer Jack Whitaker

602 The Kentucky Derby
ABC Sports Special   ABC
Program Type Sports
101st Kentucky Derby at Churchill Downs,
Louisville, Kentucky. Live coverage. 5/3/75. 60
minutes.
Executive Producer Roone Arledge
Production Company ABC Sports
Announcer Chic Anderson
Reporters Howard Cosell; Jim McKay; Chris
Schenkel
Analyst Johnny Rotz

603 Khan!   CBS
Program Type Crime Drama
Set in San Francisco's Chinatown. 60 minutes.
Friday. Premiere date: 2/7/75. Last show:
2/28/75.
Producer Laurence Heath
Production Company CBS Television Network
CAST
Khan ....Khigh Dhiegh
Anna Khan .... Irene Yah-Ling Sun
Kim Khan .... Evan Kim
Det.-Lt. Gubbins .... Vic Tayback

604 Khrushchev Remembers
Window on the World   Syndicated
Program Type Documentary/Special
60-minute special based on the book "Khrushchev Remembers." Premiere: 6/75.
Executive Producer Jack Beck
Producer Harold Mayer
Production Company Time-Life Television
Distributor Time-Life Films
Director Harold Mayer
Writer Nikita Khrushchev
Narrator Burgess Meredith

CAST
Nikita Khrushchev .... Steven Hill

605 Killer Bees
Tuesday/Wednesday Movie of the Week ABC
Program Type TV Movie
90 minutes. Premiere date: 2/26/74. Repeat
date: 3/11/75. Filmed on location in the Napa
Valley, California.
Producer Howard Rosenman; Ron Bernstein
Production Company RSO Films for ABC-TV
Director Curtis Harrington
Writer Joyce Corrington; John William Corrington
CAST
Mme. Van Bohlen .... Gloria Swanson
Edward Van Bohlen .... Edward Albert
Dr. Helmut Van Bohlen .... Roger Davis
Victoria .... Kate Jackson
Rudolph .... Craig Stevens
Mathias .... Don McGovern
Jeffreys .... John S. Ragin
Salesman .... Jack Perkins
Lineman .... Donald Gentry

606 The Killers   PBS
Program Type Educational
Five-part health series. 90 minutes each. Premiere date: 11/19/73. Repeat dates: 9/2/74;
8/18/75. Covers trauma, heart disease, genetic
defects, pulmonary disease and cancer. Specials
made possible through a grant from Bristol Myers Company.
Executive Producer David Prowitt
Production Company WNET Science Program
Group/New York
Reporter David Prowitt

607 King Lear
Theater in America   PBS
Program Type Drama
Play by William Shakespeare taped at the New
York Shakespeare Festival in 1973. 180 minutes.
Premiere date: 2/20/74. Repeat date: 3/26/75.
Series made possible by grants from Exxon Corporation and the Corporation for Public Broadcasting.
Executive Producer Jac Venza
Producer Joseph Papp
Production Company WNET/New York
Director Edwin Sherin
Host Hal Holbrook
CAST
King Lear .... James Earl Jones
Earl of Kent .... Douglass Watson
Earl of Gloucester .... Paul Sorvino
Edmund .... Raul Julia
Edgar .... Rene Auberjonois
Goneril .... Rosalind Cash
Cordelia .... Lee Chamberlain
Regan .... Ellen Holly

Fool ....Tom Aldredge
Albany .... Robert Stattel

608 King Orange Jamboree Parade NBC
Program Type Documentary/Special
41st annual parade from Miami, Florida. 60
minutes. 12/31/74.
Producer Elmer Gorry
Production Company NBC Television Network
Host Joe Garagiola; Jo Ann Pflug

Kings of the Sun *see* NBC Nights at the
Movies

Klute *see* NBC Nights at the Movies

609 Knuckle
Hollywood Television Theatre   PBS
Program Type Drama
Adapted from the play by David Hare. 120
minutes. Premiere date: 6/4/75.
Executive Producer Norman Lloyd
Production Company KCET/Los Angeles
Director Norman Lloyd
Writer David Scott Milton
                              CAST
Curley Delafield .... Michael Cristofer
Mrs. Grace Dunning .... Eileen Brennan
Patrick Delafield .... Jack Cassidy
Jenny Wilbur .... Gretchen Corbett
Chico Moreno .... Manuel Rivera
Sarah's Lover .... Jack Colvin
Sarah Delafield .... Julie McKenna
Additional Cast James Green; Jack Sahakian

610 Kodak All American Football Team
CBS Sports Special   CBS
Program Type Sports
1974 team chosen by the American Football
Coaches Association. 30 minutes. 12/14/74.
Producer Frank Chirkinian
Production Company CBS Television Network
Sports
Announcer Pat Summerall

611 Kodiak   ABC
Program Type Drama
30 minutes. Premiere date: 9/13/74. Last show:
10/11/74. Adventures of the Alaska State Pa-
trol. Created by Anthony Lawrence; Stan Shpet-
ner.
Producer Stan Shpetner
Production Company Kodiak Productions
Director Various
Writer Various
                              CAST
Cal "Kodiak" McKay .... Clint Walker
Abraham Lincoln Imhook .... Abner Biberman
Mandy .... Maggie Blye

612 Kojak   CBS
Program Type Crime Drama
Set in New York City. Created by Abby Mann.
60 minutes. Sunday. Premiere date: 10/24/73.
Season premiere: 9/15/74 (120 minute show).
Executive Producer Matthew Rapf
Supervising Producer Jack Laird
Producer James McAdams
Production Company Universal Television
Director Various
Writer Various
                              CAST
Lt. Theo Kojak .... Telly Savalas
Capt. Frank McNeil .... Dan Frazer
Det. Crocker ....Kevin Dobson
Det. Stavros ....Demosthenes

613 Korg: 70,000 B.C.!   ABC
Program Type Children's Show
30 minutes. Saturday. Premiere date: 9/7/74
Last show: 8/31/75. Survival in the Neanderthal
era.
Executive Producer William Hanna; Joseph
Barbera
Producer Richard L. O'Connor; Fred Freiberger
Production Company Hanna-Barbera Produc-
tions
Director Irving Moore; Chris Nyby
Narrator Burgess Meredith
                              CAST
Korg .... Jim Malinda
Bok .... Bill Ewing
Mara .... Naomi Pollack
Tane .... Christopher Man
Tor ....Charles Morteo
Ree ....Janelle Pransky

614 Kung Fu   ABC
Program Type Crime Drama
60 minutes. Premiere date: 1/18/73. Season
premiere: 9/14/74 (120 minutes). Last show:
6/28/75. Created by Ed Spielman; developed by
Herman Miller.
Executive Producer Jerry Thorpe
Producer Herman Miller; Alex Beaton
Production Company Warner Brothers Televi-
sion
                              CAST
Caine ....David Carradine
Master Kan .... Philip Ahn
Master Po .... Keye Luke
Young Caine ....Radames Pera

615 Kup's Show   PBS
Program Type Interview/Discussion
60 minutes. Weekly. Originally a local show
premiering in February 1958; carried by WBBM-
TV. Now carried by WMAQ-TV/Chicago. Premiere date (on PBS): 7/7/75. Continuous. Program made possible by grants from the

Kup's Show *Continued*
Corporation for Public Broadcasting, the Ford Foundation, and Public Television Stations.
Producer Paul Frumkin
Production Company KAET/Phoenix
Director Tony Verdi
Host Irv Kupcinet

616   **Ladies of the Corridor**
Hollywood Television Theatre   PBS
Program Type Drama
120 minutes. Premiere date: 4/10/75. Repeat date: 9/4/75.
Supervising Producer George Turpin
Producer Norman Lloyd
Production Company KCET/Los Angeles
Director Robert Stevens
Writer Dorothy Parker; Arnaud d'Usseau
CAST
Lulu Ames ....Cloris Leachman
Mrs. Nichols .... Jane Wyatt
Connie Mercer .... Neva Patterson
Mildred Tynan .... Zohra Lampert
Mrs. Gordon .... Barbara Baxley
Mrs. Lauterbach .... Mabel Albertson
Paul Osgood .... Mike Farrell
Charles Nichols .... Richard Lenz
Robert Ames .... Colby Chester
Betsy Ames ....Elaine Giftos
Mary Linscott ....Gertrude Flynn
Tom Linscott .... Tom Palmer
Mr. Humphries ....Dick Van Patten
Harry .... Chris Stone
Casey .... Gary Barton
Irma ....Pat Hitchcock
Announcer ....Ed Arnold
Cab Driver ....Eugene Jackson
Extra Lady .... Kathryn Janssen
Doorman .... Ben Wright

617   **The Lady Is a Champ ... A Colgate Women's Sports Special**
ABC Sports Special   ABC
Program Type Sports
Update of 1974 "Colgate Women's Sports Special." 60 minutes. Premiere date: 8/28/75.
Executive Producer Roone Arledge
Producer Eleanor Riger
Production Company ABC Sports
Director Lou Volpicelli
Host Billie Jean King
Guests Chris Evert; Shirley Babashoff; Francie Larrieu; Sandra Palmer; Amy Alcott; Genia Fuller; Donna de Varona

Lady Liberty *see* The ABC Sunday Night Movie

618   **The Lady's Not for Burning**
Hollywood Television Theatre   PBS
Program Type Drama
Adapted from the stage play by author Christopher Fry. 105 minutes. Premiere date: 11/18/74. Repeat date: 7/3/75.
Executive Producer Norman Lloyd
Producer George Turpin
Production Company KCET/Los Angeles
Director Joseph Hardy
Writer Christopher Fry
CAST
Thomas Mendip ....Richard Chamberlain
Jennet Jourdemayne .... Eileen Atkins
Hebble Tyson ....Keene Curtis
Nicholas Devise ....Stephen McHattie
Humphrey Devise .... Scott Hylands
Margaret Devise .... Rosemary Murphy
Richard .... Kristoffer Tabori
Alizon .... Laurie Prange
Chaplain .... Tom Lacy
Edward Tappercoom .... Jacques Aubuchon
Matthew Skipps ....John Carradine

619   **Lamp Unto My Feet**   CBS
Program Type Educational
Premiered on the CBS Network in November 1948. 30 minutes. Sunday. Continuous.
Executive Producer Pamela Ilott
Producer Various
Production Company CBS News Presentation
Host Various

620   **Land of the Free**
From Sea to Shining Sea   Syndicated
Program Type Drama
Second of seven-part miniseries for the bicentennial. 60 minutes. Premiere: 12/74. Music composed by Michel Legrand; lyrics by Hal David. Title song sung by Tommy Overstreet.
Producer John H. Secondari; Helen Jean Secondari
Production Company John H. Secondari Productions, Ltd.
Distributor The Hughes Television Network
Director Leo Penn
Writer John H. Secondari
Musical Director Michel Legrand
CAST
John Freeborn .... Robert Culp
Pres. John Adams .... Burgess Meredith
Gen. Andrew Jackson .... Jeff Corey
Jamie MacGillivray .... Jeff Conaway
Thomas Pickering .... Thayer David
Mrs. Adams ....Kate Wilkinson
Weatherford .... Robert Pastene

621   **Land of the Lost**   NBC
Program Type Children's Show
30 minutes. Saturday. Premiere date: 9/7/74.
Executive Producer Albert J. Tenzer

Producer Sid Krofft; Marty Krofft
Production Company Sid and Marty Krofft Productions
Director Bob Lally; Dennis Steinmetz
Story Editor David Gerrold
Writer Various
CAST
Forest Ranger Rick Marshall .... Spencer Milligan
Will Marshall .... Wesley Eure
Holly Marshall .... Kathy Coleman
Sleestack .... John Lambert; Bill Laimbeer;
Dave Greenwood
Paku .... Sharon Baird; Joe Giamalva
Paku (Cha-ka) ....Philip Paley
Colley .... Walker Edmiston

The Landlord see The ABC Saturday
Night Movie

622   Larry
General Electric Theatre   CBS
Program Type Drama
Special. Dramatization of "Larry: Case History
of a Mistake" by Dr. Robert McQueen. Filmed
on location at Camarillo State Hospital, California. 90 minutes. Premiere date: 4/23/74. Repeat
date: 5/15/75.
Executive Producer Herbert Hirschman
Producer Mitchell Brower; Robert Lovenheim
Production Company Tomorrow Entertainment,
Inc.
Director William A. Graham
Writer David Seltzer
CAST
Larry Herman .... Frederic Forrest
Nancy Hockworth .... Tyne Daly
Dr. McCabe .... Michael McGuire
Mrs. Whitten .... Katherine Helmond
Tom Corman .... Robert Walden

623   The Las Vegas Entertainment
Awards   NBC
Program Type Awards Show
Special. Taped at Caesar's Palace, Las Vegas,
Nevada. 60 minutes. Premiere date: 11/20/74.
Producer of stage show: Breck Wall.
Executive Producer Bob Hope
Producer Mort Lachman; Norman Sedawie
Production Company Bob Hope Enterprises
Host Bob Hope

624   Lassie's Rescue Rangers   ABC
Program Type Animated Film
Based on "Lassie" character of Wrather Corporation and Rudd Weatherwax. 30 minutes. Sunday. Premiere date: 9/8/73. Reruns: 9/8/74.
Last show: 8/30/75.
Producer Norm Prescott; Lou Scheimer
Production Company Filmation Associates
Director Hal Sutherland

Writer Jim Ryan; Bill Danch
Art Director Don Christensen
Voices Ted Knight; Keith Sutherland; Jane
Webb; Lane Scheimer; Hal Harvey

625   The Last American Supper
The Quarterly Report   PBS
Program Type Documentary/Special
Third in series. 120 minutes. Premiere date:
4/17/75. Panel discussion plus interviews with
nutritional and agricultural experts.
Producer Lincoln Furber
Production Company NPACT (National Public
Affairs Center for Television)
Host Jim Lehrer; Paul Duke

626   The Last Bride of Salem
ABC Afternoon Playbreak   ABC
Program Type TV Movie
Special. 90 minutes. Premiere date: 5/8/74. Repeat date: 6/12/75.
Executive Producer Bob Lewis
Producer George Paris
Production Company 20th Century-Fox Television
Director Tom Donovan
Writer Rita Lakin
CAST
Matt Clifton .... Bradford Dillman
Jennifer Clifton .... Lois Nettleton
Kelly Clifton .... Joni Bick
Sebastian .... Paul Harding
Seth .... Ed McNamara
Fletcher .... Murray Westgate
Grace .... Susan Rubis
Dr. Glover .... James Douglas
Rebecca .... Patricia Hamilton
Elsbeth .... Moya Fenwick
Master .... Rex Hagon
Abner .... Jim Barron
Thomas .... Robert Hawkins
First Son ....Rick Bennett
Second Son ....John Candy

627   The Last Day
NBC Nights at the Movies   NBC
Program Type TV Movie
120 minutes. Premiere date: 2/15/75. Repeat
date: 8/21/75. Based on a story by Steve Fisher
and A. C. Lyles.
Producer A. C. Lyles
Production Company A. C. Lyles and Paramount
Television
Director Vincent McEveety
Writer Jim Byrnes; Steve Fisher
Narrator Harry Morgan
CAST
Will Spence ....Richard Widmark
Betty Spence .... Barbara Rush
Bob Dalton .... Robert Conrad
Daisy .... Loretta Swit
Emmet Dalton .... Tim Matheson

The Last Day *Continued*
Grat Dalton .... Richard Jaeckel
Dick Broadwell .... Christopher Connelly
Bill Powers .... Tom Skerritt
Connelly ....Gene Evans
Munson .... Rex Holman
Payne .... Morgan Woodward
Additional Cast Kathleen Cody; Logan Ramsey

628   The Last Frontier   Syndicated
Program Type Animal Documentary
Filmed in Kenya. Special with Robert F. Kennedy, Jr. and Norman Myers, wildlife photographer and ecologist. 60 minutes. Premiere: 9/75.
Executive Producer Roger E. Ailes
Producer Tom Shachtman
Production Company Roger Ailes & Associates
Distributor TVN Enterprises
Director Roger E. Ailes
Writer Tom Shachtman
Host Robert F. Kennedy, Jr.

629   Last Hours Before Morning
NBC Nights at the Movies   NBC
Program Type TV Movie
90 minutes. Premiere date: 4/29/75. Repeat date: 7/30/75.
Executive Producer Charles Fries
Producer Malcolm Stuart
Production Company Charles Fries Productions, Inc. in association with MGM Television and NBC-TV
Director Joseph Hardy
Writer Robert Garland; George Yanok
CAST
Bud Delaney .... Ed Lauter
Yolanda Marquez .... Victoria Principal
Mrs. Pace ....Rhonda Fleming
Bruno .... Michael Baseleon
Shirley .... Sheila Sullivan
Justice ....Thalmus Rasulala
Peter Helms .... Peter Donat
Ty Randolph ....Kaz Garas
Lucky English .... Robert Alda
Elmo .... William Finley
Westover .... John O'Leary
Mr. Pace .... Don Porter
Buck ....Art Lund
Sgt. Hagen .... George Murdock
Owings .... George Dicenzo
Cashman .... John Harkins
Muscleman .... Michael Stearns
Korbett ....John Quade
Max .... Philip Bruns
Hopkins .... Redmond Gleeson
Dancer .... Elaine Pepparde

Last of the Wild *see* Lorne Greene's Last of the Wild

The Last Picture Show *see* The ABC Sunday Night Movie

The Last Run *see* The CBS Thursday/Friday Night Movies

630   The Last Survivors
NBC World Premiere Movie   NBC
Program Type TV Movie
Based on a true story. 90 minutes. Premiere date: 3/4/75. Repeat date: 7/22/75.
Executive Producer Bob Banner
Producer Tom Egan
Production Company Bob Banner Associates
Director Lee Katzin
Writer Douglas Day Stewart
CAST
Alexander Holmes .... Martin Sheen
Marilyn West .... Diane Baker
Marcus Damian ....Tom Bosley
Duane Jeffries .... Christopher George
Michael Larrieu .... Bruce Davison
Helen Dixon .... Anne Francis
Inez .... Bethel Leslie
Rudy Franco .... Percy Rodriguez
Susie Mansham .... Anne Seymour
Mrs. Peters ....Beulah Quo
Prosecutor ....Eugene Roche

631   The Law
NBC World Premiere Movie   NBC
Program Type TV Movie
Based on the experiences of Alvin Nierenberg in the Los Angeles Public Defender's Office. Story by William Sackheim; Joel Oliansky. 150 minutes. Premiere date: 10/22/74. Repeat date: 8/19/75.
Producer William Sackheim
Production Company Universal Television in association with NBC-TV
Director John Badham
Writer Joel Oliansky
CAST
Murray Stone .... Judd Hirsch
Gene Carey .... John Beck
William Bright .... Gary Busey
Judge Fornier .... Barbara Baxley
Bobbie Stone .... Bonnie Franklin
Jules Benson ....Sam Wanamaker
Thomas Q. Rachel ....John Hillerman
Leonard Caproni .... Allan Arbus

632   The Law (miniseries)   NBC
Program Type Drama
Three-part series based on "NBC World Premiere Movie" of the same name. 60 minutes. Created by William Sackheim and Joel Oliansky. Premiere date: 3/19/75. Second show: 3/26/75. Third show: 4/16/75.
Producer William Sackheim

Production Company Universal Television in association with NBC-TV
Director Various
Writer Various
CAST

Atty. Murray Stone	Judd Hirsch
Michael	Fiona Guinness
Van Lorn	Alex Nicol
Hiller	Gerald McRaney

Lawmen *see* The CBS Thursday/Friday Night Movies

633 The Lawrence Welk Show

Syndicated
Program Type Music/Dance
Began on 7/2/55 as "The Dodge Dancing Party." In syndication since 9/71. 60 minutes. Season premiere: 9/74. Lawrence Welk is M.C. and host. Weekly.
Executive Producer Sam J. Lutz
Producer James Hobson
Distributor Don Fedderson Productions, Inc.
Director James Hobson
Musical Director George Cates
Host Lawrence Welk
Regular Anaconi; Ava Barber; Bobby Burgess; Henry Cuesta; Dick Dale; Ken Delo; Arthur Duncan; Gail Farrell; Jo Feeney; Myron Floren; Sandi Griffiths; Charlotte Harris; Clay Hart; Larry Hooper; Guy Hovis; Radna Hovis; Jack Imel; Cissy King; Bob Lido; Mary Lou Metzger; Tom Netherton; Bob Ralston; Jim Roberts; Tanya Welk; Norma Zimmer

634 Legacy

NBC
Program Type Documentary/Special
Special. 300 years of Dutch painting. 60 minutes. Premiere date: 1/21/73. Repeat date: 6/1/75. Music performed by David Amram.
Producer Doris Ann
Production Company NBC Television Religious Programs Unit
Director Joseph Vadala
Host Alexander Scourby
Camera Joseph Vadala

635 The Legend of Lizzie Borden

Special Movie Presentation   ABC
Program Type TV Movie
Based on the 1892 Fall River, Massachusetts ax murders. 120 minutes. Premiere date: 2/10/75. Repeat date: 8/25/75.
Producer George Le Maire
Production Company Paramount Television
Director Paul Wendkos
Writer William Bast
CAST

Lizzie Borden	Elizabeth Montgomery
Emma Borden	Katherine Helmond
Bridget Sullivan	Fionnuala Flanagan
Hosea Knowlton	Ed Flanders
George Robinson	Don Porter
Andrew Borden	Fritz Weaver
Sylvia Knowlton	Bonnie Bartlett
Dr. Bowen	John Beal
Abby Borden	Helen Craig
Mayor	Alan Hewitt
Alice	Gail Kobe

636 The Legendary Curse of the Hope Diamond

A Smithsonian Institution Special   CBS
Program Type Drama
Special. 60 minutes. Premiere date: 3/27/75. Dramatization of the history of the Hope Diamond. Epilogue and summation by S. Dillon Ripley. Coordinator for the Smithsonian: Nazaret Cherkezian.
Executive Producer George Lefferts
Producer Delbert Mann
Production Company Wolper Productions and The Smithsonian Institution
Director Delbert Mann
Writer George Lefferts
Narrator Rod Serling
CAST

Edward McLean	Bradford Dillman
Evalyn Walsh McLean	Samantha Eggar
Marie Antoinette	Claudine Longet
Willem Fals	Oscar Homolka
Louis XVI	Robert Clary
Hendrik	Robert Wolders
Mummie	Martha Scott
Harriet Goelet	Joan Tetzel
Lord Hope	Christopher Gary
"Monsignor"	Henry Wilcoxon
Herbert Hoover	Eric Lord
Cartier	Maurice Marsac
Pres. Harding	Harry Stanton
Maggie	Donna Sullivan
Beaulieu	Galen Thompson
Princess Lamballe	Ren Turner
Attendant	Maurina Maubert
Dancer	Elaine Boulton
Albert Fall	Jim Boles
May Yohe	Lezlie Dalton
Eliason	Edgar Daniels
Butler	John McKee
Chief Justice Hughes	William Remick

L'eggs World Series of Tennis *see* World Series of Women's Tennis

637 L'Enfance du Christ

CBS
Program Type Religious Program
CBS News religious special. Repeat of December 1964 program. The oratorio by Hector Berlioz; orchestra conducted by Alfredo Antonini. 60 minutes. Repeat date: 12/22/74.
Executive Producer Pamela Ilott
Production Company CBS News

L'Enfance du Christ *Continued*
Director Jerome Schnur
Host Madeleine Carroll

638   Let's Grow a Garden   PBS
Program Type Educational
24 programs. 30 minutes. Weekly. Premiere date: 6/30/75.
Executive Producer Carol Brodtrick
Producer Carol Brodtrick
Production Company WMUL/Huntington, West Virginia
Director Don Harvey; Adrian Lawson
Writer Carol Brodtrick
Host Matt Hanna; Carol Brodtrick

639   Let's Make a Deal   ABC
Program Type Game Show
30 minutes. Monday-Friday. Continuous. Premiere date: 12/63 (on NBC). Moved to ABC 12/30/68.
Executive Producer Stefan Hatos
Production Company Hatos-Hall Productions
Director Joseph Behar
Host Monty Hall
Announcer Jay Stewart
Model Carol Merrill

640   Let's Make a Deal   Syndicated
Program Type Game Show
30 minute evening version of daytime show. Twice weekly. Premiere date: 9/71.
Executive Producer Stefan Hatos
Production Company Hatos-Hall Productions
Director Joseph Behar
Host Monty Hall
Announcer Jay Stewart
Model Carol Merrill

641   Let's Switch!
Tuesday/Wednesday Movie of the Week ABC
Program Type TV Movie
90 minutes. Premiere date: 1/7/75. Repeat date: 7/22/75. Based on a story by Peter Lefcourt.
Producer Bruce Johnson
Production Company Universal Television
Director Alan Rafkin
Writer Peter Lefcourt; Ruth Court Flippen; Andy Chubby Williams; Sid Arthur
CAST
Lacy Colbert .... Barbara Eden
Kate Fleming .... Barbara Feldon
Sidney King .... George Furth
Ross Daniels .... Richard Schaal
Randy Colbert .... Pat Harrington
Morgan Ames .... Barra Grant
Alice Wright ....Penny Marshall
Linette Robbin .... Joyce Van Patten
Flo Moore ....Kaye Stevens
Greta Bennett .... Barbara Cason

LaRue Williams .... Ron Glass
Inez Dulin .... Bella Bruck
Bill Ballance .... Bill Ballance
Missy .... Tanya Matarazzo
Rex .... Jerry Bishop

642   Letters from Three Lovers
Tuesday/Wednesday Movie of the Week ABC
Program Type TV Movie
90 minutes. Premiere date: 10/3/73. Repeat date: 12/24/74. Sequel to "The Lovers" telecast in March 1973 on the "Movie of the Week." Trilogy consists of "Dear Vincent," "Dear Monica," "Dear Maggie."
Producer Aaron Spelling; Leonard Goldberg
Production Company Spelling/Goldberg Production
Director John Erman
Writer Ann Marcus; Jerome Kass
CAST
Monica ....June Allyson
Jack ....Ken Berry
Maggie .... Juliet Mills
Angie .... Belinda Montgomery
Vincent .... Martin Sheen
Bob .... Robert Sterling
Joshua ....Barry Sullivan
Sam .... Lyle Waggoner
Messenger .... Lawrence Rosenberg
The Postman .... Henry Jones

643   Liberty Bowl
ABC Sports Special   ABC
Program Type Sports
16th Liberty Bowl in Memphis, Tennessee. Live coverage. 12/16/75. Maryland Terrapins versus Tennessee Volunteers.
Executive Producer Roone Arledge
Production Company ABC Sports
Announcer Keith Jackson

644   Life at the End of the World
The Undersea World of Jacques Cousteau
                                                ABC
Program Type Documentary/Special
Special. Filmed in the South Atlantic Chilean channels and off Tierra del Fuego. 60 minutes. Premiere date: 11/14/74. (Season premiere of series.) With Jacques Cousteau and the crew of the *Calypso.*
Executive Producer Jacques Cousteau; Marshall Flaum
Producer Andy White
Production Company A Marshall Flaum Production in association with The Cousteau Society and MPC Metromedia Producers Corporation and ABC News
Director Philippe Cousteau
Writer Andy White
Host Jacques Cousteau

Narrator Joseph Campanella
Photographer Philippe Cousteau

645 The Life of Leonardo da Vinci   PBS
Program Type Documentary/Special
Five-part series. Weekly. 90 minutes. Premiered
in 1972. Repeat dates: 11/20/74; 7/20/75. Pre-
sented in the United States by WGBH/Boston:
Henry Morgenthau, producer. Series made possi-
ble by a grant from Alitalia.
Production Company RAI Radiotelevisione Ital-
iana - ORTF - TVE Instituto Luce
Director Renato Castellani
Host Ben Gazzara
CAST
The Guide .... Guilio Bosetti
Leonardo da Vince (as an adult) .... Phillipe Leroy

646 Lights, Camera, Monty!   ABC
Program Type Comedy/Variety
Special. Filmed on the Universal Studios back
lot. 60 minutes. Premiere date: 4/24/75.
Producer Bob Wynn
Production Company Monty Hall Enterprises
Director Bob Wynn
Writer Bob Arnott; Coslough Johnson; Marilyn
Hall
Musical Director Harper MacKay
Host Monty Hall
Special Guest Star Steve Lawrence
Guest Stars Michele Lee; Marty Feldman; Len-
non Sisters; Carl Jablonski Dancers

647 Lilias, Yoga and You   PBS
Program Type Exercise Program
30 minutes. Monday-Thursday. Season
premiere: 9/23/74. Series made possible by
grants from the Corporation for Public Broad-
casting, the Ford Foundation, and Public Televi-
sion Stations.
Executive Producer Charles Vaughan
Producer Len Goorian
Production Company WCET/Cincinnati
Director Bill Gustin
Writer Lilias Folan
Teacher Lilias Folan

648 Lily   ABC
Program Type Comedy/Variety
Special. 60 minutes. Premiere date: 2/21/75.
Executive Producer Irene Pinn
Producer Jane Wagner; Lorne Michaels
Production Company Omnipotent, Inc.
Director John Moffitt
Writer Sybil Adelman and Barbara Gallagher;
Gloria Banta and Pat Nardo; Stuart Birnbaum
and Matt Newman; Lorne Michaels; Marilyn
Miller; Earl Pomerantz; Rosie Ruthchild; Lily
Tomlin; Jane Wagner

Musical Director Peter Matz
Host Lily Tomlin
Costume Designer Ray Aghayan
Guests Richard Dreyfuss; Frank Blair; Dr.
Demento; Valri Bromfield; Archie Hahn;
Lady Rowlands; Billy Zuckert; Benji (the dog)

649 Lily Tomlin   ABC
Program Type Comedy/Variety
Special. 60 minutes. Premiere date: 7/25/75. Re-
peat date: 9/6/75.
Executive Producer Irene Pinn
Producer Jane Wagner; Lorne Michaels
Production Company Omnipotent, Inc.
Director Jay Sandrich
Writer Jane Wagner; Lorne Michaels; Ann El-
der; Christopher Guest; Earl Pomerantz; Jim
Rusk; Lily Tomlin; Rod Warren; George
Yanok
Musical Director Peter Matz
Choreographer Walter Painter
Host Lily Tomlin
Special Guest Star John Byner
Guests Betty Beaird; Valri Bromfield; Christo-
pher Guest; Doris Roberts; Richard Tomlin;
Gary Weis; Bill Zuckert

650 The Little Drummer Boy   NBC
Program Type Animated Film
Special. Title song by Katherine Davis; Henry
Onorati; Harry Simeone. New songs by Maury
Laws; Jules Bass. 30 minutes. Seventh consecu-
tive year on television. Repeat date: 12/15/74.
Producer Arthur Rankin, Jr.; Jules Bass
Production Company Videocraft-International
Production in association with NBC-TV
Director Arthur Rankin, Jr.; Jules Bass
Writer Romeo Muller
Narrator Greer Garson
VOICES
Haramed .... Jose Ferrer
Aaron, The Little Drummer Boy .... Teddy Eccles
Ali/Other Voices .... Paul Frees
Additional Voices The Vienna Choir Boys

651 Little House on the Prairie   NBC
Program Type Drama
Based on "Little House" books by Laura Ingalls
Wilder. 60 minutes. Wednesday. Premiere date:
9/11/74. Set in southwestern Minnesota in 1878.
Carrie Ingalls is played by twin sisters Lindsay
and Sidney Greenbush.
Executive Producer Ed Friendly; Michael Lan-
don
Producer John Hawkins; Winston Miller
Production Company NBC Television Produc-
tion in association with Ed Friendly
Director Bill Claxton; Alf Kjellin; Leo Penn; Mi-
chael Landon
Writer Various

Little House on the Prairie *Continued*
Costume Designer (for men) Andrew Mat Yasi
Costume Designer (for women) Richalene Kelsay
CAST
Charles Ingalls .... Michael Landon
Caroline Ingalls .... Karen Grassle
Mary Ingalls .... Melissa Sue Anderson
Laura Ingalls .... Melissa Gilbert
Carrie Ingalls   Lindsay Greenbush; Sidney Greenbush

652   The Little Mermaid   CBS
Program Type Animated Film
Special. Adapted from the fairy tale by Hans
Christian Andersen. Music composed by Ron
Goodwin. 30 minutes. Premiere date: 2/4/74.
Repeat date: 1/31/75.
Producer Christine LaRocque; Murray Shostak
Production Company Reader's Digest Presenta-
tion in association with Potterton Productions,
Inc.
Director Peter Sander
Writer Peter Sander; Christine LaRocque
Musical Director Ron Goodwin
Narrator Richard Chamberlain

653   Locusts
Tuesday/Wednesday Movie of the Week   ABC
Program Type TV Movie
90 minutes. Premiere date: 10/9/74. Repeat
date: 8/27/75. Filmed on location in Alberta,
Canada.
Executive Producer Michael Donohew
Producer Herbert Wright
Production Company Carson/Paramount Pro-
duction
Director Richard T. Heffron
Writer Robert Malcolm Young
CAST
Amos Fletcher .... Ben Johnson
Donny Fletcher .... Ron Howard
Claire Fletcher .... Katherine Helmond
Cissy Fletcher .... Lisa Gerritsen
Janet .... Belinda Balaski
Aaron .... Rance Howard
Cully .... Robert Cruse
Ace .... William Speerstra
Klauser .... Bob Koons
Tom .... Robert Hoffman

654   The Log of the Black Pearl
NBC Nights at the Movies   NBC
Program Type TV Movie
120 minutes. Premiere date: 1/4/75. Repeat
date: 5/31/75.
Executive Producer Jack Webb
Producer William Stark
Production Company Mark VII Productions and
Universal Television
Director Andrew V. McLaglen
Writer Harold Jack Bloom

CAST
Capt. Fitz .... Ralph Bellamy
Christopher Sand .... Kiel Martin
Lila Bristol .... Anne Archer
Jock Roper .... Jack Kruschen
Devlin .... Glenn Corbett
Kort .... John Alderson
Additional Cast Henry Wilcoxon; Edward Faulkner;
Pedro Armendariz, Jr.; Jose Angel Espinosa

655   Look Up and Live   CBS
Program Type Educational
Began on the CBS Television Network in 1954.
30 minutes. Continuous.
Executive Producer Pamela Ilott
Producer Various
Production Company CBS News Presentation

656   Lorne Greene's Last of the Wild
                                                 Syndicated
Program Type Animal Documentary
30 minutes. Weekly. Premiere: 9/74. Based on
"Animal Lexicon" series created and produced
by Ivan Tors.
Executive Producer Skip Steloff
Producer Julian J. Ludwig
Production Company Ivan Tors Productions
Distributor Heritage Enterprises, Inc.
Director Various
Writer Ivan Tors; Anthony Jay
Narrator Lorne Greene

657   Love Among the Ruins
ABC Theatre   ABC
Program Type Drama
120 minutes. Premiere date: 3/6/75. Music by
John Barry; lyrics by Don Black.
Producer Allan Davis
Production Company ABC Circle Films
Director George Cukor
Writer James Costigan
CAST
Jessica Medlicott .... Katherine Hepburn
Sir Arthur Granville-Jones, K.C. .... Laurence Olivier
J. F. Devine, K.C. .... Colin Blakely
Druce .... Richard Pearson
Fanny Pratt .... Joan Sims
Alfred Pratt .... Leigh Lawson
Hermione Davis .... Gwen Nelson
The Judge .... Robert Harris
Additional Cast Peter Reeves; John Blythe; Arthur
Hawlett; John Dunbar; Frank Forsyth; John Heller

658   Love Nest
Comedy Special   CBS
Program Type Comedy
30 minutes. Pilot film. Premiere date: 3/14/75.
Sequel to 1973–74 season pilot. Set in Florida
trailer camp.
Producer Saul Ilson; Ernest Chambers

Production Company Ilson-Chambers Productions
Director Mel Ferber
Writer Austin Kalish; Irma Kalish
CAST
Jenny Ludlow .... Florida Friebus
Ned Cooper ....Charles Lane
Mary Francis .... Alice Nunn
Dickie Ewing .... Burt Mustin
Mort .... Dana Elcar
Dorothy .... Dee Carroll

659   Love of Life   CBS
Program Type Daytime Drama
Second longest running daytime drama, it premiered on 9/24/51 with regular 15-minute shows. Present format: 4/14/58. 25 minutes. Monday-Friday. Continuous. Set in "Rosehill, U.S.A." Theme song, "The Life That You Live" by Carey Gold. Cast information: spring 1975. Margaret De Priest replaced headwriters Claire Labine and Paul Mayer.
Executive Producer Darryl Hickman
Producer Jean Arley
Production Company CBS Television
Director Larry Auerbach; Jerry Evans
Head Writer Claire Labine and Paul Avila Mayer; Margaret De Priest
Announcer Ken Roberts
CAST
Linda Crawford .... Romola Robb Allrud
Hank Latimer ....David Carlton
Caroline Aleata .... Deborah Courtney
David Hart ....Brian Farrell
Dr. Paul Bryson .... Earle Hyman
Betsy Crawford .... Elizabeth Kemp
Rick Latimer ....Jerry Lacy
Felicia Flemming ....Pamela Lincoln
Prof. James Crawford .... Kenneth McMillan
Charles Lamont .... Jonathan Moore
Vanessa Dale Sterling ....Audrey Peters
Johnny Prentiss .... Trip Randall
Ben Harper .... Christopher Reeve
Sarah Caldwell .... Joanna Roos
Diana Lamont .... Diane Rousseau
Arlene Lovett ....Birgitta Tolksdorf
Bruce Sterling .... Ron Tomme
Meg Dale Hart .... Tudi Wiggins
Jamie Rollins ....Ray Wise

660   The Loyal Opposition
NBC News Special   NBC
Program Type Documentary/Special
Special. 60 minutes. Panel discussion with Democrats. Premiere date: 3/2/75.
Producer Frank Jordan
Production Company NBC News
Anchor Douglas Kiker
Panel Catherine Mackin; Ray Scherer

661   Lucas Tanner   NBC
Program Type Drama
Based on TV movie shown 5/8/74. 60 minutes. Wednesday. Premiere date: 9/11/74. Last show: 9/3/75. Set in Harry S. Truman Memorial High School, Webster Grove, Missouri. John Randolph replaced Rosemary Murphy as school superintendent.
Executive Producer David Victor
Producer Jay Benson
Production Company A Groverton Productions Ltd. in association with Universal Television and NBC-TV
Director Various
Writer Various
CAST
Lucas Tanner .... David Hartman
Mrs. Margaret Blumenthal .... Rosemary Murphy
Hamilton ....John Randolph
Glendon ....Robbie Rist
Jaytee ....Alan Abelew
Terry .... Kimberly Beck
Cindy .... Trish Soodik
Michael .... Michael Dwight-Smith

662   Lucia   PBS
Program Type Feature Film
Special. 160 minute-film; 50 minutes of historical background about 1969 film made in Cuba. Premiere date on PBS: 2/27/75.

663   A Lucille Ball Special Starring Lucille Ball and Dean Martin   CBS
Program Type Comedy
Special. 60 minutes. Premiere date: 3/1/75.
Executive Producer Lucille Ball
Producer Gary Morton
Production Company Lucille Ball Productions, Inc.
Director Jack Donohue
Writer Robert O'Brien
Musical Director Nelson Riddle
CAST
Lucy Collins .... Lucille Ball
Dean Martin .... Dean Martin
Gus Mitchell ....Jackie Coogan
Max Vogel ....Bruce Gordon
Eddie ....Joey Forman
Antonio .... Gino Conforti
Packy West .... Paul Picerni
Gladys .... Vanda Barra
Chuck Murdock .... Lee Delano

664   Mac
ABC Comedy Special   ABC
Program Type Comedy
Special. Created by Lila Garrett. 30 minutes. Premiere date: 5/28/75.
Executive Producer Byron Paul
Producer Lila Garrett
Director Robert Morse

Mac *Continued*
Writer Lila Garrett; George Bloom
CAST
MacLeish .... Dick Van Dyke
Hal Stark ....Shelley Berman
Augie ....Jimmy Baio
Suzy ....Marcia Rodd
Adcock ....John Myhers
Waiter .... Joe Wong

665   The Mac Davis Show   NBC
Program Type Comedy/Variety
60 minutes. Thursday. Premiere date: 12/19/74.
Last show: 5/22/75.
Executive Producer Sandy Gallin
Producer Arnie Rosen; Bob Ellison
Production Company Dream, Inc.
Director Tim Kiley
Writer Stan Burns; Don Hinckley; Arthur
  Julian; Mike Marmer
Musical Director Mike Post
Host Mac Davis

MacKenna's Gold *see* The CBS
  Thursday/Friday Night Movies

666   Macy's Thanksgiving Day Parade
                                          NBC
Program Type Documentary/Special
48th annual Macy's Parade from New York
City. 120 minutes. 11/28/74.
Producer Dick Schneider
Production Company NBC Television Network
Director Dick Schneider
Host David Hartman; Karen Grassle

**667   Macy's Thanksgiving Day Parade
Preview**   NBC
Program Type Documentary/Special
60 minutes. 11/28/74. Preview of 48th annual
Macy's parade from New York City.
Producer Dick Schneider
Production Company NBC Television Network
Director Dick Schneider
Host Rita Moreno; Mason Reese

668   Magazine   CBS
Program Type News Magazine
CBS News daytime series. 60 minutes. Premiere
date: 5/2/74. 1974–75 season: five programs -
10/22/74; 12/17/74; 1/29/75; 2/26/75; 4/2/75.
Executive Producer Perry Wolff
Producer Phyllis Bosworth; Judy Crichton; Vern
  Diamond; Mary Drayne; Irina Posner
Production Company CBS News
Director Vern Diamond
Host Sylvia Chase; Hughes Rudd

669   Maggie and the Beautiful Machine
                                          PBS
Program Type Exercise Program
30 munutes. Weekly. Premiere date: 7/11/72.
12-part series. Repeats shown 1974–75.
Producer Rick Hauser
Production Company WGBH/Boston
Director David Atwood
Instructor Maggie Lettwin

**670   The Magical Mystery Trip Through
Little Red's Head**
ABC Afterschool Specials   ABC
Program Type Animated Film
Special. Musical cartoon based on "Little Red
Riding Hood." Music by Dean Elliott; lyrics by
Johnny Bradford. 60 minutes. Repeat date:
12/11/74.
Producer David H. DePatie; Friz Freleng
Production Company Depatie-Freleng Enter-
  prises
Director Herbert Klein
Writer Larry Spiegel
VOICES
Timer .... Lennie Weinrib
Carol .... Diane Murphy
Larry .... Ike Eisenmann
Little Red .... Sarah Kennedy
Mother/Adeline/Diane .... Joan Gerber

671   The Magnificent Marble Machine
                                          NBC
Program Type Game Show
30 minutes. Monday-Friday. Premiere date:
7/7/75. Continuous.
Executive Producer Robert Noah
Producer Bob Synes
Production Company Merrill Heatter-Bob Quig-
  ley Productions
Director Jerome Shaw
Host Art James
Announcer Johnny Gilbert

672   Magnificent Monsters of the Deep
                                          CBS
Program Type Animal Documentary
Special. 60 minutes. Filmed in the Gulf of San
Matias in Southern Argentina (Patagonia). Fea-
turing Dr. Roger Payne of the New York Zoo-
logical Society, and his family studying the
southern right whale. Premiere date: 4/30/75.
Producer Aubrey Buxton
Production Company Survival Anglia Ltd., in as-
  sociation with the World Wildlife Fund
Writer Colin Willock
Photographers Des Bartlett; Jen Bartlett
Narrator Orson Welles

673 Make a Wish   ABC
Program Type Children's Show
25 minutes. Sunday. Premiere date: 9/12/71.
Season premiere: 9/8/74. Information series for
children.
Executive Producer Lester Cooper
Production Company ABC News Public Affairs
Director Lester Cooper
Writer Lester Cooper
Host Tom Chapin

674 The Making of the President, 1972
                              Syndicated
Program Type Documentary/Special
Based on book by Theodore H. White. 90
minutes. Premiere: 5/75. Introduction by Theo-
dore White.
Producer Al Wasserman
Production Company Time-Life Television
Writer Theodore White

675 Making Things Grow   PBS
Program Type News Magazine
30 minutes. Weekly. Premiered in 1970. Avail-
able through the Public Television Library. Se-
ries made possible by a grant from Clairol.
Producer Richard Hauser
Production Company WGBH/Boston
Director Richard Hauser
Host Thalassa Cruso

**676 Male Menopause: The Pause That
Perplexes**   PBS
Program Type Documentary/Special
Special. 60 minutes. Premiere date: 6/24/74. Re-
peat dates: 9/16/74; 6/27/75.
Producer Richard V. Brown
Production Company NPACT (National Public
  Affairs Center for Television)
Writer Michael De Guzman
Host William Windom
Guests Anne Meara; Oscar Brand

The Man *see* The ABC Sunday Night
  Movie

677 Man Builds, Man Destroys   PBS
Program Type Documentary/Special
13-part series on environmental problems composed of new and old programs. 30 minutes.
Weekly. Premiere date: 7/4/73. Season
premiere: 7/9/75.
Executive Producer Peter Hollander
Production Company New York State Department of Education and United Nations Television
Distributor Great Plains National ITV Library

Man in the Wilderness *see* The ABC
  Sunday Night Movie; Special Movie
  Presentation

678 The Man of Destiny
Hollywood Television Theatre   PBS
Program Type Comedy
60 minutes. Repeat date: 6/26/75.
Executive Producer Norman Lloyd
Production Company KCET/Los Angeles
Director Joseph Hardy
Writer George Bernard Shaw
                   CAST
Napoleon Bonaparte .... Stacy Keach
Mysterious Woman .... Samantha Eggar
Lieutenant .... William H. Bassett
Innkeeper .... Gino Conforti

679 Man on the Outside
The ABC Sunday Night Movie   ABC
Program Type TV Movie
120 minutes. Premiere date: 6/29/75.
Executive Producer David Victor
Producer George Eckstein
Production Company Universal Television
Director Boris Sagal
Writer Larry Cohen
                   CAST
Wade Griffin .... Lorne Greene
Nora ....Lorraine Gary
Mark ....Lee H. Montgomery
Ellen .... Jean Allison
Gerald .... James Olson
Ames .... William C. Watson
Sandra Ames ....Brooke Bundy
Lt. Matthews .... Ken Swofford
Detective ....Alan Fudge
Scully .... Bruce Kirby
Arnold ....Charles Knox Robinson
Benny .... Garry Walberg
Stella ....Ruth McDevitt
Ruben .... Scat Man Crothers

680 The Man Without a Country ABC
Program Type Drama
Special. Adapted from the book by Edward Ever-
ett Hale. 90 minutes. Premiere date: 4/24/73.
Repeat date: 12/6/74.
Producer Norman Rosemont
Production Company A Norman Rosemont En-
  terprises, Inc. Production
Director Delbert Mann
Writer Sidney Carroll
Costume Designer Noel Taylor
                   CAST
Philip Nolan .... Cliff Robertson
Frederick Ingham ....Beau Bridges
Arthur Danforth .... Peter Strauss
Lt. Cmdr. Vaughan .... Robert Ryan
Col. Morgan .... Walter Abel
Slave .... Geoffrey Holder
Secy. of the Navy .... Shepperd Strudwick

The Man Without a Country *Continued*
Aaron Burr .... John Cullum
Mrs. Griff .... Patricia Elliott
Counsel .... Laurence Guittard

The Manchurian Candidate *see NBC Nights at the Movies*

681   Mandolinist: Frank Wakefield   PBS
Program Type Music/Dance
Special. The bluegrass music of Frank Wakefield taped in Pittsburgh in 1971. 30 minutes. Premiere date: 3/26/73. Repeat date: 1/22/75.
Producer James Sweenie
Production Company WQED/Pittsburgh
Director David Chen

682   The Manhattan Transfer   CBS
Program Type Comedy/Variety
Four-part summer series. 60 minutes. Sunday. Premiere date: 8/10/75. Last show: 8/31/75. The Manhattan Transfer members: Tim Hauser; Laurel Masse; Alan Paul; Janis Siegel. Archie Hahn appears as Dougie Dick in comedy sequences.
Executive Producer Aaron Russo
Executive Producer Bernard Rothman; Jack Wohl
Production Company Aaron Russo Productions, Inc. in association with Rothman-Wohl Productions, Inc.
Director Ron Field; Tom Trbovich
Writer Sidney Reznick; Jeffrey Barron
Musical Director Ira Newborn

683   The Manhunter   CBS
Program Type Crime Drama
60 minutes. Wednesday. Premiere date: 9/11/74. Last show: 4/9/75. Based on pilot "The Manhunter" shown on the "CBS Tuesday Night Movies" 2/26/74.
Executive Producer Quinn Martin
Producer Sam C. Rolfe
Production Company Quinn Martin Productions
CAST
Dave Barrett .... Ken Howard
Paul Tate .... Robert Hogan

684   Mannix   CBS
Program Type Crime Drama
60 minutes. Sunday. Premiere date: 9/16/67. Season premiere: 9/22/75. Last show: 8/27/75.
Executive Producer Bruce Geller
Producer Ivan Goff; Ben Roberts
Production Company Paramount Pictures Corporation for CBS-TV.
CAST
Joe Mannix .... Mike Connors
Peggy .... Gail Fisher

685   Many Unhappy Returns - A Report on Your Taxes
NBC News Special   NBC
Program Type Documentary/Special
Special. 60 minutes. Premiere date: 4/6/75
Producer Wallace Westfeldt
Production Company NBC News
Director Stanley Losak
Anchor David Brinkley

686   Marcus Welby   ABC
Program Type Drama
60 minutes. Tuesday. Premiere date: 9/23/69. Season premiere: 9/10/74. Set in Marcus Welby's home and in the Family Practice Center, Lang Memorial Hospital, Santa Monica, California.
Executive Producer David Victor
Producer David J. O'Connell
Production Company Universal Television for the ABC Television Network
Director Various
Writer Various
CAST
Dr. Marcus Welby .... Robert Young
Dr. Steven Kiley .... James Brolin
Consuelo Lopez .... Elena Verdugo
Kathleen Faverty .... Sharon Gless

687   The Mark of Zorro
Tuesday/Wednesday Movie of the Week; The ABC Summer Movie   ABC
Program Type TV Movie
90 minutes. Premiere date: 10/29/74. Repeat date: 8/22/75. Based on a book by Johnston McCulley.
Producer Robert C. Thompson; Rodrick Paul
Production Company 20th Century-Fox Television Production
Director Don McDougall
Writer Brian Taggert
CAST
Don Diego Vega/Zorro .... Frank Langella
Capt. Esteban .... Ricardo Montalban
Don Alejandro Vega .... Gilbert Roland
Inez Quintero .... Louise Sorel
Don Luis Quintero .... Robert Middleton
Teresa .... Anne Archer
Fray Filipe .... Tom Lacy
Isabella Vega .... Yvonne DeCarlo
Sgt. Gonzales .... George Cervera, Jr.
Duenna Maria .... Inez Perez
Rodrigo .... John Rose
Antonio .... Jay Hammer
Miguel .... Alfonso Tafoya
Dock Worker .... Robert Carricart

688   Markheim   PBS
Program Type Music/Dance
Special. One-act opera by Carlisle Floyd based on a short story by Robert Louis Stevenson. Uni-

versity of Washington Sinfonietta conducted by Samuel Krachmalnick. 70 minutes. Premiere date: 6/11/75.
Executive Producer Robert Hagopian
Production Company KCTS/Seattle in cooperation with the School of Music of the University of Washington
Director Ralph Rosinbum; Ronald Ciro
Musical Director Samuel Krachmalnick
Scenic Designer Dick Kinsman
CAST
Markheim ....Leon Liechner
Creech .... Robert Julien
Tess ....Carol Webster
Mysterious Stranger .... Larry Scalf

689 Marlo Thomas and Friends in Free to Be ... You and Me   ABC
Program Type Children's Show
Special. Based on record of the same name. 60 minutes. Premiere date: 3/11/74. Repeat date: 1/12/75. Film sequences directed by Len Steckler. Animation sequences directed by Fred Wolf. Puppet and animation voices directed by Alan Alda. 18 songs, stories and poems.
Producer Marlo Thomas; Carole Hart
Production Company A Free to Be Production in association with Murakami-Wolf
Director Bill Davis
Writer Various
Musical Director Stephen Lawrence
Choreographer Donald McKayle
Costume Designer Frank Thompson
Stars Alan Alda; Harry Belafonte; Mel Brooks; Rita Coolidge; Billy DeWolfe; Roberta Flack; Rosey Grier; Dustin Hoffman; Michael Jackson; Kris Kristofferson; Bobby Morse; The New Seekers; Tom Smothers; Marlo Thomas; Cicely Tyson; Voices of East Harlem; Dionne Warwicke

690 Marshall Efron's Illustrated, Simplified and Painless Sunday School   CBS
Program Type Children's Show
Primarily reruns of series in 1973–74 season; four new shows. 30 minutes. Sunday. Season premiere: 12/15/74.
Executive Producer Pamela Ilott
Producer Ted Holmes
Production Company CBS News
Director Alvin Thaler
Writer Marshall Efron; Alfa-Betty Olsen
Narrator Marshall Efron

691 Martin Agronsky: Evening Edition   PBS
Program Type Interview/Discussion
30 minutes. Monday-Friday. Continuous. Series made possible by grants from the Corporation for Public Broadcasting, the Ford Foundation, and Public Television Stations.
Producer John Larkin
Production Company WETA/Washington, D.C.
Host Martin Agronsky

692 Mary Jane Grows Up: Marijuana in the 70's
NBC News Special   NBC
Program Type Documentary/Special
Special. 60 minutes. Premiere date: 8/3/75.
Producer Joan Konner
Production Company NBC News
Director Joan Konner
Writer Joan Konner
Reporter Jack Perkins

Mary, Queen of Scots *see* NBC Nights at the Movies

693 The Mary Tyler Moore Show   CBS
Program Type Comedy
Set in Minneapolis, at WJM-TV. Created by James L. Brooks; Allan Burns. 30 minutes. Saturday. Premiere date: 9/19/70. Season premiere: 9/14/74.
Executive Producer James L. Brooks; Allan Burns
Producer Ed. Weinberger; Stan Daniels
Production Company MTM Enterprises, Inc.
Director Various
Writer Various
CAST
Mary Richards .... Mary Tyler Moore
Lou Grant ....Ed Asner
Ted Baxter .... Ted Knight
Murray Slaughter .... Gavin MacLeod
Georgette ....Georgia Engel
Sue Ann Nivens
(The Happy Homemaker) ....Betty White
Phyllis Lindstrom ....Cloris Leachman

694 M*A*S*H   CBS
Program Type Comedy
Based on the 1970 motion picture "M*A*S*H." The 4077th unit during the Korean War. 30 minutes. Tuesday. Premiere date: 9/17/72. Season premiere: 9/10/74.
Producer Gene Reynolds; Larry Gelbart
Production Company 20th Century-Fox Television
Director Various
Writer Various
CAST
Hawkeye .... Alan Alda
Trapper John ....Wayne Rogers
Lt. Col. Henry Blake .... McLean Stevenson
Hot Lips Houlihan .... Loretta Swit
Maj. Frank Burns .... Larry Linville

M*A*S*H *Continued*

Radar .... Gary Burghoff
Klinger ....Jamie Farr
Father Mulcahy .... William Christopher

M*A*S*H (feature film) *see* The CBS Thursday/Friday Night Movies

695   Masquerade Party   Syndicated
Program Type Game Show
New evening version of show originally produced 7/14/52. 30 minutes. Weekly. Premiere: 9/74.
Executive Producer Stefan Hatos; Monty Hall
Producer Alan Gilbert
Production Company Hatos-Hall Productions
Distributor 20th Century-Fox Television
Director Joseph Behar
Writer Alan Gilbert; Bernie Gould; Nat Ligerman; Roger Wright
Host Richard Dawson
Announcer Jay Stewart
Regular Bill Bixby; Lee Meriwether; Nipsey Russell

696   Mass–A Theatre Piece for Singers, Players and Dancers
Theater in America   PBS
Program Type Music/Dance
Written by Leonard Bernstein. Taped live at the Vienna Konzerthaus; performed by students of Yale University and a Viennese choir in a version conceived by John Mauceri. 120 minutes. Premiere date: 2/27/74. Repeat date: 4/23/75. Series made possible by grants from Exxon Corporation and the Corporation for Public Broadcasting.
Executive Producer Jac Venza; Harry J. Kraut
Producer David Griffiths
Production Company WNET/New York; Amberson Production
Director Brian Large
Host Hal Holbrook
CAST
Celebrant .... Michael Hume

697   Masterpiece Theatre   PBS
Program Type Drama
Umbrella title for a variety of programs which differ each season. 60 minute programs. Weekly. Premiere: 9/69. Season premiere: 10/6/74. Theme: "Fanfare" by J. J. Mouret. Produced in the United States by Joan Sullivan for WGBH/Boston. Programs made possible by a grant from the Mobil Oil Corporation. 1974–75 season: "Country Matters," "Murder Must Advertise," "The Nine Tailors," "Upstairs, Downstairs," "Vienna 1900: Games with Love and

Death." (*See* individual titles for credits.)
Host Alistair Cooke

698   Masters Tournament
CBS Sports Special   CBS
Program Type Sports
39th annual Masters Tournament. Televised live 4/12/75; 4/13/75 from the Augusta, Georgia National Golf Course.
Producer Frank Chirkinian
Production Company CBS Television Network Sports
Announcer Frank Glieber; Henry Longhurst; Pat Summerall; Jack Whitaker; Ben Wright

699   Match Game '74/'75   CBS
Program Type Game Show
Title changes yearly. 30 minutes. Monday-Friday. Continuous. Premiere date: 7/2/73. Six celebrities each week; three permanent.
Producer Ira Skutch
Production Company Goodson-Todman Production
Director Marc Breslow
Host Gene Rayburn
Announcer Johnny Olson
Regular Richard Dawson; Brett Somers; Charles Nelson Reilly

700   Matt Helm
Tuesday/Wednesday Movie of the Week ABC
Program Type TV Movie
Pilot for ABC series 1975–76 season. Premiere date: 5/7/75. Based on the novels of Donald Hamilton.
Executive Producer Irving Allen
Producer Buzz Kulik
Production Company Meadway Productions in association with Columbia Pictures Television
Director Buzz Kulik
Writer Sam H. Rolfe
CAST
Matt Helm .... Tony Franciosa
Sgt. James .... Val Bisoglio
Sgt. Hanrahan .... Gene Evans
Charlie Danberry .... Michael C. Gwynne
Col. Shawcross .... Patrick Macnee
Seki .... Hari Rhodes
Thomas McCauley III .... James Shigeta
Claire Kronski .... Laraine Stephens
Harry Paine .... John Vernon
Maggie Gantry .... Ann Turkel
Alice .... Catherine Bach
Drone .... Richard Butler
Taybor .... Frank Campanella
Champion .... Charles Picerni
Saleslady ....Joan Shawlee

701 A Matter of Justice: Lawyers and the Public Interest PBS
Program Type Documentary/Special
Special. 60 minutes. Premiere date: 6/16/75.
Production Company WNET/New York
Host Rep. Peter Rodino
Narrator Rep. Peter Rodino

702 A Matter of Wife ... and Death
NBC Nights at the Movies NBC
Program Type TV Movie
Based on the motion picture "Shamus" (1973).
90 minutes. Premiere date: 5/3/75. Repeat date:
7/14/75.
Producer Robert M. Weitman
Production Company Robert M. Weitman Production in association with NBC-TV and Columbia Pictures Television
Director Marvin Chomsky
Writer Don Ingalls
CAST
Shamus .... Rod Taylor
Lt. Vince Promuto .... Joe Santos
Heavy .... Dick Butkus
Springy .... Larry Block
Joe Ruby .... John Colicos
Carol .... Anne Archer
Snell .... Luke Askew
Paulie Baker .... Tom Drake
Dottore .... Cesare Danova
Helen Baker .... Anita Gillette
Blinky .... Eddie Firestone
Zelda .... Lynda Carter
Angie .... Marc Alaimo

703 Maude CBS
Program Type Comedy
Series created by Norman Lear. 30 minutes.
Monday. Premiere date: 9/12/72. Season
premiere: 9/9/74. Set in Tuckahoe, N.Y.
Executive Producer Norman Lear
Producer Rod Parker
Production Company Bud Yorkin-Norman Lear Tandem Productions
Director Hal Cooper
Writer Various
CAST
Maude Findlay .... Beatrice Arthur
Walter Findlay .... Bill Macy
Carol .... Adrienne Barbeau
Dr. Arthur Harmon .... Conrad Bain
Vivian Harmon .... Rue McClanahan
Mrs. Naugatuck .... Hermione Baddeley

704 McCloud
NBC Sunday Mystery Movie NBC
Program Type Crime Drama
Some episodes 90 minutes; others 120 minutes.
Shown irregularly. Based on "NBC World
Premiere: McCloud: Who Killed Miss U.S.A.?"
shown 2/17/70. Premiere date: 9/16/70. Season

premiere: 9/22/74. Set in New York City. Ken
Lynch and Diana Muldaur have recurring roles.
Executive Producer Glen A. Larson
Producer Michael Gleason; Ron Satlof
Production Company Universal Television
Director Various
Writer Various
CAST
Marshal Sam McCloud .... Dennis Weaver
Chief Peter B. Clifford .... J. D. Cannon
Sgt. Joe Broadhurst .... Terry Carter
Det. Grover .... Ken Lynch
Chris Coughlin .... Diana Muldaur

The McKenzie Break *see* The CBS Thursday/Friday Night Movies

705 McMillan & Wife
NBC Sunday Mystery Movie NBC
Program Type Crime Drama
Created by Leonard Stern. 120 minutes. Shown
irregularly. Premiere date: 9/29/71. Season
premiere: 9/29/74. Set in San Francisco.
Executive Producer Leonard B. Stern
Producer Jon Epstein
Production Company Universal Television and Talent Associates in association with NBC-TV
Director Various
Writer Various
CAST
Police Commissioner
Stewart McMillan .... Rock Hudson
Sally McMillan .... Susan Saint James
Sgt. Charles Enright .... John Schuck
Mildred .... Nancy Walker

The Mechanic *see* NBC Nights at the Movies

706 Medical Center CBS
Program Type Drama
Set in "University Medical Center." 60 minutes.
Monday. Premiere date: 9/24/69. Season
premiere: 9/9/74.
Executive Producer Frank Glicksman; Al C. Ward
Producer Don Brinkley
Production Company Alfra Productions in association with MGM
Director Various
Writer Various
CAST
Dr. Joe Gannon .... Chad Everett
Dr. Paul Lochner .... James Daly
Nurse Wilcox .... Audrey Totter

707 Meet the Press NBC
Program Type Interview/Discussion
Longest-running show on television. Four guest

Meet the Press *Continued*
interviewers each week. 30 minutes. Sunday. Premiere date: 11/6/47. Continuous.
Producer Lawrence E. Spivak
Production Company NBC News
Moderator Lawrence E. Spivak

708   **Mele Hawaii**   PBS
Program Type Music/Dance
Six-part series. 30 minutes. Weekly. Premiere date: 10/5/74. Covers Hawaii's "unwritten poetry:" chants.
Producer Martha Carrell
Production Company KHET/Honolulu in cooperation with the Hawaiian Music Foundation
Director Nino J. Martin
Writer Martha Carrell
Host Kaupena Wong; Charles K. L. Davis

709   **Memories of Prince Albert Hunt**
                                         PBS
Program Type Documentary/Special
Special. First super 8 film on national television. Premiere date: 4/7/75. Film produced under grants from the National Endowment for the Arts and the Corporation for Public Broadcasting. Profiles the life of musician Prince Albert Hunt.
Producer Ken Harrison
Production Company KERA/Dallas-Fort Worth
Director Ken Harrison

710   **A Memory of Two Mondays**
Theater in America   PBS
Program Type Drama
Play by Arthur Miller. 90 minutes. Premiere date: 1/28/71 on "NET Playhouse." Repeat date: 8/20/75. Introduction by Arthur Miller.
Executive Producer Jac Venza
Producer Jacqueline Babbin
Production Company WNET/New York
Director Paul Bogart
CAST
Bert .... Kristoffer Tabori
Gus .... Jack Warden
Larry .... George Grizzard
Agnes .... Estelle Parsons
Patricia .... Cathy Burns
Raymond .... Dick Van Patten
Frank .... Tony Lo Bianco
Tom .... J. D. Cannon
Mechanic .... Jerry Stiller
Jim .... Barnard Hughes
Kenneth .... Dan Hamilton
William .... Earl Hindman
Jerry .... Harvey Keitel
Unemployed Man .... Tom Rosqui
Mr. Eagle .... Donald Buka

711   **The Men Who Made the Movies**
                                         PBS
Program Type Interview/Discussion
Interviews with motion picture directors and film clips from their movies. Eight-part series. 60 minutes. Weekly. Repeat date: 9/25/74. Series made possible by a grant from the Eastman Kodak Company.
Producer Richard Schickel
Production Company WNET/New York
Director Richard Schickel
Writer Richard Schickel
Host Richard Schickel
Narrator Cliff Robertson
Guests Frank Capra; George Cukor; Howard Hawks; Alfred Hitchcock; Vincente Minnelli; King Vidor; Raoul Walsh; William Wellman

712   **Menominee**   PBS
Program Type Documentary/Special
Special. 60 minutes. Premiere date: 5/30/74. Repeat date: 3/24/75. The Menominee Indians of Wisconsin and their fight for self-determination.
Executive Producer Lee O'Brien
Producer Barry Stoner
Production Company University of Wisconsin at Green Bay-WPNE/Green Bay
Director Fred Wessel; Barry Stoner

713   **A Menuhin Tribute to Willa Cather**
Special of the Week   PBS
Program Type Music/Dance
Special. Concert performed 12/7/73 in honor of Willa Cather. 120 minutes. Premiere date: 8/12/74. Repeat date: 9/1/75. Performers: Yehudi Menuhin; Hephzibah Menuhin; Yaltah Menuhin.
Production Company Nebraska Educational Television

The Mephisto Waltz *see* The CBS Thursday/Friday Night Movies

714   **The Merv Griffin Show**   Syndicated
Program Type Variety/Talk Show
Began in syndication in 1964. Went to CBS in 1969. Current syndication started in 1972. 90 minutes. Monday-Friday. Continuous.
Producer Bob Murphy
Production Company Merv Griffin Productions in association with Metromedia Producers Corporation
Director Dick Carson
Writer Merv Griffin; Bob Murphy; Tony Garofalo
Musical Director Mort Lindsey
Host Merv Griffin

**715   The Mickey Finns Finally Present
... How the West Was Lost**   Syndicated
Program Type Comedy/Variety
Special. 60 minutes. Premiere: 7/75. Filmed at
the Holiday Riverboat Casino in Las Vegas.
Producer Alan Handley
Production Company Andrews-Finn Productions
Director Alan Handley
Head Writer John Bradford
Musical Director Larry Cansler
Choreographer George LaFave
Narrators Roy Rogers; Dale Evans
Cast Fred Finn; Mickie Finn; Rob Reiner;
Charlie Callas; Foster Brooks; Diana Trask;
Alliene Flanery; Scotty Plummer

716   Middle Age Blues   Syndicated
Program Type Documentary/Special
Special. 60 minutes. A look at two men: Bert and
Bob. Premiere: 7/75.
Producer Al Korn
Production Company RKO General Television
Director Richard Shore
Writer Kermit Kahn
Narrator Art Carney

Midnight Cowboy *see* The ABC Sunday
Night Movie

717   The Midnight Special   NBC
Program Type Music/Dance
90 minutes. Saturday (1-2:30 a.m.). Premiere
date: 2/3/73. "Rock Tribute" segment added
June 1975; "Hit of the Week" added September
1975. Special filming by Chuck Braverman; animation by John Wilson.
Executive Producer Burt Sugarman
Producer Stan Harris
Production Company Burt Sugarman, Inc. Productions
Host Helen Reddy
Announcer Wolfman Jack

718   The Mike Douglas Show   Syndicated
Program Type Variety/Talk Show
In thirteenth year. 90 minutes. Monday-Friday.
Continuous. Has different guest co-host each
week.
Executive Producer Jack Reilly
Producer Woody Fraser
Production Company Group W/Westinghouse
Broadcasting Company, Inc. in association
with Mike Douglas Entertainments, Inc.
Director Ernie Sherry
Host Mike Douglas

719   Miles to Go Before I Sleep
General Electric Theater   CBS
Program Type Drama
Special. 90 minutes. Premiere date: 1/8/75.
Story by Judith Parker.
Executive Producer Philip Barry, Jr.
Producer Herbert Hirschman
Production Company Tomorrow Entertainment,
Inc.
Director Fielder Cook
Writer Judith Parker
CAST
Ben Montgomery	Martin Balsam
Robin Williams	Mackenzie Phillips
Maggie Stanton	Kitty Wynn
Lisa	Pamela Ferdin
Hattie	Dorothy Meyer
Kate	Elizabeth Wilson
Ruth	Florida Friebus
Jenny	Susan Lynn Mathews
Kathy	Wendy Wright
Susan	Alma Collins
Valerie	Vicki Kriegler
Bruce	Sheldon Allman
O'Dell	Tom Atkins

**720   The Minnesota Orchestra at
Orchestra Hall**
Special of the Week   PBS
Program Type Music/Dance
Special. Stanislaw Skrowaczewski conducts the
Minnesota Orchestra in the inaugural concert at
Orchestra Hall. 90 minutes. Premiere date:
7/14/75. Program funded by the Peavy Company, Minneapolis, the Minnesota Orchestral
Association and the Corporation for Public
Broadcasting.
Producer Larry Morrisette
Production Company KTCA/Minneapolis-St.
Paul
Director Larry Morrisette
Commentator Henry Charles Smith; Rita Shaw

721   Miracle on 34th Street   CBS
Program Type Drama
Special. Based on the 1946 movie by George Seaton. 120 minutes. Premiere date: 12/14/73. Repeat date: 11/29/74.
Producer Norman Rosemont
Production Company A Norman Rosemont Production in association with 20th Century-Fox
Television
Director Fielder Cook
Writer Jeb Rosebrook
CAST
Kris Kringle	Sebastian Cabot
Karen Walker	Jane Alexander
Bill Schaffner	David Hartman
Horace Shellhammer	Jim Backus
Dr. Sawyer	Roddy McDowall
Susan Walker	Suzanne Davidson
R. H. Macy	David Doyle

Miracle on 34th Street *Continued*
Adam Gimbel .... Roland Winters
District Attorney .... James Gregory
Judge Harper .... Tom Bosley
Celeste .... Ellen Weston
Alfred .... Jerry Greenberg
Dr. Pierre .... Conrad Janis

722   Miss America Pageant   NBC
Program Type Awards Show
Special. 55th annual pageant. Live from Convention Hall, Atlantic City, New Jersey. 120 minutes. 9/6/75. Shirley Cothran, Miss America of 1975, crowns her successor. Bert Parks sings "There She Is . . . Miss America."
Executive Producer Albert A. Marks, Jr.
Producer John L. Koushouris
Director Dave Wilson
Writer Joseph Scher
Choreographer Peter Gennaro
Host Phyllis George; Debbie Ward
Master of Ceremonies Bert Parks

723   Miss Teenage America Pageant   CBS
Program Type Awards Show
14th annual award. Live from Little Rock, Ark. 90 minutes. 11/30/74.
Producer Charles Andrews
Director Sid Smith
Host Sally Field; Lori Matsukawa
Master of Ceremonies Ken Berry
Special Guest Abigail Van Buren

724   Miss Universe Beauty Pageant   CBS
Program Type Awards Show
24th annual pageant; from San Salvador, El Salvador. Winner crowned by Miss Universe 1974 Amparo Munoz. 120 minutes. 7/19/75.
Executive Producer Charles E. Andrews
Producer Charles Raymond
Director Sidney Smith
Host Bob Barker; Helen O'Connell

725   Miss U.S.A. Beauty Pageant   CBS
Program Type Awards Show
24th annual pageant; from Niagara Falls, N.Y. Winner crowned by Miss U.S.A. 1974 Karen Morrison. 120 minutes. 5/17/75.
Executive Producer Charles E. Andrews
Producer Charles Raymond
Director Sidney Smith
Writer Donald K. Epstein
Host Bob Barker; Helen O'Connell
Featured Guests The Lettermen; West Point Glee Club

726   The Missiles of October
ABC Theatre   ABC
Program Type Drama
Special. Dramatization of the 1962 Cuban missile crisis. 180 minutes. Premiere date: 12/18/74.
Executive Producer Irv Wilson
Producer Buzz Berger; Herbert Brodkin
Production Company Viacom Enterprises
Director Anthony Page
Writer Stanley R. Greenberg
CAST
Pres. John F. Kennedy .... William Devane
Robert F. Kennedy .... Martin Sheen
Nikita Khrushchev .... Howard da Silva
Adlai Stevenson .... Ralph Bellamy
Tom Hughes .... Earl Bowen
David F. Powers .... James Callahan
Dean Acheson .... John Dehner
John McCone .... Keene Curtis
Theodore C. Sorensen .... Clifford David
Senator No. 2 .... Francis De Sales
David Ormsby-Gore .... Peter Donat
Gen. Maxwell D. Taylor .... Andrew Duggan
Gen. David M. Shoup .... Richard Eastham
Robert McNamara .... Dana Elcar
Presidium Member No. 2 .... Gene Elman
Charles de Gaulle .... Ronald Feinberg
Soviet Marshal .... Michael Fox
Charles A. Halleck .... Arthur Franz
Dean Rusk .... Larry Gates
American General .... Ted Hartley
Chief Presidium No. 1 .... Bern Hoffman
U Thant .... James Hong
Richard B. Russell .... Wright King
Valerian A. Zorin .... Will Kuluva
John Scali .... Paul Lambert
Pierre Salinger .... Michael Lerner
Gen. Curtis LeMay .... Robert P. Lieb
Kenneth J. O'Donnell .... Stewart Moss
McGeorge Bundy .... James Olson
Anatoly Dobrynin .... Albert Paulsen
Llewelyn Thompson .... Dennis Patrick
Andrei Gromyko .... Nehemiah Persoff
C. Douglas Dillon .... William Prince
George Ball .... John Randolph
Presidium Member No. 3 .... Richard Karlan
W. E. Knox .... Stacy Keach, Sr.
Mrs. Lincoln .... Doreen Lang
Yevgeny Yevtushenko .... John McMurty
J. W. Fulbright .... Byron Morrow
Adm. George Anderson .... Ken Tobey
Soviet Stenographer .... Serge Tschernisch
Mario Garcia-Inchaustegui .... Jay Varela
Alexandr Fomin .... Harris Yulin

727   The Missing Are Deadly
Tuesday/Wednesday Movie of the Week ABC
Program Type TV Movie
90 minutes. Premiere date: 1/8/75. Repeat date: 6/24/75.
Executive Producer Lawrence Gordon
Producer Allen S. Epstein
Production Company A Lawrence Gordon Production
Director Don McDougall

Writer Katharyn Michaelian; Michael Michaelian
CAST
Dr. Margolin .... Ed Nelson
Dr. Durov .... Leonard Nimoy
David ....George O'Hanlon, Jr.
Jeff .... Gary Morgan
Mrs. Robertson .... Marjorie Lord
Michelle .... Kathleen Quinlan
Mr. Warren .... Jose Ferrer
Mrs. Bates .... Irene Tedrow
Grocer .... Stuart Nisbet
Dr. Martinez .... Armand Alzamora
Capt. Franklin .... John Milford

728 Mitzi and a Hundred Guys   CBS
Program Type Comedy/Variety
Special. Stars Mitzi Gaynor; Jack Albertson; Michael Landon; the 75-member University of Southern California Marching Band; the Million Dollar Chorus (see below). 60 minutes. Premiere date: 3/24/75.
Executive Producer Jack Bean
Producer Mort Green
Production Company Green Isle Enterprises, Inc.
Director Tony Charmoli
Writer Jerry Mayer
Choreographer Tony Charmoli
Host Mitzi Gaynor
Million Dollar Chorus Marty Allen; Steve Allen; Tige Andrews; Ken Berry; Carl Betz; Bill Bixby; Tom Bosley; Mike Connors; Bob Crane; Bill Dana; Clifton Davis; James Farentino; Christopher George; Andy Griffith; Monty Hall; Bob Hope; Ross Hunter; Dean Jones; Tom Kennedy; Ted Knight; Rich Little; Allen Ludden; Gavin MacLeod; Monte Markham; Peter Marshall; Ross Martin; Strother Martin; Jim McKrell; Greg Morris; Jim Nabors; Leonard Nimoy; Louis Nye; Bill Shatner; Lyle Waggoner

729 Mixed Doubles Classic
CBS Sports Special   CBS
Program Type Sports
Live coverage of mixed doubles from the John Gardiner Tennis Ranch, Scottsdale, Arizona. 5/4/75.
Production Company CBS Television Network Sports
Announcer Pat Summerall; Wendy Overton

The Molly Maguires *see* The ABC Saturday Night Movie

Money from Home *see* The ABC Saturday Night Movie; The ABC Sunday Night Movie

730 The Money Maze   ABC
Program Type Game Show
30 minutes. Monday-Friday. Premiere: 12/23/74. Last show: 7/4/75.
Producer Don Lipp
Production Company Daphne-Don Lipp Production in association with the ABC Television Network
Host Nick Clooney

731 Monkey, Monkey, Bottle of Beer, How Many Monkeys Have We Here?
Theater in America   PBS
Program Type Drama
Play by Marsha Sheiness performed by the Cincinnati Playhouse. 90 minutes. Premiere date: 5/22/74. Repeat date: 4/9/75. Series made possible by grants from Exxon Corporation and the Corporation for Public Broadcasting.
Executive Producer Jac Venza
Producer Ken Campbell
Production Company WNET/New York
Director Harold Scott; Peter Levin
Host Hal Holbrook
CAST
Evans .... Deloris Gaskins
Luther .... Diane Danzi
Amber .... Rosemary DeAngelis
Lewis .... Peggy Kirkpatrick
Todd .... Jean DeBaer
Lynn .... Helene Friedman
Joe .... Marc Jefferson

732 Monsters! Mysteries or Myths?
A Smithsonian Institution Special   CBS
Program Type Documentary/Special
Special. Focuses on the legends of the Abominable Snowman, the Loch Ness Monster and Bigfoot. 60 minutes. Premiere date: 11/25/74.
Executive Producer George Lefferts
Producer Robert Guenette
Production Company Wolper Productions in co-operation with The Smithsonian Institution
Director Robert Guenette
Writer Robert Guenette
Narrator Rod Serling
CAST
Bigfoot .... Richard Kiel

733 Monty Python's Flying Circus PBS
Program Type Comedy
30 minutes. Weekly. Premiere date: 10/6/74. Available through the Eastern Educational Network.
Producer Ian Macnaughton
Production Company British Broadcasting Corporation
Distributor Time-Life Films
Writer Eric Chapman; John Cleese; Terry Gilliam; Eric Idle; Terry Jones; Michael Palin

Monty Python's Flying Circus *Continued*
Regular Eric Chapman; John Cleese; Terry Gilliam; Eric Idle; Terry Jones; Michael Palin
Animator Terry Gilliam
Costume Designer Hazel Pethig

734   A Moon for the Misbegotten
ABC Theatre   ABC
Program Type Drama
Special. 150 minutes. Premiere date: 5/27/75.
Producer David Susskind; Audrey Maas
Production Company Talent Associates
Director Jose Quintero; Gordon Rigsby
Writer Eugene O'Neill
CAST
James Tyrone ....Jason Robards
Josie Hogan ....Colleen Dewhurst
Phil Hogan .... Ed Flanders
T. Stedman Harder .... John O'Leary
Mike Hogan .... Edwin J. McDonough

735   Moses the Lawgiver   CBS
Program Type Drama
Six-part miniseries. Filmed in Israel. Premiere date: 6/21/75. Last show: 8/2/75.
Producer Vincenzo Labella
Production Company RAI Television (Italy) in association with ATV-ITC
Director Gianfranco DeBosio
Writer Anthony Burgess; Vittorio Bonicelli
Narrator Richard Johnson
CAST
Moses .... Burt Lancaster
Aaron .... Anthony Quayle
Miriam .... Ingrid Thulin
Zipporah .... Irene Papas
Pharoah .... Laurent Terzieff
Young Moses .... Will Lancaster
Ramses II .... Mario Ferrari
Joshua ....Aharon Ipale
Pharoah's Wife .... Melba Englander
Egyptian Princess .... Mirangela Melato
Cotbi .... Simonetta Stefanelli
Eliseba .... Marina Berti
Tutor ....Paul Muller

736   Movin' On   NBC
Program Type Drama
60 minutes. Premiere date: 9/12/74. Music by Don Ellis.
Executive Producer Philip D'Antoni; Barry Weitz
Producer Joseph Gantman
Production Company D'Antoni-Weitz Television Production in association with NBC -TV
Director Various
Writer Various
CAST
Sonny Pruett .... Claude Akins
Will Chandler .... Frank Converse

737   Mr. and Mrs. Cop
CBS Pilot Film   CBS
Program Type Drama
30 minutes. Premiere date: 5/3/74. Repeat date: 4/3/75.
Producer Leonard B. Kaufman
Production Company Viacom Enterprises Production
Director Harvey Heit
Writer Howard Rodman
CAST
Paul Roscommon .... Anthony Costello
Nancy Roscommon .... Marianne McAndrews
Lt. Ocala ....Richard Angarola
Sgt. Baum ....William Campbell
Al Johnson .... Tom Falk
Chester .... Howard Platt
Mills .... Gary Barton
Mills' Partner .... Mark Boli
Irv Pyle .... Redmond Gleeson
Mrs. Salmon .... Holly Near
Krunkle .... Daniel Spelling
Chester's Mother .... Norma Connoly
Albanel ....Max Gail
Minister .... Alan Dexter
Sgt. Plantanos .... Gerald Ray

738   Mr. Rogers' Neighborhood   PBS
Program Type Children's Show
30 minutes. Monday-Friday. Continuous. Premiere date: 5/22/67. Show created by Fred Rogers. Program made possible by grants from the Sears Roebuck Foundation, the Corporation for Public Broadcasting, the Ford Foundation and Johnson & Johnson Baby Products. Fred Rogers is the puppeteer and voice of ten of the puppets.
Executive Producer Fred Rogers
Producer Bill Moates
Production Company Family Communications, Inc. in association with WQED/Pittsburgh
Director Bill Moates
Writer Fred Rogers
Musical Director John Costa
Host Fred Rogers
CAST
Lady Aberlin .... Betty Aberlin
Chef Brockett .... Don Brockett
Francois Clemmons .... Francois Clemmons
Pilot Ito ....Yoshi Ito
Mrs. McFeely .... Betsy Nadas
Elsie Neal .... Elsie Neal
Handyman Negri ....Joe Negri
Mr. McFeely .... David Newell
Audrey Cleans Everything (A.C.E.)/Audrey
   Paulifficate ....Audrey Roth
Robert Troll/Bob Dog/Bob Trow .... Bob Trow
VOICES
X the Owl/King Friday XIII/Queen Sara
   Saturday/Cornflake S. Pecially/Lady Elaine
   Fairchilde/Henrietta Pussycat/Grandpere/Edgar
   Cooke/Daniel Striped Tiger/Donkey
   Hodie .... Fred Rogers
Dr. Duckbill Platypus/Mrs. Elsie Jean
   Platypus .... William P. Barker
Harriett Elizabeth Cow .... Robert Trow

739 **Mr. Rooney Goes to Dinner**
CBS News Special   CBS
Program Type Documentary/Special
60 minutes. Premiere date: 6/24/75.
Producer Andrew A. Rooney
Production Company CBS News
Writer Andrew A. Rooney
Reporter Andrew A. Rooney

740 **Mr. Rooney Goes to Washington**
CBS News Special   CBS
Program Type Documentary/Special
Tongue-in-cheek view of Washington bureaucracy. 60 minutes. Premiere date: 1/26/75. Repeat date: 7/28/75.
Producer Andrew A. Rooney
Production Company CBS News
Director Andrew A. Rooney
Writer Andrew A. Rooney
Host Andrew A. Rooney

741 **Mrs. Lincoln's Husband**
Sandburg's Lincoln   NBC
Program Type Drama
First in series on the life of Abraham Lincoln based on biography by Carl Sandburg. 60 minutes. Premiere date: 9/6/74.
Executive Producer David L. Wolper
Producer George Schaefer
Production Company David L. Wolper Production
Director George Schaefer
Writer James Prideaux
CAST
Abraham Lincoln .... Hal Holbrook
Mary Todd Lincoln .... Sada Thompson
Salmon P. Chase .... Roy Poole
Sen. Fogelson .... John Beal
John Nicolay .... Michael Christoffer
Robert Lincoln .... James Carroll Jordan
Willie Lincoln .... Michael-James Wixted
Tad Lincoln .... John Levin
Mrs. Livingston .... Anne Seymour
Gen. Tom Thumb .... Felix Silla
Lavinia .... Patty Maloney

Mrs. Pollifax - Spy *see* The CBS
Thursday/Friday Night Movies

742 **The Muppet Show**   ABC
Program Type Comedy
Special. 70 new Muppets created by Jim Henson. 30 minutes. Premiere date: 3/19/75.
Producer Jim Henson; Jon Stone
Production Company Henson Associates, Inc.
Director Dave Wilson
Head Writer Marshall Brickman
Writer Norman Stiles; Jon Stone
Musical Director Joe Raposo
Puppeteers Frank Oz; Jerry Nelson; Richard

Hunt; Dave Goelz; John Lovelady; Fran Brill; Jim Henson

743 **Murder Must Advertise**
Masterpiece Theatre   PBS
Program Type Drama
Four-part series adapted from the novel by Dorothy L. Sayers. 60 minutes. Weekly. Presented in the United States by WGBH-TV/Boston; Joan Sullivan, producer. Premiere date: 10/6/74 (season premiere of "Masterpiece Theatre"). Repeat date: 8/10/75. Series made possible by a grant from the Mobil Oil Corporation.
Producer Richard Beynon
Production Company BBC
Director Rodney Bennett
Writer Bill Craig
Host Alistair Cooke
CAST
Lord Peter Wimsey .... Ian Carmichael
Insp. Parker .... Mark Eden
Lady Mary .... Rachel Herbert
Dian de Momerie .... Bridget Armstrong
Pym .... Peter Pratt
Tallboy .... Paul Darrow
Pamela .... Gwen Taylor
Ingleby .... John Hallam
Willis .... Christopher Timothy
Miss Meteyard .... Fiona Walker
Milligan .... Peter Bowles
Puncheon .... Ian Gelder

744 **The Music Project Presents**   PBS
Program Type Music/Dance
Six-part series. 30 minutes. Weekly. Premiere date: 4/23/75. Programs made possible by grants from the National Endowment for the Arts, the Corporation for Public Broadcasting, the Kansas City Philharmonic, the Andrew W. Mellon Foundation, Pyramid Films, the Carrie J. Loose Trust, the Harry W. Loose Trust, and the Edward F. Swinney Trust. Programs: "The Secret Life of an Orchestra," "Romeo and Juliet in Kansas City," "Music for Prague 1968," "A Wizard with Sound," "Ancient Voices of Children," "Bolero."
Producer Allan Miller
Production Company WNET/New York
Director Allan Miller; Urs Furrer

745 **Musical Chairs**   CBS
Program Type Game Show
Musical-variety show in game format, featuring special guests each week. 30 minutes. Monday-Friday. Continuous. Premiere date: 6/16/75.
Producer Bill W. Chastain, Jr.
Production Company Jerome Schnur/Don Kirshner Production
Director Lynwood King
Writer Bruce Sussman; Carol George

Musical Chairs *Continued*
Musical Director Derek Smith
Host Adam Wade

Mutual of Omaha's Wild Kingdom *see*
Wild Kingdom

746   My Darling Daughters' Anniversary
Tuesday/Wednesday Movie of the Week ABC
Program Type TV Movie
90 minutes. Premiere date: 11/7/73. Repeat
date: 12/25/74. Sequel to "All My Darling
Daughters."
Executive Producer David Victor
Producer David O'Connell
Production Company Universal Television
Director Joseph Pevney
Writer John Gay
CAST
Judge Charles Raleigh .... Robert Young
Matthew Cunningham .... Raymond Massey
Maggie Cartwright .... Ruth Hussey
Susan ....Darleen Carr
Robin .... Judy Strangis
Jennifer ....Sharon Gless
Charlotte ....Lara Parker
Andy .... Darrell Larson
Jerry .... Jerry Fogel
Brad .... Colby Chester
Biff .... Alan Vint

My Fair Lady *see* NBC Nights at the
Movies

747   My Father's House
The ABC Sunday Night Movie   ABC
Program Type TV Movie
120 minutes. Premiere date: 6/1/75. Based on
the book by Philip Kunhardt, Jr..
Executive Producer Edward S. Feldman
Producer David Sontag
Production Company Edward S. Feldman-David
Sontag Production in association with Film-
ways
Director Alex Segal
Writer David Sontag; David Seltzer
CAST
Tom, Jr. (the present) .... Cliff Robertson
Judith .... Rosemary Forsyth
Steven ....Michael Cornelison
Ellen .... Carlene Olson
Zozo .... Victoria Clark; Hilary Clark
Paula .... Gail Strickland
Father .... Robert Preston
Mother .... Eileen Brennan
Anna .... Ruth McDevitt
Tom, Jr. (the past) .... Michael-James Wixted
Brad .... Brad Savage
Susan .... Lark Geib
Noble .... Lil Greenwood
Baby Jane .... Kari Osborn; Kelli Osborn

748   My Favorite Martians   CBS
Program Type Animated Film
Reruns. Premiered September 1973. 30 minutes.
Sundays, moved to Saturdays. Last show:
8/30/75.
Producer Norm Prescott; Lou Scheimer
Production Company Filmation Associates in as-
sociation with Jack Chertog Television, Inc.
Director Hal Sutherland
Writer Ben Starr; Jim Ryan; Bill Danch; Marc
Richards
Animation Director Don Towsley; Rudy Larriva;
Bill Reed; Lou Zukor; Ed Solomon
Creative Consultant Jack Chertog
Art Director Don Christensen
Voices Jonathan Harris; Howard Morris; Jane
Webb; Lane Scheimer

Mysteries of the Deep *see* All-Disney
Night

749   The Mystery of Nefertiti   PBS
Program Type Documentary/Special
Special. 60 minutes. Premiere date: 10/15/73.
Repeat date: 1/13/75. Program made possible by
a grant from IBM Corporation.
Production Company British Broadcasting Cor-
poration
Narrator Dr. Raymond Winfield Smith

750   Mystery of the Maya   PBS
Program Type Documentary/Special
Special. 60 minutes. Premiere date: 4/1/74. Re-
peat date: 5/15/75. Program funded by grants
from the Ford Foundation and the Robert Ster-
ling Clark Foundation.
Producer Hugh Johnston; Suzanne Johnston
Production Company WNET/New York
Narrator Ricardo Montalban

751   Nakia   ABC
Program Type Crime Drama
60 minutes. Saturday. Premiere date: 9/21/74.
Last show: 12/28/74. Filmed in and around Al-
buquerque, New Mexico. Pilot "Nakia" telecast
4/17/74 on "Wednesday Movie of the Week
Double Feature."
Executive Producer Charles Larson
Producer Ernest Losso; George Sunga
Production Company David Gerber Productions,
Inc. in association with Columbia Pictures
Television
Director Various
Writer Various
CAST
Dep. Sheriff Nakia Parker .... Robert Forster
Sheriff Sam Jericho ....Arthur Kennedy
Irene James .... Gloria De Haven
Dep. Hubbel Martin ....Taylor Lacher

752 Name That Tune   NBC
Program Type Game Show
30 minutes. Monday-Friday. Continuous.
Created by Harry Salter with original premiere
9/2/54. New show premiere: 7/29/74. Last
show: 1/3/75.
Executive Producer Ralph Edwards
Producer Ray Horl
Production Company A Ralph Edwards Production in association with NBC-TV
Director Terry Kyne
Writer Richard Gottlieb
Musical Director Bob Alberti
Host Dennis James
Announcer John Harlan
Musicologist Harvey Bacal
Music Coordinator Richard Gottlieb

753 Name That Tune   Syndicated
Program Type Game Show
Evening version of daytime game show. 30
minutes. Premiere: 9/74. Weekly. Show originally created by Harry Salter in 1954.
Executive Producer Ralph Edwards
Producer Ray Horl
Production Company Ralph Edwards Productions
Distributor Station Syndication, Inc.
Director Richard Gottlieb
Writer Richard Gottlieb
Musical Director Bob Alberti
Host Tom Kennedy
Announcer John Harlan
Musicologist Harvey Bacal

754 NASL Soccer
PBS Sports Special   PBS
Program Type Sports
120 minutes. North American Soccer League
game between New York Cosmos and Boston
Minutemen from Nickerson Field, Boston. Premiere date: 8/3/75. Carried live eastern time.
Announcer Kyle Rote, Jr.; Crane Davis

**National Basketball Association All-Star
Game** *see* NBA All-Star Game

**755 National Basketball Association
Games**   CBS
Program Type Sports
Second season on CBS. Live coverage. Season
premiere: 10/27/74. Weekly coverage between
1/5/75–4/6/75. Playoffs began 4/12/75; finals
5/20/75–5/25/75. Regular announcers: Brent
Musberger and Oscar Robertson. Chuck Milton
and Sandy Grossman produced and directed
most games.
Producer Chuck Milton

Production Company CBS Television Network
Sports
Director Sandy Grossman
Announcer Brent Musburger; Oscar Robertson;
Don Criqui; Jerry West

National Collegiate Athletic Association
see NCAA

National Football Conference *see* NFC

National Football League *see* NFL

National Hockey League *see* NHL
Hockey

**National Invitational Tournament
Basketball** *see* NIT Basketball

756 National Town Meeting   PBS
Program Type Interview/Discussion
13-week series. 60 minutes. Weekly. Premiere
date: 9/29/74. Series made possible by a grant
from Mobile Oil Corporation.
Producer Bud Myers
Production Company WNET/New York
Moderator Harrison Salisbury

757 The Naturalists   PBS
Program Type Documentary/Special
Four-part series. 30 minutes. Weekly. Premiere
date: 3/11/73. Repeat date: 5/9/75. Series made
possible by a grant from the Corporation for
Public Broadcasting. Series covers Henry Thoreau, Theodore Roosevelt, John Muir, John Burroughs.
Producer James Case
Production Company Special Projects Cine Unit
of KRMA/Denver
Director James Case
Editor James Case

758 The Navajo Way
NBC News Special   NBC
Program Type Documentary/Special
60 minutes. Premiere date: 12/23/74.
Producer Robert Northshield
Production Company NBC News
Director Robert Northshield
Writer Robert Northshield

759   Navidad Encantada: Enchanted Christmas
ABC News Special Events   ABC
Program Type Religious Program
Special. 60 minutes. Premiere date: 12/25/74.
Christmas mass taped 12/23/74 at San Felipe De Meri Church, Albuquerque, New Mexico. Archbishop Robert Sanchez principal celebrant for Spanish-English service.
Producer Sid Darion
Production Company ABC News
Director Marshall Diskin

760   NBA All-Star Game
CBS Sports Special   CBS
Program Type Sports
25th annual game. Live coverage. 1/14/75.
Production Company CBS Television Network Sports
Announcer Brent Musburger; Oscar Robertson

761   NBC Midday News   NBC
Program Type News
Five minutes. Monday-Friday. Midday. Continuous.
Executive Producer Les Crystal
Production Company NBC News
Newscaster Edwin Newman

NBC Monday Nights at the Movies *see* NBC Nights at the Movies

762   NBC News Special   NBC
Program Type Documentary/Special
Live and taped coverage of special events. Programs shown during the 1974–75 season: "America Abroad," "And Who Shall Feed This World?" "Apollo-Soyuz Joint Space Mission," "A Conversation with President Ford," "A Country Called Watts," "A Handshake in Space," "Helsinki Summit: The Price of Detente," "If You Think It Was Tough to Make Ends Meet in 1974, Wait 'Til You Hear About 1975," "Jack Benny: We Remember," "Joint U.S.–U.S.S.R. Space Mission Preview," "The Loyal Opposition," "Many Unhappy Returns - A Report on Your Taxes," "Mary Jane Grows Up: Marijuana in the 70's," "The Navajo Way," "1974: The World Turned Upside Down," "The Nuclear Threat to You," "Of Women and Men," "President Ford's First 100 Days in Office," "President Ford's State of the Union Message to Congress," "Rabin and Sadat: Peace or War?" "Senate Rules Committee Hearings on the Rockefeller Nomination for Vice-President," "7382 Days in Vietnam," "A Shooting Gallery Called America," "Tornado! 4:40 P.M., Xenia, Ohio," "UFOs: Do You Believe?" "The White-

Collar Rip-Off." (*See* individual titles for credits.)
Production Company NBC News
Producer Various

763   NBC News Update   NBC
Program Type News
60 seconds. Daily. Premiere date: 8/6/75. First regularly scheduled news summary in prime time. Anchored Monday-Friday night by Tom Snyder; Saturday night by Edwin Newman; Sunday night by Chuck Scarborough; and by John Schubeck in the Western time zone.
Producer Various
Production Company NBC News
Director Various

764   NBC Nightly News   NBC
Program Type News
30 minutes. Monday-Friday. Continuous.
Executive Producer Les Crystal
Producer Joseph Angotti
Production Company NBC News
Newscaster John Chancellor
Commentator David Brinkley

765   NBC Nights at the Movies   NBC
Program Type TV Movie – Feature Film
A combination of films made for television and those previously released commercially. The made-for-television films do not include those shown on Tuesdays as "NBC World Premiere Movies" or "Ellery Queen" and "The Return of Joe Forrester" seen as an "NBC Sunday Mystery Movie" and special "Police Story" respectively. The feature films include several shown as specials: "Pollyanna," "Scrooge," "The Three Lives of Thomasina," "Willy Wonka and the Chocolate Factory," and "The Wizard of Oz" (shown for the 17th time on Easter Sunday at 6:30 Eastern time). The made-for-television films are: "The Blue Knight," "A Case of Rape," "Crossfire," "Delancey Street: The Crisis Within," "The Execution of Private Slovik," "Frankenstein: The True Story," "The Greatest Gift," "The Last Day," "Last Hours Before Morning," "The Log of the Black Pearl," "A Matter of Wife ... and Death," "Nevada Smith," "One of Our Own," "The Runaway Barge," "Sky Hei$t," "The Specialists," "Strike Force," "Target Risk," "The Turning Point of Jim Malloy," "The Underground Man," "Who Is the Black Dahlia?" "Winner Take All." (*See* individual titles for cast and credits.) The films commercially distributed before being seen on television are: "The African Queen" (1951) shown 12/2/74, "The Arrangement" (1969) shown 8/9/75, "Barefoot in the Park" (1967) shown 4/5/75, "A Big Hand for the Little Lady" (1966) shown

3/10/75, "The Bridge at Remagen" (1969) shown 5/10/75, "Buck and the Preacher" (1972) shown 5/12/75, "Butterflies Are Free" (1972) shown 2/24/75, "Cactus Flower" (1969) shown 3/22/75, "Call Me Bwana" (1963) shown 6/14/75, "The Candidate" (1972) shown 10/21/74, "The Caretakers" (1963) shown 8/7/75, "Charley Varrick" (1973) shown 10/5/74, "Chisum" (1970) shown 1/11/75, "Cold Sweat" (1971) shown 2/10/75, "Cool Hand Luke" (1967) shown 2/8/75, "Cotton Comes to Harlem" (1970) shown 6/19/75, "The Defiant Ones" (1958) shown 7/3/75, "Doctors' Wives" (1971) shown 2/3/75, "Elvis - That's the Way It Is" (1970) shown 6/5/75, "Flight from Ashiya" (1964) shown 7/31/75, "Geronimo" (1962) shown 12/21/74, "The Godfather" (1972) shown in two parts: 11/16/74 and 11/18/74, "The Great Escape" (1963) shown in two parts: 5/17/75 and 5/19/75, "The Greatest Story Ever Told" (1965) shown in two parts: 3/28/75 and 3/29/75, "Hotel" (1967) shown 4/26/75, "I Want to Live!" (1958) shown 6/28/75, "If It's Tuesday, This Must Be Belgium" (1969) shown 7/10/75, "Impasse" (1969) shown 3/17/75 and 8/2/75, "Joe Kidd" (1972) shown 9/9/74, "Kings of the Sun" (1963) shown 11/25/74, "Klute" (1971) shown 9/14/74, "The Manchurian Candidate" (1962) shown 8/16/74, "Mary, Queen of Scots" (1971) shown 12/28/74 and 6/21/75, "The Mechanic" (1972) shown 10/19/74, "My Fair Lady" (1964) shown in two parts: 12/7/74 and 12/9/74, "The New Centurians" (1972) shown 11/2/74, "Oklahoma Crude" (1973) shown 9/21/74, "The Omega Man" (1971) shown 3/15/75, "One, Two, Three" (1961) shown 7/12/75, "The Parent Trap" (1971) shown 10/26/74 as part of "All-Disney Night," "Pete 'N' Tillie" (1972) shown 11/11/74 and 6/12/75, "Play Misty for Me" (1971) shown 1/27/75, "Pollyanna" (1960) shown 3/8/75 as a special presentation, "Rachel, Rachel" (1968) shown 9/23/74 and 8/14/75, "Salt and Pepper" (1968) shown 10/7/74, "Sam Whiskey" (1969) shown 1/20/75, "The Scalphunters" (1968) shown 1/25/75, "Scorpio" (1973) shown 1/18/75, "Scrooge" (1970) shown 12/23/74 as a special presentation, "The Seventh Dawn" (1964) shown 11/30/74, "Shamus" (1973) shown 10/28/74, "Showdown" (1973) shown 10/12/74, "Solomon and Sheba" (1959) shown 7/19/75, "Start the Revolution Without Me" (1970) shown 12/16/74, "Support Your Local Sheriff" (1969) shown 9/30/74, "Theatre of Blood" (1973) shown 9/28/74, "There Was a Crooked Man" (1970) shown 2/1/75, "The Three Lives of Thomasina" (1963) shown 12/14/74 as a special presentation, "The Train Robbers" (1973) shown 2/22/75, "Two Mules for Sister Sara" (1971) shown 4/28/75, "Ulzana's Raid" (1972) shown 1/13/75 and

5/24/75, "What's the Matter with Helen?" (1971) shown 9/16/74 and 4/7/75, "Willy Wonka and the Chocolate Factory" (1971) shown 11/28/74 as a special presentation, "Winning" (1969) shown 11/9/74, "The Wizard of Oz" (1939) shown 3/30/75 as a special presentation for the 17th time, "The World of Henry Orient" (1964) shown 6/7/75, "The Young Savages" (1961) shown 7/17/75, "Yours, Mine and Ours" (1968) shown 10/14/74, "Zeppelin" (1971) shown 11/23/74.

766   NBC Saturday Night News   NBC
Program Type News
30 minutes. Saturday. Continuous.
Executive Producer Les Crystal
Production Company NBC News
Newscaster Tom Brokaw

NBC Saturday Nights at the Movies *see* NBC Nights at the Movies

767   NBC Sunday Night News   NBC
Program Type News
30 minutes. Sunday. Continuous. Tom Synder replaced Floyd Kalber in June 1975.
Executive Producer Les Crystal
Production Company NBC News
Newscaster Floyd Kalber; Tom Snyder

NBC Thursday Nights at the Movies *see* NBC Nights at the Movies

768   NBC Sunday Mystery Movie   NBC
Program Type Crime Drama
Four series shown Sundays on a rotating basis. 90-120 minutes each. "Amy Prentiss," "Columbo," "McCloud," "McMillan & Wife." "Ellery Queen" shown once as a special. (*See* individual titles for cast and credits.)
Producer Various

769   NBC World Premiere Movie   NBC
Program Type TV Movie
First-time showings of films made for television - many of them pilots for proposed series. Only television films shown on Tuesdays have been included in this listing. For other "world premiere" films, *see* "NBC Nights at the Movies" as well as the films "Ellery Queen" and "The Return of Joe Forrester" shown as an "NBC Sunday Mystery Movie" and special "Police Story" respectively. 90 minutes or 120 minutes. Tuesday. Season premiere: 9/10/74. The films are: "The Big Ripoff," "Born Innocent," "The Dead Don't Die," "Death Among Friends," "Death Stalk," "The Disappearance of Flight 412,"

NBC World Premiere Movie *Continued*
"The Dream Makers," "The Imposter," "The Invisible Man," "Journey From Darkness," "The Last Survivors," "The Law," "Punch and Jody," "The Rangers," "Sara T. - Portrait of a Teen-Age Alcoholic," "The Secret Night Caller," "A Shadow in the Street," "The Strange and Deadly Occurrence," "Strange Homecoming," "Terror on the 40th Floor," "They Only Come Out at Night," "This Is the West That Was," "The Virginia Hill Story," "Where Have All the People Gone?" (*See* individual titles for cast and credits.)
Producer Various
Production Company Various

770   NCAA Basketball Tournament
NBC Sports Special   NBC
Program Type Sports
Live coverage of National Collegiate Athletic Association Basketball play-offs between 32 teams: 3/15/75; 3/22/75. Finals: UCLA Bruins versus Kentucky Wildcats (in San Diego, California): 3/29/75; 3/31/75.
Production Company NBC Sports
Announcer Jim Simpson; Tommy Hawkins; Jay Randolph; Ross Porter; Curt Gowdy; Billy Packer; Jerry Lucas
Anchor Tim Ryan; Al McGuire

771   NCAA Football   ABC
Program Type Sports
39 national, regional and double-header games. Live coverage. Season premiere: 9/7/74. Last show of season: 12/14/74. Keith Jackson is the principal play-by-play announcer.
Executive Producer Roone Arledge
Producer Chuck Howard
Production Company ABC Sports
Announcer Keith Jackson; Chris Schenkel; Bill Flemming
Expert Commentators Bud Wilkinson; Duffy Daugherty
Feature Reporter Jim Lampley

772   NCAA Pre-Season Report
ABC Sports Special   ABC
Program Type Sports
60 minutes. Premiere date: 8/29/75. Report on football.
Executive Producer Roone Arledge
Production Company ABC Sports
Host Keith Jackson
Reporters Ara Parseghian; Bud Wilkinson

773   Nevada Smith
NBC Nights at the Movies   NBC
Program Type TV Movie
Written and created by John Michael Hayes; Martin Rackin. Based on characters created by Harold Robbins. Sequel to 1966 movie. 90 minutes. Premiere date: 5/3/75. Repeat date: 7/26/75.
Producer Martin Rackin; John Michael Hayes
Production Company A Rackin-Hayes Production in association with MGM Television and NBC-TV
Director Gordon Douglas
Writer John Michael Hayes; Martin Rackin
CAST
Jonas Cord .... Lorne Greene
Nevada Smith .... Cliff Potts
Frank Hartlee .... Adam West
Red Fickett .... Warren Vanders
Two Moon .... Jorge Luke
Brill .... Jerry Gatlin
Davey .... Eric Cord
McLane .... John McKee
Perkins .... Roger Cudney
MacBaren .... Alan George
Belva .... Lorraine Chanel

774   The New Adventures of Gilligan
                    ABC
Program Type Animated Film
Based on the characters of the series "Gilligan's Island." Created by Sherwood Schwartz. 30 minutes. Premiere date: 9/7/74.
Executive Producer Norm Prescott; Lou Scheimer
Production Company Filmation Production
Director Don Towsley; Lou Zukor; Rudy Larriva; Bill Reed
Writer Various
Creative Director Don Christensen
Executive Consultant Sherwood Schwartz
VOICES
Gilligan .... Bob Denver
Skipper .... Alan Hale
Howell .... Jim Backus
Lovey .... Natalie Schaefer
Professor .... Russell Johnson
Ginger .... Jane Webb
Maryann .... Jane Edwards

775   The New Candid Camera   Syndicated
Program Type Game Show
30 minutes. Weekly. Premiere: 9/74. Originated as "Candid Microphone" on radio in 1947. "Candid Camera" first produced on television 9/12/49.
Producer Allen Funt
Production Company Allen Funt Productions, Inc.
Distributor Firestone Program Syndication Company
Host Allen Funt; John Bartholomew Tucker

The New Centurians *see* NBC Nights at the Movies

776 The New Land   NBC
Program Type Drama
60 minutes. Saturday. Premiere date: 9/14/74. Last show: 10/19/74. Swedish immigrants in Minnesota in 1858.
Executive Producer William Blinn
Producer Philip Leacock
Production Company Warner Brothers Television
Director Philip Leacock; John Erman
CAST
Christian Larsen .... Scott Thomas
Anna Larsen .... Bonnie Bedelia
Bo Larsen .... Kurt Russell
Lundstrom .... Donald Moffat
Molly .... Gwen Arner
Tuliff Larsen .... Todd Lookinland
Annaliese Larsen ....Debbie Lytton
Murdock .... Lou Frizzell

The New Price Is Right *see* The Price Is Right

777 The New Treasure Hunt   Syndicated
Program Type Game Show
Syndicated evening version of the defunct network show created by Jan Murray. (Original premiere: 8/12/57 daytime). Syndication premiere: 9/74. 30 minutes. Weekly.
Executive Producer Chuck Barris; Walter Case
Producer Michael J. Metzger
Production Company Chuck Barris Productions
Distributor Sandy Frank Film Syndication, Inc.
Director John Dorsey
Writer Michael J. Metzger; Robert Sand
Host Geoff Edwards
Announcer Johnny Jacobs
Costume Designer Barbara Murphy

778 New Year's Eve with Guy Lombardo   CBS
Program Type Music/Dance
Special. From the Grand Ballroom of the Waldorf-Astoria in New York City. Live (in East). 90 minutes. 12/31/74. Featuring Guy Lombardo and the Royal Canadians.
Executive Producer Kevin O'Sullivan
Producer Albert G. Hartigan
Production Company World Vision Enterprises
Director Don Mischer
Host Guy Lombardo
Guest Star Helen O'Connell

New York Philharmonic Young People's Concert *see* Young People's Concert

779 New Zoo Revue   Syndicated
Program Type Children's Show
30 minutes. Monday-Friday. Premiere date: 1/24/72. Mini-musical in each show. Created by Barbara Atlas; Douglas Momary. Animal costumes by Sid & Marty Krofft Productions.
Executive Producer Stephen W. Jahn
Producer Various
Production Company FunCo Corporation
Director Various
Writer Various
Musical Director Milton Greene
CAST
Doug .... Douglas Momary
Emmy Jo .... Emily Peden
Freddie the Frog .... Yanco Inove
Henrietta Hippo .... Larri Thomas
Charlie the Owl ....Sharon Baird

780 The Newlywed Game   ABC
Program Type Game Show
30 minutes. Monday-Friday. Premiere date: 7/11/66. Continuous. Last show: 12/20/74.
Executive Producer Chuck Barris
Producer Walt Case
Production Company A Chuck Barris Production
Director John Dorsey
Host Bob Eubanks
Announcer Johnny Jacobs

781 Next Year Is Here
NBC Sports Special   NBC
Program Type Sports
Special. 60 minutes. Premiere date: 4/6/75. Start of the baseball season.
Executive Producer Joe Garagiola
Producer Don Ellis
Production Company NBC Sports and Joe Garagiola Enterprises
Director Don Ellis
Writer Frank Slocum
Host Joe Garagiola

782 NFC Championship
CBS Sports Special   CBS
Program Type Sports
National Football Conference championship covered live 12/29/74. Minnesota Vikings versus Los Angeles Rams.
Production Company CBS Television Network Sports
Announcer Pat Summerall; Tom Brookshier; Bart Starr

783 NFC Play-Offs (Game 1)
CBS Sports Special   CBS
Program Type Sports
Live coverage of the National Football Confer-

NFC Play-Offs (Game 1) *Continued*
ence play-off 12/21/74. Minnesota Vikings versus St. Louis Cardinals.
Production Company CBS Television Network Sports
Announcer Brent Musburger; Irv Cross; Johnny Unitas

784   NFC Play-Offs (Game 2)
CBS Sports Special   CBS
Program Type Sports
Live coverage of the National Football Conference play-off 12/22/74. Los Angeles Rams versus Washington Redskins.
Producer Chuck Milton
Production Company CBS Television Network Sports
Director Bob Dailey
Announcer Pat Summerall; Tom Brookshier; Bart Starr

785   NFL Football   CBS
Program Type Sports
83 regular season games. Season premiere: 9/15/74. Live. National and regional telecasts.
Producer Various
Production Company CBS Television Network Sports
Director Various
Host Jack Whitaker; Lee Leonard
Analysts Tom Brookshier; Irv Cross; Pete Retzlaff; John Sauer; Bart Starr; Pat Summerall/ Wayne Walker
Play-By-Play Commentators Jack Buck; Don Criqui; Frank Glieber; Dan Kelly; Brent Musburger; Lindsey Nelson; Dick Stockton

786   NFL Football Exhibition Season
                                                              ABC
Program Type Sports
Pre-season games. Season premiere: 8/2/75 as special "ABC's Wide World of Sports." Weekly. Last show of season: 8/23/75.
Executive Producer Roone Arledge
Production Company ABC Sports
Announcer Frank Gifford; Howard Cosell; Alex Karras; Stu Nahan

787   NFL Game of the Week   NBC
Program Type Sports
85 regular season national, regional and double-header football games. Live coverage. Season premiere: 9/15/74. Last game: 12/15/75. Announcers listed cover national games.
Producer Various
Production Company NBC Sports
Director Various

Announcer Don Meredith; Al DeRogatis; Curt Gowdy

788   NFL Monday Night Football   ABC
Program Type Sports
14 weeks. Season premiere: 9/16/74. Last show of season: 12/9/74. Monday. Live coverage. Alex Karras replaced Fred Williamson as announcer. Extra game shown Saturday 12/14/75.
Executive Producer Roone Arledge
Production Company ABC Sports
Announcer Frank Gifford; Howard Cosell; Alex Karras; Fred Williamson

789   NFL Pre-Season Games   NBC
Program Type Sports
Three pre-season football games covered live 8/23/75, 8/30/75, 9/5/75.
Production Company NBC Sports
Announcer Curt Gowdy; Al DeRogatis; Jim Simpson; John Brodie

790   NFL Pre-Season Special
CBS Sports Special   CBS
Program Type Sports
Pre-season game. Live coverage from Berkeley, California. 8/17/75. Pittsburgh Steelers versus Oakland Raiders.
Production Company CBS Television Network Sports
Announcer Lindsey Nelson; Sonny Jurgensen

791   The NFL Today/Pro Football Report   CBS
Program Type Sports
"The NFL Today" 30 minute pre-game show; "Pro Football Report" 15 minute post-game show. Season premiere: 9/15/74. (See also "NFL Football.") Live.
Executive Producer Bill Fitts
Producer Various
Production Company CBS Television Network Sports
Director Various
Host Brent Musburger

792   NHL Hockey   NBC
Program Type Sports
14 regular season games. Live coverage. 1/5/75– 4/6/75.
Production Company NBC Sports
Announcer Tim Ryan; Ted Lindsay; Brian McFarlane

Nicholas and Alexandra *see* The ABC Saturday Night Movie; The ABC Sunday Night Movie

793 Night Dreams NBC
Program Type Music/Dance
Late night musical special presented in two parts. 90 minutes each. 8/2/75; 8/9/75. (1–2:30 a.m. Eastern time.) Theme of first show: love; theme of second: dreams, illusions and fantasy.
Executive Producer Syd Vinnedge
Producer Art Fisher
Production Company Syd Vinnedge Productions in association with NBC-TV
Director Art Fisher
Guests (8/2/75) 10 C.C.; The Spinners; B.J. Thomas; Black Oak Arkansas; Tanya Tucker
Guests (8/9/75) Three Dog Night; Rod Stewart; Slade; Freddie Fender; Little Richard; Hamilton, Joe Frank and Reynolds

Night Drum see The Japanese Film

794 The Night Stalker ABC
Program Type Crime Drama
60 minutes. Premiere date: 9/13/74. Last show: 8/30/75. Series aired on Fridays until August when it moved to Saturday. Based on characters created by Jeff Rice appearing in two TV movies: "The Night Stalker" and "The Night Strangler." (*See* entry for "The Night Strangler.") Crime dramas of the supernatural.
Producer Paul Playdon
Production Company Universal Television
CAST
Carl Kolchak .... Darren McGavin
Tony Vincenzo .... Simon Oakland

795 The Night Strangler
The ABC Summer Movie ABC
Program Type TV Movie
90 minutes. Premiere date: 1/16/73. Repeat date: 8/22/75. Filmed partly on location in Seattle. (*See* "The Night Stalker" for series.) Characters created by Jeff Rice.
Producer Dan Curtis
Production Company An ABC Circle Film
Director Dan Curtis
Writer Richard Matheson
CAST
Carl Kolchak .... Darren McGavin
Louise Harper .... Jo Ann Pflug
Tony Vincenzo .... Simon Oakland
Capt. Schubert .... Scott Brady
Mr. Berry .... Wally Cox
Prof. Crabwell .... Margaret Hamilton
Llewellyn Crossbinder .... John Carradine
Charisma Beauty .... Nina Wayne
Wilma Krankheimer .... Virginia Peters

796 Nightmare
The CBS Thursday/Friday Night Movies CBS
Program Type TV Movie

90 minutes. Premiere date: 1/8/74. Repeat date: 6/5/75.
Producer Mark Carliner
Production Company Mark Carliner Productions
Director William Hale
Writer David Wiltse
CAST
Howard Faloon .... Richard Crenna
Jan Richards .... Patty Duke Astin
Det. Rausch .... Vic Morrow
Taylor .... Peter Bromilow
Superintendant .... Arch Johnson
Linda .... Arlene Golonka
George .... Richard Schaal
Louise .... Doreen Lang
Mrs. Ramsey .... Mary Esther Denver
Albert .... Norbert Schiller

797 The Nine Tailors
Masterpiece Theatre PBS
Program Type Drama
Four-part series. 60 minutes. Weekly. Adaptation of story by Dorothy L Sayers. Premiere date: 4/13/75. Repeat date: 9/7/75. Produced in the United States by Joan Sullivan, for WGBH/Boston. Series made possible by a grant from the Mobil Oil Corporation.
Production Company BBC
CAST
Lord Peter Wimsey .... Ian Carmichael
Bunter .... Glyn Houston
Rev. Theodore Venables .... Donald Eccles
Deacon .... Keith Drinkel
Sir Charles Thorpe .... Desmond Llewelyn
Cranton .... Patrick Jordan
Sir Hector Geffe .... Anthony Roye
Lady Wilbraham .... Anne Blake
Susan .... Jane Cussons
Mrs. Tebbut .... Maryann Turner
Mary Deacon .... Elizabeth Proud
Jim Thoday .... David Jackson
Ezra .... Dan Meaden
Dr. Baines .... Bill Gavin
Hilary .... Gail Harrison
Warder .... Edwin Brown
Sergeant .... Michael Stainton
Shorty .... Keith James
Dowson .... Ronald Adam
Will Thoday .... Neil McCarthy
Gotobed .... Charles Lamb
Insp. Parker .... Mark Eden

798 1974: A Television Album
CBS News Special CBS
Program Type Documentary/Special
Summary of the year's highlights by CBS News correspondents. 60 minutes. Premiere date: 12/29/74.
Executive Producer Leslie Midgley
Producer Hal Haley; Bernard Birnbaum
Production Company CBS News
Director James Clevenger
Writer John Hart
Anchor John Hart

1974: A Television Album *Continued*
Correspondents Dan Rather; Bob Schieffer; Mitchell Krauss; Nelson Benton; Marvin Kalb

799   1974: The World Turned Upside Down
NBC News Special   NBC
Program Type Documentary/Special
Special. Discussion of year's events. 90 minutes. Premiere date: 1/5/75.
Producer Wallace O. Westfeldt
Production Company NBC News
Moderators Edwin Newman; Douglas Kiker; Garrick Utley

800   The 93rd Congress: Restoring the Balance   PBS
Program Type Interview/Discussion
Special. 60 minutes. Premiere date: 12/28/74.
Production Company NPACT (National Public Affairs Center for Television)
Interviewers Paul Duke; Carolyn Lewis
Guests Sen. Edmund Muskie; Sen. Jacob Javits; Rep. James Mann

801   NIT Basketball
CBS Sports Special   CBS
Program Type Sports
Semifinal and final games of the National Invitational Tournament. Live coverage from Madison Square Garden, New York. 3/22/75; 3/23/75.
Production Company CBS Television Network Sports
Announcer Don Criqui; Sonny Hill

North American Soccer League *see* NASL Soccer

Norwood *see* The ABC Saturday Night Movie

802   Not for Women Only   Syndicated
Program Type Interview/Discussion
Preceded by "For Women Only" with Aline Saarinen. Became "Not for Women Only" with Barbara Walters 9/71. 30 minutes. Monday-Friday.
Executive Producer Lawrence Johnson
Producer Madeline Amgott
Production Company WNBC-TV
Distributor Syndicast Services, Inc.
Director Paul Freeman
Host Barbara Walters

803   Nourish the Beast
Hollywood Television Theatre   PBS
Program Type Comedy
90 minutes. Premiere date: 6/5/75. Repeat date: 9/11/75.
Executive Producer Norman Lloyd
Producer George Turpin
Production Company KCET/Los Angeles
Director Norman Lloyd
Writer Steve Tesich
CAST
Goya .... Eileen Brennan
Mario .... John Randolph
Bruno .... John Beck
The Criminal .... Randy Kim
Sylvia .... Pamela Bellwood
The Old Man .... Will Lee
Studley .... Geoffrey Scott
Adolph .... Ken Tigar
The Client .... James Greene

804   Nova   PBS
Program Type Documentary/Special
60 minutes. Weekly. Premiere date: 3/3/74. Season premiere: 11/3/74. Repeat date: 4/27/75. Programs captioned for the deaf as of 7/19/75. Series made possible by grants from the Carnegie Corporation of New York, the Corporation for Public Broadcasting, the National Science Foundation, and Polaroid Corporation. Produced with the advice and cooperation of the American Association for the Advancement of Science.
Executive Producer Michael Ambrosino
Production Company WGBH/Boston
Science Editor Graham Credd

805   Now You See It   CBS
Program Type Game Show
30 minutes. Monday-Friday. Continuous. Premiere date: 4/1/74. Last show: 6/13/75. Created by Frank Wayne.
Executive Producer Frank Wayne
Producer Buck D'Amore
Production Company Goodson-Todman Productions
Director Marc Breslow
Host Jack Narz
Announcer Johnny Olson

806   The Nuclear Energy Debate   PBS
Program Type Interview/Discussion
Special. 30 minutes. Premiere date: 3/26/75. Debate between Ralph Nader and Prof. Norman Rasmussen. Legislative perspective by Rep. Anthony Moffett. Program made possible by a grant from the U.S. Department of Health, Education and Welfare.
Production Company WGBY/Springfield, Massachusetts

807 The Nuclear Threat to You
NBC News Special   NBC
Program Type Documentary/Special
Special. 60 minutes. Premiere date: 2/2/75.
Producer Wallace Westfeldt
Production Company NBC News
Director Stanley Losak
Writer Kenneth C. Donoghue; Wallace West-
feldt
Anchor John Chancellor

**808 The Nursing Home Scandals: The
Old Folks Aren't at Home**   PBS
Program Type Documentary/Special
Special. 60 minutes. Premiere date: 5/21/75.
Production Company WNET/New York
Host Robert Sam Anson

809 The Odd Couple   ABC
Program Type Comedy
30 minutes. Thursday. Premiere date: 9/27/70.
Season premiere: 9/12/74. Last show: 7/4/75.
Based on characters created by Neil Simon in
"The Odd Couple."
Executive Producer Garry Marshall; Sheldon
Keller
Producer Tony Marshall
Production Company Paramount Television
Director Various
Writer Various
CAST
Felix Unger .... Tony Randall
Oscar Madison ....Jack Klugman
Myrna ....Penny Marshall
Miriam .... Elinor Donahue
Murray .... Al Molinaro

The Odd Couple (feature film) *see* The
ABC Sunday Night Movie

810 Of Pure Blood   PBS
Program Type Documentary/Special
Special. 90 minutes. Premiere date: 3/9/75.
Story of Nazi breeding camps.
Producer Clarissa Henry; Marc Hillel
Distributor Agence Franchaise d'Images (Paris)

811 Of Women and Men
NBC News Special   NBC
Program Type Documentary/Special
Special. 180 minutes. Premiere date: 1/9/75. 25
minifeatures. Readings by Viveca Lindfors;
songs by The Deadly Nightshade.
Executive Producer Eliot Frankel
Producer Thomas Tomizawa
Host Tom Synder; Barbara Walters

812 Offstage with Beverly Sills   PBS
Program Type Interview/Discussion
Special. Taped at the Hollywood Bowl. 30
minutes. Premiere date: 9/2/75. Music critic
Martin Bernheimer talks with Beverly Sills.
Producer Price Hicks
Production Company KCET/Los Angeles
Director Jerry Hughes

813 Oh! Baby, Baby, Baby ...
ABC Afternoon Playbreak   ABC
Program Type TV Movie
Special. 90 minutes. Premiere date: 12/5/74. Re-
peat date: 8/14/75.
Executive Producer Alan Landsburg; Laurence
D. Savadove
Producer Kay Hoffman
Production Company Alan Landsburg Produc-
tions, Inc.
Director Howard Morris
Writer Ruth Brooks Flippen
CAST
Rick Stoner .... Bert Convy
Stacy Stoner .... Judy Carne
Ceil ....Nina Foch
Dr. Fisher .... King Moody
Dr. Roth ....Henry Corden
Gwen .... Boni Enten
Cab Driver .... Frank Campanella
Dr. Burkeholder .... Parley Baer
Arthur Booth .... John Furlong
Mrs. Cook .... Dodo Denney
Ms. Phillips .... Lora Kaye
Mrs. Tusher ....Reta Shaw
Mrs. Hoffman ....Reva Rose

814 O. J. Simpson: Juice on the Loose
ABC Sports Special   ABC
Program Type Documentary/Special
Profile of O. J. Simpson. 60 minutes. Premiere
date: 12/28/74.
Executive Producer Roone Arledge
Producer Richard Rubinstein
Production Company ABC Sports
Guests Richard Burton; Howard Cosell; Lee
Marvin; John McKay

Oklahoma Crude *see* NBC Nights at the
Movies

815 Old Is Somebody Else   Syndicated
Program Type Documentary/Special
Special. 60 minutes. Premiere: 8/75. Hosted by
Wayland Flowers and his puppet, Madame.
Producer Herbert Danska
Production Company WNEW/New York, in co-
operation with the National Council on Aging
Distributor Metromedia
Director Herbert Danska
Writer Herbert Danska

Old Is Somebody Else *Continued*
Guests Gloria Steinem; Dick Gregory; Dr. Benjamin Spock; Margaret Mead; Mary Calderone

Oliver! *see* The ABC Sunday Night Movie

The Omega Man *see* NBC Nights at the Movies

816   On Death and Dying   NBC
Program Type Interview/Discussion
Special. 60 minutes. Premiere date: 11/24/74. Interview with Dr. Elisabeth Kubler-Ross.
Executive Producer Doris Ann
Producer Martin Hoade
Production Company NBC Television Religious Programs Unit
Director Martin Hoade

817   On the Road with Charles Kuralt
CBS News Special   CBS
Program Type Documentary/Special
CBS News special documentary. A collection of reports originally featured on the "CBS Evening News with Walter Cronkite." 60 minutes. Premiere date: 6/16/75.
Executive Producer Leslie Midgley
Producer Charles Kuralt; Bernard Birnbaum
Production Company CBS News
Writer Charles Kuralt
Host Charles Kuralt

818   Once Upon a Horse
Call It Macaroni   Syndicated
Program Type Children's Show
Real-life adventure. Two Maryland youngsters learning show riding in Middleburg, Va. 30 minutes. Premiere 5/75. Producer for WJZ-TV/Baltimore: Peter Virsis.
Executive Producer George Moynihan
Producer Gail Frank
Production Company WJZ-TV/Baltimore; Group W Productions
Distributor Westinghouse Broadcasting Company
Director Gail Frank
Cinematographer Dick Roy

One Is a Lonely Number *see* The CBS Thursday/Friday Night Movies

819   One Life to Live   ABC
Program Type Daytime Drama
30 minutes. Monday-Friday. Premiere date:

7/15/68. Continuous. Set in Llanview, U.S.A. Created by Agnes Nixon.
Producer Doris Quinlan
Production Company ABC Television Network Presentation
Director David Pressman; Gordon Rigsby
Head Writer Gordon Russell
Writer Sam Hall; Ted Dazan; Don Wallace

CAST

Anna Craig	Doris Belack
Tim Siegel	Tom Berenger
Wanda Webb	Marilyn Chris
Lt. Ed Hall	Al Freeman, Jr.
Sister Jenny	Katherine Glass
Steven Burke	Bernard Grant
Eileen Siegel	Alice Hirson
Carla Gray Hall	Ellen Holly
Dr. Mark Toland	Tom Lee Jones
Cathy Craig	Dorrie Kavanaugh
Julie Siegel Toland	Leonie Norton
Joe Riley	Lee Patterson
Dr. Dorian Cramer	Nancy Pinkerton
Dr. James Craig	Nat Polen
Vince Wolek	Antony Ponzini
Susan Barry	Lisa Richards
Victoria Lord Riley	Erika Slezak
Dr. Larry Wolek	Michael Storm
Victor Lord	Shepperd Strudwick

One More Time *see* The CBS Thursday/Friday Night Movies

820   One of a Kind   PBS
Program Type Music/Dance
30 minutes. Weekly. Premiere date: 2/4/73. Repeat date: 12/31/74. A combination of new and old programs featuring country and folk musicians.
Producer Alan Baker
Production Company KCET/Los Angeles
Director Allan Muir

821   One of Our Own
NBC Nights at the Movies   NBC
Program Type TV Movie
Pilot for "Doctors Hospital" series (1975–76 season). 120 minutes. Premiere date: 5/5/75.
Executive Producer Matthew Rapf
Producer Jack Laird
Production Company Universal Television in association with NBC-TV
Director Richard Sarafian
Writer Jack Laird

CAST

Dr. Jake Goodwin	George Peppard
Dr. Moresby	William Daniels
Carole Simon	Louise Sorel
LeRoy Atkins	Strother Martin
Dr. Norah Purcell	Zohra Lampert
Dr. Ortega	Victor Campos
Dr. Madison	Peter Hooten
Dr. Janos Varga	Albert Paulsen

Sanantonio .... Giorgio Tozzi
Frances Hollander .... Jacqueline Brookes
Felix Needham .... Ben Masters
Scotty .... Maxine Stuart
Dr. Helmut Von Schultheis .... Oscar Homolka
Grace Chang .... Mary Mon Toy
Rose Sanantonio .... Rose Gregorio
Bill Hinshaw .... William Traylor
Mavis Porter .... Eleanor Lee
Sabina .... Trisha Noble
Adrian Hollander .... Scott McKay
Debbie Hinshaw .... Wendy Phillips
Muriel Emhardt .... Frances Osborne
Dr. Korngold .... Milt Kogan
Myrna .... Karen Knotts
Glick .... Larry Gelman

One, Two, Three see NBC Nights at the Movies

The Only Game in Town see The ABC Monday Night Movie

822 Only With Married Men
Tuesday/Wednesday Movie of the Week ABC
Program Type TV Movie
90 minutes. Premiere date: 12/4/74. Repeat dates: 6/25/75.
Executive Producer Aaron Spelling; Leonard Goldberg
Producer Jerome L. Davis
Production Company A Spelling-Goldberg Production
Director Jerry Paris
Writer Jerome L. Davis
CAST
Dave Andrews .... David Birney
Jill Garrett .... Michele Lee
Dr. Harvey Osterman .... John Astin
Murray West .... Dom DeLuise
Jordan Robbins .... Gavin MacLeod
Mr. Tolan .... Dan Tobin
Tina .... Simone Griffeth
Sheila Osterman .... Yolanda Galardo
Chef .... Fritz Feld
Alfreda .... Jan Narramore
Charlotte .... Royce Wallace
Maitre D' .... Mike Perrotta
Doris .... Lora Kaye
The Minister .... John Hart
Ann West .... Michele Stacy
Peter West .... Patrick Laborteaux

823 Opryland U.S.A.-1975   ABC
Program Type Comedy/Variety
Special. Taped at Opryland U.S.A. (music-theme park) in Nashville, Tenn. 60 minutes. Premiere date: 5/14/75. Special musical material by Billy Barnes.
Executive Producer Ray Canady; Irving Waugh
Producer Bob Wynn

Production Company A Mellodan Production, Inc. with facilities by Compact Video Systems
Director Bob Wynn
Writer Bob Arnott
Musical Director Bill Walker
Choreographer Carl Jablonski
Host Dennis Weaver; Sandy Duncan
Costume Designer Bill Hargate
Guests Jonelle Allen; Tanya Tucker; Jim Stafford

824 Orange Bowl
NBC Sports Special   NBC
Program Type Sports
Live coverage of the 75th Orange Bowl in Miami, Florida. Notre Dame Fighting Irish versus Alabama Crimson Tide. 1/1/75.
Producer Don Ellis; Ted Nathanson
Production Company NBC Sports
Director Ted Nathanson
Announcer Jim Simpson; John Brodie

825 Ordeal
Tuesday/Wednesday Movie of the Week ABC
Program Type TV Movie
90 minutes. Premiere date: 10/30/73. Repeat date: 3/18/75. Based on a story by Francis Cockrell. Filmed partly in Red Rock Canyon in the Mojave Desert, California.
Producer William Bloom
Production Company 20th Century-Fox Television
Director Lee H. Katzin
Writer Francis Cockrell; Leon Tokatyan
CAST
Richard Damian .... Arthur Hill
Kay Damian .... Diana Muldaur
Andy Folsom .... James Stacy
Eliot Frost .... Macdonald Carey
Sheriff Geeson .... Michael Ansara
Dep. Sheriff Fred .... Arch Whiting
Dep. Sheriff Joe .... Bill Catching

The Organization see The ABC Saturday Night Movie

826 Ormandy International   PBS
Program Type Music/Dance
Special. 60 minutes. Premiere date: 11/4/74. Program funded by the International Union. Eugene Ormandy conducts the Philadelphia Orchestra.
Producer Norman Marcus
Production Company WHYY/Philadelphia
Director Robert Hankal

827 The Orphan and the Dude
ABC Comedy Special   ABC
Program Type Comedy

The Orphan and the Dude *Continued*
Special. Created by Joseph A. Goodson. 30
minutes. Premiere date: 7/18/75.
Producer Jim Parker; Arnold Margolin
Production Company Parker-Margolin Production in association with MGM Television
Director James Frawley
Writer Jim Parker; Arnold Margolin
CAST

Oliver Smith	Oliver Clark
Curtis Brown	Art Evans
Sam Brodsky	Ed Barth
Mr. Brown	Bill Henderson
Amber	Lynne Holmes
Leonard Brown	Todd Bridges
Fast Freddie	Frank McRae
Dan	David Moody

828   **The Oscar Awards**   NBC
Program Type Awards Show
Special. 47th annual awards presented by the
Academy of Motion Picture Arts and Sciences.
Live. Approximately 120 minutes. 4/8/75.
Sammy Davis, Jr. sang and danced a salute to
Fred Astaire; Aretha Franklin, Jack Jones and
Frankie Laine sang the nominated songs.
Producer Howard W. Koch
Director Marty Pasetta
Writer Hal Kanter; William Ludwig; Leonard
Spigelgass
Musical Director John Green
Choreographer Anita Mann
Emcees Sammy Davis, Jr.; Bob Hope; Shirley
MacLaine; Frank Sinatra
Singers Sammy Davis, Jr.; Aretha Franklin; Jack
Jones; Frankie Laine

829   **The Osmonds Special**   CBS
Program Type Music/Dance
Special. 60 minutes. Premiere date: 11/20/74.
The Osmonds: Alan, Wayne, Merrill, Jay,
Donny, Marie, Jimmy. Special music by Earl
Brown.
Executive Producer Raymond Katz
Producer Alan Blye; Chris Bearde
Production Company Skyjay Productions, Inc. in
association with Oshro Productions, Inc.
Director Jeff Margolis
Writer Chris Bearde; Alan Blye
Choreographer Jaime Rogers
Special Guests Andy Williams; Isaac Hayes

The Other *see* The CBS Thursday/Friday
Night Movies

830   **The Other Half of the Sky: A
China Memoir**   PBS
Program Type Documentary/Special
Special. 75 minutes. Premiere date: 4/15/75. 10-
women tour of mainland China. Presented by
WNET/New York.
Producer Shirley MacLaine
Director Claudia Weill; Shirley MacLaine
Writer Shirley MacLaine
Narrator Shirley MacLaine

831   **The Other Half of the Sky: A
China Memoir: Discussion**   PBS
Program Type Interview/Discussion
Special. 45 minutes. Premiere date: 4/15/75.
Follow-up discussion to film "The Other Half of
the Sky: A China Memoir."
Production Company WNET/New York
Moderators Audrey Topping; O. Edmund Clubb

832   **Out of the Huddle and Into the
Booth with Don Meredith and the NBC
All-Stars**
NBC Sports Special   NBC
Program Type Sports
Special preceding Thanksgiving Day football
games. 30 minutes. 11/28/74.
Producer Don Ellis
Production Company NBC Sports
Host Don Meredith; Curt Gowdy; Al DeRogatis

833   **Out to Lunch**   ABC
Program Type Comedy/Variety
Special. With characters from "Sesame Street,"
the Muppets, and cast of "The Electric Company." 60 minutes. Premiere date: 12/10/74.
Music by Joe Raposo.
Executive Producer David D. Connell
Producer Norton W. Wright
Production Company CTW Productions
Director Bill Davis
Writer Christopher Cerf; Tom Dunsmuir; Clark
Gessner; Bryan Joseph; Norman Stiles; Jim
Thurman; Tom Whedon
Choreographer Patricia Birch
Guest Stars Barbara Eden; Elliott Gould
Guests Luis Avalos; Jim Boyd; Morgan Freeman;
Judy Graubart; Skip Hinnant; Rita Moreno;
Hattie Winston
Puppeteers Frank Oz; Jerry Nelson; Richard
Hunt; Carroll Spinney

834   **Pagliacci**
Great Performances   PBS
Program Type Music/Dance
Special. 90 minutes. Premiere date: 3/22/75.
Presented in the United States by WNET/New
York; David Griffiths coordinating producer.
Opera staged at La Scala, Milan, Italy; Herbert
von Karajan conducting.
Producer Paul Hager
Production Company Cosmotel S.A. Production

Guests Artists: Jon Vickers; Raina Corsi-Kabaivanska; Peter Glossop

835   Palm Sunday Service   NBC
Program Type Religious Program
Palm Sunday Mass from the National Shrine of the Immaculate Conception, Washington, D.C. The Rev. William W. Baum, Archbishop of Washington, principal celebrant.
Producer Doris Ann
Production Company NBC Television Religious Programs Unit
Director Richard Cox

836   Panic on the 5:22
Tuesday/Wednesday Movie of the Week ABC
Program Type TV Movie
90 minutes. Premiere date: 11/20/74.
Executive Producer Quinn Martin
Producer Anthony Spinner
Production Company Quinn Martin Productions
Director Harvey Hart
Writer Eugene Price
CAST
Countess Hedy Maria Tovarese	Ina Balin
Wendell Weaver	Bernie Casey
Tony Ebsen	Linden Chiles
Harlan Jack Gardner	Andrew Duggan
Hal Rodgers	Dana Elcar
Jerome Hartford	Eduard Franz
Mary Ellen Lewis	Lynda Day George
Lawrence Lewis	Laurence Luckinbill
Emil Linz	Reni Santoni
Frankie Seamantini	James Sloyan
Eddie Chiario	Robert Walden
Dudley Stevenson	Dennis Patrick
Dr. Cruikshank	Robert Mandan

837   Paper Moon   ABC
Program Type Comedy
30 minutes. Thursday. Premiere date: 9/12/74. Last show: 1/2/75. The Midwest in the 1930s. Based on the motion picture "Paper Moon."
Executive Producer Anthony Wilson
Producer Robert Stambler
Production Company Paramount Television
CAST
Moze Pray	Christopher Connelly
Addie Pray	Jodie Foster

The Parent Trap *see* All-Disney Night

838   Paris Open
NBC Sports Special   NBC
Program Type Sports
Taped coverage 6/14/75; 6/15/75 from Paris of French tennis championships. 90 minutes each.
Production Company NBC Sports

839   Partridge Family: 2200 A.D.   CBS
Program Type Animated Film
The singing Partridges in animation. 30 minutes. Saturday. Premiere date: 9/7/74. Last show: 3/1/75.
Executive Producer William Hanna; Joseph Barbera
Producer Iwao Takamoto
Production Company William Hanna-Joseph Barbera Productions
Director Charles A. Nichols
Writer Barry Blitzer; Larz Bourne; Dick Conway and Buddy Atkinson; Rance Howard and Jim Begg; Jack Mendelsohn; John Fenton Murray; Ray Parker; Bill Raynor
Voices Sherry Alberoni; Danny Bonaduce; Suzanne Crough; Susan Dey; Mickey Dolenz; Brian Forster; Joan Gerber; Dave Madden; Chuck McLennan; Julie McWhirter; Allan Melvin; Alan Oppenheimer; Mike Road; Hal Smith; John Stephenson; Lennie Weinrib; Franklin Welker

840   Password   ABC
Program Type Game Show
30 minutes. Monday-Friday. Premiere date: 4/5/71. Last show: 6/27/75. Revival of "Password" which premiered in 1961 and ran for six years hosted by Allen Ludden. During the season, show changed name to "Password All Stars" and back again to "Password."
Producer Frank Wayne
Producer Howard Felcher
Production Company Goodson-Todman Production
Director Stuart W. Phelps
Host Allen Ludden

841   Paul Hornung's Greatest Sports Legends   Syndicated
Program Type Sports
30 minutes. Weekly. Premiere: 2/75. Guests for the series: "Red" Auerbach; Roy Campanella; Don Carter; Joe DiMaggio; Elroy "Crazylegs" Hirsch; Jack Kramer; Bobby Layne; Marion Motley; Joe Perry; Bob Pettit; Oscar Robertson; Kyle Rote; Gale Sayers; Secretariat and Helen Tweedy; Sam Snead; Bart Starr; Roger Ward
Executive Producer Berl Rotfeld
Producer Berl Rotfeld
Distributor SyndiCable, Inc.
Director Tony Verna
Host Paul Hornung

842   Paul Sand in Friends and Lovers   CBS
Program Type Comedy
Set in Boston. Paul Sand portrays a bass violinist for the Boston Symphony Orchestra. 30 minutes.

Paul Sand in Friends and Lovers
Continued
Saturday. Premiere date: 9/14/74. Last show: 1/4/75.
Executive Producer James L. Brooks; Allan Burns
Producer Steve Pritzker
Production Company MTM Enterprises, Inc.
Director Various
Writer Various
CAST
Robert Dreyfuss .... Paul Sand
Charlie Dreyfuss .... Michael Pataki
Janice Dreyfuss ....Penny Marshall
Fred Meyerbach .... Steve Landesberg
Jack Riordan ....Dick Wesson
Mason Woodruff .... Craig Richard Nelson

843   **Pebbles and Bamm-Bamm**   CBS
Program Type Animated Film
Reruns. Action revolves around children of Flintstone characters. Originally presented 1971–72 season. Return date: 3/8/75. 30 minutes. Saturday.
Executive Producer Joseph Barbera; William Hanna
Production Company Hanna-Barbera Productions
Writer Joel Kane; Woody Kling; Howard Morganstern; Joe Ruby; Ken Spears
Musical Director Ted Nichols
Animation Director Charles A. Nichols

844   **A Peculiar Treasure**
The Eternal Light   NBC
Program Type Religious Program
Dramatization of the childhood of Edna Ferber. 60 minutes. Premiere date: 2/17/74. Repeat date: 7/20/74.
Executive Producer Doris Ann
Producer Martin Hoade
Production Company NBC Television Religious Programs Unit
Director Martin Hoade
CAST
Edna Ferber (as an adult) .... Bobo Lewis
Edna (as a child) .... Jill Chodor
Mother .... Louise Troy
Father .... Norman Rose
Fannie ....Toni Kalem

845   **People Just Don't Whistle No More**
                                           PBS
Program Type Music/Dance
Special. 8th annual Old-Time Fiddlers Contest. Filmed in Friendsville, Maryland and Dunbar, Pennsylvania. 30 minutes. Premiere date: 1/2/75. Repeat date: 1/2/75. Guest fiddlers: Jim Bryner; Jonah Hughes; Lawrence Fluharty; Reuben Bittinger; William Deal; Pinkie Shoemaker.

Producer Laurence Wiseman
Production Company WQED/Pittsburgh for the Pennsylvania Public Television Network
Camera Dusty Nelson; Pasquale Buba

The People Next Door *see* The CBS Thursday/Friday Night Movies

846   **The People's Choice Awards**   CBS
Program Type Awards Show
First entertainment awards determined by a survey of the American public. 120 minutes. Premiere date: 3/4/75.
Executive Producer Robert Stivers
Producer Paul W. Keyes
Production Company Super Award Show, Inc. and Robert Stivers Company
Director Stan Harris
Writer Paul W. Keyes; Marc London; Bob Howard
Musical Director Donn Trenner
Host Richard Crenna; Army Archerd
Announcer Johnny Gilbert

847   **Performance: Jazz**   PBS
Program Type Music/Dance
Three specials. 30 minutes each. First available through the Eastern Educational Network 10/1/73.
Production Company Maryland Center for Public Broadcasting
Artists Sheilah Ross; Errol Robinson; Fred Thaxton

848   **The Perry Como Christmas Show**
                                           CBS
Program Type Comedy/Variety
Special. 60 minutes. Premiere date: 12/17/74.
Executive Producer Perry Como
Producer Nick Vanoff
Production Company Rancom Productions
Director Nick Vanoff
Host Perry Como
Guests Peggy Fleming; Rich Little; The Carpenters

849   **The Perry Como Springtime Special**
                                           CBS
Program Type Comedy/Variety
Special. 60 minutes. Premiere date: 3/27/75. Choral direction and special musical material by Ray Charles.
Producer Bob Finkel
Production Company Roncom Productions, Inc. in association with Teram Productions, Inc.
Director Jack Regas
Writer Herbert Baker
Musical Director Nick Perito

Host Perry Como
Guests Olivia Newton-John; Pat Boone and family
Special Guest Bob Newhart

850   Perry Como's Summer of '74   CBS
Program Type Comedy/Variety
Special. 60 minutes. Premiere date: 9/12/74.
Choral direction and special musical material by
Ray Charles.
Producer Nick Vanoff
Production Company Roncom Productions, Inc.
Director Nick Vanoff
Writer Bob Ellison; Jay Burton; Mort Scharfman
Host Perry Como
Guests Paul Lynde; Michele Lee; Jimmie Walker

Pete 'N' Tillie *see* NBC Nights at the Movies

851   Petrocelli   NBC
Program Type Crime Drama
60 minutes. Wednesday. Premiere date: 9/11/74.
Set in San Remo. (Filmed in Tucson, Arizona.)
Based on motion picture "The Lawyer" and tv
movie "Night Games." Created by Sidney J. Furie; Harold Buchman. Developed for television
by E. Jack Neuman.
Executive Producer Thomas L. Miller; Edward
K. Milkis
Producer Leonard Katzman
Production Company Paramount Television in
association with Miller-Milkis Productions
Director Various
Writer Various
CAST
Tony Petrocelli .... Barry Newman
Maggie Petrocelli .... Susan Howard
Pete Ritter .... Albert Salmi

852   PGA Golf Championship
ABC Sports Special   ABC
Program Type Sports
57th annual tournament. Second, third and final
round play from the Firestone Country Club,
Akron, Ohio. 8/8/75; 8/9/75; 8/10/75.
Executive Producer Roone Arledge
Producer Chuck Howard
Production Company ABC Sports
Director Terry Jastrow; Jim Jennett
Announcer Chris Schenkel; Jim McKay; Frank
Gifford; Bill Flemming; Dave Marr

853   The Phil Donahue Show   Syndicated
Program Type Variety/Talk Show
60 minutes. Monday-Friday. Continuous. Premiered 1968.
Executive Producer Dick Mincer

Producer Patricia McMillen
Production Company Avco Broadcasting
Director Ron Weiner
Host Phil Donahue

854   Philadelphia Folk Festival   PBS
Program Type Music/Dance
13-part series. 60 minutes. Premiere date:
7/10/75. Concerts taped at the 1974 Philadelphia Folk Festival at Old Pool Farm, Schwenksville, Pa. and made possible by a grant from the
Pennsylvania Public Television Network.
Executive Producer Norman Marcus
Producer Doug Bailey
Production Company WHYY/Wilmington-
Philadelphia
Director Various

855   A Pin to See the Peepshow   PBS
Program Type Drama
Special. Four 50-minute episodes shown in one
evening. Premiere date: 3/8/75. Based on the
novel by Friniwyd Tennyson Jesse.
Producer Rex Tucker
Production Company British Broadcasting Corporation
Director Raymond Menmuir
Writer Elaine Morgan
CAST
Julia Starling .... Francesca Annis
Herbert Starling .... Bernard Hepton
Leo Carr ....John Duttine
Almond .... Ron Pember
Alfie .... Keith Drinkel
Anne .... Petronella Barker
George .... John Nettleton
Mildred .... Maggie Flint
Mrs. Almond .... Mary Chester
Bertha .... Georgine Anderson
Elsa .... Rosemary Blake
Mrs. Humble .... Queenie Watts
Marian .... Marian Melford
Policeman .... Frank Jarvis
Inspector .... Victor Brooks
Crown Counsel .... Kenneth Breda
Julia's Counsel .... Anthony Rowe

856   The Pink Panther   NBC
Program Type Animated Film
30 minutes. Saturday. Premiere date: 9/6/69.
Season premiere: 9/7/74 (reruns). Created by
Blake Edwards. "Pink Panther Theme" by
Henry Mancini.
Producer David H. DePatie; Friz Freleng
Production Company Mirisch-Geoffrey-DePatie-
Freleng Production
Director Hawley Pratt; Gerry Chiniquy; Arthur
Davis
Writer John Dunn; William Lutz; Don Christensen

857 A Place for No Story   PBS
Program Type Documentary/Special
Special. An aerial portrait of California without narration. 60 minutes. Premiere date: 3/26/74. Repeat date: 5/10/75.
Executive Producer Richard O. Moore; Zev Putterman
Producer Richard Greene
Production Company KQED/San Francisco

858 Planet of the Apes   CBS
Program Type Science Fiction
Based on the book and motion picture by Pierre Boule. 60 minutes. Friday. Premiere date: 9/13/74. Last show: 12/27/74.
Executive Producer Herbert Hirschman
Producer Stan Hough
Production Company 20th Century-Fox Television
CAST
Galen .... Roddy McDowall
Alan Virdon ....Ron Harper
Pete Burke ....James Naughton
Urko .... Mark Lenard
Zaius ....Booth Colman

Planet of the Apes (feature film) *see* The CBS Thursday/Friday Night Movies

859 Play Bridge with the Experts   PBS
Program Type Educational
26-program series. Created by W. Edward Allen. 30 minutes. Weekly. Premiere date: 9/29/74. 15 master-player members of the American Contract Bridge League are featured.
Production Company KUHT/Houston; Educational TV Productions, Inc.
Director Jack Veres
Writer George S. Dawkins; Anita "Pidgeon" Davis; Carolyn Flornouy; Bobby Goldman; George Pisk; Rennie Sharfstein
Host Nathan Ostrich
Consultant John Gerber

Play Misty for Me *see* NBC Nights at the Movies

860 Playmates
Tuesday/Wednesday Movie of the Week ABC
Program Type TV Movie
90 minutes. Premiere date: 10/3/72. Repeat date: 10/15/74.
Producer Lillian Gallo
Production Company An ABC Circle Film
Director Theodore J. Flicker
Writer Richard Baer
CAST
Marshall Burnett .... Alan Alda
Patty Holvey .... Connie Stevens

Kermit Holvey .... Doug McClure
Lois Burnett ....Barbara Feldon
Johnny Holvey .... Tiger Williams
Eric Burnett ....Bryan Scott
Amy .... Eileen Brennan
Gallery Patron .... Severn Darden
Father .... Roger Bowen
Estelle .... Eloise Hardt
Bikini No. 1 ....Valerie Fitzgerald
Bikini No. 2 ....Debbie Dozier

861 The Point
Special Movie Presentation   ABC
Program Type Animated Film
First full-length animated feature made for television. 90 minutes. Premiere date: 2/2/71. Repeat date: 12/7/74. Based on a story by Harry Nilsson; music composed and performed by Harry Nilsson.
Production Company Nilsson House Music, Inc. and Murakami-Wolf Productions, Inc.
Director Fred Wolf
Writer Norman Lenzer
Animation Director Fred Wolf
Narrator Alan Barzman
VOICES
The Father ....Alan Barzman
Son/Oblio .... Michael Lookinland
The King/Leafman/Oblio's Father .... Paul Frees
The Count .... Lenny Weinrib
Rockman .... Bill Martin
Oblio's Mother .... Joan Gerber
The Count's Son .... Buddy Foster

862 Police Story   NBC
Program Type Crime Drama
Anthology series created by Joseph Wambaugh. Developed for television by E. Jack Neuman. 60 minutes. Tuesday. Premiere date: 10/2/73. Season premiere: 9/10/74. (*See* special episode, "The Return of Joe Forrester.")
Executive Producer Stanley Kallis
Producer Christopher Morgan
Production Company David Gerber Production in association with Columbia Pictures Television
Director Various
Writer Various
Story Consultants Mark Rodgers; Liam O'Brien

863 Police Surgeon   Syndicated
Program Type Crime Drama
30 minutes. Weekly. Premiere: 9/72. Season premiere: 9/74.
Executive Producer Wilton Schiller
Producer Chester Krumholz
Production Company Addison, Goldstein & Walsh, Inc.
Director Various
Writer Various

CAST

Dr. Simon Locke .... Sam Groom
Det. Jack Gordon .... Larry D. Mann

864 Police Woman   NBC
Program Type Crime Drama
Spinoff from "Police Story." 60 minutes. Friday.
Premiere date: 9/13/74.
Executive Producer David Gerber
Producer Douglas Benton
Production Company David Gerber Productions
in association with Columbia Pictures Televi-
sion
Director Various
Writer Various

CAST

Sgt. Pepper Anderson .... Angie Dickinson
Sgt. Bill Crowley .... Earl Holliman
Det. Joe Styles .... Ed Bernard
Pete Royster .... Charles Dierkop

Pollyanna *see* NBC Nights at the Movies

865 Pop! Goes the Country   Syndicated
Program Type Comedy/Variety
Country music show. 30 minutes. Weekly. Sea-
son premiere: 9/74. Theme sung by The Statler
Brothers.
Executive Producer Bill Graham
Producer J. Reginald Dunlap
Production Company Show Biz, Inc.
Director Bill Turner
Writer Bill Graham
Musical Director Jerry Whitehurst
Host Ralph Emery

866 Popi
Comedy Special   CBS
Program Type Comedy
30 minutes. Pilot film. Based on 1969 motion
picture of the same name. Premiere date: 5/2/75.
Producer Herbert B. Leonard
Production Company International Television
Productions
Director E. W. Swackhamer
Writer Tina Pine; Lester Pine

CAST

Abraham .... Hector Elizondo
Lupe .... Liz Torres
Maggio .... Lou Criscuolo
Junior .... Anthony Perez
Luis .... Dennis Vasquez
Jackson .... Herb Jefferson, Jr.
Principal .... McIntyre Dixon
Doorman .... Santos Morales
Flower Seller .... Matt Russo
Ambulance Driver .... Ron McClarty

867 Portrait - The Man From
Independence   ABC
Program Type Drama
Special. 60 minutes. Premiere date: 3/11/74. Re-
peat date: 12/28/74.
Executive Producer David Victor
Producer Jon Epstein
Production Company Universal Television in as-
sociation with Groverton Productions for
ABC-TV
Director Jack Smight
Writer Edward DeBlasio

CAST

Harry S Truman .... Robert Vaughn
Tom Pendergast .... Arthur Kennedy
Bess Truman .... June Dayton
Mama Truman ....Martha Scott
Margaret Truman .... Tasha Lee
Bud Linaver .... Russell Johnson
Constance .... Ronne Troup
Bob Mooney .... Alan Fudge
Werner ....Leonard Stone
The Stranger .... James Luisi
Additional Cast Lou Frizzell; Michael Vandever; Alice
Backes; Jay Varela

The Poseidan Adventure *see* The ABC
Sunday Night Movie

Potemkin *see* Humanities Film Forum

868 Prairie Lawyer
Sandburg's Lincoln   NBC
Program Type Drama
Third show in Lincoln series based on biography
by Carl Sandburg. 60 minutes. Premiere date:
4/7/75.
Executive Producer David L. Wolper
Producer George Schaefer
Production Company David L. Wolper Produc-
tion
Director George Schaefer
Writer Emmet Lavery; Irene Kamp; Louis
Kamp

CAST

Abraham Lincoln .... Hal Holbrook
Maj. John Stuart .... Robert Foxworth
Mary Owens .... Catherine Burns
Judge Davis ....Richard Dysart
Stephen Douglas .... Walter McGinn
Kitty Cavan .... Martine Bartlett
Judge Thomas .... Paul Fix
Henry Truett .... James Greene
Mary Todd .... Michele Marsh
William Butler ....Iggie Wolfington

869 The Preakness
CBS Sports Special   CBS
Program Type Sports
100th running of the Preakness from Pimlico

The Preakness *Continued*
Race Course, Baltimore, Maryland. Live coverage. 5/17/75. 60 minutes.
Production Company CBS Television Network Sports
Director Tony Verna
Announcer Chic Anderson
Reporters Jack Whitaker; Heywood Hale Broun; Frank Wright

870   Prescription: Take with Caution
CBS Reports   CBS
Program Type Documentary/Special
Special. Documentary dealing with the health hazards of prescription drugs. 60 minutes. Premiere date: 1/10/75.
Executive Producer Burton Benjamin
Producer Al Wasserman
Production Company CBS News
Anchor Dan Rather
Reporter Daniel Schorr

871   President Ford's Address on Amnesty and Pardon
CBS News Special   CBS
Program Type Documentary/Special
Live coverage. 9/16/74. Address of Pres. Gerald Ford from Washington, D.C. Followed by summary and analysis by Eric Sevareid.
Executive Producer Leslie Midgley
Production Company CBS News

872   President Ford's Address on the Economy Before Congress
CBS News Special   CBS
Program Type Documentary/Special
Live coverage from Washington, D.C. 10/8/74. Address of Pres. Gerald Ford to Congress. Summary and analysis by George Herman.
Executive Producer Leslie Midgley
Producer Sanford Socolow
Production Company CBS News
Anchor Bob Schieffer

873   President Ford's Address to Sigma Delta Chi Convention
CBS News Special   CBS
Program Type Documentary/Special
Live coverage from Phoenix. Address of Pres. Gerald Ford to professional journalists on Rockefeller nomination for the vice-presidency. 11/14/74.
Executive Producer Leslie Midgley
Production Company CBS News

874   President Ford's Address to the Future Farmers of America
CBS News Special   CBS
Program Type Documentary/Special
Live coverage from Kansas City, Mo. Speech by Pres. Gerald Ford on inflation 10/15/74. Summary and analysis by George Herman.
Executive Producer Leslie Midgley
Production Company CBS News
Anchor Barry Serafin

875   President Ford's Address to the United Nations
CBS News Special   CBS
Program Type Documentary/Special
Live coverage from New York City. Address of Pres. Gerald Ford to the United Nations. Commentary by Richard C. Hottelet; Bob Schieffer. 9/18/74.
Executive Producer Leslie Midgley
Production Company CBS News
Anchor Roger Mudd

876   President Ford's Appearance Before the House Judiciary Committee's Subcommittee on Criminal Justice
CBS News Special   CBS
Program Type Documentary/Special
Live coverage from Washington, D.C. Historic appearance of Pres. Gerald Ford at House Committee. 10/17/74.
Executive Producer Leslie Midgley
Producer Sanford Socolow
Production Company CBS News
Anchors Walter Cronkite; Bob Schieffer
Correspondent Bruce Morton

877   President Ford's Economic Address to the Nation
CBS News Special   CBS
Program Type Documentary/Special
Live coverage of Pres. Gerald Ford from Washington, D.C. Address followed by analysis by George Herman. 1/13/75.
Executive Producer Leslie Midgley
Production Company CBS News
Anchor Bob Schieffer

878   President Ford's First 100 Days in Office
NBC News Special   NBC
Program Type Documentary/Special
Special. 60 minutes. Assessment of Pres. Gerald Ford after 100 days by NBC news correspondents. Premiere date: 11/17/74.
Production Company NBC News

879   President Ford's State of the Union Message to Congress
ABC News Special Events; CBS News Special; NBC News Special   ABC; CBS; NBC; PBS
Program Type Documentary/Special
Live coverage of State of the Union by Pres. Gerald Ford. 1/15/75.
Production Company ABC News; CBS News; NBC News; PBS

880   The President in Asia
ABC News Special Events   ABC
Program Type Documentary/Special
Two specials. 30 minutes each. Premiere dates: 11/19/74; 11/22/74.
Executive Producer Walter J. Pfister, Jr.
Producer Elliott L. Bernstein
Production Company ABC News
Director Robert Delaney

Pressure Point *see* CBS Tennis Classic/Pressure Point

881   The Price Is Right   CBS
Program Type Game Show
Originally appeared in 1956. New show premiered 9/4/72. 30 minutes. Monday-Friday. Continuous.
Executive Producer Frank Wayne
Producer Jay Wolpert
Production Company Goodson-Todman Productions
Director Marc Breslow
Host Bob Barker
Announcer Johnny Olson

882   The Price Is Right   Syndicated
Program Type Game Show
Evening version of daytime game show. 30 minutes. Weekly. Premiere: 9/72. Season premiere: 9/74.
Executive Producer Frank Wayne
Producer Jay Wolpert
Production Company Goodson-Todman Productions
Distributor Viacom Enterprises
Director Marc Breslow
Host Dennis James
Announcer Johnny Olson

883   The Price of Knowledge   PBS
Program Type Interview/Discussion
Special. 30 minutes. Premiere date: 1/6/75. Follow-up to "Primate," cinema-verite film by Frederick Wiseman shown 12/5/74.
Production Company "Nova" Science Unit-WGBH/Boston

Moderator Graham Credd
Panelists Frederick Wiseman; Dr. Adrian Perachio; Richard Lervantin; David Baltimore

884   Primal Man: The Human Factor
                                 ABC
Program Type Documentary/Special
Last in four-part series presented over one and a half years. 60 minutes. Premiere date: 5/22/75.
Producer Jack Kaufman
Production Company A David L. Wolper Production
Narrator Alexander Scourby

885   Primate   PBS
Program Type Documentary/Special
Special. Cinema-verite film of experiments on apes photographed at the Yerkes Primate Research Center, Atlanta, Georgia. 105 minutes. Premiere date: 12/5/74. (*See also* "The Price of Knowledge," a follow-up discussion to the film.)
Producer Frederick Wiseman
Production Company Zipporah Films and WNET/New York
Director Frederick Wiseman
Editor Frederick Wiseman

Pro Bowl *see* AFC-NFC Pro Bowl

Pro Football Report *see* The NFL Today/Pro Football Report

886   Professional Bowlers Tour   ABC
Program Type Sports
16 events. Show premiered in 1962. Season premiere: 1/4/75. Last show of season: 4/19/75. 90 minutes. Live coverage. Saturday.
Executive Producer Roone Arledge
Producer Bob Goodrich
Production Company ABC Sports
Director Roger Goodman; Jim Jennett
Host Chris Schenkel
Announcer Chris Schenkel
Commentator Nelson Burton, Jr.

Professional Golf Association Championship *see* PGA Golf Championship

The Professionals *see* The CBS Thursday/Friday Night Movies

887   Profile in Music: Beverly Sills PBS
Program Type Music/Dance

Profile in Music: Beverly Sills *Continued*
Special. 90 minutes. Premiere date: 3/10/75. Interview and performance by Beverly Sills.
Producer Patricia Foy
Production Company British Broadcasting Corporation
Interviewer/Narrator Bernard Levin

888   Promise Him Anything . . .
Tuesday/Wednesday Movie of the Week ABC
Program Type TV Movie
90 minutes. Premiere date: 5/14/75.
Producer Mitchell Brower; Robert Lovenheim
Production Company An ABC Circle Film
Director Edward Parone
Writer David Freeman
CAST
Pop .... Eddie Albert
Marjorie .... Meg Foster
Paul .... Frederic Forrest
Silver .... William Schallert
Judge .... Tom Ewell
Chuck .... Steven Keats
Tom .... Edward Bell
Cop .... Aldo Ray
Housewife .... Ellen Blake
Helen .... Judy Cassmore
Mother ....Peggy Rea
Lyle ....Hunter von Leer
Lucille .... Joyce Jameson
O'Brien .... Tom Hatten
Seaplane Attendant .... Pearl Shear
Crazy Lady .... Mary Jane Canfield
Karen .... Patty Regan

889   Pssst! Hammerman's After You!
ABC Afterschool Specials   ABC
Program Type Children's Show
Special. Based on "The 18th Emergency" by Betsy Byars. 60 minutes. Premiere date: 1/16/74. Repeat date: 1/8/75.
Producer D. Martin Tahse
Production Company Entertainment Media Productions
Director Jack Regas
Writer Bob Rodgers
CAST
Mouse Fawley ....Christian Juttner
Marv Hammerman .... Jim Sage
Ezzie .... Lance Kerwin
Mr. Casino .... Titos Vandis
Mr. Stein .... Jack Manning
Mouse's Mother .... Jay MacIntosh
Mrs. Schwartz .... Lillian Adams
Viola .... Lark Geib
Margy .... Ann D'Andrea

890   Punch and Jody
NBC World Premiere Movie   NBC
Program Type TV Movie
90 minutes. Premiere date: 11/26/74. Repeat date: 5/27/75.
Executive Producer Dick Berg
Producer Doug Benton
Production Company Metromedia Producers Corporation
Director Barry Shear
Writer John McGreevey
CAST
Punch .... Glenn Ford
Jody ....Pam Griffin
Lil .... Ruth Roman
Midget .... Billy Barty

891   The Quality of Life   PBS
Program Type Interview/Discussion
Special. Round table forum on the impact of the economy on the quality of life. 60 minutes. Premiere date: 12/30/74. Program made possible by grants from the National Economists Club Educational Fund, National Science Foundation, Ford Motor Company Fund, Equitable Life Assurance Company of the United States, Continental Bank Foundation, and Bankers Trust Company.
Executive Producer David Prowitt
Production Company Science Program Group, Inc. in cooperation with WCET/Cincinnati
Host David Prowitt
Panelists Sar Laviton; John Quarles; Dr. Theodore Cooper; John Barnum

892   The Quarterly Report   PBS
Program Type Documentary/Special
Reports on America. Two shows shown during 1974–75: "America in Transition" and "The Last American Supper." (*See* individual titles for credits.)
Producer Various
Production Company NPACT (National Public Affairs Center for Television)

893   QB VII   ABC
Program Type TV Movie
Special. Based on the novel by Leon Uris. Filmed in the United States, Belgium, England and Israel. 210 minutes. Premiere dates: 4/29/74; 4/30/74. Repeat dates: 4/22/75 (90 minutes); 4/23/75 (60 minutes); 4/24/75 (60 minutes).
Producer Douglas S. Cramer
Production Company Screen Gems and The Douglas S. Cramer Company
Director Tom Gries
Writer Edward Anhalt
CAST
Abe Cady .... Ben Gazzara
Dr. Adam Kelno .... Anthony Hopkins
Angela Kelno .... Leslie Caron
Lady Margaret ....Lee Remick
Justice Gilroy .... Jack Hawkins
Samantha Cady .... Juliet Mills
Shawcross .... Dan O'Herlihy
Dr. Parmentier .... Edith Evans

Bannister	Anthony Quayle
Highsmith	Robert Stephens
Clinton-Meek	John Gielgud
Lotaki	Milo O'Shea
Stephen Kelno	Anthony Andrews
Natalie	Judy Carne
Lena Kronska	Signe Hasso
Dr. Tressler	Sam Jaffe
Semple	Alan Napier
King McAvoy	Lee Phillips
Ben Cady	Kristoffer Tabori
Morris Cady	Joseph Wiseman

894 Queen of the Stardust Ballroom
CBS
Program Type Drama
Special. Drama with music. 120 minutes. Premiere date: 2/13/75. Music by Billy Goldenberg; lyrics by Marilyn Bergman; Alan Bergman.
Producer Robert W. Christiansen; Rick Rosenberg
Production Company Tomorrow Entertainment, Inc.
Director Sam O'Steen
Writer Jerome Kass
Choreographer Marge Champion
Costume Designer Bruce Walkup
CAST

Bea Asher	Maureen Stapleton
Al Green	Charles Durning
David	Michael Brandon
Jack	Michael Strong
Helen	Charlotte Rae
Angie	Jacquelyn Hyde
Diane	Beverly Manners
Louis	Alan Fudge
Jennifer	Elizabeth Berger
Singer	Martha Tilton
M.C.	Orrin Tucker

895 The Questions of Abraham
CBS
Program Type Religious Program
CBS News religious special. Oratorio for Passover by Ezra Laderman; Joseph Darion; conductor: Alfredo Antonini. 60 minutes. Premiere date: 9/30/73. Repeat date: 3/23/75.
Executive Producer Pamela Ilott
Production Company CBS News
Director Jerome Schnur
CAST

Abraham	Sherrill Milnes
Master of Ceremonies	Morley Meredith
Sarah	Johanna Meier
Hagar	Hilda Harris

896 Rabin: Action Biography
Action Biography　　ABC
Program Type Documentary/Special
Special. 60 minutes. Premiere date: 4/15/75.
Producer Margery Lipton; Eileen Russell
Production Company ABC News

Correspondents Howard K. Smith; William Seamans
Reporter William Seamans

897 Rabin and Sadat: Peace or War?
NBC News Special　　NBC
Program Type Documentary/Special
Special. 60 minutes. Premiere date: 4/5/75.
Producer Les Crystal
Production Company NBC News
Host John Chancellor
Reporters Richard Valeriani; John Palmer

898 Rachel, La Cubana
PBS
Program Type Music/Dance
Special. Opera by Hans Werner Henze based on "La Cancion de Rachel" by Miguel Barnet. 90 minutes. Originally shown on "WNET Opera Theater" 3/4/74. Repeat date: 6/30/75.
Executive Producer Peter Herman Adler
Producer David Griffiths
Production Company WNET/New York
Director Kirk Browning
CAST

Young Rachel	Lee Venora
Eusebio/Paco/Federico	Alan Titus
Old Rachel	Lili Darvas
Lucile/Rosita	Susanne Marsee
Yarini/Alberto	Ronald Young
Telescope Man	David Rae Smith

Rachel, Rachel *see* NBC Nights at the Movies

899 A Rachmaninoff Festival
Special of the Week　　PBS
Program Type Music/Dance
Special. Concert of works by Sergei Rachmaninoff performed by the Mormon Youth Symphony and Choir. 90 minutes. Premiere date: 1/20/75. Repeat date: 8/23/75.
Executive Producer Byron Openshaw
Production Company KUED/Salt Lake City

Rage *see* The ABC Sunday Night Movie

900 Ragtime
PBS
Program Type Music/Dance
Special. 60 minutes. Premiere date: 9/30/74. Scott Joplin music performed by Eubie Blake; E. Power Biggs; The New England Conservatory Ragtime Ensemble conducted by Gunther Schuller. Jerilyn Dana; Alphonse Poulin dance.
Production Company WGBH/Boston
Host Max Morath

901 The Rangers
NBC World Premiere Movie   NBC
Program Type TV Movie
Pilot for "Sierra." 90 minutes. Premiere date:
12/24/74. Repeat date (as "NBC Nights at the
Movies"): 7/14/75.
Producer Edwin Self
Production Company Mark VII Ltd. in associa-
tion with Universal Television and NBC-TV
Director Chris Nyby, Jr.
Writer Robert A. Cinader; Michael Donovan;
Preston Wood
                        CAST
Ranger Tim Cassidy .... James G. Richardson
Ranger Matt Harper .... Colby Chester
Chief Ranger Jack Moore ....Jim B. Smith
Edie .... Laraine Stephens
Bob ....Laurence Delaney
Frank .... Michael Conrad
Sam .... Roger Bowen
Additional Cast Roger Breedlove; Dave Birkoff

902 Really Rosie: Starring the Nutshell
Kids   CBS
Program Type Animated Film
Special. Based on characters by Maurice Sendak
in "The Nutshell Books." Music composed and
sung by Carole King; lyrics by Lou Adler.
Producer Sheldon Riss
Production Company Sheriss Productions, Inc.
Director Maurice Sendak
Writer Maurice Sendak
                        VOICES
Rosie .... Carole King
Additional Voices Baille Gerstein; Mark Hampton; Al-
ice Playten; Dale Soules

903 The Reasoner Report   ABC
Program Type News Magazine
30 minutes. Saturday. Premiere date: 2/24/73.
Season premiere: 9/14/74. Last show: 6/28/75.
Executive Producer Albert T. Primo
Producer Various
Production Company ABC News
Host Harry Reasoner

904 The Rebel
Benjamin Franklin   CBS
Program Type Drama
Third of four-part series dealing with the life of
Benjamin Franklin. 90 minutes. Premiere date:
1/9/75.
Executive Producer Lewis Freedman
Producer Glenn Jordan
Production Company CBS Television
Director Glenn Jordan
Writer David Shaw
                        CAST
Benjamin Franklin ....Richard Widmark
Margaret Stevenson .... Honor Blackman
John Church .... Hurd Hatfield

Mrs. Peachum .... Georgia Brown
Wedderburn .... Ian Holm
Hillsborough .... John Neville
Dartmouth .... Anthony Quayle
Dunning ....Roger Livesey
William Whateley .... John Bird
William Franklin .... David Knight
Bishop Shipley ....David Markham
Mrs. Shipley ....Vivian Pickles

905 The Red Badge of Courage   NBC
Program Type Drama
Special. Adaptation of novel by Stephen Crane.
90 minutes. Premiere date: 12/3/74.
Executive Producer Norman Rosemont
Producer Charles FitzSimons
Production Company Norman Rosemont Pro-
ductions in association with 20th Century-Fox
Television
Director Lee Philips
Writer John Gay
                        CAST
Henry Fleming ....Richard Thomas
Wilson .... Wendell Burton
Jim Conklin .... Michael Brandon
The Sergeant ....Lee DeBroux
The Tattered Man .... Charles Aidman
The Cheery Soldier .... Warren Berlinger
The General ....Hank Kendrick
The Colonel .... George C. Sawaya
The Fat Soldier ....Tiny Wells
The Mother .... Francesca Jarvis

906 Reflections of Murder
The ABC Sunday Night Movie   ABC
Program Type TV Movie
120 minutes. Premiere date: 11/24/74. Based on
a novel by Pierre Boileau and Thomas Narcejac
on which the 1955 film "Diabolique" was based.
Producer Aaron Rosenberg
Production Company An Aaron Rosenberg-
Charles Lederer Production for ABC Circle
Film
Director John Badham
Writer Carol Sobieski
                        CAST
Vicky ....Tuesday Weld
Claire Elliott ....Joan Hackett
Michael Elliott .... Sam Waterston
Mrs. Turner .... Lucille Benson
Jerry Steele .... Michael Lerner
Coroner .... Ed Bernard
Mr. Turner .... R. G. Armstrong
"Chip" .... Lance Kerwin
"Keith" .... John Levin
Cop on Freeway .... Jesse Vint
Mr. Griffiths ....William Turner
Peter .... James A. Newcombe
David .... Sam Henriot
Photographer .... Don Sparks
Woman .... Sandra Coburn
Maid .... Rita Conde

907 **Renior** PBS
Program Type Documentary/Special
Special. 30 minutes. Premiere date: 5/17/74. Repeat date: 6/11/75. Profile of the artist Pierre Auguste Renoir.
Producer Donald Knox
Production Company WTTW/Chicago
Director Donald Knox
Writer Donald Knox
Narrator Marty Robinson

908 **Requiem for a Nun**
Hollywood Television Theatre PBS
Program Type Drama
Adapted from the novel by William Faulkner. 90 minutes. Premiere date: 2/10/75. Repeat date: 8/21/75.
Executive Producer Norman Lloyd
Producer George Turpin
Production Company KCET/Los Angeles
Director Larry Yust
Writer Ruth Ford
CAST
Temple Drake .... Sarah Miles
Nancy Mannigoe .... Mary Alice
Judge .... Stacy Keach, Sr.
Gowan Stevens .... Lawrence Pressman
Gavin Stevens .... Lester Rawlins
Governor .... Sam Edwards
Pete .... Kiel Martin
Mr. Tubbs .... Ed Lauter

909 **The Restless Earth** PBS
Program Type Documentary/Special
Special. 1972 geological study of the earth's plates. 120 minutes. Premiere: 12/72. Repeat date: 12/16/74.
Production Company WNET/New York; BBC/England; Swedish Television; Australian Broadcasting Commission; Bavarian Television
Writer Nigel V. Calder
Reporter David Prowitt

910 **The Return of Joe Forrester** NBC
Program Type TV Movie
Pilot for "Joe Forrester" series, 1975-76 season. Special 90-minute "Police Story" episode. Premiere date: 5/6/75. Repeat date: 9/2/75.
Executive Producer Stanley Kallis; David Gerber
Producer Christopher Morgan
Production Company Columbia Pictures Television in association with NBC-TV
Director Virgil W. Vogel
Writer Mark Rodgers
CAST
Joe Forrester .... Lloyd Bridges
Georgia Cameron .... Patricia Crowley
Jake Mandel .... Jim Backus
Jolene Jackson .... Dwan Smith
Sgt. Callan .... Dean Stockwell

Lt. Eaher .... Dane Clark
Claudine .... Della Reese
Irene .... Janis Paige
The Golfer .... Tom Drake
Massage Parlor Owner .... Edie Adams
Plums .... Don Stroud
Malone .... Eddie Egan

911 **Returning Home**
Tuesday/Wednesday Movie of the Week ABC
Program Type TV Movie
90 minutes. Premiere date: 4/29/75. Based on the film "The Best Years of Our Lives" by Robert E. Sherwood from the novel by MacKinlay Kantor.
Executive Producer Lee Rich
Producer Herbert Hirschman
Production Company Lorimar Productions
Director Daniel Petrie
Writer John McGreevey
CAST
Sgt. Al Stephenson .... Dabney Coleman
Capt. Fred Derry .... Tom Selleck
Homer Parrish .... James R. Miller
Miller Stephenson .... Whitney Blake
Peggy Stephenson .... Joan Goodfellow
Marie Derry .... Sherry Jackson
Wilma .... Laurie Walters
Butch .... Lou Frizzell

912 **Rex Humbard** Syndicated
Program Type Religious Program
Syndicated for over 22 years from the Cathedral of Tomorrow. 60 minutes. Weekly. Featured guests on monthly basis.
Executive Producer Rex Humbard, Jr.
Production Company The Cathedral of Tomorrow-World Outreach Ministry
Director Bob Anderson
Host Pastor Rex Humbard
Regular The Rex Humbard Family Singers; Cathedral Choir
Featured Soloists Maude Aimee Humbard; Elizabeth Humbard

913 **Rhoda** CBS
Program Type Comedy
Spin-off from "The Mary Tyler Moore Show." Created by James L. Brooks; Allan Burns. 30 minutes. Monday. Set in New York City. "Rhoda's Wedding" 60 minute special 10/28/74.
Executive Producer James L. Brooks; Allan Burns
Producer David Davis; Lorenzo Music
Production Company MTM Enterprises, Inc.
Director Various
Writer Various
CAST
Rhoda Morgenstern Gerard .... Valerie Harper
Joe Gerard .... David Groh
Brenda Morgenstern .... Julie Kavner
Ida Morgenstern .... Nancy Walker

Rhoda *Continued*
Martin Morgenstern .... Harold Gould
VOICES
Carlton, the Doorman .... Lorenzo Music

914   **Rhyme and Reason**   ABC
Program Type Game Show
30 minutes. Monday-Friday. Premiere date:
7/7/75. Continuous. Nipsey Russell is called
"Resident Poet."
Executive Producer Steven Friedman
Producer Walt Case
Production Company W.T. Naud Production
Director John Dorsey
Host Bob Eubanks
Announcer Jim Thompson
Regular Nipsey Russell

915   **The Rich Little Show**   NBC
Program Type Comedy
Special. 60 minutes. Premiere date: 9/3/75.
Executive Producer Jerry Goldstein
Producer Rich Eustis; Al Rogers
Production Company A Dudley Enterprises, Inc.
Director Walter Miller
Head Writer Ron Clark
Writer Barry Blitzer; Ron Clark; Rudy DeLuca;
Ray Jessel; Jack Kaplan; Barry Levinson; Jim
Mulligan
Musical Director Robert E. Hughes
Host Rich Little
Costume Designer Bill Belew
Guests Sandy Duncan; Glen Campbell; George
Burns; Peter Marshall

916   **Rikki-Tikki-Tavi**   CBS
Program Type Animated Film
Special. Adapted from "The Jungle Books" by
Rudyard Kipling. 30 minutes. Premiere date:
1/9/75.
Producer Chuck Jones
Production Company Chuck Jones Enterprises,
Inc.
Director Chuck Jones
Writer Chuck Jones
Narrator Orson Welles
VOICES
Rikki-Tikki-Tavi ....Orson Welles
Additional Voices June Foray; Les Tremayne; Michael
Le Clair; Len Weinrib; Shep Menken

917   **The Rimers of Eldritch**
Theater in America   PBS
Program Type Drama
Play by Lanford Wilson. 90 minutes. Premiere
date: 11/4/72. Repeat date: 8/27/75. Filmed in
Pittsville, Maryland.
Producer Matthew N. Herman
Production Company WNET/New York

Director Davey Marlin-Jones
CAST
Cora Groves .... Rue McClanahan
Wilma Atkins .... Frances Sternhagen
Skelly Mannor .... Will Hare
Eva Jackson ....Carol Williard
Robert Conklin .... James Staley
Evelyn Jackson .... K. Callan
Nelly Winrod ....Sarah Cunningham
Mary Winrod .... Joanna Roos
Patsy Johnson .... Susan Sarandon
Mavis Johnson .... Helen Stenborg
Peck Johnson .... Cliff Carpenter
Josh Johnson ....Vance Sorrells
Lena Truit ....Kathleen Doyle
Martha Truit .... Kate Harrington
Judge/Preacher ....Roberts Blossom
Walter .... Ernest Thompson
Trucker .... Cliff Pellow

The Rise of Louis XIV *see* Humanities
Film Forum

918   **The Rivals of Sherlock Holmes** PBS
Program Type Crime Drama
60 minutes. Weekly. Anthology based on stories
edited by Sir Hugh Greene in "The Rivals of
Sherlock Homes," "The Further Rivals of Sher-
lock Holmes," and "Cosmopolitan Crimes: Eu-
ropean Rivals of Sherlock Holmes." Theme mu-
sic by Robert Sharples. Premiere date: 7/1/75.
Executive Producer Shirley Lloyd
Producer Various
Production Company Thames Television (En-
gland)
Distributor Eastern Educational Television Net-
work
Director Various
Writer Various

919   **Robinson Crusoe**   NBC
Program Type Drama
Special. Based on the novel by Daniel Defoe.
Filmed in Tabago, West Indies. Dog played by
Rex.
Producer Cedric Messina
Production Company BBC-TV Production with
NBC-TV
Director James MacTaggart
Writer James MacTaggart
CAST
Robinson Crusoe .... Stanley Baker
Friday ....Ram John Holder
Sea Captain .... Jerome Willis

920   **The Rock Music Awards**   CBS
Program Type Awards Show
Special. Live from the Santa Monica Civic Audi-
torium. First Rock Music Awards. 90 minutes.
Premiere: 8/9/75.
Executive Producer Don Kirshner

Producer Bob Wynn
Director Stanley Dorfman
Writer Arnie Kogen
Musical Director Nelson Riddle
Choreographer Carl Jablonski
Host Diana Ross; Elton John
Costume Designer Ray Aghayan
Entertainers and/or Presenters Ann-Margret;
Cher; Alice Cooper; Roger Daltrey; Kiki Dee;
Michael Douglas; Labelle; Olivia Newton-
John; Tony Orlando and Dawn; Brenda Vac-
caro; Raquel Welch; Edgar Winter

921 The Rockford Files   NBC
Program Type Crime Drama
Created by Roy Huggins; Stephen J. Cannell.
Theme music by Mike Post; Peter Carpenter. 60
minutes. Friday. Premiere date: 9/13/74.
Executive Producer Meta Rosenberg
Supervising Producer Stephen J. Cannell
Producer Roy Huggins
Production Company Universal Television,
Cherokee Productions and Public Arts Pro-
duction
Director Various
Writer Various
CAST
Jim Rockford .... James Garner
Joseph "Rocky" Rockford .... Noah Beery
Det. Becker .... Joe Santos

922 Roll, Freddy, Roll
Tuesday/Wednesday Movie of the Week; The
ABC Summer Movie   ABC
Program Type TV Movie
90 minutes. Premiere date: 12/17/74. Repeat
date: 9/5/75.
Producer Bill Persky; Sam Denoff
Production Company ABC Circle Films
Director Bill Persky
Writer Bill Persky; Sam Denoff
CAST
Freddy Danton .... Tim Conway
"Big Sid" Kane .... Jan Murray
Tommy Danton .... Moosie Drier
Sidni Kane .... Barra Grant
Adm. Norton .... Scott Brady
Don Talbert .... Robert Hogan
Evelyn Danton Kane .... Ruta Lee
Theodore Menlo .... Henry Jones
Skating Rink Attendant .... Danny Wells
Rita .... Edwina Gough
Gas Station Attendant .... Sam Denoff

923 The Romagnolis' Table   PBS
Program Type Food/Cooking/Nutrition
Classic Italian cooking. 13-program series. 30
minutes. Weekly. Series made possible by grants
from the Corporation for Public Broadcasting,
the Ford Foundation, and Public Television Stations.

Production Company WGBH/Boston
Host Margaret Romagnoli; Franco Romagnoli

Romance of a Horsethief see The ABC
Monday Night Movie

924 The Romantic Rebellion   PBS
Program Type Documentary/Special
15-part series. 30 minutes. Weekly. Premiere
date: 1/13/74 (60 minute show). Series made
possible by a grant from the American Can Com-
pany. Presented in the United States by WNET/-
New York. Covers late 18th century and early
19th century artists.
Producer Colin Clark
Production Company Visual Programme Sys-
tems
Distributor Reader's Digest Association
Director Colin Clark
Writer Kenneth Clark
Host Kenneth Clark
Narrator Kenneth Clark

925 Rona Looks at Raquel, Liza, Cher
and Ann-Margret   CBS
Program Type Interview/Discussion
Special. 60 minutes. Interviews with Raquel
Welch; Liza Minnelli; Cher; Ann-Margret. Pre-
miere date: 5/28/75.
Executive Producer William Trowbridge
Producer Larry Einhorn
Production Company Martin Ransohoff Produc-
tions, Inc. in association with Miss Rona En-
terprises, Inc.
Director Larry Einhorn
Interviewer Rona Barrett

926 Rookie of the Year
ABC Afterschool Specials   ABC
Program Type Children's Show
Special. Emmy-award winner. Based on "Not
Bad for a Girl" by Isabella Taves. 60 minutes.
Premiere date: 10/3/73. Repeat date: 3/12/75.
Producer Daniel Wilson
Production Company Daniel Wilson Productions
Director Lawrence S. Elikann
Writer Gloria Banta
CAST
Sharon Lee .... Jodie Foster
Mark .... Dennis McKiernan
Kenny .... Joey Marvel
Charlie .... David Perkins
Paul .... Mike Scheer
Greg .... Mitchell Spera

927 The Rookies   ABC
Program Type Crime Drama
60 minutes. Monday. Premiere date: 9/11/72.

The Rookies *Continued*
Season premiere: 9/9/74. 120-minute special
2/17/75 introduced characters of "S.W.A.T."
series.
Producer Hal Sitowitz; Rick Husky
Production Company Spelling/Goldberg Pro-
ductions
CAST
Off. Terry Webster .... Georg Stanford Brown
Off. Mike Danko .... Sam Melville
Off. Chris Owens .... Bruce Fairbairn
Lt. Eddie Ryker .... Gerald S. O'Loughlin
Jill Danko .... Kate Jackson

928   Rose Bowl
NBC Sports Special   NBC
Program Type Sports
Live coverage of the 61st Rose Bowl at Pasadena,
California. Ohio State Buckeyes versus USC Tro-
jans. 1/1/75.
Producer Dick Auerbach
Production Company NBC Sports
Announcer Curt Gowdy; Al DeRogatis

**929   Rose Kennedy Remembers - The
Best of Times ... The Worst of Times**
Window on the World   Syndicated
Program Type Interview/Discussion
Special. Rose Kennedy interviewed by Robert
MacNeil. 60 minutes. Premiere: 3/75.
Producer David Gerrard
Production Company BBC-TV And Time-Life
Television
Distributor Time-Life Films
Narrator Burgess Meredith

Rosemary's Baby *see* The ABC Saturday
Night Movie

930   Rosenthal and Jones
Comedy Special   CBS
Program Type Comedy
30 minutes. Pilot film. Premiere date: 4/11/75.
Repeat date: 7/11/75.
Executive Producer Ira Barmak
Producer Lawrence Kasha
Production Company Filways Production
Director H. Wesley Kenney
Writer Robert Klane
CAST
Nate Rosenthal .... Ned Glass
Henry Jones .... George Kirby
David Rosenthal .... Jerry Fogel
Marge Rosenthal .... Nedra Deen
Lucille .... Dee Timberlake

931   Rudolph the Red-Nosed Reindeer
                                                          CBS
Program Type Animated Film
Special. Based on the song by Johnny Marks.
Additional music and lyrics by Johnny Marks;
orchestration by Maury Laws. Adapted from a
story by Robert L. May. 60 minutes. Premiere
date: 12/64. Repeat date: 12/13/74.
Producer Arthur Rankin, Jr.; Jules Bass
Production Company Videocraft International
Production
Director Larry Roemer
Writer Romeo Muller
Narrator Burl Ives
VOICES
Sam the Snowman .... Burl Ives
Rudolph .... Billie Richards
Yukon Cornelius .... Larry Mann
Santa Claus .... Stan Frances
Hermy the Elf .... Paul Soles
Clarice .... Janet Orenstein
Additional Voices Alfie Scopp; Paul Klugman; Corinne
Connely; Peg Dixon

**932   Ruffian-Foolish Pleasure Match
Race**
CBS Sports Special   CBS
Program Type Sports
Live coverage from Belmont Park, Elmont, New
York. 60 minutes. 7/6/75.
Producer Chuck Milton
Production Company CBS Television Network
Sports
Director Tony Verna
Announcer Chic Anderson
Reporters Jack Whitaker; Heywood Hale Broun;
Frank Wright; Eddie Arcaro; Phyllis George

933   The Rules of the Game
Theater in America   PBS
Program Type Drama
Play by Luigi Pirandello. Translated by William
Murray. Performed by the New Phoenix Reper-
tory Company, New York City. 90 minutes. Pre-
miere date: 4/30/75. Series funded by Exxon
Corporation and the Corporation for Public
Broadcasting.
Executive Producer Jac Venza
Producer Ken Campbell
Production Company WNET/New York
Director Stephen Porter; Kirk Browning
Host Hal Holbrook
CAST
Leone Gala .... John McMartin
Silia Gala .... Joan Van Ark
Guido .... David Dukes
Marquis .... Peter Friedman
Coco .... Nicholas Hormann
Dr. Spiga .... Charles Kimbrough

934 Run, Joe, Run   NBC
Program Type Children's Show
30 minutes. Saturday. Premiere date: 9/7/74.
Executive Producer William P. D'Angelo
Producer Robert Williams; Bill Schwartz
Production Company William P. D'Angelo Productions, Inc.
Director Various
Writer Various
CAST
Sgt. Cory .... Arch Whiting
Joe (the German shepherd) .... Heinrich of Midvale

935 Runaway!
Tuesday/Wednesday Movie of the Week ABC
Program Type TV Movie
90 minutes. Premiere date: 9/29/73. Repeat date: 1/22/75.
Producer David Lowell Rich
Production Company Universal Television
Director David Lowell Rich
Writer Gerald DiPego
CAST
Holly Gibson .... Ben Johnson
Les Reaver .... Ben Murphy
Nick Staffo .... Ed Nelson
Carol Lerner ....Darleen Carr
Mark ....Lee H. Montgomery
John Shedd ....Martin Milner
Ellen Staffo ....Vera Miles
Prof. Dunn .... Ray Danton
Dispatcher ....Frank Marth
Conductor .... John McLiam
Brakeman .... Lou Frizzell
Chief Dispatcher .... Frank Maxwell
Fireman .... Bing Russell

936 The Runaway Barge
NBC Nights at the Movies   NBC
Program Type TV Movie
90 minutes. Premiere date: 3/24/75. Repeat date: 7/5/75. Story based on an idea by Sara Macon.
Executive Producer Lee Rich
Producer Boris Sagal
Production Company Lorimar Productions
Director Boris Sagal
Writer Stanford Whitmore
CAST
Ezel Owens ....Bo Hopkins
Danny Worth .... Tim Matheson
Capt. Buckshot Bates .... Jim Davis
Ray Blount .... Nick Nolte
June Bug .... Devon Ericson
Reba .... Christina Hart
Bingo .... James Best
Madge .... Lucille Benson
Sooey .... Clifton James

937 The Runaways
ABC Afterschool Specials   ABC
Program Type Children's Show
Special. 60 minutes. Premiere date: 3/27/74. Repeat date: 1/22/75.
Producer Bill Schwartz
Production Company Hanna-Barbera Productions
Director John Florea
Writer Clyde Ware
CAST
Cindy Britton .... Belinda Balaski
Francis .... Claudio Martinez
Louise Britton ....Patricia Blair
Turner .... Anthony Eisley
Detective .... William Bryant
Freddie ....Moosie Drier
Policeman .... Skip Reilly
Vitina ....Helene Nelson
Simpson .... Hal Bokar

938 The Runaways   CBS
Program Type Drama
Special. 90 minutes. Premiere date: 4/1/75. Based on Victor Canning novel. With Yarra, the leopard.
Executive Producer Lee Rich
Producer Philip Capice
Production Company Lorimar Productions, Inc.
Director Harry Harris
Writer John McGreevey
CAST
Angela Lakey ....Dorothy McGuire
Joe Ringer .... Van Williams
George Collingwood .... John Randolph
Alice Collingwood .... Neva Patterson
Johnny Miles ....Josh Albee
Mrs. Wilson .... Lenka Peterson
Lew Brown .... Steve Ferguson
Haines .... Don Matheson
Bob Davis .... Tierre Turner
Mrs. Pickerel .... Janice Carroll
Al Pritchard ....John Pickard
Rita Armijo .... Gina Alvarado
Capt. Baker ....Leonard Stone
Kelly .... George Reynolds
Mr. Morgan ....Norman Andrews
Capt. Cole ....Ray A. Stephens
Sgt. Coonan .... Wayne A. Jones
Soldier ....Tony Huston

939 Ryan's Hope   ABC
Program Type Daytime Drama
30 minutes. Monday-Friday. Premiere date: 7/7/75. Created by Claire Labine; Paul Avila Mayer. Set in the upper west side of New York City; much of the action occurs in Ryan's Bar and Restaurant and in Riverside Hospital.
Executive Producer Claire Labine; Paul Avila Mayer
Producer George Lefferts
Production Company Labine-Mayer Production

Ryan's Hope *Continued*
in association with the ABC Television Network

Director Lela Swift; Bob Myhrum
Head Writer Claire Labine; Paul Avila Mayer
CAST
Jillian Coleridge ....Nancy Addison
Johnny Ryan .... Bernard Barrow
Dr. Faith Coleridge .... Faith Catlin
Dr. Bucky Carter .... Justin Deas
Nick Szabo .... Michael Fairman
Seneca Beaulac ....John Gabriel
Maeve Ryan .... Helen Gallagher
Dr. Pat Ryan .... Malcolm Groome
Nurse Ramona Gonzalez .... Rosalinda Guerra
Dr. Roger Coleridge .... Ronald Hale
Frank Ryan .... Michael Hawkins
Bob Reid ....Earl Hindman
Delia Reid Ryan ....Ilene Kristen
Dr. Ed Coleridge .... Frank Latimore
Jack Fenelli ....Michael Levin
Mary Ryan ....Kate Mulgrew
Clem Moultrie .... Hannibal Penney, Jr.
Dr. Nell Beaulac .... Diana Van Der Vlis

940   Sad Figure, Laughing
Sandburg's Lincoln   NBC
Program Type Drama
Second show in Lincoln series based on biography by Carl Sandburg. 60 minutes. Premiere date: 2/12/75.
Executive Producer David L. Wolper
Producer George Schaefer
Production Company David L. Wolper Production
Director George Schaefer
Writer Jerry McNeely
CAST
Abraham Lincoln .... Hal Holbrook
Mary Todd Lincoln .... Sada Thompson
Kate Chase Sprague ....Elizabeth Ashley
Salmon P. Chase .... Roy Poole
Gideon Welles .... Severn Darden
John Nicolay .... Michael Cristofer
Secy. Stanton ....Bert Freed
Robert Lincoln .... James Carroll Jordan
Gen. Ulysses S. Grant .... Normann Burton

941   Sadat: Action Biography
Action Biography   ABC
Program Type Documentary/Special
Special. 60 minutes. Premiere date: 12/19/74. Repeat date: 2/16/75. Filmed in Egypt, Israel, Morrocco and the United States.
Executive Producer Av Westin
Producer Stan Opotowsky; Peter Jennings
Production Company ABC News
Correspondents Howard K. Smith; Peter Jennings

942   Sail on the Wind's Time
Call It Macaroni   Syndicated
Program Type Children's Show
Real-life adventures of Massachusetts youngsters apprenticing on replica of 19th-century schooner. 30 minutes. Premiere 4/75. Co-producer for WBZ/Boston: Tanya Hart.
Executive Producer George Moynihan
Producer Stephanie Meagher
Production Company WBZ/Boston; Group W Productions
Distributor Westinghouse Broadcasting Company
Director Stephanie Meagher
Cinematographer Dick Roy
Editor David E. Roland

943   Salt and Pepe
Comedy Special   CBS
Program Type Comedy
30 minutes. Pilot film. Created by Duke Vincent; Bob Arnott. Premiere date: 4/18/75.
Executive Producer Duke Vincent
Production Company Warner Brothers Television
Director Jack Shea
Writer Duke Vincent; Bob Arnott
CAST
Jeremiah Salt .... Mel Stewart
Pepe .... Frank La Loggia
Abigail Salt ....Dorothy Meyer
Yolanda Salt ....Diane Sommerfield
Millie ....Clarice Taylor
Nadine Salt ....Sharon Brown
Additional Cast Damon Douglas; Jose Rodriguez

Salt and Pepper *see* NBC Nights at the Movies

944   Salute to Sir Lew - The Master Showman   ABC
Program Type Comedy/Variety
Special. 60 minutes. Premiere date: 6/13/75. Tribute by the New York Chapter of the National Academy of Television Arts and Sciences.
Producer Dick Schneider
Production Company ITC Production
Director Dwight Hemion
Writer Joseph Scher
Musical Director Milton DeLugg
Stars Julie Andrews; Tom Jones; Peter Sellers; John Lennon; Dave Allen; Dougie Squire's Second Generation Dancers

945   Sam Francis: These Are My Footsteps   PBS
Program Type Documentary/Special
Special. Portrait of artist Sam Francis. 30

minutes. Premiere date: 5/20/74. Repeat date: 5/10/75.
Producer Dan Healy
Production Company WNED/Buffalo
Director Dan Healy

Sam Whiskey *see* NBC Nights at the Movies

946 Sammy and Company Syndicated
Program Type Comedy/Variety
90 minutes. Weekly. Premiere: 4/75.
Executive Producer Pierre Cossette
Producer Eric Lieber
Production Company Pierre Cossette Company in association with Sammy Davis Video
Distributor Syndicast Services, Inc.
Director John Moffitt
Musical Director George Rhodes
Host Sammy Davis, Jr.
Regular William B. Williams; Johnny Brown; Avery Schreiber

947 Sammy Davis Jr.-Greater Hartford Open
CBS Sports Special CBS
Program Type Sports
Third and final round coverage from the Wethersfield (Conn.) Country Club. 8/16/75; 8/17/75.
Production Company CBS Television Network Sports

948 Sandburg's Lincoln NBC
Program Type Drama
Specials based on Carl Sandburg biography of Abraham Lincoln. 60 minutes each. Four programs shown in 1974-75 season: "Mrs. Lincoln's Husband," "Prairie Lawyer," "Sad Figure, Laughing," "The Unwilling Warrior." (*See* individual titles for cast and credits.)
Executive Producer David L. Wolper
Producer George Schaefer
Production Company David L. Wolper Production
Director George Schaefer
Writer Various

949 The Sandy Duncan Show CBS
Program Type Comedy/Variety
Special. 60 minutes. Premiere date: 11/13/74. Special music by Ray Charles.
Executive Producer Gus Schirmer
Producer Gary Smith
Production Company ATV-ITC
Director Dwight Hemion

Writer Marty Farrell; Jack Burns; Karyl Geld; Alan Thicke
Musical Director Jack Parnell
Choreographer Rob Iscove
Host Sandy Duncan
Guests Paul Lynde; John Davidson; Valerie Armstrong
Special Guest Star Gene Kelly

950 Sanford and Son NBC
Program Type Comedy
Based on "Steptoe and Son" created by Ray Galton; Alan Simpson. Music by Quincy Jones. 30 minutes. Friday. Premiere date: 1/14/72. Season premiere: 9/13/74. Set in South Central Los Angeles.
Executive Producer Bud Yorkin
Producer Saul Turteltaub; Bernie Orenstein
Production Company A Bud Yorkin-Norman Lear-Tandem Production
Director Various
Writer Various
CAST
Fred Sanford .... Redd Foxx
Lamont Sanford .... Demond Wilson
Grady ....Whitman Mayo
Aunt Esther .... LaWanda Page
Rollo .... Nathaniel Taylor
Bubba ....Don Bexley
Donna ....Lynn Hamilton

Sanjuro *see* The Japanese Film

Sansho the Bailiff *see* The Japanese Film

951 Santa Claus Is Coming to Town ABC
Program Type Animated Film
Special. Music by Maury Laws; Jules Bass. Title song by J. Fred Coots; Haven Gillespie. 60 minutes. Premiere: 12/70. Repeat date: 12/5/74. Fred Astaire narrates in the role of Postman S.D. Kluger.
Producer Arthur Rankin, Jr.; Jules Bass
Production Company Rankin/Bass Productions
Director Arthur Rankin, Jr.; Jules Bass
Writer Romeo Muller
Narrator Fred Astaire
VOICES
Kris Kringle ....Mickey Rooney
Winter Warlock .... Keenan Wynn
Burgermeister .... Paul Frees
Tanta Kringle .... Joan Gardner
Jessica .... Robie Lester
Additional Voices Dina Lynn; Andrea Sacino; Greg Thomas; Gary White; Westminster Children's Choir

952 Santiago's America

ABC Afterschool Specials   ABC
Program Type Children's Show
Special. Filmed on location in Spanish Harlem (New York City). Sequel to "Santiago's Ark." Santiago theme by Les Thompson. Music composed by Keith Avedon. 60 minutes. Premiere date: 2/19/75.
Producer Albert Waller
Production Company Windhover Productions, Inc.
Director Albert Waller
Writer Albert Waller
CAST
Santiago .... Ruben Figueroa
John, the Junkman .... Marc Jordan
Carlos .... Alex Colon
Mother .... Carmen Maya
Mr. Sands ....Bill Duke
Stevie .... Marcus Ticotin
Teacher .... Gloria Irizzary
Father .... Rene Enriquez
Father Otero .... Father Otero

953 Sara T. - Portrait of a Teen-Age Alcoholic

NBC World Premiere Movie   NBC
Program Type TV Movie
120 minutes. Premiere date: 2/11/75.
Producer David Levinson
Production Company Universal Television in association with NBC-TV
Director Richard Donner
Writer Richard Shapiro; Esther Shapiro
CAST
Sarah Travis .... Linda Blair
Jean Hodges ....Verna Bloom
Ken Newkirk ....Mark Hamill
Matt Hodges .... William Daniels
Jerry Travis .... Larry Hagman
Dr. Marvin Kittredge .... Michael Lerner
Margaret .... Hilda Haynes
Nancy .... Laurette Spang
Peterson .... M. Emmet Walsh
Marsha .... Karen Purcil

954 Sara's Summer of the Swans

ABC Afterschool Specials   ABC
Program Type Children's Show
Special. Story by Betsy Byars. 60 minutes. Premiere date: 10/2/74.
Producer Martin Tahse
Production Company An Entertainment Media Production
Director James B. Clark
Writer Bob Rodgers
Animation Director David Brain
CAST
Sara Godfrey .... Heather Totten
Joe Melby ....Chris Knight
Aunt Willie .... Priscilla Morrill
Gretchen Wyant .... Eve Plumb
Wanda .... Betty Ann Carr

Mary .... Doney Oatman
Frank .... Scott McCartor
Charlie .... Reed Diamond

955 Satan's Triangle

Tuesday/Wednesday Movie of the Week ABC
Program Type TV Movie
90 minutes. Premiere date: 1/14/75. Repeat date: 9/2/75. Special effects by Gene Grigg.
Executive Producer Paul Junger Witt; Tony Thomas
Producer James Rokos
Production Company A Danny Thomas Production
Director Sutton Roley
Writer William Reed Woodfield
CAST
Eva ....Kim Novak
Haig .... Doug McClure
P. Martin ....Alejandro Rey
Strickland .... Ed Lauter
Hal .... Jim Davis
Pagnolini .... Michael Conrad
Salao .... Titos Vandis
Juano .... Zitto Kazann
Swedish Captain ....Peter Bourne
Coast Guard Captain .... Hank Stohl
Miami Rescue Radio Officer .... Tom Dever
Miami Rescue Lieutenant .... Trent Dolan

956 The Saturday Evening Post   NBC

Program Type Comedy/Variety
Special. 90 minutes. Premiere date: 12/14/74.
Executive Producer Pierre Cossette
Producer Pierre Cossette; Eric Lieber
Production Company Pierre Cossette Company
Director Bill Davis
Writer Tom Whedon; Harry Lee Scott; John Boni
Host Peter Marshall
Guests Charlton Heston; Franklyn Ajaye; Chuck McCann; Phil Spector; Paul Williams; Kelly Lange; Jud Strunk; Joyce Maynard; Bryant Gumbel; Dave Madden; Carol Androsky; Chapter Five

957 The Saturday Preview Revue   NBC

Program Type Children's Show
Special. Preview of 1975-76 children's shows on NBC. 9/5/75. 30 minutes.
Production Company NBC Television Network
Host Michael Landon
Guests The Lockers; Billy Barty; Johnny Whitaker

958 Savages

Tuesday/Wednesday Movie of the Week ABC
Program Type TV Movie
90 minutes. Premiere date: 9/11/74. Repeat date: 4/1/75. Filmed partly on location in the

Mojave Desert, California. Based on the novel "Death Watch" by Robb White.
Producer Aaron Spelling; Leonard Goldberg
Production Company Spelling/Goldberg Productions
Director Lee H. Katzin
Writer William Wood

CAST

Horton Maddock	Andy Griffith
Ben Whiting	Sam Bottoms
George Whiting	Noah Beery
Sheriff Hamilton	James Best
Dep. Haycroft	Randy Boone
Les Hanford	Jim Antonio
The Doctor	Jim Chandler

959 Say Goodbye, Maggie Cole
Tuesday/Wednesday Movie of the Week ABC
Program Type TV Movie
90 minutes. Premiere date: 9/27/72. Repeat date: 7/15/75.
Producer Aaron Spelling; Leonard Goldberg
Production Company Spelling/Goldberg Production
Director Jud Taylor
Writer Sandor Stern

CAST

Dr. Maggie Cole	Susan Hayward
Dr. Lou Grazzo	Darren McGavin
Dr. Sweeney	Michael Constantine
Lisa Downey	Michele Nichols
Mrs. Anderson	Beverly Garland
Fergy	Maidie Norman
Hank Cooper	Dane Clark
Mrs. Downey	Jeanette Nolan
Ben Cole	Richard Anderson

The Scalphunters *see* NBC Nights at the Movies

960 The School for Scandal
Theater in America   PBS
Program Type Comedy
Play by Richard Brinsley Sheridan performed by the Guthrie Theater Company, Minneapolis, Minnesota. 120 minutes. Premiere date: 4/2/75. Series made possible by grants from Exxon Corporation and the Corporation for Public Broadcasting.
Executive Producer Jac Venza
Producer David Griffiths
Production Company WNET/New York; KTCA/St. Paul
Director Michael Langham; Nick Havinga
Writer Michael Bawtree
Host Hal Holbrook

CAST

Lady Sneerwell	Patricia Conolly
Joseph	Nicholas Kepros
Charles	Kenneth Welsh
Sir Oliver Surface	Larry Gates
Sir Peter Teazle	Bernard Behrens
Lady Teazle	Blair Brown
Mrs. Candour	Barbara Bryne
Backbite	Mark Lamos
Maria	Sheridan Thomas

961 School for Wives   PBS
Program Type Music/Dance
Special. Ballet created by Birgit Cullberg based on the play by Jean Baptiste Moliere. Performed by the Cullberg Balleten. 30 minutes. Premiere date: 12/30/74. Repeat date: 8/26/75. Program funded by a grant from the Corporation for Public Broadcasting.
Production Company University of Wisconsin Telecommunications Center, WHA/Madison, Wisconsin
Director Phil Samuels

962 Schoolhouse Rock   ABC
Program Type Animated Film
Four-minute animated information series shown Saturdays/Sundays throughout children's programming time. Premiered in 1972–73 season with "Multiplication Rock." "Grammer Rock" introduced 9/8/73; "America Rock" (history) premiered 9/7/74. Series conceived by David B. McCall.
Executive Producer Tom Yohe
Production Company Scholastic Rock, Inc.
Musical Director Bob Dorough
Animation Director Phil Kimmelman and Associates

963 Scooby-Doo, Where Are You? CBS
Program Type Animated Film
Originally appeared in September 1969. Reruns 1974–75 season. 30 minutes. Saturday.
Producer Joseph Barbera; William Hanna
Production Company Hanna-Barbera Productions
Director Joseph Barbera; William Hanna
Writer Ken Spears; Bill Butler; Joe Ruby; Bill Lutz
Animation Director Charles A. Nichols
Voices Stefanianna Christopherson; Nicole Jaffe; Casey Kasem; Don Messick; Vic Perrin; Hal Smith; John Stephenson; Jean VanderPyl; Frank Welker

Scorpio *see* NBC Nights at the Movies

964 Scream of the Wolf
Tuesday/Wednesday Movie of the Week ABC
Program Type TV Movie
90 minutes. Premiere date: 1/16/74. Repeat date: 3/12/75. Filmed near Malibu, California.
Executive Producer Charles Fries
Producer Dan Curtis

Scream of the Wolf *Continued*
Production Company Metromedia Producers
  Corporation and Dan Curtis Productions
Director Dan Curtis
Writer Richard Matheson
CAST

John Wetherby	Peter Graves
Byron Douglas	Clint Walker
Sandy	Jo Ann Pflug
Sheriff Bell	Philip Carey
Grant	Don Megowan
Deputy Crane	Brian Richards
Student	Lee Paul
Girl	Bonnie Van Dyke
Boy	Jim Storm
Lake	Dean Smith
Deputy Bill	Grant Owens

Scrooge *see* NBC Nights at the Movies

965   Sculpture in the Open
Special of the Week   PBS
Program Type Documentary/Special
Special. Outdoor art at Princeton University. 30
minutes. Premiere date: 3/24/75.
Producer Hugh Johnston; Suzanne Johnston
Production Company WNET/New York

966   Sea Pines Heritage Classic
CBS Sports Special   CBS
Program Type Sports
Live coverage of third and final round play from
Harbour Town Golf Links, South Carolina.
3/29/75–3/30/75.
Producer Frank Chirkinian
Production Company CBS Television Network
  Sports
Announcer Ken Venturi; Jack Whitaker; Ben
  Wright

967   A Seaful of Adventure
Call It Macaroni   Syndicated
Program Type Children's Show
Real-life adventure of youngsters studying with
a marine biologist in the Dry Tortugas and Sani-
bel Island. 30 minutes. Premiere: 7/75. Producer
at WBZ/Boston: Tanya Hart.
Executive Producer George Moynihan
Producer Stephanie Meagher
Production Company Group W Productions;
  WBZ/Boston
Distributor Westinghouse Broadcasting Com-
pany
Director Stephanie Meagher
Cinematographer Dick Roy
Supervising Editor Henry Maldonado

968   The Seagull
Theater in America   PBS
Program Type Drama
Play by Anton Chekhov performed by the Wil-
liamstown (Mass.) Festival Theatre. 120
minutes. Premiere date: 1/29/75. Series made
possible by Exxon Corporation and the Corpora-
tion for Public Broadcasting.
Executive Producer Jac Venza
Producer David Griffiths
Production Company WNET/New York
Director Nikos Psacharopoulos; John Desmond
Host Hal Holbrook
CAST

Treplev	Frank Langella
Irina Arkadina	Lee Grant
Nina	Blythe Danner
Trigorin	Kevin McCarthy
Masha	Marian Mercer
Pauline Andreevna	Olympia Dukakis
Sorin	William Swetland
Medvedenko	David Clennon

969   Search for the Gods
The ABC Sunday Night Movie; The ABC
Summer Movie   ABC
Program Type TV Movie
120 minutes. Premiere date: 3/9/75. Repeat
date: 8/29/75. Created by Herman Miller.
Filmed in Taos, New Mexico.
Executive Producer Douglas S. Cramer
Producer Wilford Lloyd Baumes
Production Company The Douglas S. Cramer
  Company in association with Warner Brothers
  Television
Director Jud Taylor
Writer Ken Pettus
CAST

Shan Mullins	Kurt Russell
Willie Longfellow	Stephen McHattie
Genara Juantez	Victoria Racimo
Raymond Stryker	Raymond St. Jacques
Tarkanian	Albert Paulsen
Dr. Henderson	Ralph Bellamy
Lucio	John War Eagle
Wheeler	Carmen Argenziano
Elder	Joe David Marcus
Council Indian	Joe Marcus, Jr.
Jailer	Larry Blake
Glenn	Jackson D. Kane

970   Search for Tomorrow   CBS
Program Type Daytime Drama
The longest-running daytime drama on television. Premiered on 9/3/51 in 15-minute format.
Created by Agnes Nixon. Theme song, "Search
for Tomorrow" by Jon Silbermann. Mary Stuart
has played Joanne Vincent since premiere. Set in
"Henderson, U.S.A." Cast information as of
April 1975. Producer Bernie Sofronski replaced
by Mary-Ellis Bunim. 30 minutes. Monday-Friday. Continuous.

Producer Bernie Sofronski; Mary-Ellis Bunim
Production Company Procter & Gamble Production
Director Ned Stark
Head Writer Ann Marcus
Announcer Dwight Weist
CAST

Liza Walton	Meg Bennett
Stephanie Wilkins	Marie Cheatham
Dr. Wade Collins	John Cunningham
John Wyatt	Val Dufour
Jennifer Pace	Morgan Fairchild
Dr. Tony Vincent	Anthony George
Stu Bergman	Larry Haines
Sam Hunter	Stephen Joyce
Dr. Bob Rogers	Carl Low
Eric Leshinsky	Christopher Lowe
Wendy Wilkins	Andrea McArdle
Amy Kalso	Pamela Miller
Bruce Carson	Steve Nisbet
Steve Kalso	Michael Nouri
Dave Wilkins	Dale Robinette
Kathy Phillips	Courtney Sherman
Scott Phillips	Peter Simon
Raney Wesner	Katherine Squire
Joanne Tate Vincent	Mary Stuart
Janet Collins	Millee Taggart
Ellie Harper	Billie Lou Watt
Eunice Martin Wyatt	Ann Williams

971   **A Season of Celebration**   PBS
Program Type Documentary/Special
Special. 30 minutes. Premiere date: 10/2/74.
Program made possible by a grant from Allstate
Foundation. Studs Terkel introduces the
Chicago Free Street Theater.
Executive Producer Robert J. Zeller
Producer Gerald T. Rogers
Production Company WTTW/Chicago

The Secret Life of an American Wife *see*
The ABC Sunday Night Movie

972   **The Secret Life of T. K. Dearing**
ABC Afterschool Specials   ABC
Program Type Children's Show
Special. Based on the book by Jean Robinson. 60
minutes. Premiere date: 4/23/75.
Producer Daniel Wilson
Production Company Daniel Wilson Productions, Inc.
Director Harry Harris
Writer Bob Rodgers
CAST

T. K. Dearing	Jodie Foster
Grandpa Kindermann	Eduard Franz
Walter Dearing	Leonard Stone
Ruth Dearing	Zoe Karant
Potato Tom	Brian Wood
Dugger	Brian Part
Alvin	Michael Link

Alice	Robin Stone
Jerry	Tierre Turner
Mrs. Witfield	Barbara Morrison
Mr. Crane	Norman Andrews
Sheriff	Ted Jordan

973   **The Secret Night Caller**
NBC World Premiere Movie   NBC
Program Type TV Movie
90 minutes. Premiere date: 2/18/75. Repeat
date: 6/24/75.
Executive Producer Florence Small
Producer Art Stolnitz
Production Company Penthouse Productions,
Inc. in association with Charles Fries Productions, Inc.
Director Jerry Jameson
Writer Robert Presnell, Jr.
CAST

Durant	Robert Reed
Pat Durant	Hope Lange
Jan Durant	Robin Mattson
Dr. Mayhill	Michael Constantine
Kitty	Sylvia Sidney
Chloe	Elaine Giftos

974   **Secret Sleuth**   Syndicated
Program Type Comedy/Variety
30 minutes. Premiere: 8/75.
Executive Producer Hal B. Belfer
Production Company Premore, Inc.
Director Art Fisher; Jeff Margolis
Writer Bob Arnott; Howard Johnson; Hal B.
Belfer; Grace Bernstein
Musical Director D'Vaughn Pershing
Choreographer Bob Thompson
Special Dancer Teo Morca
CAST

Journalist	Dora Hall
Scatman	Scat Man Crothers
Chief of Intelligence	Dave Barry
Sylvester	Sid Melton
Hawkins	Larry Wilde

Additional Cast Muriel Landers; Dante Di Paolo; Joe
Ploski; Gerald Jann; Cory Rand; Danny Butch

975   **The Seeds**   NBC
Program Type Religious Program
Special. Traces the rise of early Christianity
through a tour of Mediterranean ruins. 60
minutes. Premiere date: 12/2/74. Repeat date:
6/15/75.
Producer Doris Ann
Production Company NBC Television Religious
Programs Unit
Director Joseph Vadala
Host Hugh Downs
Camera Joseph Vadala

976   Senate Rules Committee Hearings on the Rockefeller Nomination for Vice-President
ABC News Special Events; CBS News Special; NBC News Special   ABC; CBS; NBC
Program Type Documentary/Special
Live coverage of Nelson Rockefeller testifying before the Senate Rules Committee. Covered by networks in rotation: ABC 11/13/74; CBS 11/14/74; NBC 11/15/74.
Production Company ABC News; CBS News; NBC News

977   Senior Bowl
NBC Sports Special   NBC
Program Type Sports
26th Senior Bowl from Mobile, Alabama. Live coverage. 1/11/75. North versus South.
Producer Larry Cirillo
Production Company NBC Sports
Announcer Jim Simpson; John Brodie

The Sentry Collection Presents *see* Funny Girl to Funny Lady; Herb Alpert & The TJB

978   Sesame Street   PBS
Program Type Children's Show
30 minutes. Monday-Friday. Premiere date: 11/10/69. Season premiere: 11/4/74. Muppets created by Jim Henson. Series made possible by a grant from the U.S. Dept. of Health, Education and Welfare, Office of Education.
Executive Producer Jon Stone
Producer Bob Cuniff
Production Company Children's Television Workshop
CAST
David .... Northern J. Calloway
Luis .... Emilio Delgado
Mr. Hooper .... Will Lee
Susan .... Loretta Long
Maria .... Sonia Manzano
Bob .... Bob McGraw
Gordon .... Roscoe Orman

979   7382 Days in Vietnam
NBC News Special   NBC
Program Type Documentary/Special
Special. 60 minutes. Premiere date: 4/29/75. Retrospective on the war with NBC news correspondents.
Production Company NBC News
Correspondent John Chancellor
Reporters Jim Laurie; Mike Jackson; Arthur Lord; David Brinkley; Tom Brokaw; Charles Quinn; Jack Reynolds; John Cochran; Garrick Utley

The Seventh Dawn *see* NBC Nights at the Movies

980   The Sex Symbol
Tuesday/Wednesday Movie of the Week ABC
Program Type TV Movie
90 minutes. Premiere date: 9/17/74. Repeat date: 7/16/75. Based on the novel "The Symbol" by Alvah Bessie.
Producer Douglas S. Cramer
Production Company Douglas S. Cramer Company Production in association with Screen Gems
Director David Lowell Rich
Writer Alvah Bessie
CAST
Kelly Williams .... Connie Stevens
Agatha Murphy .... Shelley Winters
Manny Foxe .... Jack Carter
J. P. Harper .... William Castle
Grant O'Neal .... Don Murray
Calvin Bernard .... James Olson
Nikos Fortis .... Nehemiah Persoff
Joy Hudson .... Madlyn Rhue
Buck Wischnewski .... William Smith
Phil Bamberger .... Milton Selzer
Rick Roman .... Tony Young
Director .... Joseph Turkel
Ted Brown .... Jack Collins
P.R. Man .... Bing Russell
Investigator .... Frank Loverde

981   A Shadow in the Street
NBC World Premiere Movie   NBC
Program Type TV Movie
90 minutes. Premiere date: 1/28/75. Repeat date: 7/1/75.
Executive Producer Edward L. Rissien
Producer John D. F. Black; Richard D. Donner
Production Company Playboy Productions
Director Richard D. Donner
Writer John D. F. Black
CAST
Pete Mackey .... Tony Lo Bianco
Gina .... Sheree North
Len Raeburn .... Dana Andrews
Siggie .... Ed Lauter
Debby .... Jesse Welles
Leroy Benson .... Bill Henderson
Bense .... Dick Balduzzi

Shaft *see* The CBS Thursday/Friday Night Movies

982   The Shakers   PBS
Program Type Documentary/Special
Special. 30 minutes. Premiere date: 4/21/75. Program funded by grants from the American Crafts Council and the National Endowment for the Humanities.
Producer Tom Davenport; Frank DeCola

Production Company Maryland Center for Public Broadcasting

Shakespeare Wallah *see* Hollywood Television Theatre

Shamus *see* NBC Nights at the Movies

983 Shark . . . Terror, Death, Truth
ABC News Special Events   ABC
Program Type Documentary/Special
Special. 30 minutes. Premiere date: 9/7/75.
Executive Producer Av Westin
Producer Tom Bywaters
Production Company ABC News
Host Peter Benchley; Peter Jennings
Narrator Peter Benchley
Correspondent Peter Jennings

984 Shazam!   CBS
Program Type Children's Show
Based on characters in "Shazam!" Magazine.
Live action. 30 minutes. Saturday. Premiere date: 9/7/74.
Executive Producer Lou Scheimer; Norm Prescott
Producer Arthur H. Nadel
Production Company Filmation Associates
Director Various
Writer Various
Creative Director Don Christensen
CAST
Billy Batson .... Michael Gray
Mentor .... Les Tremayne
Captain Marvel .... John Davey

985 Shell Game
The CBS Thursday/Friday Night Movies CBS
Program Type TV Movie
90 minutes. Premiere date: 5/9/75. Repeat date: 8/29/75.
Producer Harold Jack Bloom
Production Company Thoroughbred Productions
Director Glenn Jordan
Writer Harold Jack Bloom
CAST
Max Castle .... John Davidson
Stoker Frye .... Tommy Atkins
Stephen Castle .... Robert Sampson
Lola Ramirez .... Maria O'Brien
Lyle Rettig .... Jack Kehoe
Shirley .... Joan Van Ark
Mrs. Margolin .... Louise Latham
Susan .... Karen Machon
Carruthers .... Robert Symonds
Bellhop .... Gary Sandy
Carmichael .... Cliff Emmich
Sammy .... Lance Taylor, Sr.
Tim Carson .... Gary Pagett

Louie .... Pete Gonneau
Countess .... Signe Hasso
Bonnie .... Deborah Sherman
Klein .... Jason Wingreen
Short Man .... Frank Corsentino
Mugger .... Mike Tillman
Chauffeur .... Don Diamond

986 Shirley MacLaine: If They Could See Me Now   CBS
Program Type Comedy/Variety
Special. 60 minutes. Premiere date: 11/28/74.
Music by Cy Coleman.
Producer Robert Wells
Production Company MacLaine Enterprises
Director Robert Scheerer
Writer Robert Wells; John Bradford; Cy Coleman
Musical Director Donn Trenner
Choreographer Alan Johnson
Host Shirley MacLaine
Guest Star Carol Burnett

987 A Shooting Gallery Called America
NBC News Special   NBC
Program Type Documentary/Special
Special. 60 minutes. Premiere date: 4/27/75.
Producer Lucy Jarvis
Production Company NBC News
Director Tom Priestley
Writer Rafael Abramovitz; Carl Stern
Reporter Carl Stern

Showdown *see* NBC Nights at the Movies

988 Showoffs   ABC
Program Type Game Show
30 minutes. Monday-Friday. Premiere date: 6/30/75.
Producer Howard Felcher
Production Company Goodson-Todman Production
Director Paul Alter
Host Bobby Van
Announcer Gene Wood

989 Sierra   NBC
Program Type Drama
60 minutes. Thursday. Premiere date: 9/12/74.
Last show: 12/12/74. Set in "Sierra National Park." For pilot, *see* "The Rangers."
Executive Producer Robert A. Cinader
Producer Bruce Johnson
Production Company Mark VII Ltd. and Universal Television
CAST
Tim Cassidy .... James G. Richardson
Matt Harper .... Ernest Thompson
Jack .... Jack Hogan

Sierra Continued

P. J. .... Mike Warren
Julie .... Susan Foster

990 Sigmund and the Sea Monsters NBC

Program Type Children's Show
30 minutes. Saturday. Premiere date: 9/8/73.
Season premiere: 9/7/74.
Executive Producer Si Rose
Producer Sid Krofft; Marty Krofft; Tom Hill
Production Company Sid and Marty Krofft Production
Director Bob Lally
Writer Si Rose; John Fenton Murray; Jack Raymond; Fred Fox; Seaman Jacobs
CAST
Johnny .... Johnny Whitaker
Scott .... Scott Kolden
Sigmund .... Billy Barty
Zelda .... Mary Wickes
Sheldon .... Rip Taylor

991 Since the American Way of Death
PBS

Program Type Documentary/Special
Special. 60 minutes. Originally telecast on WTTW/Chicago 12/18/74. Premiere date on PBS: 5/22/75. The funeral business in the decade following publication of "The American Way of Death" by Jessica Mitford.
Producer Michael Hirsh
Production Company WTTW/Chicago
Director Dave Erdman
Writer Michael Hirsh
Narrator Martin Agronsky
Guests Peter Hawley; Jessica Mitford

992 The Sinners
PBS

Program Type Drama
13 programs. 60 minutes. Weekly. Premiere date: 11/4/74. Repeat date: 2/2/75. Adaptations of stories by Brian Friel: "The Highwayman and the Saint;" James Joyce: "The Dead;" Frank O'-Connor: "The Best Man," "The Holy Door," "Legal Aid," The Little Mother," "The Mad Lomasneys;" Sean O'Faolain: "Dividends," "In the Bosom of the Country," "Mother Matilda's Book/The Man Who Invented Sin," "One Man, One Boat, One Girl ...," "A Thousand Pounds for Rosebud;" James Plunkett: "The Wearin' of the Green."
Producer Brian Armstrong
Production Company Granada Television (England)
Distributor Eastern Educational Television Network

The Best Man
Director Barry Davis
Writer Hugh Leonard

CAST
Rosaline .... Gillian McCutcheon
Frank Daly .... Patrick Laffan
Kate .... Josie Kidd
Jim Hourigan .... Tony Doyle

The Dead
Director Donald McWhinnie
Writer Hugh Leonard
CAST
Gabriel Conroy .... Ray McAnally
Kate Morkan .... Nora Nicholson
Gretta Conroy .... Pauline Delany
Miss Power .... Mary Hignett

Dividends
Director Barry Davis
Writer Hugh Leonard
CAST
Anna Maria .... Nora Nicholson
Sean Whelan .... Denys Hawthorne
Mel Meldrum .... Desmond Perry
Sheila .... Finnuala O'Shannon

The Highwayman and the Saint
Director Carol Wilks
Writer Brian Armstrong
CAST
Andy Kelly .... James Berwick
Mrs. Wilson .... Marie Kean
Madge Wilson .... Pauline Delany
Cissy Cassidy .... Marjorie Hogan

The Holy Door
Director Donald McWhinnie
Writer Hugh Leonard
CAST
Polly Conegan .... Sinead Cusack
Charlie Cashman .... Ray McAnally
Nora Lawlor .... Brigit Forsyth
Father Ring .... Eddie Byrne
Mrs. Cashman .... Elizabeth Begley
Molly .... Molly Gogan
Countryman (Tom) .... Mike Hayden

In the Bosom of the Country
Director Barry Davis
Writer Brian Armstrong
CAST
Anna Mohan .... Barbara Jefford
The Monsignor .... Cyril Cusack
The Priest .... Will Leighton
Maj. Frank Keene .... John Carson
Mabel Tallant .... Elizabeth Tyrell

Legal Aid
Director Barry Davis
Writer Hugh Leonard
CAST
Tom Flynn .... Jim Norton
Delia Carty .... Mary Larkin
Ned Flynn .... Ronnie Walsh
Mr. O'Grady .... Martin Dempsey

The Little Mother
Director Barry Davis
Writer Brian Armstrong

CAST

Joan Twomey	Brenda Fricker
May Twomey	Biddy White-Lennon
Mick Twomey	Cecil Sheehan
Kitty Twomey	Anita Reeves
Dick Gordon	Clive Geraghty

The Mad Lomasneys
Director Donald McWhinnie
Writer Hugh Armstrong
CAST

Ned Lowry	Donal McCann
Nellie	Fidelma Murphy
Mrs. Lomasney	Ronnie Masterson
Mr. Lomasney	Derry Power
Rita	Brigit Forsyth
Kitty	Eileen Murphy

The Man Who Invented Sin
Director Donald McWhinnie
Writer Hugh Leonard
CAST

Lispeen	Ronald Lacey
Sister Magdalen	Evin Crowley
Brother Majellan	Eamon Morrissey
Brother Virgilius	Aidan Murphy
Whelan	Denys Hawthorne
Sister Chrysostom	Mary Larkin

Mother Matilda's Book
Director Michael Apted
Writer Hugh Leonard
CAST

Mother Matilda	Elizabeth Begley
Mother John	Eileen Kennally
The Bishop	Leo McCabe
Mother Philomena	Kitty Fitzgerald
Father Colgan	Devin Flynn

One Man, One Boat, One Girl ...
Writer Hugh Leonard
CAST

Al Flood	Eamon Morrissey
T. J. Mooney	Donal McCann
Janey Anne	Kaye Binchy
Fan	Barbara Brennan
Olly Carson	David Battley

A Thousand Pounds for Rosebud
Director Michael Apted
Writer Hugh Leonard
CAST

Rosebud	Patricia Brake
Milo	Donal Cox
Clarence	Joseph Pilkington
Customs Officer	Edward Golden

The Wearing' of the Green
Director Brian Mills
Writer Hugh Leonard
CAST

Purcell	James Caffrey
John Sweeney	Barry Keegan
Sally McGuire	Evin Crowley

993 The Six Million Dollar Man   ABC
Program Type Crime Drama
60 minutes. Friday. Premiere date: 1/14/74. Season premiere: 9/13/74. Based on the novel "Cyborg" by Martin Caidin. Pilot "The Six Million Dollar Man" aired 3/7/73 on the "Wednesday Movie of the Week" followed by two "ABC Suspense Movies" in October and November '73.
Executive Producer Harve Bennett
Producer Lionel E. Siegel; Joe L. Cramer
Production Company Universal Television
Director Various
Writer Various
CAST

Steve Austin	Lee Majors
Oscar Goldman	Richard Anderson

994 Sixty Minutes   CBS
Program Type News Magazine
60 minutes. Sunday. Premiere date: 9/24/68. Season premiere: 1/5/75. Moved to prime time 7/6/75. Last show of season 9/7/75. "Point-Counter-Point" features Shana Alexander; James J. Kilpatrick.
Executive Producer Don Hewitt
Producer Various
Production Company CBS News
Host Mike Wallace; Morley Safer

995 The Skating Rink
ABC Afterschool Specials   ABC
Program Type Children's Show
Special. Based on the book by Mildred Lee. Music by Glenn Paxton. Skating choreographer: Bill Blackburn. 60 minutes. Premiere date: 2/5/75.
Producer Martin Tahse
Production Company Martin Tahse Productions, Inc.
Director Larry Elikann
Writer Bob Rodgers
CAST

Pete Degley	Jerry Dexter
Lilly Degley	Devon Ericson
Ida Faraday	Betty Beaird
Myron Faraday	Rance Howard
Tuck Faraday	Stewart Petersen
Elva Grimes	Cindy Eilbacher
Tom Faraday	Billy Bowles
Clete Faraday	Robert Clotworthy
Karen Faraday	Tara Talboy
Mrs. Bayliss	Molly Dodd
Tuck's Real Mother	Patricia Stevens
Young Tuck	Sparky Marcus

996 Skiing Free
ABC Sports Special   ABC
Program Type Sports
The Colgate women's freestyle ski championships at Stowe, Vermont. 30 minutes. Premiere date: 3/30/75.
Executive Producer Roone Arledge

Skiing Free *Continued*
Producer Eleanor Riger
Production Company ABC Sports
Announcer Donna de Varona; Billy Kidd

Skin Game *see* The CBS
Thursday/Friday Night Movies

Skullduggery *see* The ABC Saturday
Night Movie

997   Sky Hei$t
NBC Nights at the Movies   NBC
Program Type TV Movie
120 minutes. Premiere date: 5/26/75.
Executive Producer Andrew J. Fenady
Producer Rick Rosner
Production Company A. J. Fenady Associates in
association with Warner Brothers Television
Director Lee H. Katzin
Writer William F. Nolan; Rick Rosner
CAST
Sgt. Doug Trumbell .... Don Meredith
Capt. Monty Ballard .... Joseph Campanella
Schiller .... Larry Wilcox
Pat Connelly .... Ken Swofford
Terry Hardings .... Stefanie Powers
Ben Hardings .... Frank Gorshin
Lisa .... Shelley Fabares
Additional Cast Ray Vitte; Nancy Belle Fuller; James
Daris; Steve Franken; Alex Colon

998   The Sleeping Sharks of Yucatan
The Undersea World of Jacques Cousteau
                                                                      ABC
Program Type Animal Documentary
Special. 60 minutes. Premiere date: 4/6/75. With
Jacques Cousteau and the men of the *Calypso.*
Executive Producer Jacques Cousteau; Marshall
Flaum
Producer Andy White
Production Company A Marshall Flaum Produc-
tion in association with The Cousteau Society
and MPC Metromedia Producers Corporation
and ABC News
Director Philippe Cousteau
Writer Andy White
Musical Director Walter Scharf
Underwater Camera Philippe Cousteau; Michel
De Loire
Narrator Joseph Campanella

999   Small Claims   PBS
Program Type Documentary/Special
Special. New York City's Small Claims Court,
Judge Beatrice Shainswit presiding. Shown lo-
cally on WNET/New York 5/6/74. Repeat date
on national PBS: 6/22/75.
Producer Paul Smirnoff

Production Company Consumer Help Center-
WNET/New York in cooperation with New
York University School of Law

1000   The Small Miracle
Hallmark Hall of Fame   NBC
Program Type Drama
Special. Adapted from the story by Paul Gallico.
Filmed in Assisi and Rome. Premiere date:
4/11/73 in 90-minute form. Repeat date:
3/19/75 edited to 60 minutes.
Producer Duane C. Bogie
Production Company FCB Productions in associ-
ation with Alan Landsburg Productions
Director Jeannot Szwarc
Writer John Patrick; Arthur Dales
CAST
Pepino .... Marco Della Cava
Father Damico .... Vittorio De Sica
Father Superior .... Raf Vallone
Salesman .... Guidarini Guidi
First Guard .... Jan Larsson
Second Guard .... Paolo Malco

1001   Smile, Jenny, You're Dead   ABC
Program Type TV Movie
Second pilot for series "Harry O." 90 minutes.
Premiere date: 2/3/74. Repeat date: 7/31/75.
Producer Jerry Thorpe
Production Company Warner Brothers Televi-
sion
Director Jerry Thorpe
Writer Howard Rodman
CAST
Harry Orwell .... David Janssen
Col. John Lockport, U.S.A. (ret.) ...... John Anderson
Police Lt. Humphrey Kenney .... Howard Da Silva
Meade De Ruyter .... Martin Gabel
Det. Milt Bosworth .... Clu Gulager
Roy St. John .... Zalman King
Jennifer English .... Andrea Marcovicci
Charley English .... Tim McIntire
Liberty .... Jodie Foster
Portrait Photographer .... Harvey Jason
Mildred .... Barbara Leigh
Police Lt. Richard Marum .... Victor Arco
Julia .... Ellen Weston
Asst. Photographer .... Chet Winfield

1002   A Smithsonian Institution Special
                                                                      CBS
Program Type Documentary/Special
Three specials shown during the 1974-75 season:
"Flight: The Sky's the Limit," "The Legendery
Curse of the Hope Diamond," "Monsters! Mys-
teries or Myths?" (*See* individual titles for cred-
its.) 60 minutes each. Season premiere:
11/25/74.
Executive Producer George Lefferts
Producer Various
Production Company Wolper Productions in co-
operation with The Smithsonian Institution

1003 **The Smothers Brothers** NBC
Program Type Comedy/Variety
60 minutes. Monday. Premiere date: 1/13/75.
Last show: 5/26/75.
Executive Producer Joe Hamilton
Producer Gail Parent; Kenny Solms
Production Company Jocar Productions in association with NBC-TV
Director Mack Bing; Bill Foster
Writer Kenny Solms; Gail Parent; Mickey Rose; Ray Jessel; Mason Williams; Rod Warren; Jim Mulligan; James R. Stein; Robert Illes; Chevy Chase; Pat Proft
Musical Director Marty Paich
Choreographer Walter Painter
Host Tom Smothers; Dick Smothers
Regular Don Novello; Bob Einstein; Pat Paulsen

1004 **Soccer Bowl '75**
CBS Sports Special CBS
Program Type Sports
Live coverage of the North American Soccer League Championship from San Jose, California. Tampa Bay Rowdies versus Portland Timbers. 8/24/75.
Production Company CBS Television Network Sports

1005 **Sojourner**
The American Parade CBS
Program Type Drama
Sixth show of series. 60 minutes. Premiere date: 3/30/75. Based on the career of Sojourner Truth.
Executive Producer Joel Heller
Producer Lois Bianchi
Production Company CBS News for the CBS Television Network
Director Peter Levin
Writer Bill Gunn
Narrator James Earl Jones
CAST
Sojourner Truth .... Vinnette Carroll
Harriet Beecher Stowe .... Frances Sternhagen
Sophia .... Minnie Gentry
Ned .... Anthony Chisholm
Esquire Chip .... Robert Dryden
Peter .... Lawrence Jacobs
Jamie ....Damien Leake
David Ruggles .... Charles Peques
Dr. Strain .... Frederick Rolf
Mr. Dumont .... Nicholas Saunders
Frederick Douglass .... Thurman Scott
Pres. Lincoln .... Fred Stuthman

1006 **Solar Energy** PBS
Program Type Documentary/Special
Six-part series. 30 minutes. Weekly. Premiere date: 3/25/75.
Producer Carl Manfredi

Production Company KNME/Albuquerque (University of New Mexico)
Host David Prowitt

Solomon and Sheba *see* NBC Nights at the Movies

1007 **Someone I Touched**
Tuesday/Wednesday Movie of the Week ABC
Program Type TV Movie
90 minutes. Premiere date: 2/26/75. Story by Patricia Winter; James Henerson.
Executive Producer Dick Berg
Producer Wayne Weisbart
Production Company Charles Fries/Stonehenge Production
Director Lou Antonio
Writer James Henerson
CAST
Laura Hyatt .... Cloris Leachman
Sam Hyatt .... James Olson
Paul Livermore .... Kenneth Mars
Terry Warner .... Glynnis O'Connor
Frank Berlin .... Andy Robinson
Dr. Klemperer .... Peggy Feury
Eddie .... Richard Guthrie
Jean .... Allyn Ann McLerie
Enid .... Lenka Peterson

1008 **Somerset** NBC
Program Type Daytime Drama
Began as "Another World-Somerset." 30 minutes. Monday-Friday. Continuous. Premiere date 3/30/70. Set in "Somerset, U.S.A." (Cast as of 9/16/74.)
Executive Producer Lyle B. Hill
Producer Sid Sirulnuck
Production Company Procter & Gamble Productions
Director Joseph K. Chomyn; Jack Coffey
CAST
Marion Parker .... Ellen Barber
Eve Lawrence .... Bibi Besch
Julian Cannell .... Joel Crothers
Warren Parker .... Bruce Gray
Ginger Cooper .... Fawne Harriman
Teri Martin .... Gloria Hoye
Bill Greeley .... Bill Hunt
Tony Cooper .... Barry Jenner
Ellen Grant .... Georgeann Johnson
Heather Lawrence .... Audrey Landers
Stan Kurtz .... Michael Lipton
Jill Farmer .... Susan McDonald
Becky Winkle .... Jane Rose
Freida Lang .... Polly Rowles
Kate Thornton .... Tina Sloan
Lt. Price .... Eugene Smith
Rex Cooper .... Paul Sparer
Greg Mercer .... Gary Swanson
Additional Cast James Congdon; Ted Danson; James O'Sullivan

1009 Songs and Stones   CBS
Program Type Religious Program
CBS News religious special. The music of lutanist Rodrigo DeZayas and mezzo-soprano Anne Perret; also interview with guitarist Andres Segovia. 60 minutes. Premiere date: 5/18/75.
Executive Producer Pamela Ilott
Producer Ben Flynn
Production Company CBS News

1010 The Sonny Comedy Revue   ABC
Program Type Comedy/Variety
60 minutes. Sunday. Premiere date: 9/22/74. Last show: 12/29/74.
Producer Alan Blye; Chris Bearde
Production Company A Skyjay, Inc. & Gank, Inc. Production/Blye-Bearde Productions, Inc.
Director Art Fisher
Writer George Burditt; Coslough Johnson; Bob Arnott; David Panich; Ronny Graham; Chris Bearde; Alan Blye; Bob Einstein
Musical Director Lex De Azevedo
Choreographer Jaime Rogers
Host Sonny Bono
Regular Ted Zeigler; Billy Van; Peter Cullen; Freeman King; Murray Langston; Teri Garr

1011 Sons and Daughters   CBS
Program Type Drama
The 1950's at Southwest High. 60 minutes. Wednesday. Premiere date: 9/11/74. Last show: 11/6/74.
Executive Producer David Levinson
Producer Michael Gleason
Production Company Universal Television
CAST

Jeff Reed	Gary Frank
Anita Cramer	Glynnis O'Connor
Stash	Scott Colomby
Moose	Barry Livingston
Charlie	Lionel Johnston
Evie	Debralee Scott
Lucille Reed	Jay W. MacIntosh
Walter Cramer	John S. Ragin
Ruth Cramer	Jan Shutan
Danny Reed	Michael Morgan
Cody	Christopher Nelson
Mary Anne	Laura Siegel

1012 The Sorrow and the Pity   PBS
Program Type Documentary/Special
1970 documentary by Marcel Ophuls shown on PBS 8/75.

1013 Soul!   PBS
Program Type Music/Dance
Repeat of series featuring black musicians and singers. 60 minutes. Weekly. Series premiered in 1970. Repeat date: 11/7/74.

Executive Producer Ellis Haizlip
Production Company WNET/New York

1014 A Sound of Dolphins
The Undersea World of Jacques Cousteau
                                      ABC
Program Type Animal Documentary
Special. Photographed in the Mediterranean. 60 minutes. Premiere date: 2/25/72. Repeat date: 5/28/75. With Jacques Cousteau and the crew of the *Calypso.*
Executive Producer Jacques Cousteau; Marshall Flaum
Producer Andy White
Production Company Metromedia Producers Corporation and The Cousteau Society in association with ABC News
Writer Andy White
Narrator Rod Serling

1015 Soundstage   PBS
Program Type Music/Dance
15-part series of pop music concerts. 60 minutes. Weekly. Premiere date: 11/12/74. Series made possible by grants from Public Television Stations, the Ford Foundation, and the Corporation for Public Broadcasting.
Executive Producer Kenneth J. Ehrlich
Producer David Erdman
Production Company WTTW/Chicago
Director David Erdman

Soylent Green *see* The CBS
Thursday/Friday Night Movies

1016 Space for Man?   PBS
Program Type Documentary/Special
Special. 120 minutes. Premiere date: 7/17/75. Program made possible by a grant from the Xerox Corporation.
Executive Producer Al Vecchione
Producer Richard V. Brown
Production Company NPACT (National Public Affairs Center for Television); European Broadcasting Union
Director Duke Struck
Correspondents Paul Duke; Jim Lehrer; Carolyn Lewis

1017 Spaulding International Mixed Doubles Classic
PBS Sports Special   PBS
Program Type Sports
Live coverage of semifinal and final matches from Dallas, Texas. 1/4/75; 1/5/75. Program made possible by grants from the Commercial

Metals Company, Mead Paper, and Fidelity Union Life Insurance.
Executive Producer Ron Devillier
Producer Renate Cole
Production Company KERA/Dallas-Fort Worth
Announcer Bud Collins; Judy Dixon

1018   Special Movie Presentation   ABC
Program Type TV Movie – Feature Film
A combination of feature films and made-for-television films. The television films are: "Brian's Song," "A Dream for Christmas," "Friendly Persuasion," "The Legend of Lizzie Borden," "The Point," and "The Story of Jacob and Joseph." (*See* individual titles for cast and credits.) The feature films are: "For a Few Dollars More" (1964) shown 11/2/74, "Godspell" (1973) shown 11/27/74, "The Guns of Navarone" (1961) shown 10/18/74, "Hang 'Em High" (1968) shown 10/26/74, "Hatari" (1962) shown 10/25/74, "Man in the Wilderness" (1971) shown 8/26/75, "True Grit" (1969) shown 10/11/74, "Valdez Is Coming" (1971) shown 11/23/74, "Where Eagles Dare" (1969) shown 11/16/74.

1019   The Specialists
NBC Nights at the Movies   NBC
Program Type TV Movie
Filmed in part at the Center for Disease Control in Atlanta, Georgia. 90 minutes. Premiere date: 1/6/75. Repeat date: 6/26/75.
Executive Producer Robert A. Cinader
Production Company Mark VII Ltd. and Universal Television
Director Richard Quine
Writer Preston Wood; Robert A. Cinader
CAST
Dr. William Nugent .... Robert York
Dr. Christine Shofied ....Maureen Reagan
Dr. Edward Gray .... Jack Hogan
Dick Rawdon ....Jed Allan
Dr. Al Marsdan ....Alfred Ryder
Dr. Burkhart ....Harry Townes
Eileen .... Anne Whitefield
Additional Cast Lillian Lehman; Corinne Camacho; 'ackie Coogan; Tom Scott; Chris Anders

1020   Speed Buggy   CBS
Program Type Animated Film
30 minutes. Saturday. Premiere: 9/73. Season reruns: 9/7/74.
Executive Producer William Hanna; Joseph Barbera
Producer Iwao Takamoto
Production Company Hanna-Barbera Productions
Director Charles A. Nichols
Writer Jack Mendelsohn; Larz Bourne; Len Jan-

son; Joel Kane; Jack Kaplan; Woody Kling; Norman Maurer; Chuck Menville; Ray Parker; Larry Rhine
Musical Director Hoyt Curtin
Voices Chris Allen; Michael Bell; Mel Blanc; Ron Feinberg; Arlene Golonka; Virginia Gregg; Phil Luther, Jr.; Jim MacGeorge; Sid Miller; Alan Oppenheimer; Michael Road; Charles Martin Smith; Hal Smith; John Stephenson; Janet Waldo

1021   Spin-Off   CBS
Program Type Game Show
30 minutes. Monday-Friday. Continuous. Premiere date: 6/16/75. Last show: 9/5/75.
Executive Producer Nick Nicholson; E. Roger Muir
Producer Willie Stein
Production Company Nicholson-Muir Productions, Inc.
Director Bob Schwarz
Host Jim Lange

1022   Split Second   ABC
Program Type Game Show
30 minutes. Monday-Friday. Premiere date: 3/20/72. Continuous. Last show: 6/27/75.
Executive Producer Stu Billet
Producer Bob Synes
Production Company Stefan Hatos-Monty Hall Productions
Host Tom Kennedy

1023   Stalin   PBS
Program Type Documentary/Special
Special. 150 minutes. Premiere date: 5/14/73. Repeat date: 5/28/75. Adapted from book by George Paloczi-Horvath.
Production Company KCET/Los Angeles; British Broadcasting Corporation
Writer Robert Vas
First Narrator Sebastian Shaw
Second Narrator Lee Montague
Third Narrator Peter Copley
CAST
Author ....Michael Gough
Anna Akhmatova ....Jill Balcon

The Stalking Moon see The CBS Thursday/Friday Night Movies

1024   Stanley Cup Play-Offs/Championship
NBC Sports Specials   NBC
Program Type Sports
Live coverage of hockey play-offs 4/13/75–5/11/75. Finals: 5/20/75–5/25/75. Finals

Stanley Cup Play-Offs/Championship
Continued
played in Philadelphia and Buffalo between Philadelphia Flyers and Buffalo Sabres.
Production Company NBC Sports
Announcer Tim Ryan; Ted Lindsay; Brian McFarlane

Star! *see* The ABC Sunday Night Movie

1025   Star Trek   NBC
Program Type Animated Film
Created by Gene Roddenberry; based on the live-action series. Adventures of the crew of the *U.S.S. Enterprise*. 30 minutes. Saturday. Premiere date: 9/8/73. Season premiere: 9/7/74. Last show: 8/30/75.
Producer Norm Prescott; Lou Scheimer
Production Company Filmation Associates in association with NBC-TV
Director Hal Sutherland
Writer Various
VOICES
Capt. James T. Kirk .... William Shatner
Mr. Spock .... Leonard Nimoy
Dr. McCloy .... DeForest Kelley
Scotty .... James Doohan
Lt. Uhura .... Michele Nichols
Lt. Sulu .... George Takei
Nurse Chapel .... Majel Barrett

1026   Stars and Stripes Show   NBC
Program Type Comedy/Variety
Special. Fourth annual show. Taped at Oklahoma City's Myriad Convention Center. 60 minutes. 7/3/75.
Executive Producer Lee Allan Smith
Producer Dick Schneider
Production Company Dick Schneider in association with the Oklahoma City Association of Broadcasters
Director Bill Thrash
Writer Barry Downes
Stars Bob Hope; Charley Pride; Anita Bryant; John Davidson; Juliet Prowse

1027   Starsky and Hutch
Tuesday/Wednesday Movie of the Week ABC
Program Type TV Movie
Pilot for ABC series 1975–76 season. Premiere date: 4/30/75. Repeat date: 9/3/75.
Executive Producer Aaron Spelling; Leonard Goldberg
Producer Joseph P. Naar
Production Company Spelling/Goldberg Productions
Director Barry Shear
Writer William Blinn

CAST
Det. Sgt. Ken Hutchinson .... David Soul
Det. Sgt. Dave Starsky ....Paul Michael Glaser
Fat Rolly .... Michael Lerner
Capt. Doby ....Richard Ward
Tallman .... Gilbert Green
Henderson .... Albert Morganstern
Zane .... Richard Lynch
Cannell .... Michael Conrad
Coley .... Buddy Lester
Huggy Bear ....Antonio Fargas
Gretchen .... Carol Ita White

Start the Revolution Without Me *see*
NBC Nights at the Movies

1028   Stat!
CBS Pilot Film   CBS
Program Type Drama
30 minutes. Premiere date: 5/15/75. Repeat date: 7/31/75.
Producer E. Jack Neuman
Director Richard Donner
Writer E. Jack Neuman
CAST
Ben Voorhees .... Frank Converse
Nick Candros .... Michael Delano
Nurse Ellen Quayle .... Marian Collier
Dr. Jan Cavanaugh .... Casey MacDonald
Dr. Neil Patricks .... Henry Brown
Nurse Dolores Payne .... Marcy Lafferty
Mary Ann Murphy .... Monika Henreid
Doris Runyon ....Penny Rea

1029   State of the Democratic Process
PBS
Program Type Interview/Discussion
Four programs edited from proceedings sponsored by the Center for the Study of Democratic Institutions 6/74. Shows aired 9/74. Various lengths. Programs made possible by a grant from the Businessmen's Educational Fund.
Producer Jerry Hughes
Production Company KCET/Los Angeles
Director Jerry Hughes
Host Sander Vanocur

State of the Union *see* President Ford's
State of the Union Message to
Congress

1030   The Statesman
Benjamin Franklin   CBS
Program Type Drama
Fourth and last show of series. 90 minutes. Premiere date: 1/28/75.
Executive Producer Lewis Freedman
Producer Glenn Jordan
Production Company CBS Television
Director Glenn Jordan

Writer Edward Adler

CAST

Benjamin Franklin	Melvyn Douglas
Sara Bache	Michael Learned
Benny Bache	Kristoffer Tabori
Dr. Benjamin Rush	William Shatner
Arthur·Lee	David Wayne
James Wilson	Donal Donnelly
Keil	Anthony Zerbe
Temple Franklin	Stephen McHattie

1031   Steambath
Hollywood Television Theatre   PBS
Program Type Comedy
Adapted from the stage play by Bruce Jay Friedman. 90 minutes. Premiere date: 5/4/73. Repeat dates: 3/14/75; 8/20/75.
Executive Producer Norman Lloyd
Producer Norman Lloyd
Production Company KCET/Los Angeles
Director Burt Brinckerhoff
Writer Bruce Jay Friedman

CAST

Attendant	Jose Perez
Tandy	Bill Bixby
Meredith	Valerie Perrine
Broker	Kenneth Mars
Bieberman	Herb Edelman
Oldtimer	Stephen Elliott
Young Men	Neil Schwartz; Patrick Spohn
Gottlieb	Peter Kastner
Longshoreman	Art Metrano
Young Girl	Shirley Kirkes
Flanders	Biff Elliott

The Sterile Cuckoo *see* The ABC Monday Night Movie

1032   Stone in the River   NBC
Program Type Religious Program
Special. 60 minutes. Premiere date: 9/8/74. Repeat date: 8/3/75.
Executive Producer Doris Ann
Producer Martin Hoade
Production Company NBC Television Religious Programs Unit
Director Martin Hoade
Writer Allan Sloane

CAST

Sawyer Burke	Harold Miller
Raider	Roy Poole
Mrs. Burke	Roxie Roker
Homer	Kenneth McMillan

1033   The Story of Jacob and Joseph
Special Movie Presentation; The ABC Sunday Night Movie   ABC
Program Type Drama
120 minutes. Premiere date: 4/7/74. Repeat date: 3/23/75. Filmed in Israel. Music by Mikis Theodorakis.

Producer Mildred Freed Alberg
Production Company Milberg Theatrical Productions in association with Screen Gems
Director Michael Cacoyannis
Writer Ernest Kinoy
Costume Designer Judy Moorcroft
Consultant Dr. David Noel Freedman
Narrator Alan Bates

CAST

Jacob	Keith Michell
Joseph	Tony Lo Bianco
Rebekah	Colleen Dewhurst
Laban	Herschel Bernardi
Isaac	Harry Andrews
Esau	Julian Glover
Pharaoh	Yoseph Shiloah
Butler	Yossi Grabber
Rachel	Yona Elian
Potiphar's Wife	Rachel Shore
Baker	Amnon Meskin
Potiphar	Bennes Maarden
Reuben	Yehuda Efroni
Judah	Shmuel Atzmon

1034   The Story of Pretty Boy Floyd
Tuesday/Wednesday Movie of the Week ABC
Program Type TV Movie
Based on the life of Charley Arthur Floyd. Premiere date: 5/7/74. Repeat date: 4/9/75.
Executive Producer Roy Huggins
Producer Jo Swerling, Jr.
Production Company Universal Television
Director Clyde Ware
Writer Clyde Ware

CAST

Charley Arthur Floyd	Martin Sheen
Ruby Hardgraves	Kim Darby
Bradley Floyd	Michael Parks
Ma Floyd	Ellen Corby
Dominic Morell	Abe Vigoda
Phil Donnati	Frank Christi
Bill Miller	Bill Vint
George Birdswell	Rod McCary
E. W. Floyd	Joseph Estevez
Mr. Suggs	Ford Rainey
Richetti	Steven Keats
Decker	Ted Gehring
Mary Floyd	Kitty Carl
Secretary	Ann Doran
Rose	Sandra Escamilla
Farm Woman	Amzie Strickland
Melvin Purvis	Geoffrey Binney
Deputy	Roy Applegate
Blonde	Misty Rowe
Shine Rush	Mills Watson

1035   Stowaway to the Moon   CBS
Program Type Drama
Special. Children's drama from the novel by William R. Shelton. 120 minutes. Premiere date: 1/10/75.
Producer John Cutts
Production Company 20th Century-Fox Television

Stowaway to the Moon *Continued*
Director Andrew V. McLaglen
Writer John Boothe; William R. Shelton
CAST

Charlie Englehardt	Lloyd Bridges
Eli "E. J." Mackernutt, Jr.	Michael Link
Dr. Jack Smathers	James Callahan
Jacob	John Carradine
Joey	Stephen Rogers
TV News Commentator	Charles "Pete" Conrad
Astronaut Pelham	Jim McMullan
Astronaut Anderson	Morgan Paull
Astronaut Lawrence	Jeremy Slate
Whitehead	Walter Brooke
Tom Estes	Keene Curtis
Jans Hartman	Jon Cedar
Mrs. Mackernutt	Barbara Faulkner
Eli Mackernutt, Sr.	Edward Faulkner

1036　The Strange and Deadly Occurence
NBC World Premiere Movie　　　　NBC
Program Type TV Movie
Story by Sandor Stern; Lane Slate. Filmed at the Brentwood home of the late actor Robert Taylor. 90 minutes. Premiere date: 9/24/74. Repeat date: 6/10/75.
Executive Producer Charles Fries
Producer Sandor Stern
Production Company A Charles Fries Production for Alpine Productions in association with World Vision and NBC-TV
Director John Llewellyn Moxey
Writer Sandor Stern
CAST

Michael Rhodes	Robert Stack
Christine Rhodes	Vera Miles
Melissa Rhodes	Margaret Willock
Sheriff Berlinger	L. Q. Jones
Felix	Herb Edelman
Audrey	Dena Dietrich
Dr. Gilgreen	Ted Gehring
Ardie Detweiller	James McCallion

1037　Strange Homecoming
NBC World Premiere Movie　　　　NBC
Program Type TV Movie
90 minutes. Premiere date: 10/29/74. Repeat date: 4/1/75.
Executive Producer Charles Fries
Producer Eric Bercovici; Jerry Ludwig
Production Company A Charles Fries Production for Alpine Productions in association with Worldvision and NBC-TV
Director Lee H. Katzin
Writer Jerry Ludwig; Eric Bercovici
CAST

Jack Halsey	Robert Culp
Bill Halsey	Glen Campbell
Elaine Halsey	Barbara Anderson
Peggy Harwood	Whitney Blake
Earl Gates	Gerrit Graham

Additional Cast Leif Garrett; John Crawford; Victor Brandt; Tara Talboy; Arch Whiting; Bill Burton

1038　Strange New World
The ABC Sunday Night Movie　　　　ABC
Program Type TV Movie
120 minutes. Premiere date: 7/13/75.
Executive Producer Walon Green; Ronald F. Graham
Producer Robert Larson
Production Company Warner Brothers Television
Director Robert Butler
Writer Walon Green; Ronald F. Graham; Al Ramrus
CAST

Capt. Anthony Vico	John Saxon
Dr. Allison Crowley	Kathleen Miller
Dr. Scott	Keene Curtis
The Surgeon	James Olson
Tana	Martine Beswick
Sprang	Reb Brown
Sirus	Ford Rainey
Badger	Bill McKinney
Daniel	Gerrit Graham

1039　The Stranger Within
Tuesday/Wednesday Movie of the Week　ABC
Program Type TV Movie
90 minutes. Premiere date: 10/1/74. Repeat date: 8/6/75. Based on a short story by Richard Matheson.
Executive Producer Philip Capice; Lee Rich
Producer Neil T. Maffeo
Production Company Lorimar Productions, Inc.
Director Lee Philips
Writer Richard Matheson
CAST

Ann Collins	Bàrbara Eden
David Collins	George Grizzard
Phyllis	Joyce Van Patten
Bob	David Doyle
Dr. Klein	Nehemiah Persoff

1040　The Streets of San Francisco　ABC
Program Type Crime Drama
60 minutes. Thursday. Premiere date: 9/16/72 (120-minute special). Season premiere: 9/12/74. Filmed in and around San Francisco.
Executive Producer Quinn Martin
Producer John Wilder
Production Company Quinn Martin Productions
Director Various
Writer Various
CAST

Lt. Mike Stone	Karl Malden
Insp. Steve Keller	Michael Douglas

1041 Strike Force
NBC Nights at the Movies   NBC
Program Type TV Movie
90 minutes. Premiere date: 4/12/75. Repeat
date: 7/25/75. Created by Sonny Grosso.
Producer Philip D'Antoni; Barry Weitz
Production Company D'Antoni-Weitz Television
    Production in association with NBC-TV
Director Barry Shear
Writer Roger Hirson
CAST

Det. Joey Gentry	Cliff Gorman
Jerome Ripley	Donald Blakely
Walter Spenser	Richard Gere
Capt. Peterson	Edward Grover
Sol Terranova	Joe Spinell

Additional Cast Marilyn Chris; Mimi Cecchini; Billy
    Longo

1042 Sugar Bowl
ABC Sports Special   ABC
Program Type Sports
42nd Sugar Bowl in New Orleans. Live coverage.
12/31/74. Nebraska Cornhuskers versus Florida
Gators.
Executive Producer Roone Arledge
Production Company ABC Sports
Announcer Keith Jackson; Barry Switzer

1043 The Sullivan Years: A Tribute to Ed
     CBS
Program Type Comedy/Variety
Special. Edited 60-minute version of Ed Sulli-
van's 1971 special. Footage highlights the 23-
year variety series. Premiere date: 2/2/75.
Producer Robert Precht
Production Company Sullivan Productions
Director Russ Petranto
Host Dick Cavett

Summer of '42 *see* The ABC Saturday Night Movie

1044 Summer Semester
     CBS
Program Type Educational
Two courses; 24 lectures each. First course given
Monday, Wednesday, Friday. Second: Tuesday,
Thursday, Saturday. Summer premiere:
5/19/75. "Science and Society: A Humanistic
View" with Dr. Philip C. Dolce. "The Web of
Population, Inflation, Energy and Environment"
with Winston L. Kirby.
Producer Roy Allen
Production Company WCBS/New York
Director Roy Allen

1045 Sun Bowl
CBS Sports Special   CBS
Program Type Sports
40th Sun Bowl at El Paso, Texas. North Carolina
Tar Heels versus Mississippi State Bulldogs. Live
coverage. 12/28/74.
Production Company CBS Television Network
    Sports
Announcer Lindsey Nelson; John Sauer; Jane
    Chastain

1046 Sunrise Semester
     CBS
Program Type Educational
Local New York City show for six years. Pre-
miered on CBS network 9/23/63. Two courses
given each semester by professors at New York
University. "History of African Civilization"
Monday, Wednesday, Friday premiere date:
9/23/74 with Prof. Richard W. Hull. "The
Meaning of Death" Tuesday, Thursday, Satur-
day premiere: 9/24/74 with Prof. James P.
Carse. Spring "Music of the Romantic Era" with
Prof. Elaine Brody premiere date: 1/27/75; "The
Near East in Modern Times" with Prof. L. Carl
Brown; premiere date: 1/28/75. 30 minutes
daily.
Producer Roy Allen
Production Company WCBS/New York
Director Roy Allen

1047 Sunshine
     NBC
Program Type Comedy
Based on journal appearing in *Los Angeles Times,*
and on TV movie by Carol Sobieski. 30 minutes.
Friday. Premiere date: 3/6/75. Last show:
6/19/75.
Producer George Eckstein
Production Company Universal Television
Director Various
Writer Various
CAST

Sam Hayden	Cliff DeYoung
Jill Hayden	Elizabeth Cheshire
Weaver	Bill Mumy
Givits	Corey Fischer
Nora	Meg Foster

1048 Sunshine (TV Movie)
The CBS Thursday/Friday Night Movies CBS
Program Type TV Movie
Pilot for the series on NBC. 120 minutes. Pre-
miere date: 11/9/73. Repeat date: 10/17/74.
Based on journal that appeared in the *Los Ange-
les Times.*
Producer George Eckstein
Production Company Universal Television
Director Joseph Sargent
Writer Carol Sobieski
CAST

Kate Hayden	Cristina Raines

Sunshine (TV Movie) Continued

Sam Hayden	Cliff DeYoung
Dr. Carol Gillman	Brenda Vaccaro
Nora	Meg Foster
Weaver	Bill Mumy
Givits	Corey Fischer
Tony	Jimmy McNichol
Nurse	Adrian Ricard
Jill Hayden	Lindsay Greenbush

1049 Super Bowl IX

NBC Sports Special   NBC
Program Type Sports
Ninth Super Bowl. Pittsburgh Steelers versus
Minnesota Vikings from New Orleans. Live coverage. 1/12/75.
Producer George Finkel; Ted Nathanson
Production Company NBC Sports
Director Ted Nathanson
Announcer Curt Gowdy; Al DeRogatis; Don
Meredith

1050 Supercops

CBS Pilot Film   CBS
Program Type Drama
30 minutes. Premiere date: 3/21/75. Repeat
date: 8/28/75. Based on a book by L. H. Whittemore.
Executive Producer Bruce Geller
Producer James David Buchanan; Ronald Austin
Production Company Unit Productions in association with MGM Telesion
Director Bernard L. Kowalski
Writer Austin Kalish; Irma Kalish

CAST

Bobby Hantz	Alan Feinstein
Dave Greenberg	Steven Keats
Dawson	Cliff Osmond
Capt. McLain	Dick O'Neill
Bessie	Peggy Rea
Rugged Guy	Michael Lieberman
Delgado	George Loros
Lt. Gorney	Byron Morrow
Lt. Vanesian	Tony Brande
Sgt. Falcone	Lou Tiano

1051 Superfriends

ABC
Program Type Animated Film
Reruns. Animated adventures of Superman,
Wonderwoman, Aquaman, Batman and Robin
et al. 60 minutes. Saturday. Last show: 8/30/75.
Executive Producer William Hanna; Joseph
Barbera
Producer Iwao Takamoto
Production Company Hanna-Barbera Productions
Director Charles A. Nichols
Writer Fred Freiberger; Willie Gilbert; Bernie
Kahn; Dick Robbins; Ken Rotcop; Henry
Sharp; Art Weiss; Marshall Williams

Musical Director Hoyt Curtin
Voices Sherry Alberoni; Norman Alden; Danny
Dark; Shannon Farnon; Casey Kasem; Ted
Knight; Olan Soule; John Stephenson; Franklin Welker

1052 The Superstars

ABC
Program Type Sports
Third season premiere: 1/5/75. Times vary: 90
minutes-120 minutes. Sunday. "Superstars"
(male athletes) shown 1/5/75; 1/16/75; 2/9/75;
2/23/75. New event "The Women Superstars"
shown 1/19/75 and 2/2/75. Expert commentator for event: Donna de Varona. New event
"Superteams" shown 3/2/75; 3/9/75; 3/16/75,
with expert O. J. Simpson. "The Celebrity Superstars" shown 3/23/75.
Executive Producer Roone Arledge
Producer Don Ohlmeyer
Production Company ABC Sports
Director Bernie Hoffman
Host Keith Jackson
Expert Commentators Donna de Varona; O. J.
Simpson

Support Your Local Gunfighter *see* The
CBS Thursday/Friday Night Movies

Support Your Local Sheriff *see* NBC
Nights at the Movies

1053 S.W.A.T.

ABC
Program Type Crime Drama
60 minutes. Monday. Premiere date: 2/24/75.
Show originally aired as a 120-minute special
2/17/75 on "The Rookies." Activities of the Special Weapons and Tactics team of police officers
in an unnamed city in California. Created by
Robert Hamner.
Executive Producer Aaron Spelling; Leonard
Goldberg
Production Company Spelling/Goldberg Productions

CAST

Lt. Dan "Hondo" Harrelson	Steve Forrest
Sgt. David "Deacon" Kay	Rod Perry
Jim Street	Robert Urich
Dominic Luca	Mark Shera
T. J. McCabe	James Coleman

1054 The Swiss Family Robinson

Tuesday/Wednesday Movie of the Week;
Special Tuesday Movie of the Week   ABC
Program Type TV Movie
120 minutes. Premiere date: 4/15/75. Based on
the book by Johann Wyss. Pilot for series
1975–76 season.
Producer Irwin Allen

Production Company An Irwin Allen Production in association with 20th Century-Fox Television
Director Harry Harris
Writer Ken Trevey

CAST

Karl Robinson	Martin Milner
Lotte Robinson	Pat Delaney
Jeremiah Worth	Cameron Mitchell
Fred Robinson	Michael-James Wixted
Ernie Robinson	Eric Olson
Helga Wagner	Cindy Fisher
Charles Forsythe	John Vernon
Suramin	George DiCenzo
Nate Bidwell	John Crawford
Allang	Peter Kulha
First Malay	Tom Rosales

1055 Switch
The CBS Thursday/Friday Night Movies CBS
Program Type TV Movie
Pilot for series 1975–76 season. 90 minutes. Premiere date: 3/ 21/75. Repeat date: 8/28/75.
Producer Glen Larson
Production Company Glen Larson Productions in association with Universal Television
Director Robert Day
Writer Glen Larson

CAST

Pete Ryan	Robert Wagner
Frank MacBride	Eddie Albert
Phil Beckman	Charles Durning
Maggie	Sharon Gless
Capt. Griffin	Ken Swofford
Malcolm	Charlie Callas
Alice	Jaclyn Smith
Murray Franklin	Alan Manson
Chuck Powell	Greg Mullavey

Additional Cast Marc Lawrence; Roger Mosley

1056 Take Kerr Syndicated
Program Type Food/Cooking/Nutrition
Food information. 5 minutes. Monday-Friday. Premiere: 1/75.
Producer Treena Kerr
Production Company The Fremantle Corporation of Canada
Distributor JWT Syndication
Host Graham Kerr

1057 Take Me Home Again Syndicated
Program Type Interview/Discussion
60 minutes. Premiere 12/74. Special. Interview and discussion with Burt Reynolds in his home town of Palm Beach, Fla.
Executive Producer Merv Griffin
Producer Betty Bitterman
Production Company Merv Griffin Productions in association with Metromedia
Distributor Western International
Director James V. Bradley

Writer Andrew Smith
Host Burt Reynolds

1058 A Tale of Two Irelands
CBS Reports CBS
Program Type Documentary/Special
Special. Protestant and Catholic Northern Ireland. 60 minutes. Premiere date: 3/20/75. Repeat date: 8/3/75.
Executive Producer Perry Wolff
Producer Howard Stringer
Production Company CBS News
Director Howard Stringer
Writer Howard Stringer
Interviewer John Lawrence

1059 Target Risk
NBC Nights at the Movies NBC
Program Type TV Movie
90 minutes. Premiere date: 1/6/75. Repeat date: 6/26/75.
Executive Producer Jo Swerling, Jr.
Producer Robert F. O'Neill
Production Company Roy Huggins/Public Arts Production in association with Universal Television and NBC-TV.
Director Robert Scheerer
Writer Don Carlos Dunaway

CAST

Lee Driscoll	Bo Svenson
Linda Frayly	Meredith Baxter
Ralph Sloan	John P. Ryan
Julian Ulrich	Robert Coote
Simon Cusack	Keenan Wynn
Marty	Philip Bruns
Harry	Lee Paul

Additional Cast Charles Shull; William Hansen; Jack Bender

1060 Tattletales CBS
Program Type Game Show
Three guest celebrity couples each week. 30 minutes. Monday-Friday. Premiere date: 2/18/74. Continuous.
Executive Producer Ira Skutch
Producer Paul Alter
Production Company Goodson-Todman Productions
Director Paul Alter
Host Bert Convy
Announcer Gene Wood

The Ten Commandments *see* The ABC Saturday Night Movie: The ABC Sunday Night Movie

1061   The $10,000 Pyramid   ABC
Program Type Game Show
Show originated on CBS 3/26/73; went to ABC 5/6/74. 30 minutes. Monday-Friday. Continuous. (For evening version of show, *see* "The $25,-000 Pyramid.")
Executive Producer Bob Stewart
Producer Anne Marie Schmitt
Production Company Bob Stewart Productions
Director Mike Gargiulo
Host Dick Clark

1062   The Tender Grass
The Eternal Light   NBC
Program Type Religious Program
Special. Drama. 30 minutes. Premiere date: 3/30/69. Repeat date: 3/23/75.
Executive Producer Doris Ann
Producer Martin Hoade
Production Company NBC Television Religious Programs Unit
Director Martin Hoade
Writer Morton Wishengrad
CAST
Shalom .... Boris Tumarin
Shulamith/Narrator .... Marian Seldes
Elijah ....Norman Atkins
Fledgling .... Nancy Franklin
Shalom (as a boy) .... Jody Rocco

1063   Tennessee Ernie's
Nashville-Moscow Express   NBC
Program Type Comedy/Variety
Special. 60 minutes. Premiere date: 1/8/75. Concerts taped in September in the U.S.S.R. with singers and dancers from Opryland U.S.A.
Producer Bob Wynn
Production Company Mellodan Productions
Director Bob Wynn
Writer Howard Leeds
Host Tennessee Ernie Ford
Guests Sandi Burnett; Beriozka Troupe

1064   Terror on the 40th Floor
NBC World Premiere Movie   NBC
Program Type TV Movie
120 minutes. Premiere date: 9/17/74. Repeat date (as "NBC Night at the Movies"): 5/29/75.
Story by Jack Turley; Ed Montagne.
Executive Producer Charles Fries
Producer Ed Montagne
Production Company Montagne Productions in association with Metromedia Producers Corporation and NBC-TV
Director Jerry Jameson
Writer Jack Turley
CAST
Dan Overland ....John Forsythe
Howard Foster ....Joseph Campanella
Kelly Freeman .... Don Meredith

Darlene Porter .... Anjanette Comer
Betty Carson .... Kelly Jean Peters
Thelma Overland .... Pippa Scott
Lee Parker .... Lynn Carlin
Ginger .... Laurie Heineman
Capt. Harris .... Mark Tapscott

1065   Texas Tenderfoot
Call It Macaroni   Syndicated
Program Type Children's Show
Real-life adventures of youngsters on Texas ranch. 30 minutes. Premiere: 6/75. Producer for KPIX/San Francisco: Bill Hazelwood.
Executive Producer George Moynihan
Producer Stephanie Meagher
Production Company KPIX/San Francisco; Group W Productions
Distributor Westinghouse Broadcasting Company
Director Stephanie Meagher
Cinematographer Dick Roy
Supervising Editor David E. Roland

1066   The Texas Wheelers   ABC
Program Type Comedy
30 minutes. Friday. Premiere date: 9/13/74. Last show: 10/4/74. Returned as summer replacement on Thursday 6/26/75–7/31/75. Created by Dale McRaven.
Executive Producer Dale McRaven
Producer Chris Hayward
Production Company MTM Enterprises, Inc.
CAST
Zack Wheeler ....Jack Elam
Truckie Wheeler .... Gary Busey
Doobie Wheeler ....Mark Hamill
T. J. Wheeler .... Tony Becker
Boo Wheeler ....Karen Oberdiear
Sally ....Lisa Eilbacher
Herb ....Dennis Burkley
Bud .... Bill Burton

Thanksgiving Day Parade *see* CBS All-American Thanksgiving Day Parade; Macy's Thanksgiving Day Parade

1067   The Thanksgiving Treasure   CBS
Program Type Drama
Special. Based on a story by Gail Rock. Continuing the saga of the Mills family. (*See also* "The House without a Christmas Tree," and "The Easter Promise.") 60 minutes. Premiere date: 11/18/73. Repeat date: 11/17/74.
Producer Alan Shayne
Production Company CBS Television Network
Director Paul Bogart
Writer Eleanor Perry
CAST
James Mills ....Jason Robards

Grandmother	Mildred Natwick
Addie Mills	Lisa Lucas
Mr. Rhenquist	Barnard Hughes
Cora Sue	Franny Michel
Miss Thompson	Kathryn Walker
Uncle Will	Larry Reynolds
Aunt Nora	Kay Hawtrey
Cousin Henry	David Stambaugh
Billy Wild	Brady MacNamara
Aaron Burkhart	Cecil Linder

1068   That Good Ole Nashville Music
Syndicated
Program Type Comedy/Variety
From the Grand Old Opry House, Nashville, Tenn. 30 minutes. Weekly. Guest M.C.s and performers. Regulars: Sound Seventy Singers; Johnny Gimble on fiddle; and square dancers Ralph Sloan and The Tennessee Travelers. Premiere: fall 1969. Season premiere: 9/74.
Executive Producer Bill Fisher
Producer Elmer Alley
Director Bayron Binkley
Regular Sound Seventy Singers; Johnny Gimble; Ralph Sloan

1069   That Uncertain Paradise   PBS
Program Type Documentary/Special
Two-part special. 30 minutes each. Premiere dates: 6/2/75; 6/9/75. Documentary on the islands of Macronesia.
Producer Georgia WGTV/Athens-Atlanta

1070   That's My Mama   ABC
Program Type Comedy
30 minutes. Wednesday. Premiere date: 9/4/74. Set in a black community in Washington, D.C. Created by Dan T. Bradley; Allan Rice. Title song by Alan Blye; Chris Bearde; Gene Farmer. Ed Bernard played Earl in first episode.
Executive Producer Alan Blye; Chris Bearde
Producer Walter N. Bien; Gene Farmer
Production Company Blye/Bearde Productions in association with Columbia Pictures Television
Director Various
Writer Various
CAST
Clifton Curtis	Clifton Davis
"Mama" Eloise Curtis	Theresa Merritt
Earl	Theodore Wilson
Wildcat	Jester Hairston
Josh	DeForest Covan
Tracy	Lynne Moody
Junior	Ted Lange
Leonard	Lisle Wilson

1071   Theater in America   PBS
Program Type Drama
Plays by repertory companies. Times vary. Weekly. Premiere date: 1/23/74. Season

premiere: 1/8/75. Series made possible by grants from Exxon Corporation and the Corporation for Public Broadcasting. Plays shown during the 1974-75 season: "Brother to Dragons," "The Ceremony of Innocence," "The Contractor," "Cyrano de Bergerac," "Enemies," "Feasting with Panthers," "Forget-Me-Not Lane," "In Fashion," "June Moon," "King Lear," "Mass - A Theatre Piece for Singers, Players and Dancers," "A Memory of Two Mondays," "Monkey, Monkey, Bottle of Beer, How Many Monkeys Have We Here?" "The Rimers of Eldritch," "The School for Scandal," "The Seagull," "To Be Young, Gifted and Black," "A Touch of the Poet," "Who's Happy Now?" "The Widowing of Mrs. Holroyd," "The Year of the Dragon," "Zalmen or the Madness of God." (*See* individual titles for cast and credits.)
Executive Producer Jac Venza
Production Company WNET/New York
Host Hal Holbrook

Theatre of Blood *see* NBC Nights at the Movies

1072   There Shall Be Heard Again   CBS
Program Type Religious Program
CBS News religious special. Music written by prisoners of Nazi concentration camp at Terezin. Alfredo Antonini conducts. 60 minutes. Premiere date: 9/26/71. Repeat date: 9/22/74.
Executive Producer Pamela Ilott
Producer Chalmers Dale
Production Company CBS News
Director Portman Paget
Writer Arnold Walton
Host Ida Kaminska

There Was a Crooked Man *see* NBC Nights at the Movies

1073   These Are the Days   ABC
Program Type Animated Film
30 minutes. Saturday. Premiere date: 9/7/74. Small-town America at the turn of the century.
Executive Producer William Hanna; Joseph Barbara
Producer Iwao Takamoto
Production Company A Hanna-Barbera Production
Director Charles A. Nichols
Story Editor Ed Jurist
Writer Bernard M. Kahn; Sam Locke and Milton Pascal; Leo Rifkin; Gene Thompson; Dick Wesson
Musical Director Hoyt Curtin
Executive Story Consultant Myles Wilder

These Are the Days *Continued*
VOICES

Martha Day ....June Lockhart
Kay Day .... Pamelyn Ferdin
Danny Day .... Jack E. Haley
Grandpa Day .... Henry Jones
Ben Day ....Andrew Parks

They Call Me Trinity *see* The CBS
Thursday/Friday Night Movies

**1074 They Don't Laugh at Hoboken
Any More**
Special of the Week   PBS
Program Type Documentary/Special
Special. 30 minutes. Premiere date: 12/9/74. Repeat date: 6/25/75. Urban renewal in Hoboken, New Jersey.
Executive Producer Ken Stein
Production Company WNJT/Trenton

1075 They Only Come Out At Night
NBC World Premiere Movie   NBC
Program Type TV Movie
Based on a true story. 90 minutes. Premiere date: 4/29/75. Repeat date (as "NBC Nights at the Movies"): 7/26/75.
Executive Producer Everett Chambers
Producer Robert Monroe
Production Company MGM Television in association with NBC-TV
Director Daryl Duke
Writer Al Martinez
CAST

"Jigsaw John" St. John ....Jack Warden
Dep. Tallchief .... Charles Ynfante
Lt. Baylor ....Joe Mantell
Dep. Lee Mathews .... Tim O'Connor
Helen St. John .... Madeleine Thornton-Sherwood
David Rudd ....Richard Dinman
Mrs. Eichman ....Lili Valenty
Receptionist .... Barbara Luna
Petulia .... Kine Solomon III
Mrs. Owens .... Melendy Britt
Eichman Daughter .... Constance Pfeifer
Woman Pharmacist ....Dorothy Dells
Elderly Woman .... Nedra Volz
Pharmacy Clerk .... Adele Yoshioka

They Only Kill Their Masters *see* The
CBS Thursday/Friday Night Movies

1076 They Search for Survival Syndicated
Program Type Documentary/Special
Special. 60 minutes. Premiere: 12/74. Produced for World Vision International; filmed in Niger, Bangladesh, Cambodia.
Producer Russ Reid
Production Company Russ Reid Productions for World Vision International

Director Herbert L. Strock
Writer Gary Evans
Musical Director Amindav Aloni
Host Art Linkletter; Dr. Stan Mooneyham

1077 The Thin Edge   PBS
Program Type Educational
Five specials on mental health: depression, aggression, guilt, anxiety and sexuality. 60 minutes. Biweekly. Premiere date: 3/31/75. Repeat date: 7/7/75. Series made possible by a grant from Bristol Myers Company.
Executive Producer David Prowitt
Producer Stephen Gilford
Production Company WNET Science Program Group/New York
Director Al Miselow
Host David Prowitt

1078 Things in Their Season
General Electric Theater   CBS
Program Type Drama
Special. 90 minutes. Premiere date: 11/27/74. Season premiere of GE Theater.
Executive Producer Philip Barry, Jr.
Producer Herbert Hirschman
Production Company Tomorrow Entertainment, Inc.
Director James Goldstone
Writer John Gay
CAST

Peg Gerlach ....Patricia Neal
Carl Gerlach .... Ed Flanders
Andy Gerlach .... Marc Singer
Judy Pines .... Meg Foster
Willie McCreevy ....Charles Haid
Miller Havemeyer ....Doreen Lang
John Tillman ....Med Flory
M.C. .... Jim Kasten
Clifford Canby ....Oliver Jacques
Harold Redman .... A. R. Bowles
Auctioneer .... James Esch
Harvey .... Ron Tomme
Mrs. Weldy .... Sharon Rybacki
Vera Steelwright .... Marcie Reichel

1079 This Is the Life   Syndicated
Program Type Religious Program
30 minutes. Weekly dramas. Premiere: 9/52. Continuous.
Executive Producer Dr. Martin J. Neeb, Jr.
Producer Rev. Ardon D. Albrecht
Production Company Lutheran Television
Director Various
Writer Various

1080 This Is the West That Was
NBC World Premiere Movie   NBC
Program Type TV Movie

90 minutes. Premiere date: 12/17/74. Repeat date: 4/22/75.
Executive Producer Roy Huggins
Producer Jo Swerling, Jr.
Production Company Roy Huggins/Public Arts and Universal Television
Director Fielder Cook
Writer Sam H. Rolfe
Narrator Roger Davis
CAST

Wild Bill Hickok	Ben Murphy
Calamity Jane	Kim Darby
Bill Cody	Matt Clark
Sarah	Jane Alexander
J. W. McCanies	Tony Franciosa
Blind Pete	Stuart Margolin
Oscar Wellman	Bill McKinney

Additional Cast Roger Robinson; Stefan Gierasch; W. L. LeGault; Luke Askew

1081 This Week in the NFL   Syndicated
Program Type Sports
60 minutes (also 30 minute shows). 15 week series. Highlights of the National Football League action of the preceding week. Season premiere: 9/21/74.
Producer Various
Production Company NFL Films, Inc.
Distributor The Hughes Television Network
Host Tom Brookshier; Pat Summerall

1082 Three By Balanchine with the New York City Ballet
Great Performances   PBS
Program Type Music/Dance
Special. 60 minutes. Premiere date: 5/21/75. Taped in Europe for German television in 1973. Presented in the United States by WNET/New York; Emile Ardolino, coordinating producer; Jac Venza; executive producer. Robert Irving conducts the Orf Symphony Orchestra. "Serenade," "Tarantella," and "Duo Concertant" by George Balanchine.
Production Company RM Productions, Munich, in cooperation with Unitel
Guest Artists Peter Martins; Kay Mazzo; Patricia McBride; Edward Villella

The Three Lives of Thomasina *see* NBC Nights at the Movies

1083 Three Women Alone   Syndicated
Program Type Documentary/Special
Special. 60 minutes. Premiere: 3/75. Report focuses on Anne, a single woman; Starr, a divorced woman; Elaine, a widow.
Producer Al Korn
Production Company RKO General Television in association with Richard Shore

Distributor JWT
Director Richard Shore
Writer Joyce Daly
Narrator Colleen Dewhurst

Thunderball *see* The ABC Sunday Night Movie

1084 Thursday's Game
The ABC Saturday Night Movie   ABC
Program Type TV Movie
120 minutes. Premiere date: 4/14/74. Repeat date: 5/31/75. Produced as a feature film in 1971; never released commercially.
Producer James Brooks
Production Company ABC Circle Film
Director Robert Moore
Writer James Brooks
CAST

Harry Evers	Gene Wilder
Marvin Ellison	Bob Newhart
Lynn Evers	Ellen Burstyn
Lois Ellison	Cloris Leachman
Mother	Martha Scott
Mrs. Bender	Nancy Walker
Joel Forester	Rob Reiner
Ann Menzente	Valerie Harper
Melvin Leonard	Norman Fell
David Evers	Gerald Michenaud
Bob	Richard Schaal
Dick	Jed Allen
Mike	Gino Conforti
Dave	Robert Sampson
Mr. Wood	John Archer
Secretary	Barbara Barnett
Cabbie	Bill Callaway
Camp Director	Sidney Clute
Waiter	Jonathan Kidd
Camp Counselor	Chris Sarandon
TV Announcer	Charles Shull
Contestant	Carol Worthington
Bartender	Ric Mancini

1085 Tim Weisberg: Jazz Rock   PBS
Program Type Music/Dance
Special. 30 minutes. Premiere date: 5/12/75. Repeat date: 7/26/75. Tim Weisberg and group: Lynn Blessing; Marty Foltz; Todd Robinson; Doug Anderson.
Producer Neil Heller
Production Company KPBS/San Diego
Director Paul Marshall

Timex Presents Opryland U.S.A. - 1975 *see* Opryland U.S.A. - 1975

1086 To Be Young, Gifted and Black
Theater In America   PBS
Program Type Drama
Based on the works of Lorraine Hansberry by

To Be Young, Gifted and Black
Continued
Robert Nemiroff. 90 minutes. Originally telecast
on "NET Playhouse" 1971–72 season. Repeat
date: 9/3/75.
Producer Robert M. Fresco
Production Company WNET/New York
Director Michael Schultz
Writer Robert M. Fresco
Stars Ruby Dee; Claudia McNeil; Barbara Bar-
rie; Al Freeman, Jr.; Roy Scheider; Blythe
Danner; Lauren Jones

1087   **To Tell the Truth**   Syndicated
Program Type Game Show
Revival of show originally produced 12/18/56
which ran for 12 years; in syndication since 9/69.
30 minutes. Monday-Friday. (Also weekly ver-
sion.) Return: 9/74. Three regular panelists and
one guest celebrity each week.
Producer Bruno Zirato
Production Company Goodson-Todman Produc-
tions
Distributor Firestone Program Syndication
Company
Director Lloyd Gross
Host Garry Moore
Regular Kitty Carlisle; Bill Cullen; Peggy Cass

1088   **Today**   NBC
Program Type News Magazine
120 minutes. Monday-Friday. Premiere date:
1/14/52. Continuous. Lew Wood replaced
Frank Blair 3/14/75. On 7/4/75, "Today" be-
gan a weekly (Friday) 120-minute bicentennial
salute to each state. Series began in Washington,
D.C. and will end in Philadelphia. Presented spe-
cial 90-minute program "Today at Night: Amer-
ica the Humorous" 7/5/75.
Executive Producer Stuart Schulberg
Production Company NBC News
Host Barbara Walters; Jim Hartz
Newscaster Frank Blair; Lew Wood
Regular Gene Shalit

1089   **Today Is Ours**
The CBS Festival of Lively Arts for Young
People   CBS
Program Type Children's Show
Based on "Glowchild," a collection of poems by
young black poets. 60 minutes. Repeat date:
8/16/75. Cast: Ossie Davis; Ruby Dee; Harry
Belafonte.
Executive Producer Aaron Beckwith
Producer Anthony Mascucci
Production Company Beckwith Presentations,
Inc.
Director Ossie Davis
Writer Ossie Davis; Ruby Dee

1090   **Tom T. Hall: The Storyteller** PBS
Program Type Music/Dance
Special. 60 minutes. Originally telecast on KCET
in April 1973. Premiere date on PBS: 3/12/75.
Tom T. Hall at the Palomino Club in North
Hollywood.
Producer Alan Baker
Production Company KCET/Los Angeles
Director Allan Muir

1091   **Tomorrow**   NBC
Program Type Variety/Talk Show
60 minutes. Monday-Thursday (1-2 a.m. Eastern
time). Premiere date: 10/15/73. Continuous.
Show moved from Burbank, California to New
York City 12/2/74. Presented special six-hour
live program 7/4/75 as bicentennial salute.
Producer Joel Tator
Production Company NBC
Director Joel Tator
Host Tom Snyder

1092   **The Tonight Show Starring Johnny
Carson**   NBC
Program Type Variety/Talk Show
90 minutes. Monday-Friday. Premiere date:
12/27/54 (with Steve Allen.) Johnny Carson
became host 10/1/62. Continuous.
Producer Fred de Cordova
Director Bobby Quinn
Musical Director Doc Severinsen
Host Johnny Carson
Announcer Ed McMahon

1093   **Tony Awards**   ABC
Program Type Awards Show
Special. 29th annual awards presented by the
American Theatre Wing to the best performers
and productions on Broadway. 120 minutes.
4/20/75.
Producer Alexander H. Cohen
Production Company Bentwood Television Cor-
poration
Director Clark Jones
Writer Hildy Parks
Musical Director Elliott Lawrence
Host/Performers Larry Blyden; Larry Kert;
Carol Lawrence; Michele Lee; Bernadette Pe-
ters; Charles Nelson Reilly; Bobby Van

1094   **Tony Orlando and Dawn**   CBS
Program Type Comedy/Variety
Dawn: Telma Hopkins; Joyce Vincent Wilson.
60 minutes. Wednesday. Premiere date: 12/4/74.
Producer Saul Ilson; Ernest Chambers
Production Company Ilson-Chambers Produc-
tions, Inc., and Yellow Ribbons Productions,
Inc.

Director Jeff Margolis
Head Writer Al Gordon; Hal Goldman
Musical Director Bob Rozario
Choreographer Jerry Jackson
Host Tony Orlando; Telma Hopkins; Joyce Vincent Wilson

1095 The Toothpaste Millionaire
ABC Afterschool Specials   ABC
Program Type Children's Show
Special. Based on the book by Jean Merrill. Music by Charles Bernstein. 60 minutes. Premiere date: 11/27/74.
Executive Producer Irv Wilson
Producer Harold Schneider; Ronald Rubin
Production Company The Great American Film Factory in association with Viacom Enterprises
Director Richard Kinon
Writer Ronald Rubin
CAST
Rufus Mayflower .... Tierre Turner
Kate MacKinstrey .... Shelly Juttner
Oscar Hobarth .... David Pollack
Joe Smiley .... Wright King
Mr. Evers ....Mel Stevens
Mr. Porter .... Cliff Emmich
Mr. Conti .... Claude Johnson
Mrs. Mayflower ....Helena Hatcher
Mr. Mayflower .... Reuben Collins

1096 Tornado! 4:40 P.M., Xenia, Ohio
NBC News Special   NBC
Program Type Documentary/Special
Special. 60 minutes. Premiere date: 10/10/74.
Producer George F. Murray
Production Company NBC News
Director George F. Murray
Writer Patrick Trese
Narrator Floyd Kalber

1097 Touch of Gold '75   Syndicated
Program Type Music/Dance
Special. 60 minutes. Premiere 3/75. Spotlights gold records of the year.
Executive Producer Kip Walton
Producer Sam Riddle
Production Company S.R.O. Productions and Kip Walton Productions in cooperation with the NBC Television Stations
Producer Kip Walton
Producer Jimmy Abell
Musical Director Gene Page
Choreographer Jess Kutesh
Host Dusty Springfield; Mac Davis
Guests David Gates; Ray Charles; The Miracles; Bo Donaldson and The Heywoods; Thelma Houston; Ted Neeley; De Franco Family; Vicki Lawrence; David Essex; Eric Weissberg and Deliverance; Coven; Al Wilson; Edward

Bear; Alex Harvey; Stevie Wonder; Love Unlimited Orchestra

1098 A Touch of the Poet
Theater in America   PBS
Program Type Drama
Play by Eugene O'Neill. 150 minutes. Premiere date: 4/24/74. Repeat date: 7/23/75. Series made possible by grants from Exxon Corporation and the Corporation for Public Broadcasting.
Executive Producer Jac Venza
Producer David Griffiths
Production Company WNET/New York
Director Stephen Porter; Kirk Browning
Host Hal Holbrook
CAST
Cornelius Melody ....Fritz Weaver
Sara Melody .... Roberta Maxwell
Nora Melody .... Nancy Marchand
Deborah Harford .... Carrie Nye
Jamie Cregan .... Donald Moffat
Mickey Maloy ....Robert Phalen
Dan Roche .... Tom Clancy
Paddy O'Dowd ....John Heffernan
Patch Riley .... Howland Chamberlain
Nicholas Gadsby .... Humphrey Davis

1099 Tournament of Champions
ABC Sports Special   ABC
Program Type Sports
Third and final round play from the La Costa Country Club, Carlsbad, California. Live coverage: 4/26/75; 4/27/75.
Executive Producer Roone Arledge
Production Company ABC Sports
Announcer Chris Schenkel; Keith Jackson; Dave Marr; Frank Gifford

1100 Tournament of Roses Parade NBC
Program Type Documentary/Special
Special. 150 minutes. Live coverage from Pasadena, California. 1/1/75. Henry Aaron: Grand Marshal of parade; Robin Carr: 1975 Rose Queen.
Producer Dick Schneider
Production Company NBC Television Network
Host Ed McMahon; Kelly Lange

1101 The Tournament of Roses Parade
CBS
Program Type Documentary/Special
86th annual parade live from Pasadena, California. First televised 1/1/57. 150 minutes. 1/1/75. Henry Aaron: Grand Marshal of Parade; Robin Carr: 1975 Rose Queen.
Producer Vern Diamond
Production Company CBS Television
Director Vern Diamond
Writer Rene Alkoff
Host Bob Barker; Betty White; Ted Knight

1102   The Tournament of Roses Preview
CBS
Program Type Documentary/Special
Special. Preview of 86th annual parade from Pasadena, California. 30 minutes. 1/1/75.
Producer Vern Diamond
Production Company CBS Television
Director Vern Diamond
Host Bob Barker; Betty White; Ted Knight

1103   Tournament Players Championship
ABC Sports Special   ABC
Program Type Sports
Third and final round play live from the Colonial Country Club, Fort Worth, Texas. 8/23/75; 8/24/75.
Executive Producer Roone Arledge
Production Company ABC Sports

1104   The Toy Pony   Syndicated
Program Type Children's Show
Special. 30 minutes. Premiere: 8/75. Musical. Songs sung by Dora Hall.
Producer Win Opie
Production Company Premore Productions
Director Win Opie
Writer Win Opie
Choreographer Ward Ellis
CAST
Jonathan Moore III	Poindexter
Jonathan Moore II	Kip Yothers
Miss Heffelfinger	Brandy Carson
Miss Tiddly	Ina Gould
Dr. Dugan	Charles Woolf

The Train Robbers *see* NBC Nights at the Movies

1105   Trapped Beneath the Sea
Tuesday/Wednesday Movie Movie of the Week; The ABC Summer Movie   ABC
Program Type TV Movie
Based on the events of 6/17/73. 120 minutes. Premiere date: 10/22/74. Repeat date: 7/25/75. Special effects by Cliff Wenger.
Producer Frank Capra, Jr.
Production Company An ABC Circle Film
Director William Graham
Writer Stanford Whitmore
Underwater Photographer John Lamb
Narrator Howard K. Smith
CAST
Victor Bateman	Lee J. Cobb
T. C. Hollister	Martin Balsam
Sam Wallants	Joshua Bryant
Jack Beech	Paul Michael Glaser
Grace Wallants	Barra Grant
Cmdr. Prestwick	Warren Kemmerling
Gordon Gaines	Cliff Potts
Chris Moffet	Laurie Prange

Cmdr. Hanratty	Phillip R. Allen
P.O. Stanton	Redmond Gleeson
Jeff Turley	Roger Kern
Capt. Osborn	S. John Launer
Jimmy	Rod Perry
Cmdr. Robbins	William Wintersole
Dr. Lewison	Simon Deckard
Howard Wynter	Fredric Franklyn
Sailor No. 1	Norman Honath
Sailor No. 2	Andy Knight
Seaman Schrier	Hunter Von Leer

1106   The Treasure Chest Murder   ABC
Program Type TV Movie
Continuation of the saga of Sam Adams (*see* "Adams of Eagle Rock.") 60 minutes. Premiere date: 1/26/75. Repeat date: 8/30/75.
Executive Producer Richard O. Linke
Producer Walter Grauman; Charles Stewart
Production Company MGM Television
Director Lawrence Dobkin
Writer John Michael Hayes
CAST
Sam Adams	Andy Griffith
Cap Leighton	David Wayne
Tracey	Jack Kruschen
Doc	Jack Dodson
Kalmus	Lloyd Bochner
Jerry Troy	Nick Nolte
Kelly	Abby Dalton
Jubal Hammond	Iggie Wolfington
Monty	Paul Winchell
Quinn	Sheldon Allman
Leonard	Eldon Quick
Lucas Pratt	William Mims

1107   The Trial of Chaplain Jensen
Tuesday/Wednesday Movie of the Week ABC
Program Type TV Movie
90 minutes. Premiere date: 2/11/75. Repeat date: 8/20/75. Based on the book "The Trial of Chaplain Jensen" by Andrew Jensen; Martin Abrahamson.
Executive Producer Paul Monash
Producer Ron Preissman
Production Company A Monash/Preissman Production in association with 20th Century-Fox Television
Director Robert Day
Writer Loring Mandel
CAST
Chaplain Jensen	James Franciscus
Kathleen Jensen	Joanna Miles
Louise Kennelly	Lynda Day George
Adrienne Hess	Dorothy Tristan
Budd Rogers	Charles Durning
Lt. Levin	Howard Platt
Capt. Atherton	Alan Manson
Clark Jensen	Dennis Larson
Donald Jensen	Steven Kunz
Jane A. Johnston	Betty Ulrich
Irene Daniels	Sally Carter Ihnat

1108   **The Trial of Mary Lincoln**   PBS
Program Type Music/Dance
Opera composed by Thomas Pasatieri; libretto
by Anne Howard Bailey. 60 minutes. Premiere
date: 2/14/72 on "NET Opera Theater." Repeat
date: 9/16/74.
Producer Peter Herman Adler
Production Company WNET/New York
Director Kirk Browning
Musical Director Peter Herman Adler
CAST
Mary Lincoln .... Elaine Bonazzi
Robert Lincoln .... Wayne Turnage
Elizabeth .... Carole Bogarde
Additional Cast Chester Watson; Lizabeth Pritchett;
Louise Parker; Alan Titus

1109   **The Tribe**
Tuesday/Wednesday Movie of the Week   ABC
Program Type TV Movie
90 minutes. Premiere date: 12/11/74. Repeat
date: 8/1/75. Filmed on location in Beaumont,
California.
Producer George Eckstein
Production Company Universal Television
Director Richard A. Colla
Writer Lane Slate
Costume Designer Yvonne Wood
CAST
Mathis .... Victor French
Gorin .... Warren Vanders
Cana .... Henry Wilcoxon
Jen .... Adriana Shaw
Gato .... Stewart Moss
Rouse .... Sam Gilman
Sarish .... Tani Phelps Guthrie
Perron .... Mark Gruner
Hertha .... Meg Wyllie
Ardis .... Nancy Elliot
Orda .... Jeannie Brown
Kiska .... Dominique Pinassi
Neanderthal Leader .... Jack Scalici

1110   **A Tribute to George Gershwin**   PBS
Program Type Music/Dance
Special. 90 minutes. Premiere date: 8/20/73. Re-
peat date: 9/23/74. A 75th birthday salute by the
Mormon Youth Symphony and Chorus and the
Mormon Tabernacle Choir.
Executive Producer Byron Openshaw
Production Company KUED/Salt Lake City in
cooperation with KSL-TV
Director Dr. Jay Welch

1111   **A Tribute to Jack Benny**
CBS News Special   CBS
Program Type Documentary/Special
60 minutes. Premiere date: 12/29/74.
Executive Producer Leslie Midgley
Production Company CBS News
Writer Charles Kuralt

Anchor Charles Kuralt
Guests Eddie Anderson; Mel Blanc; Dennis Day;
Danny Kay; Don Wilson; Frank Wilson

1112   **Trilogy of Terror**
Tuesday/Wednesday Movie of the Week   ABC
Program Type TV Movie
90 minutes. Premiere date: 3/4/75. Based on sto-
ries by Richard Matheson. "Millicent and The-
rese" and "Julie" written by William F. Nolan;
"Amelia" written by Richard Matheson.
Producer Dan Curtis
Production Company ABC Circle Film
Director Dan Curtis
Writer William F. Nolan; Richard Matheson
CAST
Millicent/Therese/Julie/Amelia .... Karen Black
Chad .... Robert Burton
Thomas Anman .... John Karlen
Dr. Ramsey .... George Gaynes
Eddie Nells .... Jim Storm
Arthur Moore .... Gregory Harrison
Anne Richards .... Kathryn Reynolds
Tracy .... Tracy Curtis
Motel Clerk .... Orin Cannon

1113   **Triple Crown LPGA Championship**
CBS Sports Special   CBS
Program Type Sports
First and final round play. Live coverage from
the Doral Country Club, Miami Beach, Florida.
1/18/75; 1/19/75.
Producer Frank Chirkinian
Production Company CBS Television Network
Sports
Announcer Jack Whitaker; Ken Venturi; Jane
Chastain

1114   **Trouble Comes to Town**
The ABC Summer Movie   ABC
Program Type TV Movie
90 minutes. Premiere date: 1/10/73. Repeat
date: 7/18/75. Filmed on location in the Yuba
City-Marysville-Colusa area, California.
Producer Everett Chambers
Production Company An ABC Circle Film
Director Daniel Petrie
Writer David Westheimer
CAST
Sheriff Porter Murdoch .... Lloyd Bridges
Tabor .... Pat Hingle
Horace Speare .... Hari Rhodes
Naomi Speare .... Janet MacLachlan
Mrs. Murdoch .... Sheree North
Stacy Garrett .... Thomas Evans
Billy Keith .... Joe Bottoms
Stillman .... Morris Buchanan
Baker .... Thom Carney
Darrin Fox .... Damon Douglas
Bubba Speare .... Wilbert Gowdy
Buchanan .... James Wheaton

True Grit *see* Special Movie Presentation

1115   **Truth Or Consequences**   Syndicated
Program Type Game Show
Started on radio in 1948, came to tv in 1952.
Syndicated in 1967 season. 30 minutes. Monday-
Friday. Continuous.
Executive Producer Ralph Edwards
Producer Ed Bailey
Production Company A Ralph Edwards Produc-
tion in association with Metromedia Pro-
ducers Corporation
Director Bill Chestnut
Writer Jerry Payne; Mark Smith and Milt
Larsen; Ed Bailey
Musical Director Hal Hidy
Host Bob Barker
Announcer Charles Lyon

1116   **Tuesday/Wednesday Movie of the
Week**   ABC
Program Type TV Movie
Series of made-for-television films shown each
Tuesday and Wednesday. Generally 90 minutes
each; some 120 minutes. Premiere date: 9/69.
Season premiere: 9/10/74. The films are: "The
Abduction of Saint Anne," "All My Darling
Daughters," "All the Kind Strangers," "All To-
gether Now," "The Bait," "Bad Ronald," "Be-
trayal," "The California Kid," "Cry for Help,"
"A Cry in the Wilderness," "The Daughters of
Joshua Cabe," "The Daughters of Joshua Cabe
Return," "The Day the Earth Moved," "Dead
Man on the Run," "Death Be Not Proud,"
"Death Cruise," "Death Sentence," "The Des-
perate Miles," "Every Man Needs One," "The
Family Nobody Wanted," "The First 36 Hours
of Dr. Durant," "The Girl Most Like To . . . ,"
"The Girl Who Came Gift Wrapped," "The
Godchild," "The Great Ice Rip-Off," "The
Great Niagara," "Guess Who's Sleeping in My
Bed?" "The Gun," "The Hatfields and the
McCoys," "Heatwave," "Hit Lady," "Hurri-
cane," "Isn't It Shocking?" "It Couldn't Happen
to a Nicer Guy," "Killer Bees," "Let's Switch!"
"Letters From Three Lovers," "Locusts," "The
Mark of Zorro," "Matt Helm," "The Missing
Are Deadly," "My Darling Daughters' Anniver-
sary," "Only With Married Men," "Ordeal,"
"Panic on the 5:22," "Playmates," "Promise
Him Anything . . . ," "Returning Home," "Roll,
Freddy, Roll," "Runaway!" "Satan's Triangle,"
"Savages," "Say Goodbye, Maggie Cole,"
"Scream of the Wolf," "The Sex Symbol,"
"Someone I Touched," "Starsky and Hutch,"
"The Story of Pretty Boy Floyd," "The Stranger
Within," "The Swiss Family Robinson,"
"Trapped Beneath the Sea," "The Trial of Chap-

lain Jensen," "The Tribe," "Trilogy of Terror,"
"Unwed Father," "You Lie So Deep, My Love."
(*See* individual titles for cast and credits.)

1117   **Tune in America**   ABC
Program Type Documentary/Special
Special live Democratic Party telethon. 20- 1/2
hours. 7/26/75–7/27/75. Democratic senators,
representatives, governors, mayors plus perform-
ers.
Executive Producer Eric Lieber
Producer Peggy Lieber
Host Alan Alda; Edward Asner; Lorne Greene;
Helen Reddy; Della Reese; Susan Saint James

1118   **The Turning Point of Jim Malloy**
NBC Nights at the Movies   NBC
Program Type TV Movie
Based on "The Doctor's Son" by John O'Hara.
90 minutes. Premiere date: 4/12/75. Repeat
date: 7/25/75.
Executive Producer David Gerber
Producer Peter Katz; James H. Brown
Production Company David Gerber Productions
in association with Columbia Pictures Televi-
sion
Director Frank D. Gilroy
Writer Frank D. Gilroy
CAST
Jim Malloy .... John Savage
Ray Whitehead .... Gig Young
Dr. Malloy .... Biff McGuire
Mrs. Malloy .... Peggy McCay
Edith Evans .... Kathleen Quinlan
Lintzie .... Frank Campanella
Lonnie .... Janis Paige
Dr. Enright .... Allan Miller
Mr. Kelly .... John McLiam
Bo-Peep .... Rosalind Miles
Terry ....Janis Hansen
Mrs. Ingram ....Sarah Cunningham
Mr. Evans .... Noah Keen
Mrs. Evans .... Dolores Dorn
Mr. Longden ....John Hoyt
Arthur Pond .... Robert Ginty
Mr. Winfield .... Wallace Rooney
Mr. Pell .... Ivor Francis
Mr. Conrad .... Byron Morrow

1119   **'Twas the Night Before Christmas**
CBS
Program Type Animated Film
Special. Adapted from "A Visit From St. Nicho-
las" by Clement Moore. Music by Maury Laws;
Jules Bass. Artist: Paul Cohen, Jr.. 30 minutes.
Premiere date: 12/8/74.
Producer Arthur Rankin, Jr.; Jules Bass
Production Company Rankin-Bass Productions
Director Arthur Rankin, Jr.; Jules Bass
Writer Jerome Coopersmith
Narrator Joel Grey

VOICES
Albert Mouse ....Tammy Grimes
Mayor of Junctionville ....John McGiver
Father Mouse .... George Gobel
Additional Voices Patricia Bright; Alan Swift; Robert McFadden; Christine Winter; Scott Firestone

1120   **The $25,000 Pyramid**   Syndicated
Program Type Game Show
Evening version of "The $10,000 Pyramid." 30 minutes. Weekly. Premiere: 9/74.
Producer Bob Stewart
Production Company Bob Stewart Productions
Distributor Viacom Presentation
Director Mike Gargiulo
Host Bill Cullen

Twenty Four Eyes *see* The Japanese Film

1121   **Twigs**   CBS
Program Type Drama
Special. Television adaptation by George Furth of his four-act play. 90 minutes. Premiere date: 3/6/75.
Producer Joe Hamilton
Production Company Jocar Productions, Inc.
Director Alan Arkin; Clark Jones
Writer George Furth
CAST
Emily/Celia/Dorothy/Ma .... Carol Burnett
Frank .... Alex Rocco
Phil ....Edward Asner
Swede .... Conrad Bain
Lou ....Pat Hingle
Ned .... Jack Gilford
Pa .... Liam Dunn
Clergyman .... Gary Burghoff

Two Mules for Sister Sara *see* NBC Nights at the Movies

1122   **Two Plays**
Hollywood Television Theatre   PBS
Program Type Drama
60 minutes. Originally telecast live in December 1971. Repeat date: 11/6/74. Adaptation of two plays by Anton Chekhov.
Executive Producer Norman Lloyd
Production Company KCET/Los Angeles
Director Rip Torn; Robert Hopkins

The Bear
CAST
Elena Ivanovna Popova .... Geraldine Page
Grigory Stepanovitch Smirnov .... Rip Torn
Luka ....Muni Seroff

The Marriage Proposal
CAST
Natalya Stepanova .... Geraldine Page

Ivan Vassilevitch Lomov .... Rip Torn
Stepan Stepanovitch Chubukov .... Muni Seroff

1123   **The 2,000 Year Old Man**   CBS
Program Type Animated Film
Special. Based on the recordings by Mel Brooks; Carl Reiner. Characters designed by Leo Salkin. 30 minutes. Premiere date: 1/11/75. Repeat date: 4/11/75.
Producer Leo Salkin
Production Company Crossbow Acre Productions in association with Leo Salkin Films
Director Leo Salkin
Writer Carl Reiner; Mel Brooks
Animation Director Dale Case
VOICES
Commentator .... Carl Reiner
2,000-Year-Old Man .... Mel Brooks

1124   **Uber Cup Badminton Matches**
PBS Sports Special   PBS
Program Type Sports
Singles and doubles matches between U.S. and Canada. 90 minutes. Premiere date: 4/20/75. Taped at Waukesha, Wisconsin.
Announcer Bill Hennessy; Jim Cameron

1125   **UFOs: Do You Believe?**
NBC News Special   NBC
Program Type Documentary/Special
Special. 60 minutes. Premiere date: 12/15/74.
Producer Craig Leake
Production Company NBC News
Writer Craig Leake
Narrator Jim Hartz

Ugetsu *see* The Japanese Film

Ulzana's Raid *see* NBC Nights at the Movies

Umberto D *see* Humanities Film Forum

1126   **U.N. Day Concert**   PBS
Program Type Music/Dance
Special in honor of the 29th anniversary of the United Nations. Taped in the General Assembly Hall. Features Seiji Ozawa conducting the New Japan Philharmonic Orchestra and the Toho String Quartet. 90 minutes. Premiere date: 10/24/74. Repeat date: 5/24/75.
Executive Producer George Movshon
Production Company United Nations Television in cooperation with WNET/New York

1127   The Underground Man
NBC Nights at the Movies   NBC
Program Type TV Movie
120 minutes. Premiere date: 5/6/74. Repeat date: 8/15/75. Based on the book by Ross Macdonald. Pilot for NBC series "Archer."
Executive Producer Howard W. Koch
Producer Philip Parslow
Production Company Paramount Television Production in association with NBC-TV
Director Paul Wendkos
Writer Douglas Heyes
CAST
Lew Archer .... Peter Graves
Sheriff Tremaine ....Jack Klugman
Mrs. Snow .... Judith Anderson
Beatrice Broadhurst .... Celeste Holm
Marty ....Sharon Farrell
Eleanor Strome ....Vera Miles
Jean Broadhurst .... Jo Ann Pflug
Sue Crandall .... Kay Lenz
Stanley Broadhurst .... Jim Hutton
Fritz Snow .... Lee Paul

1128   The Undersea World of Jacques Cousteau
                                                                    ABC
Program Type Documentary/Special
Adventure specials. 60 minutes each. Premiere date: 1/8/68. Season premiere: 11/14/74. With Jacques Cousteau and the crew of the *Calypso.* Six programs shown during the 1974-75 season: "Beavers of the North Country," "Beneath the Frozen World," "The Coral Divers of Corsica," "Life at the End of the World," "The Sleeping Sharks of Yucatan," "A Sound of Dolphins." (*See* individual titles for credits.)
Executive Producer Jacques Cousteau; Marshall Flaum
Producer Andy White
Production Company Metromedia Producers Corporation and Les Requins Associes in association with ABC News
Director Philippe Cousteau
Writer Andy White
Host Jacques Cousteau
Photographer Philippe Cousteau

1129   Unfinished Business: A Conversation with Theodore Hesburgh
                                                                    CBS
Program Type Religious Program
CBS News religious special. Discussion by Rev. Theodore Hesburgh. 60 minutes. Premiere date: 12/29/74.
Executive Producer Pamela Ilott
Producer Ted Holmes
Production Company CBS News

1130   Union in Space
ABC News Special Events   ABC
Program Type Documentary/Special
Coverage of Apollo-Soyuz flight from liftoff 7/15/75 through docking 7/17/75 to splashdown 7/24/75. Coverage continuous throughout. Frank Reynolds reports from Moscow; Jules Bergman from U.S. Mission Control Center, Houston; Peter Jennings from New York.
Executive Producer Walter J. Pfister, Jr.
Production Company ABC News Special Events Unit
Anchors Jules Bergman; Peter Jennings; Frank Reynolds

1131   Union in Space (Preview)
ABC News Special Events   ABC
Program Type Documentary/Special
Pre-launch report on Apollo-Soyuz. 60 minutes. 7/13/75.
Producer Phil Lewis
Production Company ABC News Special Events Unit
Reporter Jules Bergman

United Nations Day Concert *see* U.N. Day Concert

United States Lawn Tennis Association Men's National Indoor Tennis Championships *see* USLTA Men's National Indoor Tennis Championships

United States Men's Amateur Golf Championship *see* U.S. Men's Amateur Golf Championship

United States Open see U.S. Open

1132   United States Open Tennis Championships
CBS Sports Special   CBS
Program Type Sports
Eighth year on CBS. 8/30/75; 8/31/75; 9/6/75; 9/7/75. Live coverage from the West Side Tennis Club, Forest Hills, New York.
Producer Frank Chirkinian
Production Company CBS Television Network Sports
Director Bob Dailey
Host Jack Whitaker
Announcer Pat Summerall
Expert Analysts Tony Trabert; Julie Heldman
Roving Reporter Rick Barry
Expert Guest Commentator Jimmy Connors

1133 **United States Open Tennis Report**
CBS Sports Special   CBS
Program Type Sports
10-minute highlights. Monday-Friday (11:30
p.m. eastern time). 9/1/75–9/5/75. Supplement
to the "United States Open Tennis Champion-
ships."
Production Company CBS Television Network
Sports
Host Jack Whitaker
Announcer Pat Summerall; Tony Trabert
Analysts Pat Summerall; Tony Trabert

United States Ski Jumping
Championships *see* U.S. Ski Jumping
Championships

United States Women's Open *see* U.S.
Women's Open

1134 **The Unquiet Death of Julius and**
Ethel Rosenberg   PBS
Program Type Documentary/Special
Special. 90 minutes. Premiered in February 1974.
Repeat date: 9/30/74.
Producer Alvin Goldstein
Production Company NPACT (National Public
Affairs Center for Television)
Narrator Barton Heyman

1135 **The Unwanted**
From Sea to Shining Sea   Syndicated
Program Type Drama
Third of a seven-part miniseries for the bicenten-
nial. 60 minutes. Premiere: 4/75. Filmed in Ire-
land. "Come with Me, Molly" composed and
sung by Michael Jesse Owens.
Producer Helen Jean Secondari; John H. Sec-
ondari
Production Company John H. Secondari Produc-
tions
Distributor The Hughes Television Network
Director Lawrence Doheney
Writer J. P. Miller
CAST
Capt. Horace Banderling .... Richard Boone
John Freeborn ....David Huffman
Judge Kinner .... Ray Milland
Mary Kennedy .... Fionnuala Flanagan
Father O'Reilly .... Donal Donnelly
Tim Kennedy .... Des Keogh
Constable ....Ty Hardin
Annie ....Mildred Mayne

1136 **Unwed Father**
Tuesday/Wednesday Movie of the Week ABC
Program Type TV Movie

90 minutes. Premiere date: 2/27/74. Repeat
date: 7/23/75.
Producer Stan Margulies
Production Company Wolper Productions
Director Jeremy Kagan
Writer W. Hermanos; Carol McKeand
CAST
Peter ....Joseph Bottoms
Vicky .... Kay Lenz
Scott ....Joseph Campanella
Judy .... Kim Hunter
Estelle .... Beverly Garland
Waitress .... Joan Crosby
Gloria ....Jan Hill
Donna .... Michele Art
Judge .... William Hansen
Corey .... Michael Talbott
Jeff .... Richard Gilliland
Karen .... Marni Alexander
Mrs. Howell .... Gina Alvarado

1137 **The Unwilling Warrior**
Sandburg's Lincoln   NBC
Program Type Drama
Fourth in Lincoln series based on the biography
by Carl Sandburg. 60 minutes. Premiere date:
9/3/75.
Executive Producer David L. Wolper
Producer George Schaefer
Production Company David L. Wolper Produc-
tion
Director George Schaefer
Writer Jerome Lawrence; Robert E. Lee
CAST
Abraham Lincoln .... Hal Holbrook
Mary Todd Lincoln .... Sada Thompson
Gen. McClellan .... Ed Flanders
Secy. Wm. Seward .... Lloyd Nolan
Elmer Ellsworth ....David Huffman
Simon Cameron .... John Randolph
Gen. Ulysses S. Grant .... Normann Burton
John Nicolay .... Michael Cristofer
Gen. Scott .... Robert Emhardt
Gen. Weitzel .... Frank Maxwell
Allan Pinkerton .... Brendon Dillon
The Assassin .... John Chandler
Tad Lincoln .... John Levin
Cavalryman ....Ron Hajek
Congressman .... Peter Hobbs

1138 **The Ups and Downs of Henry**
Kissinger
CBS News Special   CBS
Program Type Documentary/Special
60 minutes. Premiere date: 5/25/75.
Executive Producer Leslie Midgley
Producer Hal Haley; Bernard Birnbaum
Production Company CBS News
Director Richard Knox
Host Charles Collingwood
Reporters Charles Collingwood; Marvin Kalb;
Bernard Kalb; Dan Rather

1139   **Upstairs, Downstairs**
Masterpiece Theatre   PBS
Program Type Drama
13-part series. Weekly. Created by Jean Marsh;
Eileen Atkins. Series set at 165 Eaton Place, Lon-
don. Premiere date: 1/6/74. Season premiere:
11/3/74. Repeat date: 5/11/75. Series made pos-
sible by a grant from the Mobil Oil Corporation.
Produced by Joan Sullivan for WGBH/Boston.
At the conclusion of each episode, host Alistair
Cooke introduces a turn-of-the-century English
music hall number from the Players' Theatre in
London.
Executive Producer Rex Firkin
Producer John Hawkesworth
Production Company London Weekend Televi-
   sion
Host Alistair Cooke
                          CAST
Richard Bellamy .... David Langton
Lady Marjorie .... Rachel Gurney
James Bellamy .... Simon Williams
Hazel Forrest .... Meg Wynn Owen
Hudson .... Gordon Jackson
Rose .... Jean Marsh
Mrs. Bridges ....Angela Baddeley
Edward .... Christopher Beeny
Ruby .... Jenny Tomasin
Roberts ....Patsy Smart
Daisy .... Jacqueline Tong
Georgina Worsley ....Lesley-Anne Down
Sir Geoffrey .... Raymond Huntley
Lady Southwold .... Cathleen Nesbitt

1140   **U.S. Men's Amateur Golf
Championship**
ABC Sports Special   ABC
Program Type Sports
Live coverage from the Country Club of Vir-
ginia. 90 minutes. 8/31/75.
Executive Producer Roone Arledge
Producer Terry Jastrow
Production Company ABC Sports
Director Jim Jennett
Announcer Jim McKay; Bill Flemming; Dave
   Marr; Bob Rosburg

1141   **U.S. of Archie**   CBS
Program Type Animated Film
Based on characters originally designed by Bob
Montana; the "Archie" comic book series was
created by John Goldwater. 30 minutes. Pre-
miere date: 9/7/74 (Saturday). Went to Sundays
1/19/75.
Producer Lou Scheimer; Norm Prescott
Production Company A Filmation Production
Director Don Towsley; Lou Zukor; Rudy Lar-
   riva; Bill Reed
Writer Sherman Labby; Mike O'Connor; Paul
   Fennell; Phil Babet
Creative Director Don Christensen

Storyboard Supervisor Kay Wright
Voices Dal McKennon; Howard Morris; John
   Erwin; Jane Webb

1142   **U.S. Open**
ABC Sports Special   ABC
Program Type Sports
Live coverage of the third and final round play
of the U.S. Open from the Medinah Country
Club, Medinah, Illinois, 6/21/75; 6/22/75.
Executive Producer Roone Arledge
Production Company ABC Sports
Announcer Jim McKay; Chris Schenkel; Dave
Marr

1143   **U.S. Ski Jumping Championships**
PBS Sports Special   PBS
Program Type Sports
Highlights of the 1975 championships held
2/22/75–2/23/75 at Brattleboro, Vermont. 60
minutes. Premiere date: 3/2/75.
Production Company Vermont Educational
   Television
Announcer Jim Bauer; Al Merrill; Jim Shea

1144   **U.S. Women's Open**
ABC Sports Special   ABC
Program Type Sports
Third and final round play of the 30th U.S.
Women's Open from the Atlantic City Country
Club, Northfield, New Jersey. 3/19/75;
3/30/75.
Executive Producer Roone Arledge
Production Company ABC Sports

1145   **USLTA Men's National Indoor
Tennis Championships**
PBS Sports Special   PBS
Program Type Sports
Singles and doubles finals live from Wicomico
Civic Center, Salisbury, Maryland. 2/16/75.
Producer Mike Styer
Production Company Maryland Center for Pub-
lic Broadcasting/Owings Mills
Announcer Fred Perry; Clark Graebner

The Valachi Papers *see* The ABC Sunday
   Night Movie

Valdez Is Coming *see* Special Movie
   Presentation

1146   **Valley of the Dinosaurs**   CBS
Program Type Animated Film
30 minutes. Saturday. Premiere date: 9/7/74. A

modern family, the Butlers, thrust into the Stone Age.
Executive Producer William Hanna; Joseph Barbera
Producer Iwao Takamoto
Production Company Hanna-Barbera Productions
Director Charles A. Nichols
Story Editor Sam Roeca
Writer Peter Dixon; Peter Germano; James Henderson; Bernie Kahn; Ben Masselink; Dick Robbins; Henry Sharp; Jerry Thomas
Musical Director Hoyt Curtin
Executive Story Consultant Myles Wilder
Voices Melanie Baker; Shannon Farnon; Joan Gardner; Kathy Gori; Jack E. Haley; Alan Oppenheimer; Andrew Parks; Mike Road; Franklin Welker

1147 Van Cliburn International Piano Competition PBS
Program Type Music/Dance
Two specials. 30 minutes each. First special: the 1973 winner Vladimir Viardo; second special: second-prize winner Christian Zacharias. Specials shown 12/25/74; 1/1/75. Funded by General Telephone and Electronics Corporation.
Producer Tom Turk
Production Company WKAR/East Lansing, Michigan
Director John Weaver

1148 Vaudeville Syndicated
Program Type Comedy/Variety
Variety acts reminiscent of vaudeville. 60 minutes. Monthly. Guest hosts. Card girl: Donna Jean Young.
Executive Producer Burt Rosen
Producer Mort Green
Production Company Metromedia Producers Corporation
Distributor Kaymor Productions, Carbie Productions and Metromedia Producers Corporation
Director Jack Scott
Writer Mort Green
Musical Director George Wyle

1149 A Very Merry Cricket ABC
Program Type Animated Film
Special. Sequel to "The Cricket in Times Square." Music by Dean Elliott; additional lyrics by Marian Dern. Christmas scene by Bill Hajee; David Hanan. Violinist: Israel Baker. 30 minutes. Premiere date: 12/14/73. Repeat date: 11/29/73.
Producer Chuck Jones
Production Company Chuck Jones Enterprises for ABC-TV

Director Chuck Jones
Writer Chuck Jones
VOICES
Chester C. Cricket/Harry the Cat ...... Les Tremayne
Tucker the Mouse/Alley Cat .... Mel Blanc

1150 Vibrations Encore PBS
Program Type Music/Dance
Seven-part music series. 30 minutes. Weekly. Based on series "Vibrations." Premiere date: 9/26/74. Repeat date: 3/27/75. Series made possible by a grant from Exxon Corporation.
Executive Producer Donald Skelton
Producer Bud Myers
Production Company WNET/New York
Director Bud Myers
Host Noel Harrison

1151 Video: The New Wave PBS
Program Type Experimental Program
Special. Anthology of experimental works by 30 video artists. 60 minutes. Premiere date: 6/3/74. Repeat date: 5/29/75. Program funded by a grant from the National Endowment for the Arts.
Producer Fred Barzyk
Production Company WGBH/Boston
Narrator Brian O'Doherty

1152 Video Visionaries PBS
Program Type Experimental Program
13-part series. A compilation of work from experimental television projects at WGBH/Boston, the Television Lab at WNET/New York, and the National Center for Experiments in Television (NCET)/San Francisco. Funded by the National Endowment for the Arts. 30 minutes. Weekly. Premiere date: 8/7/74. Producers for WGBH: Dorothy Chiesa; Fred Barzyk; for WNET: David Loxton; for NCET and KQED: Ann Turner.

1153 Vienna 1900: Games with Love and Death
Masterpiece Theatre PBS
Program Type Drama
Six-part series. 60 minutes. Weekly. Premiere date: 3/2/75. Adaptations of five stories by Arthur Schnitzler. "A Confirmed Bachelor" is in two parts. Presented by WGBH/Boston. Series made possible by a grant from the Mobil Oil Corporation. Each episode is followed by the Boston Symphony Orchestra's string section performing Strauss waltzes from the period.
Producer Richard Beynon
Production Company BBC
Director Herbert Wise
Writer Robert Muller
Host Alistair Cooke

Vienna 1900: Games with Love and Death Continued

A Confirmed Bachelor
CAST

Doktor Graesler .... Robert Stephens
Sabine Schleheim .... Fiona Walker
Frau Schleheim .... Fanny Rowe
Friederike Graesler .... Pam Saire
Karl Schleheim .... Christopher Gable
Herr Schleheim .... Peter Copley
Dr. Bohlinger ....John Bennett
Katharina Rebner .... Susan Littler
Waiter .... Neville Phillips
Frau Rebner .... Elizabeth Stewart
Herr Rebner .... John Dearth
Frau Sommer .... Susan Field
Frau Graesler .... Sheila Brennan

The Gift of Life
CAST

Doktor Graesler .... Robert Stephens
Marie .... Maureen O'Brien
Karl Schleheim .... Christopher Gable
Waiter .... Neville Phillips
Anna Rupius .... Jacqueline Pearce
Her Lover .... Ron Daniels
Baritone .... John Barrow

A Man of Honour
CAST

Doktor Graesler .... Robert Stephens
Alfred Beratoner ....Norman Eshley
Adele .... Vanessa Miles
Elise .... Cheryl Murray
Waiter .... Neville Phillips
Adele's Father ....Bruce Purchase
Lt. Franz von Schall .... Jeremy Clyde
Postmistress .... Una Brandon-Jones
The Baron .... Robin Bailey
Doctor.. Manning Wilson
Apothecary .... George Howe
Tenor .... Peter Bamba
Cabaret Girls .... The Baker Twins

Mother and Son
CAST

Doktor Graesler .... Robert Stephens
Beate Heinold .... Dorothy Tutin
Hugo Heinold ....Christopher Guard
Fritz Weber .... Richard Morant
Baroness Fortunata .... Adrienne Corri
Herr Arbesbacher .... Christopher Benjamin
Frau Arbesbacher .... Doreen Mantle
Lilli ....Barbara Ogilvie
Wilhelmina Fallehn ....Jennifer Croxton
Alfred Beratoner ....Norman Eshley
Herr Welponer .... Bernard Lee
Companion .... Ron Daniels
Frau Welponer .... Dona Martyn

The Spring Sonata
CAST

Doktor Graesler .... Robert Stephens
Berta Garlan .... Lynn Redgrave
Anna Rupius .... Jacqueline Pearce
Her Lover .... Ron Daniels
Waiter .... Neville Phillips

Franzl .... Peter Marshall
Herr Klingmann .... Sydney Tafler
Richard Garlan .... Peter Settelen
Herr Rupius .... Lyndon Brook
Herr Garlan .... Alan Foss
Elly Garlan .... Janet Davies
Frau Graesler .... Sheila Brennan
Her Daughter .... Rebecca Saire
Emil Lindbach ....Sandor Eles

1154   The Vienna Symphony Orchestra
PBS

Program Type Music/Dance

Special. 60 minutes. Premiere date: 3/10/75. Repeat date: 8/21/75. New Year's Eve concert by the Vienna Philharmonic Orchestra conducted by Willi Boskovsky, with the Vienna State Opera Ballet Corps and the Vienna Volksoper Ballet. Production Company ORF (Austrian Television System) and ZDF (The Second German Television Network)

1155   Vietnam: A War That Is Finished
CBS News Special   CBS

Program Type Documentary/Special

Special report. 150 minutes. Premiere date: 4/29/75. Analysis and reporting by correspondents in U.S. and Southeast Asia.
Executive Producer Russ Bensley; Leslie Midgley
Production Company CBS News
Anchor Walter Cronkite

1156   Villa Alegre (Happy Village)   PBS
Program Type Children's Show

Bilingual (Spanish/English) show. 30 minutes. Monday–Friday. Premiere date: 9/23/74. Repeat date: 12/23/74. Series made possible by grants from the U.S. Department of Health, Education and Welfare, Office of Education, Exxon Corporation, U.S.A. Foundation and the Ford Foundation.
Producer Mario Guzman
Production Company BC/TV (Bilingual Children's Television, Inc., Oakland, California)

1157   Violin   PBS
Program Type Music/Dance

Special. 30 minutes. Premiere date: 8/14/72. Repeat date: 6/8/75. Profiles the chamber music players of the Boston Symphony Orchestra and their instruments. (See also "Double Reed.")
Executive Producer Syrl A. Silberman
Producer Bill Cosel
Production Company WGBH/Boston and the Massachusetts Council for the Humanities, Inc. with the cooperation of the Boston Symphony Orchestra

1158 The Virginia Hill Story
NBC World Premiere Movie   NBC
Program Type TV Movie
90 minutes. Premiere date: 11/19/74. Repeat date: 4/15/75. Filmed at the Harold Lloyd estate, Beverly Hills, and the Biltmore Hotel, Los Angeles. Story by Juleen Compton.
Executive Producer Deanne Barclay; Howard Rosenman
Producer Aaron Rosenberg
Production Company RSO Films, Inc. in association with NBC-TV
Director Joel Schumacher
Writer Joel Schumacher; Juleen Compton
CAST
Virginia Hill .... Dyan Cannon
Bugsy Siegel .... Harvey Keitel
Leroy Small .... Robby Benson
Leo Ritchie .... Allen Garfield
Nick Rubanos .... John Vernon
Sen. Kefauver .... Herbert Anderson
Mousie .... John Quade
Additional Cast Liam Dunn; Conrad Janis

Walking Tall *see* The ABC Saturday Night Movie

1159 Wall Street Week   PBS
Program Type Interview/Discussion
30 minutes. Weekly. Premiere date: 1/7/72. Continuous. Music "Twelve Bars for TWX" by Donald Swartz. Weekly guest plus panel of stock market experts. Series made possible by grants from the Corporation for Public Broadcasting, the Ford Foundation, and Public Television Stations.
Producer Anne Truex Darlington
Production Company WMPB/Baltimore
Director Steve McCullough
Host Louis Rukeyser

1160 Walsh's Animals   PBS
Program Type Children's Show
13-part series. 30 minutes. Weekly. Premiere date: 11/11/74. Series underwritten in part by a grant from the Latham Foundation.
Production Company WGBH/Boston
Host John Walsh

1161 The Waltons   CBS
Program Type Drama
Based on book by Earl Hamner and TV drama "The Homecoming" (*see* credits). 60 minutes. Thursday. Premiere date: 9/14/72. Season premiere: 9/12/74 (120-minute special "The Conflict.") Repeat specials: Thanksgiving (11/25/74); Valentine's Day (2/9/75); Easter (3/30/75). Set in West Virginia on Walton's Mountain.

Executive Producer Lee Rich
Producer Robert L. Jacks
Production Company Lorimar Productions
Director Various
Writer Various
CAST
John-Boy .... Richard Thomas
John .... Ralph Waite
Olivia .... Michael Learned
Grandpa .... Will Geer
Grandma .... Ellen Corby
Mary Ellen .... Judy Norton
Jason .... Jon Walmsley
Erin .... Mary McDonough
Ben .... Eric Scott
Jim-Bob .... David W. Harper
Elizabeth .... Kami Cotler
Ike .... Joe Conley
Mike .... Ted Eccles

Wanda *see* Hollywood Television Theatre

1162 Washington Straight Talk   PBS
Program Type Interview/Discussion
30 minutes. Weekly. Premiere date: 12/3/73. Season premiere: 10/7/74.
Production Company NPACT (National Public Affairs Center for Television)
Host Paul Duke
Regular Carolyn Lewis; Jim Lehrer; Paul Duke

1163 Washington Week in Review   PBS
Program Type Interview/Discussion
30 minutes. Weekly. Premiere date: 2/22/67. Continuous. Series made possible by grants from the Corporation for Public Broadcasting, the Ford Foundation, and Public Television Stations.
Producer Lincoln Furber
Production Company NPACT (National Public Affairs Center for Television)
Host Paul Duke
Regular Peter Lisagor; Neil McNeil; Charles Corddry

1164 The Way It Was   PBS
Program Type Sports
13-part series. 30 minutes. Weekly. Premiere date: 10/3/74. Repeat date: 5/6/75. Programs underwritten by Mobil Oil Corporation. Series covers: 1951 New York Giants/Brooklyn Dodgers playoff; 1958 Baltimore Colts/New York Giants NFL championship; 1952 Sugar Ray Robinson/Rocky Graziano fight; 1946 Army/Navy football game; 1947 New York Yankees/Brooklyn Dodgers World Series (two parts); 1961/62 Los Angeles Lakers/Boston Celtics NBA championship; 1960 Green Bay Packers/Philadelphia Eagles NFL championship; 1946 St. Louis Cardinals/Boston Red Sox World Se-

The Way It Was *Continued*
ries; 1941 Joe Louis/Billy Conn heavyweight fight; 1950 Cleveland Browns/Los Angeles Rams NFL championship; 1953 Detroit Red Wings/Montreal Canadiens Stanley Cup playoffs; 1956 New York Yankees/Brooklyn Dodgers World Series.
Production Company Gerry Gross Productions at KCET in association with Syndicast Services, Inc.
Host Curt Gowdy

1165   The Wayne Newton Special   NBC
Program Type Comedy/Variety
Special. 90 minutes. Premiere date: 9/28/74.
Executive Producer Henry Jaffe; Jay Stream
Producer Bob Booker, Jr.; George Foster
Production Company Burt Reynolds-Henry Jaffe Productions in association with Waynco Productions
Director Harold Tulchin
Writer Bob Booker, Jr.; George Foster; George Yanok; Howard Albrecht and Sol Weinstein
Host Wayne Newton
Guests Burt Reynolds; Robert Goulet; Carol Lawrence; Lee Majors; Farah Fawcett; Freda Payne; Barbara Mandrell

1166   WCT Challenge Cup   NBC
Program Type Sports
11 regular games of championship tennis covered live. Season premiere: 3/2/75. Last show of season: 5/11/75. Sunday.
Production Company NBC Sports
Announcer Bud Collins; Dan Rowan

1167   WCT Doubles Challenge Match
NBC Sports Special   NBC
Program Type Sports
90 minutes. 5/25/75. Taped coverage of WCT doubles title.
Production Company NBC Sports
Announcer Bud Collins; Dan Rowan

1168   The Weather Machine   PBS
Program Type Documentary/Special
Special. On climate and climate control. 120 minutes. Premiere date: 2/24/75. Special made possible by a grant from Champion International Corporation.
Production Company WNET/New York
Writer Nigel Calder
Correspondent David Prowitt

Wednesday Movie of the Week *see*
Tuesday/Wednesday Movie of the Week

1169   Weekend   NBC
Program Type News Magazine
90 minutes. Monthly. Premiere date: 10/20/74.
Executive Producer Reuven Frank
Producer Various
Production Company NBC News
Host Lloyd Dobyns

1170   We'll Get By   CBS
Program Type Comedy
Created by Alan Alda. Theme song by Sheldon Harnick; Joe Raposo. 30 minutes. Premiere date: 3/14/75. Last show: 5/30/75. Special 30-minute preview 3/6/75. Set in a New Jersey suburb. Two shows presented on 3/28/75, 5/30/75.
Executive Producer Marc Merson; Alan Alda
Producer Alan Alda; Allan Katz; Don Reo
Production Company Helix Productions
Director Jack Shea
CAST
George Platt .... Paul Sorvino
Liz Platt .... Mitzi Hoag
Muff Platt .... Jerry Houser
Kenny Platt .... Willie Aames
Andrea Platt .... Devon Scott

1171   What Is Noise? What Is Music?
Young People's Concert   CBS
Program Type Children's Show
Michael Tilson Thomas conducts the New York Philharmonic Orchestra. 60 minutes. Premiere date: 5/10/75.
Producer Roger Englander
Production Company CBS Television Network
Director Roger Englander
Writer Michael Tilson Thomas
Narrator Michael Tilson Thomas

1172   What Makes a Gershwin Tune a Gershwin Tune?
Young People's Concert   CBS
Program Type Children's Show
George Gershwin music analyzed and played by the New York Philharmonic Orchestra conducted by Michael Tilson Thomas. 60 minutes. Premiere date: 9/29/74.
Producer Roger Englander
Production Company CBS Television Network
Director Roger Englander
Narrator Michael Tilson Thomas
Singer Larry Marshall

1173   What Makes a Good Father?
Special of the Week   PBS
Program Type Documentary/Special
Special. 60 minutes. Premiere date: 1/6/75. Repeat date: 6/12/75. Jim Grant; Lou Watson; Sol Gittelman illustrate their approaches to child rearing.

Production Company WGBH/Boston
Host Barry Brazelton

1174 **What Will We Say To a Hungry World?** Syndicated
Program Type Documentary/Special
5-hour report/telethon. 30 filmed reports. Dr. Stan Mooneyham, President of World Vision International, host. Premiere: 6/75.
Executive Producer Russ Reid
Producer Jerry McClun
Production Company Russ Reid Productions
Director Herbert L. Strock
Writer Gary Evans

1175 **What's Apollo-Soyuz All About?**
What's It All About? CBS
Program Type Children's Show
CBS News Special for Young People. 30 minutes. Premiere date: 7/12/75.
Executive Producer Joel Heller
Producer Walter Lister
Production Company CBS News
Director Richard Knox
Writer Walter Lister
Anchor Walter Cronkite
Reporters Richard Roth; Nelson Benton

1176 **What's Going On Here? The Troubled American Economy**
CBS News Special CBS
Program Type Documentary/Special
60 minutes. Premiere date: 9/22/74.
Executive Producer Leslie Midgley
Producer Hal Haley; Bernard Birnbaum
Production Company CBS News
Director Ken Sable
Anchor John Hart
Reporters David Culhane; George Herman; Bernard Kalb; Mitchell Krauss; John Sheahan

1177 **What's Inflation All About?**
What's It All About? CBS
Program Type Children's Show
CBS News Special for Young People. 30 minutes. Premiere date: 11/30/74.
Executive Producer Joel Heller
Producer Walter Lister
Production Company CBS News
Director Richard Knox
Writer Walter Lister
Reporter Christopher Glenn

1178 **What's It All About?** CBS
Program Type Children's Show
Special informational shows for young people presented periodically. Premiered in July, 1972.

Six programs shown during 1974-75. Season premiere: 10/26/74. 30 minutes each. Saturdays. The programs are: "What's Apollo-Soyuz All About?" "What's Inflation All About?" "What's the CIA All About?" "What's the Middle East All About?" "What's the Senate All About?" "What's This Election All About?" (*See* individual titles for credits.)
Executive Producer Joel Heller
Producer Walter Lister
Production Company CBS News
Director Various
Writer Walter Lister

1179 **What's My Line?** Syndicated
Program Type Game Show
30 minutes. Weekly. Show premiered on CBS in 1950; in syndication since September 1968. Last season of new production.
Producer Gilbert Fates
Production Company Goodson-Todman Productions
Distributor Viacom Enterprises
Director Lloyd Gross
Host Larry Blyden
Regular Arlene Francis; Soupy Sales

What's New Pussycat? *see* The ABC Sunday Night Movie

1180 **What's the CIA All About?**
What's It All About? CBS
Program Type Children's Show
CBS News Special for Young People. 30 minutes. Premiere date: 6/14/75. Repeat date: 6/24/75 (in evening for adults).
Executive Producer Joel Heller
Producer Walter Lister
Production Company CBS News
Director Vern Diamond
Writer Walter Lister
Correspondent Daniel Shorr

What's the Matter with Helen? *see* NBC Nights at the Movies

1181 **What's the Middle East All About?**
What's It All About? CBS
Program Type Children's Show
CBS News Special for Young People. 30 minutes. Premiere date: 2/22/75.
Executive Producer Joel Heller
Producer Walter Lister
Production Company CBS News
Director Vern Diamond
Reporter Christopher Glenn

1182 What's the Senate All About?
What's It All About?   CBS
Program Type Children's Show
CBS News Special for Young People. 30 minutes.
Premiere date: 4/12/75.
Executive Producer Joel Heller
Producer Walter Lister
Production Company CBS News
Director Richard Knox
Writer Walter Lister
Host Roger Mudd

1183 What's This Election All About?
What's It All About?   CBS
Program Type Children's Show
CBS News Special for Young People. 30 minutes.
Premiere date: 10/26/74.
Executive Producer Joel Heller
Producer Joel Lister
Production Company CBS News
Director Arthur Bloom
Writer Walter Lister
Reporter Walter Cronkite

1184 Wheel of Fortune   NBC
Program Type Game Show
30 minutes. Monday-Friday. Premiere date:
1/6/75. Continuous.
Producer John Rhinehart
Production Company Merv Griffin Production
Director Jeff Goldstein
Host Chuck Woolery; Susan Stafford
Announcer Charlie O'Donnell

1185 Wheelie and the Chopper Bunch
                                        NBC
Program Type Animated Film
30 minutes. Saturday. Premiere date: 9/7/74.
Last show: 8/30/75.
Executive Producer William Hanna; Joseph
Barbera
Producer Iwao Takamoto
Production Company Hanna-Barbera Productions
Director Charles A. Nichols
Story Editor Ray Parker
Writer Larz Bourne; Len Janson; Chuck Menville; Robert Ogle; Dalton Sandifer
Musical Director Hoyt Curtin
VOICES
Wheelie/Chopper .... Frank Welker
Scrambles .... Don Messick
Revs .... Paul Winchell
Hi-Riser .... Len Weinrib
Rota .... Judy Strangis

When a Woman Ascends the Stairs *see*
The Japanese Film

1186 When Witches Hovered Near PBS
Program Type Drama
Special. 60 minutes. Premiere date: 10/24/73.
Repeat: 10/31/74.
Producer Barbara Gills; James Tober
Production Company Connecticut Public Television
Director Nelson Baker; C. Patterson Denny
Narrator John Colle

The Devil's Hopyard
                    CAST
Abe Brown .... James Quinn
Parson Straightback .... Hal Dorsey

The Machimoodus
                    CAST
Acton/Aucliffe .... Randall Feldman
Dr. Steel .... Robert Gustafson

Where Eagles Dare *see* Special Movie
Presentation

1187 Where Have All the People Gone?
NBC World Premiere Movie   NBC
Program Type TV Movie
90 minutes. Premiere date: 10/8/74. Repeat
date: 6/3/75. Based on a story by Lewis John
Carlino.
Executive Producer Charles Fries
Producer Gerald Isenberg
Production Company Jozak Company, Alpine
Productions and Metromedia Producers Corporation in association with NBC-TV
Director John Llewellyn Moxey
Writer Lewis John Carlino; Sandor Stern
                    CAST
Steven Anders .... Peter Graves
Jenny .... Verna Bloom
David Anders .... George O'Hanlon, Jr.
Deborah Anders .... Kathleen Quinlan
Michael .... Michael-James Wixted
Guide .... Noble Willingham

Where It's At *see* The ABC Sunday
Night Movie

1188 Where's the Fire?
ABC Comedy Special   ABC
Program Type Comedy
Special. 30 minutes. Premiere date: 5/17/75.
Executive Producer Douglas S. Cramer
Production Company Douglas S. Cramer Productions
Director Jerry Paris
Writer Gerald Gardner; Dee Caruso
                    CAST
Rosco .... Johnny Brown
Buck .... John Fink
Stanley .... Danny Fortus
Capt. O'Hara .... Dave Ketchum

Renaldo .... Gregory Sierra
Skipper ....J. Pat O'Malley
Trusdale .... Edward Andrews
Acropolis .... Carl Ballantine
Chief .... Roger Bowen
Angelina .... Leigh French

1189 The Whirlwind
Benjamin Franklin   CBS
Program Type Drama
Second of four-part series dealing with the life of Benjamin Franklin. 90 minutes. Premiere date: 12/17/74.
Executive Producer Lewis Freedman
Producer George Lefferts
Production Company CBS Television
Director Glenn Jordan
Writer Loring Mandel
CAST
Benjamin Franklin .... Lloyd Bridges
Benjamin Franklin (young man) ....Beau Bridges
Deborah Read .... Susan Sarandon
Deborah Franklin ....Sheree North
Josiah Franklin .... Will Geer
William Franklin .... Bruce Davison
Additional Cast Sorrell Booke; Keene Curtis; Gerald Hiken; Scott Hylands; Alan Napier; Perry King; Edward Bell

1190 The White-Collar Rip-Off
NBC News Special   NBC
Program Type Documentary/Special
Special. 60 minutes. Premiere date: 6/1/75.
Executive Producer Eliot Frankel
Production Company NBC News
Director Darold Murray
Writer Eliot Frankel; Michael B. Silber
Anchor Edwin Newman

1191 The White Seal   CBS
Program Type Animated Film
Special. From "The Jungle Books" by Rudyard Kipling. 30 minutes. Premiere date: 3/24/75. Music: Beethoven's Sixth Symphony arranged by Dean Elliott.
Producer Chuck Jones
Production Company Chuck Jones Enterprises
Director Chuck Jones
Writer Chuck Jones
Musical Director Dean Elliott
Master Animators George Nicholas; Hal Ambro
Narrator Roddy McDowall
VOICES
Kotick/Sea Catch/Sea Cow/
  Whale/Walrus ....Roddy McDowall
Matkah .... June Foray

1192 Who Is the Black Dahlia?
NBC Nights at the Movies   NBC
Program Type TV Movie
Based on a murder that took place in Los Ange-

les in 1947. Harry Hansen was technical advisor. 120 minutes. Premiere date: 3/1/75. Repeat date: 8/28/75.
Executive Producer Douglas S. Cramer
Producer Henry Colman
Production Company Douglas S. Cramer Production in association with NBC-TV
Director Joseph Pevney
Writer Robert W. Lenski
CAST
Det. Sgt. Harry Hansen .... Efrem Zimbalist, Jr.
Elizabeth Short .... Luci Arnaz
Sgt. Finis Brown .... Ronny Cox
Capt. Jack Donahoe .... MacDonald Carey
Dr. Coppin .... Linden Chiles
Susan Winters .... Donna Mills
Bevo Means ....Tom Bosley
Grandmother ....Mercedes McCambridge
Lee Jones .... Henry Jones
Mr. Short .... Frank Maxwell
Additional Cast June Lockhart

Who's Afraid of Virginia Woolf? *see* The CBS Thursday/Friday Night Movies

1193 Who's Happy Now?
Theater in America   PBS
Program Type Drama
Play by Oliver Hailey performed by the Mark Taper Forum, Los Angeles. 90 minutes. Premiere date: 5/14/75. Series made possible by grants from Exxon Corporation and the Corporation for Public Broadcasting.
Executive Producer Jac Venza
Producer Matt Herman; Tom Hill
Production Company WNET/New York
Director Gordon Davidson
Writer Oliver Hailey
Host Hal Holbrook
CAST
Horse Hallen .... Albert Salmi
Mary Hallen .... Betty Garrett
Faye Precious .... Rue McClanahan
Pop .... Guy Raymond
Richard .... John Ritter
Taylor .... John Fiedler
Mrs. Taylor .... Alice Ghostley

1194 Why Evangelism?   NBC
Program Type Religious Program
Special. Interview with Dr. Erwin Kolb. 30 minutes. Premiere date: 5/18/75.
Producer Doris Ann
Production Company NBC Television Religious Programs Unit
Director Robert Priaulx
Interviewer Mike Maus

The Wicked Dreams of Paula Schultz *see* The CBS Thursday/Friday Night Movies

1195   **Wide World of Entertainment** ABC
Program Type General
A combination of special events, rock music concerts taped live at the In Concert Theatre, Hollywood, California, and made-for-television mysteries. 90 minutes each. Season premiere: 9/10/74. Monday-Friday.
Producer Various
Director Various
Writer Various

Wide World of Sports *see* ABC's Wide World of Sports

1196   **The Widowing of Mrs. Holroyd**
Theater in America   PBS
Program Type Drama
Play by D. H. Lawrence performed by the Long Wharf Theater, New Haven, Conn. 120 minutes. Premiere date: 5/8/74. Repeat date: 2/5/75. Series funded by Exxon Corporation and the Corporation for Public Broadcasting.
Executive Producer Jac Venza
Production Company WNET/New York in association with CPTV/Connecticut
Director Arvin Brown; John Desmond
Host Hal Holbrook
                     CAST
Mrs. Holroyd .... Joyce Ebert
Blackmore .... Frank Converse
Holroyd .... Rex Robbins
Grandmother ....Geraldine Fitzgerald
Jack Holroyd .... Timmy Ousey
Minnie Holroyd .... Vicky Geyer
Clara .... Roberta Maxwell
Laura .... Veronica Castang
Rigley ....Emery Battis
Mine Manager .... William Swetland
Miners .... James Hacker; James Silverstein

The Wild Bunch *see* The CBS Thursday/Friday Night Movies

1197   **Wild Kingdom**   Syndicated
Program Type Animal Documentary
Oldest of the animal documentaries. Premiered in 1962. 30 minutes. Season premiere: 9/74. Weekly.
Producer Don Meier
Production Company Don Meier Productions, Inc.
Distributor Mutual of Omaha
Director Don Meier
Writer Allen Eckert
Host Marlin Perkins

Regular Tom Allen
Chief Wildlife Photographer Warren Garst
Wildlife Photographers Ralph Nelson; Rod Allin

1198   **The Wild Places**   NBC
Program Type Documentary/Special
Special. 60 minutes. Premiere date: 12/2/74. Paul Newman and Joanne Woodward with daughters Lissy and Clea in a variety of wilderness areas.
Producer Lee Mendelson; Walt De Faria
Production Company Lee Mendelson Production & The Sierra Club
Director Lee Mendelson
Writer Lee Mendelson
Host Paul Newman; Joanne Woodward

Wild Rovers *see* The CBS Thursday/Friday Night Movies

1199   **Wild, Wild World of Animals**
                                            Syndicated
Program Type Animal Documentary
30 minutes. Weekly. Premiere: 9/73. Season premiere: 9/74.
Producer Stanley Joseph
Production Company Time-Life Television Productions
Director Stanley Joseph
Narrator William Conrad

Willard *see* The CBS Thursday/Friday Night Movies

Willy Wonka and the Chocolate Factory *see* NBC Nights at the Movies

1200   **Wimbledon Tennis Championships**
NBC Sports Special   NBC
Program Type Sports
Taped coverage of English tennis championships. 6/28/75; 6/29/75; 7/5/75.
Production Company NBC Sports
Announcer Bud Collins; Jim Simpson

1201   **Window on the World**   Syndicated
Program Type Documentary/Special
Documentary specials. 60 minutes each. Three programs aired during 1974-75 season: "The Bronx Is Burning," "Khrushchev Remembers," "Rose Kennedy Remembers - The Best of Times . . . The Worst of Times." (*See* individual titles for credits.)
Production Company Time-Life Films and BBC-TV.
Distributor Time-Life Films

1202 Winesburg, Ohio

Hollywood Television Theatre   PBS
Program Type Drama
90 minutes. Premiere: 3/5/73. Repeat date: 10/30/74.
Producer Norman Lloyd
Production Company KCET/Los Angeles
Director Ralph Senensky
Writer Sherwood Anderson
CAST
Elizabeth Willard .... Jean Peters
Dr. Reefy .... William Windom
George Willard ....Joseph Bottoms
Tom Willard .... Albert Salmi
Old Pete .... Norman Foster
Ed Crowley .... Don Hammer
Salesman .... Alvin Hammer
Turk ....George Winters
Seth .... Chip Hand
Art .... Gary Barton
Will Henderson .... Curt Conway
Helen White .... Laurette Spang
Parcival .... Dabbs Greer
Mrs. Wilson .... Arlene Stuart
Mr. Wilson ....Pitt Herbert

1203 Winner Take All

NBC Nights at the Movies   NBC
Program Type TV Movie
120 minutes. Premiere date: 3/3/75.
Executive Producer Gerald I. Isenberg
Producer Nancy Malone
Production Company The Jozak Company
Director Paul Bogart
Writer Caryl Ledner
CAST
Eleanor Anderson .... Shirley Jones
Bill Anderson .... Laurence Luckinbill
Rick Santos .... Sam Groom
Edie Gould .... Joyce Van Patten
Beverly Craig .... Joan Blondell
Anne Barclay ....Sylvia Sidney
Leonard Fields ....John Carter

1204 Winnie the Pooh and the Blustery Day
    NBC
Program Type Animated Film
Special. Based on stories by A. A. Milne. Animation based on illustrations by Ernest H. Shepard. 1968 Oscar winner. 30 minutes. Repeat date: 11/26/74.
Production Company Walt Disney Productions
Narrator Sebastian Cabot
VOICES
Pooh .... Sterling Holloway

Winning *see* NBC Nights at the Movies

1205 Winning & Losing: Diary of a Campaign

ABC Afterschool Specials   ABC
Program Type Children's Show
Special. The real-life experiences of two young volunteers, Robin Allen and Lori Forman, on opposing sides of the George McGovern-Leo Thorsness senatorial race in South Dakota. 60 minutes. Premiere date: 11/6/74.
Producer Danny Wilson
Production Company Daniel Wilson Productions, Inc. in association with ABC News
Director Richard Slate

1206 Winning Streak   NBC

Program Type Game Show
30 minutes. Monday-Friday. Premiere date: 7/1/74. Last show: 1/3/75.
Executive Producer Bob Stewart
Producer Bruce Burmester
Production Company Bob Stewart Production
Director Mike Gargiulo
Host Bill Cullen
Announcer Don Pardo

1207 Witness to Creation   CBS

Program Type Religious Program
CBS News religious special. Christmas observance by Benedictine monks in Western Priory (Vermont). 30 minutes. Premiere date: 12/24/74.
Executive Producer Pamela Ilott
Producer Joe Clement
Production Company CBS News

1208 Wives

Comedy Special   CBS
Program Type Comedy
30 minutes. Pilot film. Premiere date: 3/21/75. Repeat date: 7/17/75. Created by Garry Marshall.
Executive Producer Garry Marshall
Producer Tony Marshall
Production Company The Henderson Production Company, Inc. in association with Paramount Television
Director Jay Sandrich
Writer Garry Marshall
CAST
Franny ....Janie Sell
Connie ....Penny Marshall
Mary Margaret ....Candy Azzara
Lillian .... Jacque Lynn Colton
Doris .... Phyllis Elizabeth Davis
Miss Chin .... Barbara Luna
Waiter .... Pat Morita
Man .... Billy Sands

The Wizard of Oz *see* NBC Nights at the Movies

1209   Woman   PBS
Program Type Interview/Discussion
30 minutes. Weekly. Second season premiere: 10/1/74. Third season premiere: 8/2/75. Series made possible by grants from Public Television Stations, the Ford Foundation, and the Corporation for Public Broadcasting.
Producer Sandra Elkin
Production Company WNED/Buffalo
Director Will George
Interviewer/Moderator Sandra Elkin

1210   Woman Alive!   PBS
Program Type Documentary/Special
Special. Originally aired in 1974, program profiles the feminist movement. 60 minutes. Repeat date: 6/25/75.
Executive Producer Doug Bailey; Ronnie Eldridge
Producer Joan Shigekawa
Production Company KERA/Dallas-Fort Worth in collaboration with Ms. Magazine
Writer Susan Lester

1211   Women of the Year, 1975   CBS
Program Type Awards Show
Special. 3rd annual awards to eight women selected by the *Ladies' Home Journal.* Live coverage (in East). 90 minutes. 4/19/75.
Executive Producer Lenore Hershey
Producer Joseph Cates
Director Walter Miller
Musical Director Milton DeLugg
Host Florence Henderson
Entertainers Florence Henderson; Diahann Carroll; Roberta Peters
Presenters Liz Carpenter; Angie Dickinson; Helen Hayes; Lynda Johnson Robb; Mary Louise Smith; Marlo Thomas; Barbara Walters

1212   Women's Professional Tennis Tour
                                                      CBS
Program Type Sports
Six tournaments. Live. Saturday. Premiere date: 2/15/75. Last date of season: 4/5/75.
Producer Bill Fitts
Production Company CBS Television Network Sports
Announcer Don Criqui

1213   The Wonderful World of Disney
                                                      NBC
Program Type Children's Show
Anthology series. 60 minutes. Sunday. Show originated as "Disneyland" 10/27/54; became "Walt Disney Presents" 9/12/58. Current format premiere date: 9/24/61. Season premiere: 9/15/74.
Executive Producer Ron Miller
Producer Various
Production Company Walt Disney Productions
Director Various
Writer Various

World Championship Tennis Challenge Cup *see* WCT Challenge Cup

World Championship Tennis Doubles Challenge Match *see* WCT Doubles Challenge Match

1214   World Heavyweight Championship Fight
ABC Sports Special   ABC
Program Type Sports
Live coverage from Las Vegas, Nevada 5/16/75. Muhammad Ali versus Ron Lyle. Preliminary bout: Victor Galindez versus Ray Elson in World Boxing Association light-heavyweight title.
Executive Producer Roone Arledge
Production Company ABC Sports
Announcer Howard Cosell

1215   World Hunger! Who Will Survive?
Special of the Week   PBS
Program Type Documentary/Special
Special. 90 minutes. Premiere date: 1/27/75. Program made possible by a grant from Hoffmann LaRoche, Inc.
Executive Producer Dick Hubert
Producer Mary King Rose; Andrew Pearson
Production Company Connecticut Educational Television Corporation
Director Paul Galan
Host Bill Moyers

1216   World Invitational Tennis Classic
                                                      ABC
Program Type Sports
Second season premiere: 5/4/75. 11 matches; 90 minutes each. Last show of season: 7/13/75. All games played at Sea Pines Plantation, Hilton Head Island, South Carolina.
Executive Producer Roone Arledge
Production Company ABC Sports
Announcer Chris Schenkel; Pancho Gonzales; Earl "Butch" Bucholtz

The World of Henry Orient see NBC Nights at the Movies

1217 **The World of Survival** Syndicated
Program Type Animal Documentary
Premiere: 9/71. 30 minutes. Weekly.
Executive Producer Aubrey Buxton
Producer Various
Production Company Survival Anglia Ltd. in association with The World Wildlife Fund
Distributor J. Walter Thompson Co.
Director Various
Writer Various
Host John Forsythe

1218 **World Press** PBS
Program Type Interview/Discussion
Weekly. Fifth series premiere: 1/11/75 in 60-minute format. Sixth series premiere: 7/20/75 in 30-minute format. Series made possible by grants from the Corporation for Public Broadcasting, the Ford Foundation, and Public Television Stations.
Executive Producer Zev Putterman
Producer Andrew Stern
Production Company KQED/San Francisco
Director Tom Cohen
Regular Leslie Lipson; Paul Zinner; Chalmers Johnson; Maurice Jonas; Gerald Feldman; Michael Nabti
Moderator John Boas

1219 **World Series**
NBC Sports Special NBC
Program Type Sports
1974 World Series between Oakland Athletics and Los Angeles Dodgers. 10/12/74, 10/13/74 at Los Angeles Dodger Stadium. 10/15/74, 10/16/74, 10/17/74 at Oakland-Alameda County Stadium. Live coverage.
Executive Producer Scotty Connal
Producer Roy Hammerman
Production Company NBC Sports
Announcer Joe Garagiola; Curt Gowdy; Tony Kubek

1220 **World Series of Golf**
NBC Sports Special NBC
Program Type Sports
14th annual world series of golf. Live coverage from the Firestone Country Club, Akron, Ohio. 9/6/75; 9/7/75.
Producer Larry Cirillo
Production Company NBC Sports
Announcer Jim Simpson; Charlie Jones; Jay Randolph; Pat Hernon; Arnold Palmer; John Brodie

1221 **World Series of Women's Tennis**
ABC Sports Special ABC
Program Type Sports
Taped at Austin, Texas. 4/19/74; 4/20/75. 90 minutes each.
Executive Producer Roone Arledge
Production Company ABC Sports
Announcer Frank Gifford

1222 **World Team Tennis Championship**
NBC Sports Special NBC
Program Type Sports
Second match in best-of-three covered live 8/24/75 from the Pittsburgh Civic Arena. 150 minutes. The Pittsburgh Triangles versus the San Francisco Golden Gaters.
Producer Dick Auerbach
Production Company NBC Sports
Director Ken Fouts
Announcer Tim Ryan; John Newcombe; Wendy Overton

1223 **World Team Tennis East-West All-Star Match**
NBC Sports Special NBC
Program Type Sports
120 minutes. 7/12/75. First World Team Tennis All-Star Match. Taped in the Los Angeles Sports Arena.
Production Company NBC Sports
Announcer Tim Ryan; John Newcombe

1224 **The World's Worst Air Crash: The Avoidable Accident?** PBS
Program Type Documentary/Special
Special. 60 minutes. Premiere date: 5/10/75. Repeat date: 7/11/75. The March 3, 1974 crash of Turkish Airlines Flight 509, a DC-10 jumbo jet.
Producer Peter Williams
Production Company WNET/New York; Thames Television/London; *Sunday Times/London*
Reporter Peter Williams

The Wrecking Crew see The CBS Thursday/Friday Night Movies

WUSA see The ABC Saturday Night Movie

1225 **Yankee Doodle Cricket** ABC
Program Type Animated Film
Special. Sequel to "The Cricket in Times Square" and "A Very Merry Cricket." 30 minutes. Premiere date: 1/16/75. Based on characters created by George Selden. Violinist: Israel Baker.

Yankee Doodle Cricket *Continued*
Producer Chuck Jones
Production Company Chuck Jones Enterprises
Director Chuck Jones
Writer Chuck Jones
Voices Les Tremayne; Mel Blanc; June Foray

1226   The Year of the Dragon
Theater in America   PBS
Program Type Drama
Performed by the American Place Theater, New
York City. 90 minutes. Premiere date: 1/15/75.
Repeat date: 4/16/75. Series funded by Exxon
Corporation and the Corporation for Public
Broadcasting.
Executive Producer Jac Venza
Production Company WNET/New York
Director Russell Treyz; Portman Paget
Writer Frank Chin
Host Hal Holbrook
CAST
Fred Eng .... George Takei
Pa .... Conrad Yama
Sissy .... Tina Chen
Ma ....Pat Suzuki
China Mama .... Lilah Khan
Johnny Eng .... Keenan Shimizu
Ross .... Doug Higgins

1227   The Year Without a Santa Claus
                                                              ABC
Program Type Animated Film
Special. Based on the book by Phyllis McGinley.
Music by Maury Laws; lyrics by Jules Bass. 60
minutes. Premiere date: 12/10/74.
Producer Arthur Rankin, Jr.; Jules Bass
Production Company Rankin/Bass Productions
Director Arthur Rankin, Jr.; Jules Bass
VOICES
Mrs. Santa Claus .... Shirley Booth
Santa Claus ....Mickey Rooney
Snowmiser .... Dick Shawn
Heatmiser ....George S. Irving
Jingle Bells .... Robert McFadden
Jangle Bells .... Bradley Bolke
Mother Nature ....Rhoda Mann
Mr. Thistlewhite .... Ron Marshall
Ignatius Thistlewhite ....Colin Duffy
"Blue Christmas" Girl ....Christine Winter
Additional Voices The Wee Winter Singers

The Yellow Submarine *see* The CBS
Thursday/Friday Night Movies

1228   Yes, Virginia, There Is a Santa
Claus   ABC
Program Type Animated Film
Special. Based on Virginia O'Hanlon's 1897 let-
ter to the editor of the *New York Sun*. 30 minutes.

Premiere date: 12/6/74. Title song sung by
Jimmy Osmond.
Executive Producer Burt Rosen
Producer Bill Melendez; Mort Green
Production Company A production of the Burt
Rosen Company and Wolper Productions
Director Bill Melendez
Writer Mort Green
Narrator Jim Backus
VOICES
Miss Taylor .... Susan Silo
Virginia .... Courtney Lemmon
Billie ....Billie Green
Specs ....Sean Manning
Mary Lou .... Tracy Belland
Arthur .... Christopher Wong
Amy ....Vickey Ricketts
Peewee .... Jennifer Green
Off. Riley ....Herb Armstrong
Sgt. Muldoon ....Arnold Moss

1229   Yogi's Gang   ABC
Program Type Animated Film
30 minutes. Saturday. Premiere date: 9/8/73.
Reruns: 9/7/74. Last show: 8/30/75.
Executive Producer Joseph Barbera; William
Hanna
Producer Iwao Takamoto
Production Company Hanna-Barbera Produc-
tions in association with Screen Gems
Director Charles A. Nichols
Story Editor Bob Ogle
Musical Director Hoyt Curtin
VOICES
Yogi Bear .... Daws Butler
Boo Boo Ranger ....Don Messick
Doggie Daddy ....John Stephenson
Paw Rugg ....Henry Corden
Additional Voices Josh Albee; Julie Bennett; Tom Bos-
ley; Walker Edmiston; Virginia Gregg; Jim Mac-
George; Rose Marie; Allan Melvin; Hal Smith; Jean
VanderPyl; Vincent Van Patten; Lennie Weinrib;
Jesse White; Paul Winchell

You Can't Win 'Em All *see* The ABC
Sunday Night Movie

1230   You Don't Say!   ABC
Program Type Game Show
New version of show which ran for seven years
in the '60's hosted by Tom Kennedy. 30 minutes.
Monday-Friday. Premiere date: 7/7/75.
Producer Bill Carruthers
Production Company Ralph Andrews Produc-
tion in association with Warner Brothers
Director Bill Carruthers
Host Tom Kennedy

1231 You Lie So Deep, My Love
Tuesday/Wednesday Movie of the Week ABC
Program Type TV Movie
90 minutes. Premiere date: 2/25/75.
Executive Producer Robert Hamner; John Neufeld
Producer David Lowell Rich
Production Company Universal Television
Director David Lowell Rich
Writer William L. Stuart
CAST
Neal Collins .... Don Galloway
Susan Collins .... Barbara Anderson
Jennifer Pierce .... Angel Tompkins
Uncle Joe Padway .... Walter Pidgeon
Foreman .... Russell Johnson
Ellen .... Anne Schedeen
Maid .... Virginia Gregg
Tom File .... Robert Rothwell
Jordan .... Pitt Herbert
Phyllis .... Bobbi Jordan

1232 The Young and the Restless CBS
Program Type Daytime Drama
Created by William J. Bell; Lee Phillip Bell. 30 minutes. Monday-Friday. Continuous. Premiere date: 3/26/73. Cast information: July 1975.
Producer John Conboy
Production Company Columbia Pictures Television
Director Dick Dunlap; Bill Glenn
Head Writer William J. Bell
CAST
Lorie Brooks .... Jamie Lyn Bauer
Mark Henderson .... Steve Carlson
Stuart Brooks .... Robert Colbert
Kay Chancellor .... Jeanne Cooper
Jill Foster .... Brenda Dickson
Snapper Foster .... William Gray Espy
William Foster, Sr. .... Charles Gray
Jennifer Brooks .... Dorothy Green
Brad Eliot .... Tom Hallick
Greg Foster .... James Houghton
Brock Reynolds .... Beau Kayzer
Leslie Brooks .... Janice Lynde
Liz Foster .... Julianna McCarthy
Peggy Brooks .... Pamela Solow
Chris Foster .... Trish Stewart

1233 Young Filmmakers' Festival PBS
Program Type Children's Show
Special. Spotlights nine films produced by young people 6–18 years old in the Fourth National Young Filmmakers' Festival. 60 minutes. Premiere date: 6/9/75. Program made possible by a grant from the National Endowment for the Arts.
Executive Producer Brian Benlifer
Producer Paul Marshall
Production Company KPBS/San Diego in cooperation with the Center for Understanding Media/New York
Director Brian Benlifer

1234 Young People's Concert CBS
Program Type Children's Show
Educational musical programs for school age children. Premiere date: 1/18/58. Two specials aired during the 1974-75 season: "What Is Noise?" "What Is Music?" and "What Makes a Gershwin Tune a Gershwin Tune?" (*See* titles for credits.)
Producer Roger Englander
Production Company CBS Television Network
Director Roger Englander
Host Michael Tilson Thomas

The Young Savages *see* NBC Nights at the Movies

1235 You're In Court PBS
Program Type Documentary/Special
Special. 90 minutes. Premiere date: 6/18/75. Boston's Housing Court, Judge Paul Garrity presiding.
Production Company WGBH/Boston
Narrator Ed Baumeister

Yours, Mine and Ours *see* NBC Nights at the Movies

1236 Zalmen or the Madness of God
Theater in America PBS
Program Type Drama
120 minutes. Premiere date: 1/8/75 (season premiere of series). Produced by Zelda Fichandler of the Arena Stage Company, Washington, D.C. Series funded by Exxon Corporation and the Corporation for Public Broadcasting.
Executive Producer Jac Venza
Producer Ken Campbell
Production Company WNET/New York
Director Alan Schneider; Peter Levin
Writer Elie Wiesel
Host Hal Holbrook
CAST
Zalmen .... Richard Bauer
Rabbi .... Joseph Wiseman
Chairman .... Robert Prosky
Srul .... Sanford Seeger
Shmuel .... Lieb Lensky
Motke .... Michael Mertz
Chaim .... David Reinhardsen
Zender .... Glenn Taylor
Doctor .... Mark Hammer
Inspector .... Howard Witt
Nina .... Dianne Wiest
Alexei .... Gary Bayer
Misha .... John Koch, Jr.
Commissar .... Scott Schofield
Secretary .... Nancy Dutton
Avrom .... Michael Gorrin
Feige .... Leslie Carr

Zalmen or the Madness of God
Continued
Guards .... Michael Harvey; Ken Kantor
Cantor .... John Jellison

1237   Zee Cooking School   PBS
Program Type Children's Show
30 minutes. Weekly. 14 programs. Premiere date:
10/1/74. Cooking for 8–16 year olds.
Executive Producer Warren Steibel
Producer Ann Delaney
Production Company South Carolina Educational Television Network
Director Larry Lancit
Host Colette Ross
Teacher Colette Ross

Zeppelin *see* NBC Nights at the Movies

Zigzag *see* The CBS Thursday/Friday
Night Movies

1238   The Zoo Gang   NBC
Program Type Drama
Six-part series. 30 minutes each. Two shows each
week. Premiere date: 7/16/75. Third and fourth
shows: 7/23/75. Fifth and sixth shows: 8/6/75.
Based on the book by Paul Gallico; developed for
television by Reginald Rose. Theme music by
Paul McCartney; Linda McCartney.
Producer Herbert Hirschman
Production Company ATV-ITC Productions for
Worldwide Distribution
Director Sidney Hayes; John Hough
Writer Reginald Rose; Howard Dimsdale; John
Kruse; William Fairchild; Peter Yeldman;
Sean Graham
Script Consultant Howard Dimsdale
CAST
Stephen Halliday (The Fox) .... Brian Keith
Capt. Tommy Devon (The Elephant) .... John Mills
Manouche Roget (The Leopard) .... Lilli Palmer
Alec Marlowe (The Tiger) .... Barry Morse

1239   Zoom   PBS
Program Type Children's Show
30 minutes. Monday-Friday. Premiere date:
1/9/72. Season premiere: 11/11/74. Show feature: Zoomcards. Last year of series. Series made
possible by grants from McDonald's Corporation, McDonald's Restaurants Fund and the
Corporation for Public Broadcasting.
Executive Producer Austin Hoyt
Production Company WGBH/Boston

1240   Zulu Romeo: Good Start
PBS Sports Special   PBS
Program Type Sports
Special. 60 minutes. Premiere date: 3/8/75.
Filmed at the 1973 International Glider Competition at Waikerie, Australia.
Producer John Walker
Director John Walker
Writer Peter Wyer
Camera John Haddy